Thinking With Data

Carnegie Mellon Symposia on Cognition
David Klahr, Series Editor

Thinking With Data

Edited by
Marsha C. Lovett
Carnegie Mellon University

Priti Shah
University of Michigan

 Lawrence Erlbaum Associates
Taylor & Francis Group

New York London

Cover design by Tomai Maridou.

Lawrence Erlbaum Associates
Taylor & Francis Group
270 Madison Avenue
New York, NY 10016

Lawrence Erlbaum Associates
Taylor & Francis Group
2 Park Square
Milton Park, Abingdon
Oxon OX14 4RN

International Standard Book Number-13: 978-0-8058-5422-0 (Softcover) 978-0-8058-5421-3 (Hardcover)

Visit the Taylor & Francis Web site at
http://www.taylorandfrancis.com

and the LEA Web site at
http://www.erlbaum.com

To Chris and Nathan—M.L.
To Jim, Kiran, and Avani—P.S.
With love and gratitude.

Contents

Contributors

Wändi Bruine de Bruin
Carnegie Mellon University

Marie Burrage
University of Michigan

Beth Chance
Cal Poly

Jammie Chang
Stanford University

Norma Chang
Carnegie Mellon University

David Danks
Carnegie Mellon

Bob delMas
University of Minnesota

Julie Downs
Carnegie Mellon University

Kevin Dunbar
Dartmouth College

Marina Epstein
University of Michigan

Baruch Fischhoff
Carnegie Mellon University

Jonathan Fugelsang
Dartmouth College

Joan Garfield
University of Minnesota

Susan Kirschenbaum
Naval Undersea Warfare Center Division

David Klahr
Carnegie Mellon University

Ken Koedinger
Carnegie Mellon

Cliff Konold
University of Massachusetts at Amherst

Joe Krajcik
Univeristy of Michigan

Jorge Larreamendy-Joerns
Universidad de los Andes, Colombia

Richard Lehrer
Vanderbilt University

Gaea Leinhardt
University of Pittsburgh

Eliza B. Littleton
Pittsburgh, PA

Yan Liu
Vanderbilt University

Marsha Lovett
Carnegie Mellon University

Amy Masnick
Hostra University

Kate McNeill
University of Michigan

Brad Morris
Grand Valley State University

Luis Saldanha
Portland State University

Lelyn Saner
University of Pittsburgh

Leona Schauble
Vanderbilt University

Christian Schunn
University of Pittsburgh

Dan Schwartz
Stanford University

David Sears
Stanford University

Peter Sedlmeier
Technische Universität Chemnitz, Germany

Priti Shah
University of Michigan

Courtney Stein
Dartmouth College

Pat Thompson
Arizona State University

Greg Trafton
Naval Research Laboratory

Susan Trickett
George Mason University

Preface

This volume presents the papers given at the 33rd Carnegie Symposium on Cognition, held June 4–6, 2004: *Thinking With Data*. What is thinking with data? It is more than just using data. One can use data automatically, but thinking with data requires understanding. It is more than just consuming data. One can consume without tasting, absorbing a vast array of disparate facts, but thinking with data requires making connections. It is more than just analyzing data. One can run an analysis without gaining insight, but thinking with data requires interpretations built upon sound statistical reasoning. Thinking with data, then, is the set of cognitive process for integrating and understanding complex numerical, categorical, and graphical information and the processes of learning all this, too. *Thinking* with data uses data, not just as a tool but as a medium.

This theme for the symposium was motivated by the confluence of three emerging trends. The first is the increasing need for people to think (effectively) with data. A relentless fact of modern life is that we are swimming in data. Scientists routinely collect more in one study than the previous generation could collect in a career. Industry processes an amount of data each day that was almost unimaginable a decade ago. And with a click, we all can access megabytes, gigabytes, and beyond. Like it or not, for a consumer, for a professional, for a citizen, even for a child, thinking with data is necessary for navigating our information-rich society.

The second trend is our increasing capacity for thinking with data. New tools and fast computing make it easier to calculate, manage, and display, freeing us to think about content in new ways. Recently developed algorithms and statistical methods make accessible a wider range of questions. Data sets may be growing in size and complexity over time, but our technologies are not far behind.

The third trend is the increasing recognition and interest in the challenge of understanding how people think with data. This cuts across many fields, including cognitive psychology, developmental psychology, statistics, computer science, education research, economics, and the decision sciences. In all these disciplines, research in this direction has been accelerating. Yet, it is rare for researchers working from these distinct perspectives to synthesize results across disciplinary boundaries and thus benefit from research in other areas.

There is thus a fertile opportunity for researchers from multiple disciplines to benefit from sharing their research and ideas and from seeking points of connection, possibly even convergence. Indeed, that is one of the main goals of 33rd Carnegie Symposium. That is precisely what the symposium aimed to do: The presenters and discussants represented the full range of disciplines, methods, and approaches, and it was our objective to bring them together to share solutions and ideas for common problems.

The current volume represents this scientific diversity well by offering a uniquely multidisciplinary presentation of research on how people think with data. Because of the different disciplines represented, the chapters in this volume illustrate many different methodological approaches, including qualitative and quantitative analysis, experimentation and classroom observation, computational modeling, and neuroimaging. The various chapters also span a range in terms of the degree of emphasis on theory versus application.

In keeping with the goals of the symposium, we eschewed an organization for this volume that emphasizes contrast—across discipline, methodology, or population—in favor of an organization that emphasizes commonality. The chapters in each part of this volume pursue a common question or activity involved in how people think with data. Part I focuses on the concepts of uncertainty and variation and on how people understand and learn these ideas in a variety of contexts. Part II focuses on working with data to understand its structure and to draw conclusions. This can range from formal statistical data analysis the practice of statistical data analysis to an informal assessment of evidence. Part III focuses on how people learn from data and how they use data to make decisions in daily and professional life. Although the chapters in each part vary on many dimensions (such as the age of people studied, the setting and domain, and the methods used), we hope that this organization will help reveal the deeper connections between these works. Each part ends with a commentary chapter that synthesizes and relates the chapters presented in that part.

What follows is a brief description of the chapters collected here. As even these brief summaries indicate, there are many recent and exciting developments in our understanding of how people think with data. The insights from this research apply broadly: in the classroom, in the office, and in daily life. And just as importantly, these chapters show how research from different perspectives, in different disciplines and contexts, can combine to illuminate common questions and solve common problems. We hope that this volume highlights the benefits of a multifaceted approach to understanding how people think with data and that it might inspire researchers in this area to forge productive connections across disciplinary boundaries. Because of the diversity represented here, this volume also offers a useful picture of the breadth and depth of research in this area. It should thus be particularly useful to researchers seeking to identify the current state of the art and to those who are new to the field.

PART I: REASONING ABOUT UNCERTAINTY AND VARIATION

Masnick, Klahr, and Morris present a chapter on the developmental trajectory—from children to undergraduates—of the understanding of variation. They present a taxonomy of the different kinds of error that relate to variation in data. Their results argue for the notion that people interpret variation differently based on many factors, including the degree of variation in the data, their expectations, and their knowledge of the logic involved in statistical reasoning.

Schunn, Saner, Kirschenbaum, Trafton, and Littleton argue that the symbolic, embodied, and neurocomputational theoretical frameworks make different predictions about the kinds of representations that are used in complex visual data analysis. They provide empirical evidence that, during the analysis of uncertain data, naval submarine operators and neuroscientists examining fMRI shift from one representationl system to another depending on the task demands, supporting the neurocomputational perspective.

In a related chapter, Trickett, Trafton, Saner, and Schunn take a second look at how individuals deal with uncertainty in data. They describe how experts in two very different domains: meteorology and cognitive neuroscience deal with uncertainty in weather data and functional neuroimaging data. They present verbal protocol and gesture data supporting the assertion that that experts' are more likely to engage in spatial processing when analyzing uncertain data.

DelMas and Liu describe research on students' understanding (and lack of understanding) of the standard deviation. They present results from students' use of an instructional tool that incorporates several different representations of the concept of standard deviation—the formula, the sum of squares contributing to the computation of standard deviation, and a graphical display of the data in histogram form. Even with this conceptual learning tool, delMas and Liu show the many different interpretations of standard deviation that students learn.

Garfield, delMas, and Chance describe the results of a classroom teaching experiment, focused on students' learning about variability and based on the methods of Japanese Lesson Study. They discuss students' initial intuitions about variability and present activities that help students build on these informal understandings. In addition, they present assessment results that characterize how students' knowledge developed and, based on these results, make several recommendations for instruction.

Lehrer and Schauble take a *data modeling* approach to considering the component skills involved in understanding statistics. According to this approach, data modeling involves posing questions, generating and selecting attributes to measure, measuring data, structuring and displaying data, and finally, making inferences. They describe a study in which students learn about variability in two different contexts that involve data modeling—a measurement context (e.g, measuring height of a flagpole), and a natural context (growth of plants). Students developed their own representational systems and "statistics," a process that leads to a deeper understanding of the concept of variation.

Leinhardt and Larreamendy-Joerns provide commentary on these chapters by highlighting the different meanings of variation, both historically—going all the way back to ancient Greeks' thinking on this topic—and across these six chapters. In addition, they identify several themes from what this set of chapters has to say about why learning and understanding variation is so difficult.

PART II: STATISTICAL REASONING AND DATA ANALYSIS

Dunbar begins this section by tackling the question of whether naïve theories ever go away, or in terms of this book's theme, how much data does it take to overcome students' prior beliefs? Using behavioral and neuroimaging data, he presents evidence that even after students have apparently changed their conceptual understanding (i.e., they can answer conceptual questions correctly), there is often still an fMRI signature of some residual contradiction. This result has interesting implications for instruction on statistical reasoning. Thompson, Liu, and Saldanha discuss the conceptual subtleties involved in statistical inference and then describe a study of teachers' understandings of these issues. They highlight the various conceptions held by teachers and discuss how those understandings evolved through a series of discussions and activities related to the topics of hypothesis testing, sampling statistics, and probability.

Konold takes on the challenge of finding ways to teach young school children (e.g., fourth- graders) to explore the patterns in data. After reviewing past approaches to this problem, he describes a new instructional tool called *TinkerPlots* that aims to revolutionize statistics instruction by placing the learner more in control of how to work with data. He then discusses the main design considerations motivating *TinkerPlots* and some results from students using it.

Lovett and Chang present two studies aimed at understanding students' underlying representations of statistics knowledge. In particular, they highlight several expert–novice differences in how students approach data-analysis problems and in the degree to which they make use of key problem features in selecting appropriate data analyses.

Finally, Schwartz, Sears, and Chang take a *preparing for future learning* perspective on the teaching of statistics. They argue that prior knowledge prepares individuals for future learning, but that, in many cases, prior knowledge is not in a form available for use because it cannot be related to other relevant information; they refer to this as incommensurate prior knowledge. In this chapter, they describe a number of studies in which they successfully teach statistics skills by helping students build from their prior knowledge and intuitions, as well as to develop relevant prior knowledge to prepare them for learning formal statistics.

Koedinger provides commentary on all six chapters in this section first by analyzing each according to its research question, hypothesis, theoretical basis, and evidence. Then, he identifies several thematic insights across these suggestions: their suggestions for instruction on data analysis, their probing into the mechanisms of student learning, and finally their use of new research methods and computational tools for better studying student learning.

PART III: LEARNING FROM AND MAKING DECISIONS WITH DATA

Danks provides a review of different mathematical models of causal reasoning, and then presents a unified framework for representing these models. This new framework allows models of causal reasoning to be explicitly compared and contrasted and examined in terms of fit with empirical data.

In his chapter, Sedlmeier argues that individuals have valid statistical intuitions about frequency, and that if these valid statistical intuitions are exploited individuals learn to solve statistical reasoning tasks that are frequently considered difficult. Specifically, Sedlmeier describes studies in which individuals are taught to re-represent Bayesian reasoning and sample size problems from probabilistic to frequency format. These students dramatically improve in their ability to perform these statistical reasoning tasks even on transfer problems.

Bruine de Bruin, Downs, and Fischhoff identify gaps and misconceptions in adolescents' knowledge about risks and benefits of sexual behaviors and then create an intervention designed to provide adolescents with the knowledge needed to make more informed decisions. They present data suggesting that their DVD intervention is highly effective and lead to better long-term outcomes such as fewer sexually transmitted infections.

Finally, Burrage, Epstein, and Shah comment on the final three chapters in the volume. They argue that although these three chapters share the similarity that they address how individuals learn from real-world data, they can be situated in a three-dimensional space of instructional value, domain-specificity, and importance of discrete versus probabilistic information. They then discuss major contributions of each chapter as well as possible future direction for research about learning and making decisions with data.

—Marsha Lovett
—Priti Shah

Acknowledgments

The 33rd Carnegie Symposium on Cognition, on which this book is based, was an opportunity to bring together researchers from many disciplines and perspectives to address the question "How do people think with data?" The event was a big success, with thought-provoking talks that generated interesting ideas, discussions, and potential collaborations. We would like to thank all the participants for making the symposium such an exciting and enjoyable event.

The symposium was generously funded by three federal agencies: the National Science Foundation (REC-0400979), the Office of Naval Research (ONR-N00014-04-1-0149), and the National Institute of Child Health and Human Development (NIH-1 R13 HD048255). We could not have conducted such a productive symposium without these funds and the help of the corresponding program officers: Susan Chipman (ONR), Gregg Solomon (NSF), and Daniel Berch (NICHD). We would also like to thank the Psychology Department at Carnegie Mellon for indispensable financial and logistical support.

Many individuals also contributed their time and effort to the symposium and this volume. The speakers and contributors produced a set of excellent papers and talks and were always patient with our requests and deadlines. David Klahr offered us his wisdom, gained by experience as Series Editor, and—very importantly—hosted the symposium party. The early-career fellows brought energy and diverse ideas to the conference. Rochelle Sherman and Audrey Russo worked hard, and did a superb job, organizing local arrangements and helping during the event. Stacey Becker, Miriam Rosenberg-Lee, and Norma Chang helped greatly with the countless tasks that needed to be done ten minutes ago. Judy Brooks created the beautiful graphic design of the program. We thank them all for giving so much and for making our jobs easier.

I

Reasoning About Uncertainty and Variation

1

Separating Signal From Noise: Children's Understanding of Error and Variability in Experimental Outcomes

Amy M. Masnick
Hofstra University

David Klahr
Carnegie Mellon University

Bradley J. Morris
Grand Valley State University

A young child eagerly awaits the day when she will pass the 100 cm minimum height requirement for riding on the "thriller" roller coaster at her local amusement park. She regularly measures her height on the large-scale ruler tacked to her closet door. As summer approaches, she asks her parents to measure her every week. A few weeks ago she measured 98 cm, last week 99.5 cm, but today only 99.0 cm. Disappointed and confused, when she gets to school, she asks the school nurse to measure her and is delighted to discover that her height is 100.1 cm. Success at last! But as she anticipates the upcoming annual class excursion to the amusement park, she begins to wonder: what is her *real* height? And more importantly, what will the measurement at the entrance to the roller coaster reveal? Why are all the measurements different, rather than the same? Because she is a really thoughtful child, she begins to speculate about whether the differences are in the thing being measured (i.e., maybe her height really doesn't increase monotonically from day to day) or the way it was measured (different people may use different techniques and measurement instruments when determining her height).

As this hypothetical scenario suggests, children often have to make decisions about data, not only in formal science classroom contexts, but also in everyday life. However, data vary. Data are imperfect both in the "real world" and in science classrooms. Learning when that variation matters and when it does not—separating the signal from the noise—is a difficult task no matter what the context. Children have two disadvantages in interpreting data. First, they have no formal statistical knowledge, which makes it impossible for them to fully assess the properties of the data in question. Second, children's limited experience makes it difficult for them to detect data patterns and to formulate coherent expectations—based on nascent theories—about natural phenomena.

In contrast, adults with formal statistical training can use those tools in the science laboratory to distinguish real effects from error, or effects caused by factors other than the ones being explored. When statistical tools reveal that observed differences are highly unlikely to have occurred by chance, those with statistical training can feel more confident about drawing conclusions from data. Another critical component to such reasoning is theory, which we define as the background knowledge and experience brought to the task that influences decisions about the importance of variability and the reasonableness of the conclusions. This theoretical context may include hypotheses about potential mechanisms that lead to observed outcomes, but may also be a simple statement that events are related or that they do not contradict explanations of other phenomena. The theoretical component involves any claims about the data, based on information other than the data themselves.

In everyday reasoning, for those with or without statistics training, deeply held beliefs require large and consistent discrepancies between expected outcomes and empirical discrepancies before theory revision can take place. From a Bayesian perspective, the impact of new evidence is modulated by the size of the prior probabilities. For example, if a person has seen 1,000 instances of events x and y co-occurring, one instance of x occurring by itself is unlikely to change the expectation that the next instance of x is likely to be paired with y. And even in the classic Fisherian statistical world of t-tests and ANOVAs, the significance of statistical results is always tempered by a theory-embedded interpretation. In all scientific disciplines, strongly held hypotheses require a lot of disconfirming evidence before they are revised, whereas those with less theoretical grounding are more easily revised so as to be consistent with the latest empirical findings.

But how does a child determine when such variation matters? As just discussed, knowledge guides interpretations of data yet data also guide the evaluation and creation of knowledge. There seem to be (at least) two plausible developmental explanations: knowledge precedes data or data precede knowledge. Although these characterizations are slightly exaggerated, it is useful to examine the implications of each. It is possible that children only begin to attend to data when they detect inconsistencies with their existing knowledge. For example, the child in our opening scenario who holds the belief that growth is a monotonic function—and that therefore her height will always increase—will use that "theory" to interpret any measurement indicating a "loss" of height, as inconsistent with the current theory. This anomaly may motivate a more careful and skeptical analysis of the discrepant measurement. She might look for and evaluate a series of possible explanations that account for the unexpected data (Chinn & Brewer, 2001). Thus, through the detection of theoretical inconsistencies, children might begin to attend to data and these data, in turn, provide information on the type and extent of knowledge change that is necessary.

Conversely, it is also possible that knowledge is the result of data accumulation. Perhaps children detect patterns in their environment and use the data as the basis for conceptual groupings. For example, it has been suggested that several facets of language acquisition (e.g., phoneme tuning) are derived from the statistical structure of the child's language environment. In phoneme learning, once the acoustical properties of a set of phonemes have been derived, children prefer these sounds to novel sounds (Jusczyk, Friederici, Wessels, Svenkerud, & Jusczyk, 1993). Once established, these conceptual units might anchor expectations about the probability of occurrences in the environment. A possible consequence of such an expectation is that deviations from the established data patterns (e.g., statistical structure) provide evidence of variation and may require changes in current knowledge.

We argue that theoretical, background knowledge and data dynamically interact in reasoning. That is, the tendency to attend to theoretical claims and explanations, or to specific data will be driven by the degree to which each element matches (or does not match) current knowledge. Many researchers have noted that theory influences the interpretation of data (e.g., Chinn & Malhotra, 2002; Koslowski, 1996; Kuhn & Dean, 2004; Schauble, 1996; see Zimmerman, 2005 for a review). For example, people often discount data that contradict their current knowledge. Yet few researchers have examined the role of data in modifying theory (cf. Dunbar, Fugelsang, & Stein, this volume). Further, there has been little research in which the interaction between reasoning about information based on prior knowledge and reasoning explicitly about data characteristics has been examined.

Beliefs based on background knowledge or context are one key component in drawing conclusions. However, another important, often overlooked component in decision making involves beliefs about characteristics of data. In the science laboratory, these beliefs are usually formalized in the use of statistics, but for children, these beliefs are based on a basic knowledge of probability and informal notions of statistics.

National Science Education standards urge teachers to develop children's critical thinking skills that include "deciding what evidence should be used and accounting for anomalous data" (NRC, 2000, p. 159). In conducting authentic scientific investigations, students encounter variability and error in data collection and need to discriminate meaningful effects from experimental errors. In addition, to "account for anomalous data," students need to understand the various sources of error (e.g., procedural errors, uncontrolled variables, experimenter bias). This knowledge provides a foundation for evaluating evidence and drawing conclusions based on scientific data. Thus, it is not sufficient (though necessary) for students to be able to analyze data using mathematical and statistical procedures. Rather, it is essential for students to be able to reason meaningfully and coherently about data variability itself.

In this chapter, we examine the relative roles of reasoning context and data characteristics when children and adults reason about error. First, we describe the framework that has guided our research in this area, and then we discuss three empirical studies of these issues.

ERROR TAXONOMY

One way to consider data use in science education is to consider data in the context of an experiment, noting that data variation can occur in any of a series of places. Variation and the interpretation of the variation can have different consequences at different stages of an experiment. To structure the approach to looking at these issues, we developed a taxonomy of types of errors, considering errors by the phase of experimentation during which they occur (Masnick & Klahr, 2003), building on Hon's earlier epistemological taxonomy of error (1989). The taxonomy is summarized in Table 1.1.

The taxonomy identifies five stages of the experimentation process and four types of error that can occur during these stages. Our description is couched in terms of a simple ramps experiment in which participants are asked to set up two ramps such that they can be used to test the effect of a particular variable, such as the surface of the ramp, on the distance a ball travels. A correct test involves setting up two ramps with identical settings on every level except surface, running the test, and then measuring and interpreting the results.

TABLE 1.1
Experimentation Phases and Error Types

Error Type	Phases of Experimentation				
	Design (Choose variables to test)	Setup (Physically prepare expt.)	Execution (Run experiment)	Outcome Measurement (Assess outcome)	Analysis (Draw conclusions)
Design Error	Undetected confounds; incorrect conceptualization & operationalization of variables.				
Measurement Error		Incorrect settings & arrangements of independent variables and measurement devices		Incorrect calibration of instruments or measurement of dependent variables.	
Execution Error			Unexpected, unknown, or undetected processes influence outcome variables.		
Interpretation Error	Flawed causal theories	Not noticing error in setup	Not noticing error in execution	Not noticing error in outcome measures	Statistical, inductive, & deductive errors.

Note. From "Error matters: An Initial Exploration of Elementary School Children's Understanding of Experimental Error" by A. M. Masnick & D. Klahr, *Journal of Cognition and Development, 4*, p. 70. Copyright © 2003 by Lawrence Erlbaum Associates. Reprinted with permission.

7

We distinguish five stages in the experimentation process: design (choosing variables to test), set-up (physically preparing the experiment), execution (running the experiment), outcome measurement (assessing the outcome), and analysis (drawing conclusions). Each stage is directly associated with a different category of error.

Design Error

Decisions about which factors to vary and which to control are made in the design stage. These decisions are based on both domain-general knowledge, such as how to set up an unconfounded experiment, and domain-specific knowledge, such as which variables are likely to have an effect and therefore should be controlled. Domain-specific knowledge is used to form the operational definitions of the experiment's independent and dependent variables.

Design error occurs in this stage of an experiment when some important causal variables not being tested are not controlled, resulting in a confounded experiment. Design errors occur "in the head" rather than "in the world," because they result from cognitive failures. These failures can result from either a misunderstanding of the logic of unconfounded contrasts, or inadequate domain knowledge (e.g., not considering steepness as relevant to the outcome of a ramps comparison).

Measurement Error

Measurement error can occur during either the set-up stage or the outcome measurement stage. Error in the set-up stage is associated with the readings and settings involved in arranging the apparatus and calibrating instruments, and error in the outcome measurement stage is associated with operations and instruments used to assess the experimental outcomes. Measurement always includes some error, producing values with some degree of inaccuracy. These inaccuracies can affect either the independent or the dependent variables in the experiment. Of the four types of error, measurement error most closely corresponds to the conventional view of an error term that is added to a true value of either the settings of the independent variables or the measurement of the dependent variables.

Execution Error

The execution stage covers the temporal interval during which the phenomenon of interest occurs: in other words the time period when the experiment is "run." For example, in the ramps experiment, this stage lasts from when the balls are set in motion until they come to rest. Execution error occurs in this stage when something in the experimental execution influences the outcome. Execution error can be random (such that replications can average out its effects) or biased (such that the direction of influence is the same on repeated trials), and it may be obvious (such as hitting the side of the ramp) or unobserved (such as an imperfection in the ball).

Interpretation Error

Although interpretation occurs during the final stage—analysis—interpretation error can be a consequence of errors occurring in earlier stages and propagated forward. That is, undetected errors in any stage of the experiment can lead to an interpretation error. For example, not noticing the ball hitting the side of the ramp as it rolls down might lead one to be more confident than warranted in drawing conclusions about the effect of the ramp design.

Even if there are no earlier errors of any importance, interpretation errors may occur in this final stage as conclusions are drawn based on the experimental outcome and prior knowledge. Interpretation errors may result from flawed reasoning strategies, including inadequate understanding of how to interpret various patterns of covariation (Amsel & Brock, 1996; Shaklee & Paszek, 1985) or from faulty domain knowledge that includes incorrect causal mechanisms (Koslowski, 1996). Both statistical and cognitive inadequacies in this stage can result in what are conventionally labeled as Type I or Type II errors, that is, ascribing an effect when in fact there is none, or claiming a null effect when one actually exists.

Operationally, the assessment of interpretation errors must involve assessing both the conclusions drawn and one's confidence in the conclusions. Sometimes this assessment is defined formally by considering whether a statistical test yields a value indicating how likely it is that the data distribution could have occurred by chance. Regardless of whether statistics are used, a final decision must be reached about (a) what conclusions can be drawn, and (b) the level of confidence appropriate to these conclusions.

BACKGROUND LITERATURE

Past research about children's understanding of experimental error and data variability has come from a range of contexts and methodologies. Some researchers have examined understanding of probability whereas others have looked at understanding in classroom contexts. Here we briefly summarize the related research.

Early research into children's understanding of data examined their conceptions of probability (Piaget & Inhelder, 1951/1975). Piaget and Inhelder suggested that children under the age of ten have difficulty with large sample sizes, often becoming more confused with increased amounts of data.

Given the complexity of a concept of experimental error, it is likely that children master different components of it along different developmental (and educational) trajectories. Indeed, the literature provides some evidence for such piecemeal growth of design error understanding. For example, Sodian, Zaitchik, and Carey (1991) demonstrated that even first-graders, when presented with a choice between a conclusive and an inconclusive experimental test, can make the correct choice, although they cannot yet design such a conclusive test. Similarly, we would expect that children might be able to recognize error-based explanations as plausible even if they are unable to generate execution or measurement error-related reasons for data variability.

Varelas (1997) examined third- and fourth-graders' reasoning about errors in the execution and outcome measurement stages, by looking at how they reasoned about repeated measurements. She found that most children expected some variability in measurements, although why they expected this variability was not always clear. Children also exhibited a range of opinions regarding the value of repeated measurements, with some believing the practice informative, and others finding it confusing and a bad idea. Many children appeared to believe that uncontrolled measurement and execution errors could affect outcomes, but they were often unable to explain the link between these error sources and the ensuing variation in data.

Schauble (1996) examined the performance of fifth-graders, sixth-graders, and noncollege adults on two different tasks in which the participants' goal was to determine the influence of various factors. One difficulty many children (and some adults) had was in distinguishing variation due to errors in measuring the results and variation due to true differences between the conditions (that is, between intended contrasts and measurement stage errors). When in doubt, participants tended to fall back on their prior theories. If they expected a variable to have an effect, they interpreted variability as a true effect. If they did not expect a variable to have an effect, they were more likely to interpret the variability as due to error. Thus, their prior beliefs sometimes led them to make interpretation errors in drawing conclusions.

In more recent work, Petrosino, Lehrer, and Schauble (2003) explored fourth-graders' understanding of data variability when they take repeated measurements in different contexts. They focused primarily on what we refer to as measurement errors, and were able to teach students to think about measurements as representative of a sample of measures. They had participants use instruments with varying levels of precision, and focused discussion on the best ways to summarize the data they collected. Students trained in this way performed significantly above the national average on assessments of how to collect, organize, read, represent, and interpret data.

Some researchers studying the phenomena of categorical induction have explored children's use of data characteristics from a different perspective, looking at children's ability to make inductions based on prior information. Gutheil and Gelman (1997) explored how children use sample size information and information about variation within categories in induction. They found that 8- and 9-year-old children were able to use diversity and sample size together in inferring whether a given property would be expected to occur in a new exemplar. Similarly, Jacobs and Narloch (2001) found that children as young as 7 years old could use sample size and variability information in inferring the likely frequency of a future event.

At the same time, there is some evidence that 11-year-old children still struggle to understand the reasons for taking repeated measurements within the context of a school science laboratory (Lubben & Millar, 1996). Some children at this age believe repeated measurements are important, but 18% thought that repeated measures are useful because they accommodate scatter in the data.

Taken as a whole, this small collection of studies leaves many important questions unanswered and does not provide a coherent picture of the way that children develop an understanding of error and data variability. There is evidence of skill at some types of error-based reasoning as early as first grade, yet also evidence of difficulty in reasoning about error into adulthood. Metz (1998) has noted that the limited literature on children's ability to interpret data variability reveals an apparent inconsistency between studies suggesting that children understand probability and statistics at a young age, and those suggesting that adults have significant difficulties with these concepts (e.g., Konold, 1991; Tversky & Kahneman, 1974). Metz argues that the difference may be due to the widely discrepant criteria for precisely what behaviors do and do not indicate a solid grasp of these concepts.

Some work done by contributors to this volume also bears relevance on these issues. For instance, Krajcik and McNeill (this volume) looked at how middle school children's reasoning changes with different kinds of content knowledge. In addition, Garfield, delMas, and Chance (this volume), and delMas and Liu (this volume) describe some of the difficulties college students have in understanding variation and the concept of a standard deviation.

In the following sections, we describe a series of studies in which we have begun a systematic, theoretically guided examination of children's understanding of error and data variability. Our aim is to learn more of what children know and understand about data and the ways in which they can use characteristics of data in drawing conclusions. Thus far, we have explored these issues in three contexts that vary in the extent to which children's a priori causal theories are correct. In one context (balls rolling down ramps) most second- to fourth-graders' initial theories are correct, at least about most of the causal factors. In the second context (pendulums), their causal theories are mainly incorrect. In the third context (presenting outcome data for comparison), there is little theoretical context to rely on, and conclusions must be drawn solely from data.

CHILDREN'S USE OF DATA IN A WELL UNDERSTOOD CONTEXT: RAMPS

One of our initial goals was to explore what children understand about different types of error in an experimental context. We presented elementary school children with a situation in which they had to work through each phase of an experiment: We asked them to design, execute, measure and interpret results from an experiment. At each of these stages, there was the possibility of error, both in the particular phase and in the possible interpretations of the outcome (Masnick & Klahr, 2003).

We used the domain of ramps because it is a familiar domain and one that yields data with consistent main effects but some variation. We presented 29 second- and 20 fourth-graders (average ages 8 and 10) with the opportunity to design several experiments with ramps to determine the effects of the height and surface of the ramp on the distance a ball travels. Children were asked to make predictions, justify their designs and predictions, and run the experiment. They were then asked to draw conclusions from the results and to speculate on what the outcome would be if the experiment were to be rerun with no changes in the setup. They were asked to assess how sure they were of their conclusions on a four-point scale (totally sure, pretty sure, kind of sure, not so sure). They were also asked to generate possible reasons for variation in data sets and to reason about the effect of different factors on hypothetical outcomes.

Results

When children designed comparisons to test target variables, most trials included a number of errors in each phase of their experiments, some avoidable, others not. Children recognized some but not all of these errors and had difficulty linking their conclusions with the empirical data. In the design phase, children often made design errors, by failing to set up unconfounded experiments (16% of the second-graders' designs were unconfounded; 40% of the fourth-graders' were). However, their justifications for their designs and their outcome predictions were associated with the accuracy of their design. In other words, participants who designed confounded experiments were likely to expect all the variables they did contrast to affect the outcome, even when that was not the stated goal of the comparison. Similarly, those children who did not vary the target variable were much less likely to cite differences in the target variable as a justification for the expected outcome. This finding suggests an understanding of the causal link between the design and outcome, even when this link was not clearly articulated.

In measuring the distance a ball traveled, the likelihood of measurement error was small due to the constrained nature of measurement in this task: the distance balls rolled was measured discretely by noting the numbered step on which the ball landed. However, nearly all of the participants were able to name sources of measurement error when asked to explain variation in data, indicating a recognition that this type of error is important to consider.

In addition, children were skilled at naming and recognizing many sources of execution-stage error across different tasks in the study, citing potential issues such as positioning of the ball at the start of the ramp, method of releasing the gate, or wind in the room. This finding indicates that they understand the idea that many variables can play a role in a final outcome. When asked explicitly about error, children found it easy to propose different possibilities. In fact, 90% of participants were able to generate at least one potential explanation for data variation throughout the study (the five children who could not name any sources were second graders). However, it is not clear if children link this understanding with their other knowledge about error. For example, children were unlikely to mention execution error (or to note its absence explicitly) in justifying their level of confidence that the target variable had an effect. Thus, although there is evidence for some understanding of the role of execution error, it may not yet be integrated fully into the child's knowledge base.

Children's interpretation errors were assessed by their confidence in and justifications for their conclusions about experimental outcomes. Interpretation errors are the most complex type of error because correct interpretation requires integration of all available sources of information, including information from prior theories, from empirical evidence, and from knowledge of all other potential errors that could influence the outcome. Second- and fourth-graders' understanding of the role of different factors in interpretation seems to be weak at best. Children were more confident about their conclusions when the data matched their prior beliefs (their predictions) than when it did not.

However, they still said they were sure of the conclusions drawn from later outcomes for 76% of their incorrect predictions, compared to 95% of their correct predictions. This difference suggests that at least some children are sensitive to conflicts between theory and data. In addition, prior domain knowledge appeared to guide their reasoning; children justified most of their predictions by referring to the expected effects of the target and nontarget variables.

Discussion

Overall, children were highly skilled at explaining their designs and in generating explanations of sources of variability, but these skills did not translate into an integrated approach that considered error at each stage of an experiment. They were not surprised by variation in the data and did not seem to be thrown off by it, but they had difficulty in using this information explicitly in drawing final conclusions about experimental outcomes.

In the ramps domain, children's prior beliefs about the effect of height and surface were almost always confirmed by the data (when the experiments were designed properly). Working in this domain allowed for an important beginning study of children's understanding of the phases of error and data variation, through examining children's reasoning through all phases of experimentation. Presumably, they all had some knowledge of the mechanics of ramps *before* they began these experiments. This knowledge may have affected their use of data—despite the variability in specific outcomes, the overall findings were almost always in the direction children expected. The data varied but still led to the same conclusions. Thus, the causes of that variability seem likely to be due to something other than the experimental manipulation.

In contrast, when children's prior beliefs are inaccurate, they have in some ways a more difficult decision to make: when is the variation due to a true effect, and when is it due to assorted errors such as measurement or execution errors? In such a situation, the data provide new information, and do not merely support existing beliefs.

CHILDREN'S USE OF DATA IN A POORLY UNDERSTOOD CONTEXT: PENDULUMS

Pendulums provide a potentially revealing context in which to explore children's understanding of data variability. Most children and adults believe (correctly) that the length of a pendulum affects its period of oscillation. However, most children and adults (!) also believe (incorrectly) that the mass of the bob, the height from which it is released and the force with which it is released all influence a pendulum's period.

Of course, length is the sole causal factor only in an idealized situation in which no extraneous forces act on the pendulum (such as flexibility in the string or the pendulum frame, air resistance, friction in the pivot point of the pendulum, and so on). Thus, in timing the period of a pendulum in a research laboratory, any of these factors can lead to small errors and variation in the data. We were interested in how the largely incorrect beliefs of children (fourth- and fifth-graders) and adults (college undergraduates) would influence their interpretation of data sets containing some error variation, and conversely, how variability in the data from repeated experiments would influence their beliefs.

All participants (28 undergraduates and 49 children) were interviewed individually in the lab, and their beliefs about what factors influence the period of a pendulum swing were assessed at three points: (a) in the pretest phase, before they ran any experiments, (b) during the test phase, immediately after they had "generated" and recorded the set of data points for each of the possible factors, and (c) in the post-test phase following all the experimental runs, when participants were asked to review the results of their experiments and state their final beliefs.

During Phase B, participants executed a series of experimenter-designed experiments in which the students timed the period of pendulums having different string lengths, bob masses, and starting heights. For any particular configuration of these three potentially causal variables, we chose one to vary whereas the other two were held constant. Participants were asked to time 10 swings of a pendulum in each of two configurations, such as 10 swings with a heavy bob and 10 swings with a light bob, while string length and release height were held constant. The participant released the pendulum, counted 10 swings, and the experimenter read out the resulting time. For each variable under investigation, this procedure was repeated 8 times: 4 for one level of the variable (e.g., a long string) and 8 for the other level (e.g., a short string). Unbeknownst to the participant, all of the times read by the experimenter were predetermined and not actual measures of the current trials. The times that we falsely presented as veridical were very close to the actual times for each pendulum trial, so that they were entirely plausible. However, this manipulation ensured that each participant was exposed to exactly the same amount of data variation. (Debriefings revealed that none of the participants suspected our deceptive manipulation.)

All of the data sets varied slightly: There were no two measurements given to participants that were identical within the set of trials for each given variable. However, because string length was the only variable that caused a

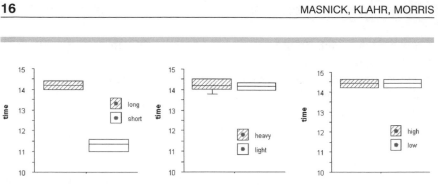

Figure 1.1 Summary of data presented to participants, showing distinct separation between times associated with long versus short strings, and complete overlap for times associated with heavy/light weights and high/low starting positions. (Y-axis shows seconds to complete 10 swings; box-plots are based on four data points for each subplot.)

true effect, the difference in the readings from the trials with a short string and those with a long string were much more pronounced. The data from these two sets of trials did not overlap. Figure 1.1 shows the box-plots for the data that were presented to each participant. (Note that the participants received the data one data point at a time, after timing each round of swings. The data were recorded in a column format, on a preprinted hand-out provided by the experimenter.)

As just noted, each participant experimented with the effects of length, weight, and height. Because we wanted to examine participants' ability to "calibrate" high versus low variability in this context, we presented the length variation as the first factor to be explored for one half of the participants, and as the last factor to be explored for the other half.

Results

Both adults and children learned from running the experiments, and there was no effect of whether the length variable was presented first or last. Figure 1.2 shows several very clear patterns: (a) With respect to initial knowledge, both adults and children tended to believe (correctly) that length matters, and (incorrectly) that weight and height also matter; (b) both adults and children

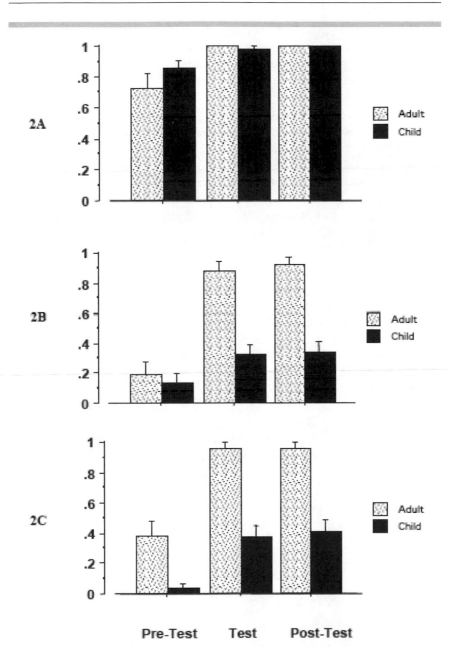

Figure 1.2 Proportion of participants (with standard error bars) in each phase and age group who correctly answered the question about whether or not a particular factor influenced the period of a pendulum. A: "Does Length matter?" (correct answer: "Yes"); B: "Does Weight matter?" (correct answer: "No"); C: "Does Height matter?" (correct answer: "No").

learned from pre-test to test phase about all three variables; (c) adults not only knew more about all three factors than did children at pre-test but also improved their knowledge more than children after seeing the data. In other words, by the end of the test phase, and through the post-test phase, most adults had revised their faulty beliefs about the effect of height and weight on the period of a pendulum. In contrast, children's gains, although statistically significant, remained at very low levels. These differences cannot be attributed to adults' being less sure of their knowledge at the outset, and thus being more responsive to data. In fact, the sureness ratings for children and adults started out at almost identical levels. By the post-test, adults were significantly more confident than they were at pre-test. They were also more confident than the children were at post-test (though their confidence increased as well).

Discussion

The results of this experiment indicate that adults are much better than children at using data to revise their beliefs when the data do not agree with prior expectations. Adults clearly differentiated the small variation in measurement of factors that do not play a role in the outcome (different weights and heights) from the large variation evident in the measurement of the one variable that did make a difference (length of the string). Children appear to have more difficulty with this process. One possible explanation is that the data variation in the noncausal variables, even though much smaller than the difference in the two levels of the causal variable, enabled them to retain their faulty beliefs. Recent work has also shown that children have much more difficulty changing inaccurate beliefs that a noncausal variable is causal than the reverse (Kanari & Millar, 2004). In the current study, the designs were set for participants, but children had difficulty in interpreting potential measurement and execution errors as causes for variability, and thus made many interpretation errors when data contradicted their beliefs. Using data to alter theory was a challenge.

CHILDREN'S USE OF DATA
WITH NO THEORETICAL CONTEXT

One method of exploring the influence of theory on conclusions drawn about data is to examine reasoning in different theoretical contexts. Although much research has examined children's understanding of data within theoretical contexts, there has not been much study of how children evaluate the data itself. That is, how do children decide when evidence is compelling or uncompelling? Once these characteristics of data are identified, we can examine the extent to which specific characteristics of data are related to theoretical change. To examine this issue, a different approach was used in which data were presented with little theoretical guidance so that the conclusions drawn would be predominantly data-driven rather than theory-driven. In this study, we examined children's reasoning in the interpretation phase of an experiment: Data were presented as results of a completed experiment, and participants were asked to draw conclusions based on the information they had available. We set up situations with minimal theoretical background information, to make the variation in data characteristics particularly salient.

Two of the most important ideas about data involve expectations about sample size and expectations about variation in data distribution, and we used these variables as the focal variables in our study. We asked participants to draw conclusions about whether there was a difference between two sets of data and to explain their reasoning (Masnick & Morris, 2002).

Thirty-nine third-graders, 44 sixth-graders, and 50 college undergraduates were presented with a cover story, and then were asked to reason about potential differences between two sets of data. Half of the participants read the following cover story about engineers who are testing new sports equipment, using robot launchers to repeatedly test different sports balls, such as tennis balls and golf balls. The other participants read an isomorphic cover story about a coach trying out two athletes vying for one slot on her team.

> Some engineers are testing new sports equipment. Right now, they are looking at the quality of different sports balls, like tennis balls, golf balls and baseballs. For example, when they want to find out about golf balls, they use a special robot launcher to test two balls from the same factory. They use a robot launcher because they can program the robot to launch the ball with the same amount of force each time. Sometimes they test the balls more than once. After they run the tests, they look at the results to see what they can learn.

After reading the cover story, participants were shown a series of data sets, one at a time. For each example, there were data for either two different balls of the same type, which were not given any distinguishing characteristics (e.g., "Baseball A" and "Baseball B") or for two athletes about which there was no information other than their names (e.g., "Alan" and "Bill"). In the robot condition, robots performed the actions with the balls, while in the athletic condition, individual athletes did. In the athlete condition, different names were used for each data set, to prevent any carry-over knowledge effect. Each page contained two lists of data: one listed the distance the first ball traveled and the second listed the distance the second ball traveled.

The data sets varied in sample size and in variability. Sample size was operationalized by the number of pairs of data presented with each story, with 1, 2, 4, or 6 pairs of data presented. Variability was operationalized by

TABLE 1.2
Examples of Datasets Shown to Participants

Example 1: Six data pairs, no overlapping data points, robot condition

Golf Ball A	Golf Ball B
466 feet	447 feet
449 feet	429 feet
452 feet	430 feet
465 feet	446 feet
456 feet	437 feet
448 feet	433 feet

Example 2: Four data pairs, one overlapping pair (3 out of 4 times Carla throws farther), athlete condition

Carla	Diana
51 feet	38 feet
63 feet	50 feet
43 feet	56 feet
57 feet	44 feet

varying whether the data in the two columns overlapped or not. In some cases ("no overlap"), all the values in one column were larger than all values in the other column. In other cases, the majority of values in one column were larger than values in the other column, but there were one or two pairs in which the pattern was reversed. Each participant received a total of 14 comparisons, with 8 trials including no overlap (two each of sample size 1, 2, 4, and 6) and 6 trials including one or two overlapping data points (sample size 4 with one overlapping data point, and sample size 6 with one or two overlapping data points). Each of the fourteen trials tested a different type of sports ball. Examples of the data sets presented are shown in Table 1.2.

For each data set, participants were asked what the engineer or coach could find out as a result of this information and to explain reasons for their answer. They were asked how sure they were about these conclusions, using the same four-level scale as in studies described earlier (totally sure, pretty sure, kind of sure, not so sure).

Results

We used participants' sureness as the dependent measure, and looked at the effect of different sample sizes and levels of variability. There were no

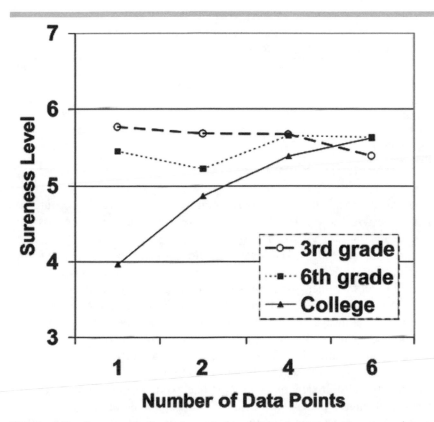

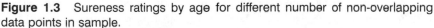

Figure 1.3 Sureness ratings by age for different number of non-overlapping data points in sample.

differences between the robot and athlete conditions on these two factors, and so data were collapsed for these analyses. When comparing across data sets in which there were no overlapping data points, we found that college students were much more sure with more data, sixth-graders had no significant differences across sample size, and third-graders were actually more sure with less data (see Fig. 1.3). Although this effect did not reach significance, as most third-graders were highly confident regardless of the amount of data, it is an intriguing finding suggesting children at this age are evaluating data by very different standards than adults.

When comparing data sets with the same sample size but different levels of variability, we found that this variation in the data affected all participants' ratings of sureness. At all grade levels, participants were more sure of conclusions when the data in the two columns did not overlap than when it did.

TABLE 1.3
Percentage Of Participants at Each Grade Level
Who Gave Each Data-Based Explanation at Least One Time.

	3rd grade	6th grade	Undergraduate
Trend	90	84	100
Sample size	10	27	96
Overlap	56	61	72
Variability	0	7	28
Magnitude of difference	36	80	90

There was a linear relationship: Participants were less sure of the outcome when there was one overlap than when there was none, and even less sure with two overlaps than with one.

Participants were also asked for justifications for their reasoning about why they felt they could be sure of conclusions. Coding of data-based reasons involved noting whether participants mentioned a trend in the data ("5 out of 6 times A went farther"); sample size ("It's only two times so it's hard to tell"); no overlap ("A always went farther than B"), variability within the column ("the numbers were really far apart in A," and magnitude of differences ("A went a lot farther than B"). There were large grade differences in the frequency of using each of the descriptions (see Table 1.3). However, all but one participant (a third-grader) made at least one explicit reference to data characteristics such as a pattern in the data or the magnitude of differences. This finding indicates that even as early as third grade, children are paying attention to some characteristics of data, and using this information in guiding their conclusions.

Additionally, reasons were also coded to take note of whether they included a mechanistic explanation for the outcome. These responses were classified as a reason based on a property of the ball ("Ball A was more aerodynamic"), of the robot or athlete ("Maybe the robot was breaking down when it threw Ball B"; "Bill was getting tired"), or of the environment ("Maybe there was wind when Ball A was thrown"). Mentioning the property of the robot or athlete was the only factor we found that did vary considerably by condition, with nearly all mentions in the athlete condition (i.e., participants sometimes said that a property of athlete was a reason for the outcome, but very rarely attributed it a property of the robot). However, there were no grade differences in frequency of providing a mechanistic explanation, with an average of 50% of participants providing at least one mechanistic explanation. In their interpretations, a sizeable number of participants were using prior background knowledge to explain the data.

Discussion

These data demonstrate that in the absence of clear domain knowledge on which to base theoretical explanations, children and college students paid attention to several features of data. Third-graders and college students responded to sample size as a key determinant of how sure they could be in their conclusions, although surprisingly, third-graders were on average less sure of conclusions with more data points. At all ages, participants responded to variation in the data as an important factor to consider in drawing conclusions.

In addition, children regularly referred to characteristics of the data in explaining their reasoning. Almost all children noticed these characteristics, and talked about them to some degree. This finding indicates that children are aware that data vary and that this variation is something to consider in reasoning. Although they did not always use the information as they described it, the fact that they would offer data-based more often than mechanism-based explanations for the results indicates that they may be using characteristics of data to develop theoretical explanations. Such interpretations indicate an understanding that many factors at different stages of the testing phase could have an impact on the outcome and are important to consider in drawing conclusions.

At the same time, there were clear age differences in many responses, indicating changes over time. The use of sample size information changed most dramatically with time, with the slight tendency for third-graders to be more sure with less data changing to a fairly consistent sureness across sample size for sixth-graders and finally, a clear pattern of increased confidence by college. This finding replicates similar findings indicating that younger children are often confused with larger quantities of data (e.g., Piaget & Inhelder, 1951/1975; Varelas, 1997).

The findings from this study suggest that students pay attention to data characteristics as early as third grade, and are able to use this information in drawing conclusions. Their knowledge of experimental processes appears to be guiding their reasoning about how to interpret experimental results. Finally, in justifying their reasoning, children and adults are relying primarily on explanations based in the data, even if these are not always fully articulated or accurately applied.

CONCLUSIONS

The results from these three studies indicate that children recognize data variation in many experimental contexts, and they use characteristics of data in their reasoning. However, the context is important. When reasoning about data in a well-understood context—when experimental outcomes match expectations—children are unlikely to change any theoretical understanding. In such contexts, they can reason to some degree about causal mechanisms that lead to variation in data. The ramps study indicates that children expect error and variation in data, and can generate many potential causes for the sources of that error. They often make design errors, but they also recognize execution and measurement errors during all phases of experimentation.

In a poorly understood context—when experimental outcomes do not match expectations—children demonstrate difficulty integrating new data that contradict their beliefs. Children seemed to be aware of the possible sources of error but had difficulty in interpreting the differences in variability as errors and not meaningful indications of a true difference between conditions.

Finally, when presented with data without a strong theoretical context, the data study indicates that children pay attention to characteristics of data and use sample size and variability as information to consider in reasoning with data. They use the key features of data in drawing conclusions, even when they cannot always articulate their justifications. However, nearly all participants talked at some point about characteristics of the data guiding their reasoning. About half the participants also develop theoretical explanations to explain the data, speculating on potential design and execution errors that may have caused the variation.

Although we have found evidence that children do use characteristics of data in their reasoning, adults are much more skilled at the integration of theory and data. The mechanisms of this developmental shift are something it seems premature to speculate about. It is clear that experience and formal education increase children's exposure to varied data. However, we are just beginning to understand what children do know about data and how they use it. We do not have data on the frequency of children's experiences with data in real life or the classroom, and how often they are asked to draw conclusions in those situations.

To return to our original question, how do children and adults separate signal from noise? In considering the somewhat exaggerated question of which comes first, the data or the theory, we are left with evidence supporting a true bootstrapping pattern, in which data and theory knowledge work together. In the ramps study, children's (mostly accurate) theories guided their reasoning—the mechanistic explanations were the most common justifications for their conclusions, regardless of the effectiveness of the design used. In the pendulum study, adults were able to use data to update their inaccurate theories without much difficulty, but only a small number of children were able to do the same. Strong theories are difficult to overcome with a brief exposure to data. In the data-only study, a small but sizeable number of participants of all ages used data characteristics to generate theoretical explanations for data patterns, without specific prompting to do so. This study demonstrated that variation is a key feature that children and adults attend to, whereas the use of sample size information is more complicated. Although adults are better able to modify theories in response to contradictory data, children show some evidence of using varied data characteristics in their reasoning and using the information both to draw conclusions and to develop causal explanations. Thus, it seems that both theory and data are important in designating what constitutes signal as well as noise.

In light of these findings, creating effective classroom materials to aid children in learning about data and experimentation needs to build on children's nascent understanding of data variation. The fact that young children do talk about data characteristics and use some data features in drawing conclusions indicates some preliminary understanding of the nature of science experimentation. The depth of this knowledge is incomplete, and future research into its limits will aid in this goal.

So what will the young roller-coaster enthusiast from our opening example conclude about her true height? That will depend in part on her age and experience. Most likely if she is in second or third grade, she will find multiple measurements confusing, and will have difficulty assessing her true height. However, because height measurement is probably a familiar context, she will have at the ready some potential theoretical explanations for the variability, considering possible measurement errors or other factors that may have gone awry. She will have difficulty integrating these theoretical beliefs with the data she sees, but she is aware that there can be variability in measurement. With increased age and experience, she will come to be more confident with increased data and to develop a more sophisticated repertoire of potential explanations for variability.

ACKNOWLEDGMENTS

This work was supported, in part, by Grant BCS-0132315 from the National Science Foundation and Grant HD25211 from the National Institute of Child Health and Human Development, both to the second author.

REFERENCES

Amsel, E., & Brock, S. (1996). The development of evidence evaluation skills. *Cognitive Development, 11*, 523–550.

Chinn, C. A., & Brewer, W. F. (2001). Models of data: A theory of how people evaluate data. *Cognition and Instruction, 19*, 323–393.

Chinn, C. A., & Malhotra, B. A. (2002). Children's responses to anomalous scientific data: How is conceptual change impeded? *Journal of Educational Psychology, 94*, 327–343.

Gutheil, G. & Gelman, S. (1997). Children's use of sample size and diversity information within basic-level categories. *Journal of Experimental Child Psychology, 64*, 159–174.

Hon, G. (1989). Towards a typology of experimental errors: An epistemological view. *Studies in History and Philosophy of Science, 20*, 469–504.

Jacobs, J. E., & Narloch, R. H. (2001). Children's use of sample size and variability to make social inferences. *Journal of Applied Developmental Psychology, 22*, 311–331.

Jusczyk, P. W., Friederici, A. D., Wessels, J. M., Svenkerud, V. Y., & Jusczyk, A. M. (1993). Infants' sensitivity to the sound patterns of native language words. *Journal of Memory and Language, 32*, 402–420.

Kanari, Z., & Millar, R. (2004). Reasoning from data: How students collect and interpret data in science investigations. *Journal of Research in Science Teaching, 41*, 748–769.

Konold, C. (1991). Information conceptions of probability. *Cognition and Instruction, 6*, 59–98.

Koslowski, B. (1996). *Theory and evidence: The development of scientific reasoning.* Cambridge, MA: MIT Press.

Kuhn, D., & Dean, D., Jr. (2004). Connecting scientific reasoning and causal inference. *Journal of Cognition and Development, 5*, 261–288.

Kuzmak, S., & Gelman, R. (1986). Children's understanding of random phenomena. *Child Development, 57*, 559–566.

Lubben, F., & Millar, R. (1996). Children's ideas about the reliability of experimental data. *International Journal of Science Education, 18*, 955–968.

Masnick, A. M., & Klahr, D. (2003). Error matters: An initial exploration of elementary school children's understanding of experimental error. *Journal of Cognition and Development, 4*, 67–98.

Masnick, A. M., & Morris, B. J. (2002). Reasoning from data: The effect of sample size and variability on children's and adults' conclusions. In W. D. Gray & C. D. Schunn (Eds.), *Proceedings of the Twenty-Fourth Annual Conference of the Cognitive Science Society* (pp. 643–648). Mahwah, NJ: Lawrence Erlbaum Associates.

Metz, K. E. (1998). Emergent understanding and attribution of randomness: Comparative analysis of the reasoning of primary grade children and undergraduates. *Cognition and Instruction, 16*, 285–365.

NRC. (2000). *Inquiry and the National Science Education Standards: A guide for teaching and learning.* Washington, DC: National Academy Press.

Petrosino, A., Lehrer, R., & Schauble, L. (2003). Structuring error and experimental variation as distribution in the fourth grade. *Mathematical Thinking and Learning, 5*, 131–156.

Piaget, J., & Inhelder, B. (1975). *The origin of the idea of chance in children* (L. Lowell,, Jr., P. Burrell, & H. D. Fishbein, Trans.). New York: W. W. Norton. (Original work published 1951)

Schauble, L. (1996). The development of scientific reasoning in knowledge-rich contexts. *Developmental Psychology, 32*, 102–119.

Shaklee, H., & Paszek, D. (1985). Covariation judgment: Systematic rule use in middle childhood. *Child Development, 56*, 1229–1240.

Sodian, B., Zaitchik, D., & Carey, S. (1991). Young children's differentiation of hypothetical beliefs from evidence. *Child Development, 62*, 753–766.

Tversky, A., & Kahneman, D. (1974). Judgment under uncertainty: Heuristics and Biases. *Science, 185*, 1124–1131.

Varelas, M. (1997). Third and fourth graders' conceptions of repeated trials and best representatives in science experiments. *Journal of Research in Science Teaching, 34*, 853–872.

Zimmerman, C. (2005). The development of scientific reasoning: *What psychologists contribute to an understanding of elementary science learning.* Paper commissioned by the National Academies of Science (National Research Council's Board of Science Education, Consensus Study of Learning Science, Kindergarten through Eighth Grade). Final report available at: http://www7.nationalacademies.org/bose/ Corinne_Zimmerman_Final _Paper.pdf

2

Complex Visual Data Analysis, Uncertainty, and Representation

Christian D. Schunn
Lelyn D. Saner
University of Pittsburgh

Susan K. Kirschenbaum
Naval Undersea Warfare Center Division

J. Gregory Trafton
Naval Research Laboratory

Eliza B. Littleton
Pittsburgh, PA

REPRESENTATIONS AND COMPLEX PROBLEM SOLVING

A core thesis of cognitive science is that representations, be they structures inside the head of the problem-solver (internal representations) or structures in the environment of the problem-solver (external representations), are fundamental to understanding problem-solving behavior (Markman, 1999). There may be some debate about the underlying nature of these representations (e.g., the relative weight that problem-solvers place on internal vs. external representations, whether the representations are symbolic or not), but all cognitive scientists endorse some form of underlying representation driving behavior (Dietrich & Marton, 2000).

The value of talking about representation is that computation (the definitional core of cognition in cognitive science) can only be meaningfully defined over some type of representation. Computation at its root consists of a data structure (for input, output, and perhaps something being stored in between) and some process. One cannot talk about the process without describing the data structure. More importantly, different data structures enable certain computations to be done easily, whereas other data structures support other computations. Thus, the choice of data structure (representation) helps explain why a problem-solver does or does not successfully engage in a given process (cognition/behavior) or perhaps why a process takes as long or as short as it does.

The goal of this chapter is to argue that representation can and should be studied directly rather than be ignored or left as an explanatory variable. We begin with a discussion of how representations can be measured. We then examine several of the main theoretical paradigms of cognitive science to see what *predictions* they make for representation choice. Finally, we present data from two studies designed to test these predictions.

MEASURING REPRESENTATIONS

Although the theoretical construct of representations are fundamental to cognitive science theorizing, the dirty secret of cognitive science is that we do not have a good theory for predicting what representations a given problem solver in a given situation will use. The most common treatment of representation is as an explanatory, intermediate (i.e., hidden) variable of performance. In other words, we observe inputs and outputs, and perhaps infer process via a description of intermediate states, but the representation is something only posited or assumed in order to explain the relationship between inputs and outputs.

To help explain why we do not have theories of how problem-solvers pick a representation, we unpack in this section the basic measurement problem for internal and external representations. On some occasions, there is some attempt to measure the representations used by the problem-solvers, to verify the assumptions that were made about the representations. Measuring representations is no easy feat. Even with external representations, the measurement task is challenging. Different observers can "see" different things in the world around them. Humans are fundamentally limited in how much information they can attend from their perceptual input (Treisman, 1969). Thus, we do not know what information in the environment to which they are attending. In a complex problem-solving situation, the external environment can be quite complex, and thus there can be a very large amount of information that is not attended. Then there are the interactions of human perception with displays. Some perceptual features are salient and easily encoded (e.g., strong color contrasts, motion onset, object appearance) whereas other perceptual features not salient or not so easily encoded (e.g., conjunctions of features, absolute pitch of sounds, etc.). Operations are easier on some external representations than on other external representations, and cognitive science talks about this interaction as affordances (Neisser, 1976).

So, to capture what external representations a problem-solver is using, we need to know what objects in the environment and what features of the objects are being attended, rather than just looking at what perceptual input is available in the environment and how it is structured. To some extent, we can measure what visual objects are being encoded through eye-tracking studies—people encode primarily what objects they foveate, and they tend to foveate objects they are thinking about (Just & Carpenter, 1976a, 1976b). But, people do encode some information from parafovea, and they sometimes do not encode information while staring blankly at the environment while their mind is elsewhere.

Another approach to measuring external representations is a mixture of ethnographic or quantitative observation and interviews (Hutchins, 1995a). The external objects that problem-solvers name or discuss while problem solving provide some good clues to what objects and features of the external environment are being attended. However, linguistics manifestations of the perceptual inputs in conversation may be systematically changed or selective, and may exclude some of the perceptual inputs that were attended. Thus, measuring external representations continues to be a challenging task.

Even more challenging is the task of measuring internal representations. Even when information is represented using a fairly perceptual-based internal representation, people are capable of recoding information from one perceptual code into another. For example, people given words visually will often transform the words into an auditory code (thereby producing auditory confusion errors rather than visual confusion errors). More problematic are recodings of input into more symbolic, abstract forms. People can build mental links between objects that aid later retrieval (Altmann & Trafton, 2002), develop new groupings of objects (called chunks) allowing them to simultaneously represent more information in mind, and categorize objects in ways unrelated to their perceptual input (e.g., the categories of "even numbers," "uncles," and "abstract categories").

Internal representations can only be measured indirectly, if "measured" is even the correct term. The basic problem is that we must typically look for some kind of external manifestation of the internal representation and that external manifestation may be only a distant echo or heavily distorted copy of the internal representation. For example, we can ask a problem-solver to draw a picture or verbally describe a given situation. The drawing may omit verbal representations, the verbal description may miss visual/spatial descriptions, both may be incomplete descriptions of those sensory-based representations, and both may be missing more abstract representations. Moreover, the act of having to describe the situation may push the problem-solver to represent features they would not have otherwise mentioned, but only looking at spontaneous produced external manifestations (e.g., spontaneous speech, gesture, or drawings) may only capture communicatively focused representations.

One approach to measuring internal representations more directly is to use neuropsychological techniques such as neuroimaging (MEG, fMRI, ERP, or PET) or single-cell recording. Although this approach holds some promise for more direct measurement, the methodological challenges of these methods (e.g., spatial and temporal resolution, extremely high noise levels) prevent their use in most complex problem-solving situations, and currently we know relatively little about the internal codes of the brain (i.e., what activation in different brain areas even means).

The reason that we discussed the basic measurement problem for internal and external representations is to help explain why we do not have theories of how problem-solvers pick a representation. The answer is that we rarely go to the trouble of measuring representations, and when we do, we are not so sure we have done it correctly. Thus, the set of results or phenomena related to representation choice is rather thin, and this would explain why we do not have much theorizing about representation choice.

THEORIZING ABOUT REPRESENTATION CHOICE

Although there are relatively few theories of representation choice (i.e., how problem-solvers choose representations) in cognitive science relative to how important representation choice is to cognitive science, there are some theories (e.g., Kaplan & Simon, 1990; Lovett & Schum, 1999). These theories can be summarized under the heading of Search and Rational Choice: Problem-solvers consider different representations when they are unsuccessful and select the representations that turn out to lead to more successful problem solving. There is also an assumption that problem-solvers start with certain salient features, but there is no theoretical specification of what features will be salient.

There is, however, considerable theorizing about the consequences of different representation choices. By applying this same general idea of rational choice, this broad theorizing about consequences can be turned into theories of choice. Specifically, with some form of rationality or asymptotic optimality assumptions, one could predict that problem-solvers will tend to select the more useful or optimal representations, especially with expertise. Although rationality and optimality are still somewhat controversial theoretical assumptions, they are not so controversial when (1) we limit ourselves to directional optimality (i.e., better is more likely than worse); and (2) we focus on the case of expert behavior. Of course, experts also likely to be limited to some form of bounded rationality (Simon, 1956), and it is possible for experts to get "stuck" using a representation chosen early but that becomes relatively successful through high levels of practice.

In terms of consequences of representation choice, we believe there are three broad theoretical camps in cognitive science: symbolic problem solving, embodied problem solving, and neurocomputational problem solving. If we apply this rationality assumption to these different theoretical camps, we can derive different predictions about representation choice. The goal of this chapter is to spell out these predictions, and explore their relative usefulness for predicting representation choice in several complex problem-solving domains in which experts work with highly uncertain visual data.

REPRESENTATIONS IN SYMBOLIC PROBLEM SOLVING

Cognitive science began with a focus on the internal and a focus on symbol processing. This approach was heavily centered in Pittsburgh and was heavily influenced by Herb Simon (Chi, Feltovich, & Glaser, 1981; Kaplan & Simon, 1990; Klahr & Dunbar, 1988; Kotovsky, Hasyes, & Simon, 1985; Larkin, McDermott, Simon, & Simon, 1980; Lovett & Schunn, 1999). The assumption of this symbolic problem-solving camp is that representation is determined by task structure (in their language, the problem space) modulo various memory limitations. More specifically, experts are assumed to have representations that strip away irrelevant details and focus on or build features that highlight the deep structure of the task at hand. For example, in a classic study, Chi, Feltovich, and Glaser (1981) found that physics experts represented simple physics problems not in their superficial terms (incline planes, pulley problems, etc), but in terms of their solution types (conservation of energy problems, $F = ma$ problems, etc).

In terms of the constraints from the external world, the symbolic problem-solving approach does not say much. Internal representations must be derivable in some ways from the external input, and it is assumed that people incur some processing costs for encoding and transformation. But there is not a detailed or higher level theory for how the external world would shape the representational choice of an expert.

In terms of constraints of the internal world (i.e., the brain), the symbolic problem-solving approach places even fewer constraints as a general theoretical approach. When one gets into particular theories, memory constraints may become apparent. For example, expertise, in some accounts, is not thought to change the number of chunks a person can hold onto in memory. However, the size of chunks is not theoretically constrained, and some theories posit that experts can learn higher order structures that allow them to circumvent the number of chunks constraint as well (Gobet & Simon, 1996). Thus, even the memory constraint is not very constraining in terms of predicting expert representation choice.

In sum, although the symbolic problem-solving approach assumes that representation choice is one of the most important issues in predicting behavior, it says relatively little about how individuals make that choice. At most, the symbolic camp makes the general prediction that people start with representations that focus on salient or superficial features and move to representations that somehow better facilitate task-relevant computations (Lovett & Schunn, 1999).

REPRESENTATIONS IN EMBODIED PROBLEM SOLVING

Beginning in the late 1970s, some researchers began to look to the structure of the external environment, and more specifically, the ways in which the human body fit into the structure of the external environment to explain human cognition and performance (Gibson, 1979; Neisser, 1976), rather than focusing so heavily on logical task structure and internal symbol manipulation. Several different lines of theorizing developed under this approach, including situated cognition (Suchman, 1987) , distributed cognition (Hutchins, 1995a, 1995b), embodied action (Fu & Gray, 2004; Gray, John, & Atwood, 1993), and perceptual symbol systems (Barsallou, 1999). For example, Ed Hutchins showed in great detail how the performance of an airplane pilot depends on being able to apply simple perceptual heuristics to correctly laid-out instruments.

An important construct in many (but not all) lines in this general approach is the notion of affordances. A display, instrument, or artifact is thought to afford certain actions and cognitions and not afford others, meaning the combination of past experiences and body/mind structure make certain actions very easy to do with a given display, instrument, or artifact. Along these lines, one might argue that experts adopt internal representations that maximize the affordances relationship between common tasks and external objects used to execute those tasks. Yet, without a very formal description of what affordances are and a predictive framework for specifying what affordances come from what tasks, the affordances framework tends to be circular in nature. Affordances are said to exist in an object when we observe smooth performance with that object. In other words, affordances are used to both describe and explain referentially to one another.

A different, more straightforward prediction of representation choice from the embodied problem-solving approach is to predict an internalization of the external. If cognition and problem solving is so heavily driven by the external world, then internal representations must be closely tied to the external world. That is, the choice of internal representation must be heavily driven by the nature of the external input (e.g., if input is 2-dimensional, then internal representations are likely to be 2-dimensional, though cf. Scaife & Rogers, 1996).

A related prediction focuses on the action rather than input side of performance. Sometimes input is in one form, but our actions occur in a different form. For example, the input a submariner gets from Sonar is very 2-dimensional, but the actions they take move the submarine in 3-dimensions. The expert problem-solver may adopt an internal representation that is close to the external input form, thereby reducing the complexity of computations going from input to cognition. Alternatively, the expert problem-solver may adopt an internal representation that is close to the external action form, thereby reducing the complexity of computations going from cognition to action. Thus, one could also predict from the embodied problem-solving perspective that choice of internal representations are driven by the external reality of the action space that the problem-solver is working within.

In sum, the embodied problem-solving perspective predicts a close match in internal representation choice to either the input representations or the output environment.

REPRESENTATIONS IN NEUROCOMPUTATIONAL PROBLEM SOLVING

Although the abstract and embodied problem-solving perspectives are themselves very different, they share a belief about the very adaptable nature of human representations—at some level, any internal representation is possible, given an appropriate task and/or appropriate external input. Or said another way, at some level, the details of the human brain are irrelevant to predicting the range of possible expert internal representations or the choice among possible representations.

At the same time, we now know a great deal about the way the human brain processes perceptual information. Since the early 1960s, we have known that the brain has very specific maps of perceptual information (Hubel

& Wiesel, 1962). Since the 1980s, we have known that the brain has elaborate pathways by which complex representations of perceptual information are gradually and carefully constructed (Ungerleider & Mishkin, 1982). Although these pathways must be rebuilt within each person through development, the general structure is very similar from individual to individual. The structure, therefore, is primarily driven by a genetic code, or at least a genetic code interacting with general features of the overall environment that are the same for everyone. Therefore, the structure of these perceptual pathways is not likely to vary significantly across individuals with different areas of expertise.

Is the way that humans process perceptual information relevant to internal representation structure? In the 1970s and 1980s, there was considerable debate about whether mental imagery was entirely symbolic or more analog in format, and about whether it relied entirely on higher level cognition or whether the basic perceptual machinery was involved (e.g., Kosslyn, Ball, & Reiser, 1978; Kosslyn, Pinter, Smith & Shwartz, 1979; e.g., Pylyshyn, 1973; Pylyshyn, 1981). By the 1990s, most researchers considered the issue resolved with the introduction of neuroscience evidence that showed clearly that mental imagery depended heavily on all the same neural structures as did perception, except the very earliest part of perceptual pathways (Kosslyn, 1994; Kosslyn et al., 1999; Kosslyn, Thompson, Kim, & Alpert, 1995), although there is still some ongoing debate Pylyshyn, 2002).

In sum, human brains have complex information processing pathways that process information in very particular ways and are common across individuals regardless of expertise, and those processing pathways are used for at least some internal representations. From that point of view, it seems plausible that the details of our neurobiology would influence the range of possible internal representations that an expert could have. This restriction of choices is particularly relevant for representations that have a perceptual or analog character rather than purely symbolic flavor, in part because we understand in great detail the perceptual systems in the brain but understand very little about the symbol manipulation systems in the brain. On the other hand, the cognitive architectures approach to modeling cognition (e.g., Anderson & Lebiere, 1998; Kieras & Meyer, 1997; Newell, 1990) also support the general idea that the underlying cognitive architecture places some restrictions, albeit relatively weak thus far (Anderson, 1990), on what kinds of representation systems are possible. Thus, there may also be neurocomputational restrictions of choices of more symbolic representations as well.

Because we have now wandered into the realm of biology, it may be worth bringing forward a framework from biology for understanding how new representations come about. In biology, the new representations are external physiological changes in a species, or creations of new species. In our case, the new representations are new internal representations with developing expertise. The symbolic problem-solving framework corresponds to the biological notion of adaptation: new representations are developed by adapting existing representations to the current task structure (Kaplan & Simon, 1990; Schunn & Klahr, 1996, 2000). The embodied problem-solving framework corresponds to notions of an analog (rather than homolog). Analogs are structures that arise from a different evolutionary source but serve similar functions, whereas homologs are structures that arise from similar evolutionary sources. The internal representation in the embodied problem-solving framework is thought to be at some level a copy of input or output representations, selected from a different neural substrate to serve a similar function (i.e., an analog). By contrast, the neurocomputational problem-solving framework corresponds to notions of exaptation (Gould & Vrba, 1982). Under this account, internal representations that were developed over evolutionary time for one set of tasks can become co-opted or exapted to a new use as new tasks occur. To be more specific, the human problem-solver is born with internal representational abilities that were there to support very traditional tasks shared with other mammals (e.g., object recognition, object manipulation, navigation, etc). The human problem-solver must make use of those fixed set of representational abilities to build representations for the range of modern tasks that humans now become expert in.

Following this line of argument further, we can then move to understanding the influence of neurocomputational constraints on the choice of particular representations for a particular task, not just on the set of possible representations. The trick is to focus on notions of efficiency or affordances, as do the abstract and embodied problem-solving frameworks. Different neuropsychological representational systems represent information in different ways in order to support different tasks (Previc, 1998; Ungerkider & Mishkin, 1982), implying that some computations are accurately or more quickly performed with some representational systems than with others. Therefore, as with exaptation in biology, we can predict that expert problem-solvers will tend to select the internal representation system whose neurocomputational abilities best support the expert's task at hand. For example, if the task requires the expert to represent themselves at the center of a full 360 degree space of mental objects placed around them, and if only one neural system supports representations in the full 360 (rather than just a frontal 120 or 180), then this approach would predict in a rather straightforward fashion that the problem-solver would use that neural system for internal representations of this task. We will say more about different possible human neural systems and their neurocomputational abilities in a later section.

TABLE 2.1
Comparison of General Predictions About Representational
Choice From Each of the Three Theoretical Camps.

Theoretical Camp	Use Affordances?	External Matters?	Internal Choices?
Symbolic	√	Maybe	Anything
Embodied	√	Yes	Anything
Neurocomputational	√	Aspects that are processed	Fixed set, Exaptation

COMPARISON OF REPRESENTATIONAL PREDICTIONS

Table 2.1 presents a comparison of the general predictions made about internal representation under the three theoretical camps. All three camps agree that affordances should matter in that experts will choose internal representations that best match the cognitions that need to be performed, and that different representations have different affordances. At some level, all three camps agree with the basic characterization provided originally by the symbolic camp that the story of affordances is best cast in computational terms—affordances reduce necessary computations by the problem-solver.

The camps do differ in exactly how the affordances are described. More specifically, they differ in the objects against which affordances are primarily defined. This focus brings us to the second dimension of comparison, the issue of whether the external world matters. The symbolic camp is somewhat neutral on this point. The external world may or may not influence internal representation choice, depending on whether there are features of the external world that are particularly helpful. In other words, if the structure of the external world is not useful for the problem-solver, then the problem-solver may choose to work entirely within an internally constructed representation that has little to no relationship to the external world. One can point to characterizations of insight problems in these terms: one core trick in solving the insight problem is to move away from the salient details of the external world and develop a new representation (Kaplan & Simon, 1990; Perkins, 1994).

By contrast, the embodied problem-solver camp predicts that the external world will have a strong role in influencing internal representations. The reason is that the embodied problem-solving perspective assumes that experts organize their external worlds such that they can make heavy use of the external world to guide their problem-solving (Hutchins, 1995a). In other words, there is a belief that real world tasks are typically embedded in complex sociotechnical systems that are influenced by the individual expert problem-solver (in which parts of their rich environment they chose to use) and by collections of expert problem-solvers (in influencing the construction of artifacts). Expert problem-solvers thereby make it possible for their internal representations to have a close affinity to the external world around them, simplifying the translation between internal and external, and yet still have very successful problem solving.

The neurocomputational problem-solver chooses a more nuanced and complex stance on the role of the external world on internal representation choice. The human perceptual system involves a division and modulation of separate perceptual features along with some integration across perceptual modalities. For example, vision can be processed separately from sound, and even within vision, color can be processed separately from orientation, and object identity can be processed separately from object location. At the same time, the brain can also integrate across very different senses, building, for example, a spatial map of the environment from visual, auditory, and tactile cues (Previc, 1998). Attention adds another layer, by being able to reduce or even remove the processing of certain streams of information (Broadbent, 1957; Pylyshyn, 1994; Treisman, 1969). The bottom line is that the neurocomputational perspective assumes that the external world has a strong influence on internal representation choice because our internal representational machinery makes heavy use of perceptual processing systems, but that the problem-solver has the ability to ignore certain perceptual inputs. Thus, only perceptually segmentable aspects of the external environment that need to be processed for the task at hand will influence internal representation choice. The perceptually segmentable constraint on what can be treated separately depends on the neurophysiological limits of our perceptual system. What is segmentable is a complex story that we cannot fully unpack here, but it is sufficient for our purposes here to say that some features can be processed separately whereas others cannot (Wolfe, 1994).

The final dimension of comparison is the space of possible choices of internal representations. For the symbolic and embodied problem-solving camps, essentially anything, in theory, is possible. For the symbolic problem-solving perspective, the set of likely choices are likely to be mostly symbolic in one way or another, although a mixture of symbolic and analog is possible (Larkin & 10 Simon, 1987; Tabachneck-Schijf, Leonardo, & Simon, 1994). For the embodied problem-solver perspective, the choices are obviously heavily influenced by the external world, but essentially anything in the external world could be mimicked internally, at least in theory. The perspective that is most distinctive on this dimension is the neurocomputational problem-solving perspective. The neurocomputational perspective holds that the problem-solver can only use a very fixed set of representational schemes. This fixed set is instantiated as human brain systems and is heavily determined by evolutionarily important tasks.

TESTING THE THEORETICAL CAMPS

No simple set of experiments can easily test between very different theoretical paradigms because of the all the additional assumptions required to account for a particular experimental situation. However, we can ask how useful the different paradigms are for explaining internal representational choice in a few cases. In this chapter, we describe two studies designed to look at internal representations of experts, and the situations of these experiments were chosen such that the different theoretical camps would make different concrete predictions for internal representation choice. In particular, we examined representation choice in how experts deal with uncertainty while analyzing complex visual/spatial data. We realize that we cannot generalize from these studies to the utility of the different theoretical camps overall. However, these studies do provide a concrete example of how one can empirically test between the utility of the different paradigms.

Both studies examine one very particular aspect of representation: how people represent visual/spatial information. The world is 3-dimensional, but most information sources that experts in complex domains interact with are 2-dimensional (e.g., paper and computer screens). The world exists relative to the problem-solver in egocentric terms, but information sources often present visual/spatial data in exocentric terms. The world is life-sized (again by definition), but expert information sources often present scaled versions, either much larger (e.g., via microscopes) or much smaller (e.g., satellite images). Given this diversity of reality and input, how will the problem-solver represent their problem-solving states internally?

The symbolic camp tells us to conduct a task analysis. Find out what strategies and representations are possible, and which are most efficient for the task at hand. The embodied problem-solving camp suggests that representations will match either the form of the external input or the external reality of the problem. What about the neurocomputational problem-solver? Here the devil is in the details—in order to develop predictions, we need to select an account (among several competing accounts) for how the brain represents visual/spatial information. We have selected the ACT-R/S theory, and explain it with just enough detail so that the predictions can be made for our current needs.

Brief Overview of ACT-R/S

ACT-R/S (Harrison & Schunn, 2002) is a neurocomputational theory of the visual/spatial representational and computational abilities of the human mind. It integrates current neuroscientific understanding of how the human brain represents visual/spatial information into the ACT-R 5.0 (Anderson, Bothell,

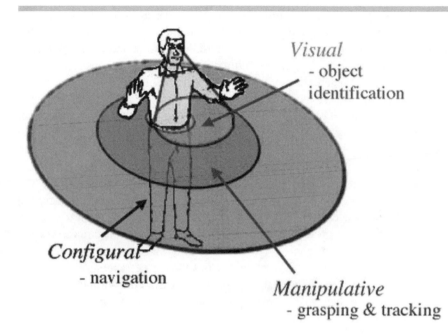

Figure 2.1 Three visual/spatial representation systems posited in ACT-R/S, the size and location of space they cover, and the basic tasks they typically support.

Byrne, Douglass & LeBiere, 2004) view of how the mind achieves complex problem solving through a rich mixture environment encoding, memory retrievals, and skill applications through goal-directed behavior. In particular, ACT-R/S posits that there are three different visual/spatial representations (see Fig. 2.1), which we call buffers. The three representations make use of different neural pathways, tend to get used for different kinds of basic perceptual/motor tasks, have fundamentally different ways of representing space, and have different strengths and weaknesses. Note that these buffers are multimodal in that they integrate spatial information coming from vision, audition, touch, locomotion, and joint sensors.

The first representation is the Visual Buffer. It is used for object identification and represents information primarily around the region that they eyes are attending to, and represents information in approximate shape terms and approximate size and location. Historically, this buffer has been called the "What" visual pathway. Its representation of the world is primarily a 2-dimensional world, with objects occupying space in the fronto-parallel plane (i.e., like on a computer screen or chart on the wall in front of you). That is, there are approximate above/below and left/right relationships, but no strong distance and exact orientation information.

The second representation is the Manipulative Buffer. Historically, it has been called the "Where" visual pathway. It is used for grasping objects and tracking of moving of objects, representing information close to within reach, but also all the way around the person. It represents spatial information in highly accurate metric terms, which is required for object manipulation, and in a true 3-D fashion. It is not good at figuring out what objects are, but it knows exactly where they are and what there component shapes are.

The third representation is the Configural Buffer. It is used for navigation in small and large spaces, figuring out where you are, where you want to go, and how to get there. It represents information in terms of egocentric range vectors to blobs (e.g., the desk is approximately so far away, with the left and right side being at such and such angles from me). Locations are configurations of such vectors (e.g., I am at the location that is so far away from the door and such distance from the window, with a given angle between the two).

COMPLEX-PROBLEM SOLVING, REPRESENTATION CHOICE, AND ACT-R/S

The strong assumption in ACT-R/S is that these three representations are the only representations (other than verbal) that a novice or expert can use for problem solving. In other words, an expert cannot invent a new visual/spatial representation that does not use one (or more) of these three representations, and that there representations will be limited computationally in the same ways as novices based on the properties of these three visual/spatial representation systems. That is, people are assumed to be fundamentally limited by their neurobiology.

ACT-R/S assumes that people can translate between the three representations. In fact, for many tasks, translation and simultaneous activation of different representations is necessary. For example, in order to figure out one's location (a Configural task), one needs to identify what the landmarks are (a Visual task). This ability to translate between representations in general is what makes much of cognitive psychology so difficult because the internal representation can differ dramatically from the input form and can vary substantially across individuals, and the choice of internal representation fundamentally influences performance. For example, people can have visual representations of auditory stimuli, producing visual confusions rather than auditory confusions. In the case of ACT-R/S, a person can take arrangements of distant objects presumably only representable in the Configural space and translate it into a miniature 3-D model in the manipulative space, or a flat visual map representation in the Visual space. The way that the person is internally representing the objects will then strongly determine how spatial features are encoded, and thus an important determiner of performance.

The choice of which representation is used will be influenced by input: things in flat displays will tend to start out as Visual; things within reach will tend to start out as Manipulative, and things out in the distant will tend to start out as Configural. However, the choice of representation will also be influenced by functional factors. ACT-R, the parent theory, assumes that people make procedural choices on the basis of past experiences of success and amount of effort with the choices. In other words, it predicts that people will tend to select choices that led more often in the past to successful attainment of goals, but also taking into account how much effort (primarily in amount of time) was required to achieve those goals. There are more formal, mathematical instantiations of the choice process and the learning of preferences, but the general understanding of this point will suffice for here. ACT-R/S, then, assumes that people will tend to move towards representations that have been generally more functional for the goal task at hand. Because the three different representations have very different basic representational form and computational abilities, the match of representation to task should be a strong influence on representation choice. Because this choice preference is embedded in a learning theory, the prediction is that this preference for a particular representation will be more pronounced with increasing expertise in a task.

UNCERTAINTY PREDICTIONS FROM ACT-R/S

With all that theoretical background on ACT-R/S and how it might apply to complex problem solving, we can now come full circle back to the issue of visual/spatial representations in complex problem solving with uncertainty. The three different spatial systems have varying degrees of match to spatial certainty. *All things being equal*, ACT-R/S then predicts that problem solving, especially in disciplines with complex visual displays, will vary as a function of spatial certainty levels of the scientist doing the data analysis: Manipulative representations will be used when spatial certainty levels are the highest because the Manipulative space represents spatial location and features in very precise terms; Visual representations will be used when spatial certainty levels are the lowest because the Visual space represents spatial location and features in very approximate terms; and the Configural representation sits somewhere in between, with precise angles, but approximate distance and very approximate shape information.

Of course, all things are not often precisely equal. Input of information will come in a particular form. The particular goals of the data analysis will influence the functional relevance of different representations, as well. Expertise will play a role here, too, as experts may be more sensitive to functional relevance and less sensitive to initial input form.

In sum, ACT-R/S makes a variety of predictions for how experts will represent visual/spatial information during data analysis, and one of those predictions involves relative uncertainty levels. We thought of this uncertainty prediction as a very novel prediction to the psychology of problem solving, in clear contrast to the predictions of the symbolic and embodied problem-solving camps. The symbolic problem-solving framework makes relatively few predictions about internal representation choice, and the embodied problem-solving framework predicts a match of internal representations to either input or action external representations; neither makes a prediction about the relationship of internal representation choice and uncertainty levels. We examine two studies of complex problem solving in a several domains to see which perspective could successfully predict (not just explain) observed (although somewhat indirectly by necessity) internal representation choices.

STUDY 1: EXPERT/NOVICE COMPARISONS IN A TRADITIONAL SUBMARINE TASK

Overview

This study examined expert, intermediate, and novice representations of 3-dimensional space while solving the complex spatial task of finding an enemy submarine using a simplified computerized environment of a traditional submarine sonar setup. We carefully examine participant spontaneous gestures as an indicator of how they are internally representing spatial locations during problem solving.

Participants

In this study, 16 submarine officers total participated: six students, six instructors, and four commanders. The students were recent graduates of the Submarine School's Submarine Officers' Basic Course (SOBC). The instructors were Junior Officers who were teaching those courses at the time of the study. The commanders were Commanding Officers (COs) and Executive Officers (XOs), three of whom were active-duty and one who was retired. In the U.S. Navy, the most expert individuals are considered too valuable to spend time teaching, and thus the instructors are the intermediate level participants.

Procedure

The procedure involved two simulated scenarios in Ned, a simulation environment built in a previous project for studying the expertise of determining a solution (see Materials). First, the participant was familiarized with the ways to gather information about potential contacts in the simulation environment. Then the participant was asked to think aloud as he solved the problem. Each officer worked for approximately 20 minutes to determine the location of an enemy submarine (called a solution). Once a solution was found, the experimenter initiated a retrospective interview. This procedure of problem solving and retrospective interview was then repeated for a second scenario.

During the retrospective interview, the participant gave a general summary of the scenario. Next, the participant was cued to explain specific moments in the simulation he just completed. Cued by predetermined screen shots or short clips of the screen at different moments in the scenario, he was asked to talk about what he was thinking, what the problem was that he was addressing, and what happened just after this moment. The participant responses were videotaped. The experimenter asked the participant to view the screen once, and then once he was ready to answer, turn away from the screen to speak to the experimenter. This physical manipulation of the screen and the participant was intended to ensure that the participant used hand gestures when he wanted to convey spatial elements and not vague points or gestures to the screen to convey explanations. In addition to the preset screen shots and clips, we generated questions opportunistically during a session, for example, when we wanted to clarify a participant's explanation.

Materials

Ned is a small-scale submarine control room simulation (Ehret, Gray, & Kirschenbaum, 2000). Although it provides the functionality to perform all the functions necessary to locate a contact, all of the data on the contact are simulated. They are not represented by a high-fidelity model, but rather by noise plus the true values for key parameters. The interface that Ned uses is a composite of common submarine display content without being a copy of any specific deployed system. As it is generic to all contemporary systems, submariners will be familiar with these displays and their functionality.

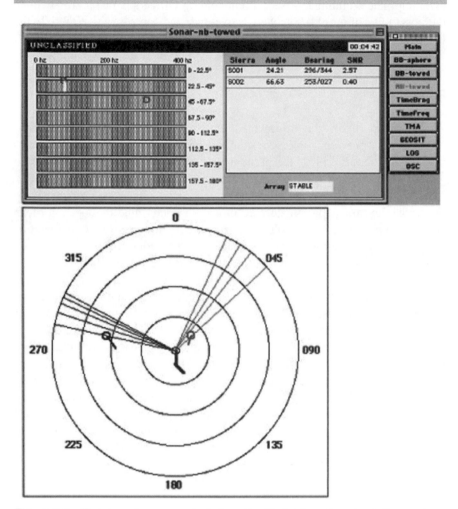

Figure 2.2 Two sample screen shots from the Ned submarine simulation environment used in Study 1.

Ned was developed with four scenarios, two of which were randomly
assigned to each participant. All scenarios have two contacts—a rather noisy
merchant and a quieter enemy submarine. In two of the scenarios, the sub-
surface contact is moving at a constant course and speed and in the other two
it is maneuvering every ten minutes, on average. The merchant ship appears
at the beginning of the scenario, and after about one minute the submerged
contact appears. In some scenarios, when the sub appears, it is dead ahead of

own-ship, necessitating a speedy maneuver on the part of own-ship to avoid the possibility of a collision and get into a more advantageous position relative to the sub. In the other scenarios, the submerged contact appears ahead of own-ship, but in not as dangerous a position, still requiring own-ship to maneuver but not as quickly as in the dead-ahead scenarios. Eventually, the submerged contact drives toward the merchant and trails it, giving the impression that the sub is threatening the merchant. Also, as the scenario progresses, the spatial relationships of the two contacts become complicated and critical as the two ships get closer to one another.

Figure 2.2 presents two sample screen shots from Ned. The left half of the top screen shot presents a diagram showing the presence of certain sound frequencies[1] at different angles of input. The right half shows information on different sound "tracks" that the problem-solver has chosen to follow. The bottom screenshot shows a geosituational view.

Predictions

Note that none of the input in Ned shows the equivalent of a view out of a window although there is a bird's-eye view with own ship in the center and lines of bearing to other platforms, and current solution, if available. The visual/spatial displays are all 2-dimensional, complex displays. At the same time, the real world being reasoned about is a very, very large, 3-dimensional world. How will problem-solvers represent this situation internally?

The symbolic perspective predicts that problem-solvers will select whatever representation minimizes mental workload and maximizes accuracy—in this complex task, we had no idea what that would be, and thus felt that no predictions were being made by the symbolic perspective other than whatever internal representation is most correlated with high performance within groups would be more likely to occur in experts. The embodied problem-solving perspective predicts that problem-solvers will use either 2-D display-based reasoning (the input) or large-scale 3-D (configural) reasoning (the real world). By contrast, the neurocomputational perspective suggests that problem-solvers will move from a display or configural representation to a manipulative (small 3-D) representation because (1) configural or display representations are more appropriate for weak initial knowledge of location and distance, and (2) manipulative representations are more appropriate when location and distance are more accurately known. The neurocomputational perspective is the only one that very clearly predicts a change in internal representation choice for this task over time.

---

[1]Because true frequencies are classified, the values used in Ned are made up and the convention used was explained to the participants during training.

Figure 2.3 A participant's configural gesture produced during his think-aloud protocol "... bearing around course oh three five, our own-ship course is about three five seven, we'll be about ... here".

Gesture Coding

Visual-spatial representations were coded from the spontaneous gestures. Configural gestures were made with the hand or arm such that the fingers are pointing in a direction without attempting to pick up or place or otherwise manipulate imaginary objects. These were usually one-handed gestures and one-dimensional, but some were two-handed when they have a quality of pointing into the distance. They can represent limited motion, for example in a single direction, but again only if it seems the motion is in far-space and not being manipulated in curves and complex dimensions. See Figure 2.3 for an example of a two-handed configural gesture in which the hands represent the angle at which the target is at relative to the heading of own-ship.

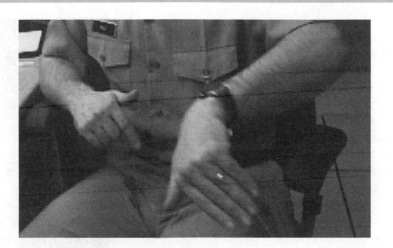

Figure 2.4 A participant's manipulative gesture produced during a hotwash, saying "I should've gone left ... come left and gone behind him ..."

Manipulative gestures placed objects and activity in a nearby space, such that the participant can actually manipulate or place the imaginary objects. Gestures include two-handed gestures showing two contacts and the relative motion involved or changes in bearing and curves in paths or course. Gestures in which the hand-shape suggests placing or holding as opposed to strictly pointing were also coded as manipulative. Figure 2.4 presents an example in which a student represents the submerged contact in a stationary position and own-ship moving forward and then turning left to follow behind the other hand (the sub). This gesture represents relative positions, motion and a complex path for own-ship.

Display-based gestures would have been gestures that involved gestures that place objects and activity on a flat surface in the fronto-parallel plane. However, in this study, those kinds of gestures did not occur, and thus are not mentioned further. There were also uncertainty-based gestures, in which participants shrugged or wiggled their hands indicating uncertainty about the situation, but those gestures do not directly indicate spatial representations and thus are not discussed further in this chapter.

Reliability of the coding was between 84% and 92% agreement depending on the category and was established with a second rater coding a randomly selected 20% of the data. The analyses reported here focus on the gestures made during the first and last maneuvers of both scenarios to show change in representations during problem solving (in addition to changes with expertise).

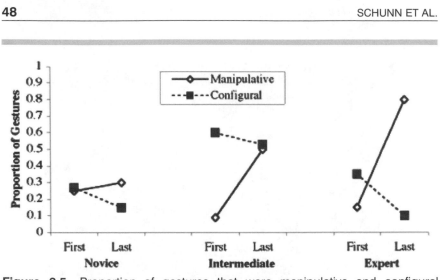

Figure 2.5 Proportion of gestures that were manipulative and configural gestures for the first and last maneuver of each scenario for novice (students), intermediates (instructors), and experts (commanders) in Study 1.

It is important to note that spontaneous gestures are an indirect measure of internal representation, and that they are likely to have biases as such a measure. For example, the gestures may be influenced by communication goals (McNeill, 1992). However, this measure of internal representation is no worse on that issue than any other measure, and gestures are particularly well suited to capturing visual-spatial representations.

Results

Figure 2.5 presents the proportion of gestures that were manipulative and configural broken down by time (first vs. last maneuver within each scenario) for each expertise group. We see the same pattern of results of change with time within each expertise group: a decrease in the proportion of configural gestures and an increase in the proportion of manipulative gestures. This pattern is exactly what was predicted by the neurocomputational account: participants would go from a representation that is appropriate for times of high uncertainty about location (configural) to a representation that is appropriate for times of lower uncertainty about location (manipulative).

As there were no gestures about the 2-D input in this situation, part of what the embodied problem-solving perspective would predict did not come true. One could argue that the presence of configural representations, especially in early problem-solving episodes, is consistent with the embodied problem-solving focus on the external reality. It is interesting that the configural gestures relative to manipulative gestures were the lowest in the experts, suggesting an especially strong movement away from external reality in experts.

Of course, all of these conclusions are very tentative, as we have only examined performance in one situation and the results can be partially explained by each of the camps (not to mention various other ad hoc possible explanations of this simple pattern). It will be important to examine spatial representations in other tasks to see whether the neurocomputational perspective provides genuine insight.

STUDY 2: EXPERT/NOVICE COMPARISONS IN MODERN SUBMARINING AND fMRI DATA ANALYSIS

Overview

This study followed (Group 1) cognitive neuroscfientists at different expertise levels analyzing Functional Magnetic Resonance Imaging (fMRI) data and (Group 2) submarine experts doing similar problem solving as in Study 1, but with a more modern interface that better affords display-based problem solving. The purpose of Group 1 was to see whether we could predict representation choice in a very different domain, with a small rather than large external reality, for example. The purpose of Group 2 was to explore what role external input had on problem solving by using a different external input for the same basic task as in Study 1.

In the Submarine domain, we had problem-solvers go through one complex scenario, as in Study 1. In the fMRI domain, we observed experts, intermediates, and novices analyzing their own data. In both domains, after 30–60 minutes of problem solving, we then stopped the data analysis activities, and showed the problem-solvers several 1-minute videotape segments of their problem solving and asked them to explain what they knew and didn't know at that point in time, so that we could examine how they were representing their data spatially and what their uncertainty levels were. We examined the speech and gestures produced by problem-solvers during those cued recall segments to measure their uncertainty levels and the way they represented their data spatially (acknowledging all along the potential dangers of relying on retrospective reports to measure internal representations). We then looked at uncertainty levels and representation choice as a function of each other as well as time and expertise.

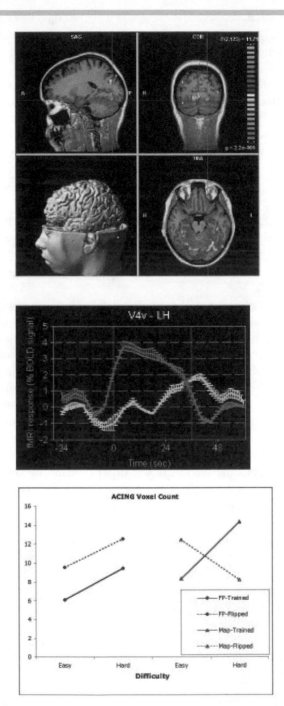

(*Continued*)

ROI	TrainedEasy Count	TrainedHard Count	FlippedEasy Count	FlippedHard Count
	1	2	3	4	5
ACING	8.33	14.33	12.44	8.33
CMLC	72.33	87.56	75.89	103.22
LCBELL	21.11	33	27.22	28.89
RCBELL	13.44	38.44	28.33	33.67
LCBELL+RCBELL	40.56	71.44	55.56	62.56
LDLPFC	42.78	55	42.77	48.56
RDLPFC	37.78	81.67	45.44	57.11
DLPFC	78.33	112.67	81.67	97.89
LFEF	5.33	6.22	4.67	7.22
RFEF	2.44	5.54	2.78	4.14
LFEF+RFEF	8.78	12.78	8.44	11.89
LHG	12.67	1.44	5.56	1.56
RHG	14	3	6	3.78
LHG+RHG	26.67	4.44	11.56	9.33
LIFG	77.56	104.89	94.78	102.44
RIFG	59.11	76.56	59.56	91.67
LIFG+RIFG	136.67	181.44	144.33	191.11
LSPL	24.44	33.22	27.33	28.67
RIPL	19.11	23.89	20.33	28.56
LIPL+RIPL	43.56	44.11	47.67	61.22
LIPS	54.67	76.56	61	75.22
RIPS	37.67	64.11	48.11	72.56
IPS	92.33	140.67	109.11	147.78

Figure 2.6 Kinds of visualizations examined in analysis of fMRI data: (a) degree of activation indicated with a color scale superimposed over a gray-scale structural brain image in three different planar slices and a surface cortex map; (b) graph of percent signal change in a brain region as a function of time relative to a stimulus presentation in two different conditions (red and green); (c) graph of number of activated voxels in an area as a function of various condition manipulations; and (d) table of number of activated voxels in different brain areas (Regions of Interest) as a function of different conditions.

fMRI Domain

The goal of fMRI is to discover both the location in the brain and the time course of processing underlying different cognitive processes. Imaging data is collected in research fMRI scanners hooked to computers that display experimental stimuli to their human subjects. Generally, fMRI uses a subtractive logic technique, in which the magnetic activity observed in the brain during one task is subtracted from the magnetic activity observed in the brain during another task, with the assumption that the resulting difference can be attributed to whatever cognitive processes occur in the one task but not the other. Moreover, neuronal activity levels are not directly measured, but rather one measures the changes in magnetic fields associated with oxygen-rich blood relative to oxygen-depleted blood. The main measured change is not

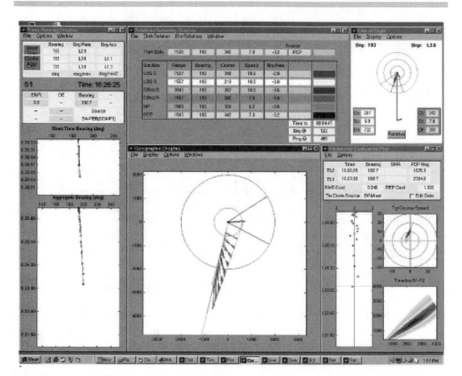

Figure 2.7   Modern submarine display used in Study 2.

the depletion due to neuronal activity but rather the delayed over-response of new oxygen-rich blood moving to active brain areas, and the delay is on the order of 5 seconds, with the delay slightly variable by person and brain area. Data is analyzed visually by superimposing color-coded activity regions over a structural image of the brain (see Fig. 2.6a), looking at graphs of mean activation level by region and/or over time (see Fig. 2.6b) or across conditions (see Fig. 2.6c), or looking at tables of mean activation levels by region across conditions (see Fig. 2.6d). Elaborate, multistepped, semi-automated computational procedures are executed to produce these various visualizations, and given the size of the data (gigabytes per subject), many steps can take up to several minutes per subject. Inferential statistical procedures (e.g., t, ANOVA) are applied to confirm trends seen visually. Note that, as in the submarine domain, the input displays are very 2-dimensional, even though the underlying reality (activation in brain regions) is 3-dimensional. Unlike the submarine domain, however, the underlying reality takes place in a very small space (smaller than a breadbasket, relatively nearby) whereas in the submarine domain, the real space is many miles in every direction, with objects being the size of medium-sized buildings.

More Realistic Submarine Interface

Although the basic task of finding other submarines using passive sonar remains fundamentally the same very difficult task, computational algorithms and visual displays designed to help the submariner have improved significantly. Figure 2.7 presents the more realistic interface that used in Study 2. It runs on a high-end Windows© personal computer, and is an unclassified simulation environment used in engineering development and training situations. It closely mirrors the actual displays used in modern U.S. Navy submarines. Explaining all the displays found in Figure 2.7 is beyond the scope of this chapter, but suffice it to say that it includes both egocentric and geosituational views, as well as alphanumeric best-guesses on target location, and that it includes explicit representations about the uncertainty in possible values of angle, distance, course, and speed of the target. Thus, in contrast to the Ned simulation used in Study 2, this environment affords better displayed-based problem solving, and thus we may see more display-based representations of space than in Study 1.

Participants

Submarine. There were 5 submarine experts who participated in Study, with similar expertise levels as the experts in Study 1.

fMRI. There were 10 fMRI participants, ranging from beginning graduate students to postdoctoral researchers. This study focused on naturalistic analysis of data, and faculty in this domain tend not to be directly involved in analysis of fMRI data, and instead work with students and postdocs after analyses have been carried out. We divided the participants into three expertise levels based on the number of studies they had carried out: four participants classified as Experts had carried out four or more fMRI studies, four participants classified as Intermediate has carried out between two and three studies, and two participants classified as Novices had carried out only one study. Because postdocs in this domain typically had earned their PhD with a technique other than fMRI, not all the postdocs were classified Experts and some of the graduate students were classified Experts. Although our fMRI Experts did not have the 10 years of focused practice that is typically required

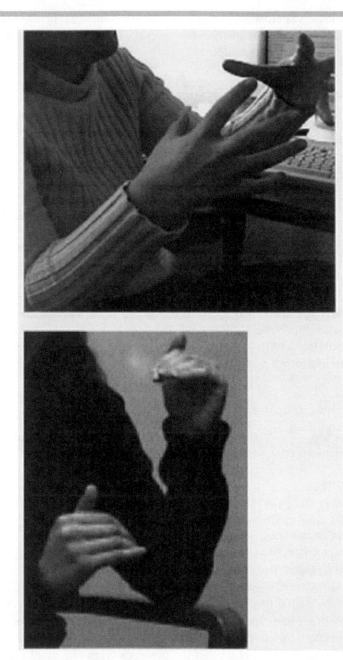

Figure 2.8   Example spatial gestures from the fMRI domain: (a) a manipulative gesture, "… if you have, like, this massive thing, the peak is really in there…", and (b) an example display-based gesture, " … I found out that, it looked like there's a difference between frontal and hippocampal activation …"

for world-class expertise, we are interested in expertise as a relative continuum, not as absolute categories.

Coding

The coding of gestures in Study 2 followed a similar procedure as in Study 1, although in this case we focused on gestures made during the various "interesting minutes" cued responses rather than on just first and last maneuvers, and we coded much more prevalent display-based gestures. Display-based gestures are gestures that described spatial relations in the discussed data, but occurred in a flat vertical (usually fronto-parallel) space, in contrast to manipulative gestures, which also took place in nearby space but gestured with 3-dimensional depth in object placement and/or size and shape, and in contrast to configural gestures, in which the hands were not representing the objects themselves but were merely pointers to objects off in a distance space. Figure 2.8b presents an example display-based gesture in which the participant takes about brain activation of two different spatial regions in terms of a flat bar-graph representation spatial region being represented one-dimensionally on the x-axis. By contrast, Figure 2.8a shows what a manipulative gestures looks like in this domain.

As in Study 1, we coded for uncertainty gestures (like shrugs and hand wiggles), but do not focus on those results here. Other gestures that were coded but not included in the current analyses were metaphorical gestures (in which space represented nonspatial dimensions like time), beating gestures (which simply keep time with speech or indicate points of emphasis in speech), and deictic gestures (point to the screen or a notebook on a desk, which is ambiguous about underlying spatial representations).

Predictions

As in Study 1, the symbolic perspective does not make obvious predictions—the adopted representation, especially by experts, could be anything, and all will depend on what representations best support problem solving. The embodied problem-solving perspective makes the following predictions. First, fMRI scientists should use manipulative (real-world) and display-based (input) representations. Second, submariners should use configural (real-world) and display-based (input) representations. The neurocomputational perspective makes different predictions. In fMRI, the end goal is not precise location, so the problem-solvers should move to less precise representations (e.g., display-based representations). In submarining, the end goal is precise location, and thus the problem-solvers should move to more precise representations (e.g., manipulative).

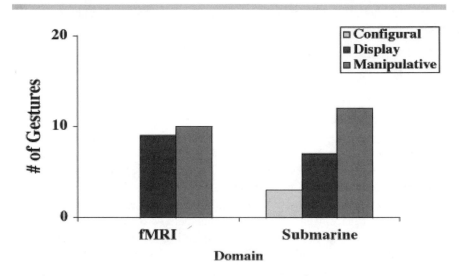

Figure 2.9   For experts only in Study 2, the number of configural, display, and manipulative gestures found in each domain.

RESULTS

Domain Differences in Expert Representations

Because we only collected data from experts in the submarine domain, to properly compare domain differences, we must focus on the expert data in the fMRI domain as well for a comparison across domains. Accordingly, Figure 2.9 presents the number of configural, display, and manipulative gestures for experts only in the fMRI and submarine domains.

Comparing the two domains, we can suggest several conclusions about expert representations. First, the underlying reality appears to matter a little. There were no configural gestures in the fMRI domain (to a large or distant brain) but there were some (although relatively few) configural gestures in the submarine domain. Second, the interface appears to matter. There were many display-based gestures in both domains, reflecting the input problem-solvers received on the screen. Moreover, comparing to the results from Study 1, changing the interface to a more modern interface appears to impact the experts in that we now see a significant presence of display-based gestures. Third, the data from the submarine domain suggest that neurocomputational factors appear to matter a lot, because the most common representation (manipulative) corresponds to neither input nor external reality.

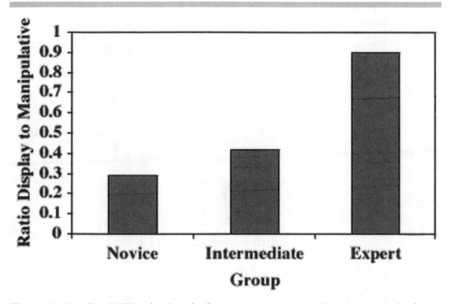

Figure 2.10   For fMRI scientists in Study 2, the ratio of display to manipulative gestures in each expertise group.

The diversity of representations within each group suggest that an account like ACT-R/S, in which there can be multiple spatial representations, is useful for highlighting representational variability. It is also the case that some participants used few spatial gestures overall. We do not think they were not thinking spatially, but rather there are large individual differences in how much and what type of gestures people use. The majority who used at least three gestures had both manipulative and display gestures, suggesting the diversity does reside within individuals rather than reflecting individual choice of a single representation to use throughout problem solving.

Expertise Effects of Representation

Focusing in on the fMRI data, we can now turn to differences in preferred representation type as a function of expertise. Figure 2.10 presents the ratio of display to manipulative gestures (large numbers indicate relatively more display gestures). We can use this ratio in this domain because there were no configural gestures. We see a gradual increase in the use of display rather than manipulative representations with expertise. This difference is consistent across participants: 3/4 experts use more display than manipulative gestures, whereas 0/4 intermediate and 0/2 of novices use more displays than manipulative gestures).

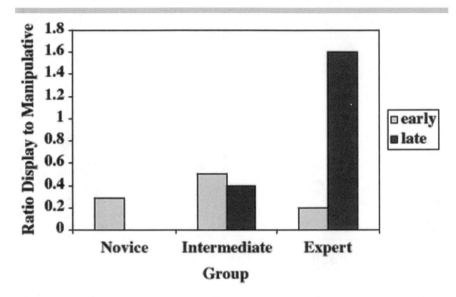

Figure 2.11   For fMRI scientists in Study 2, the ratio of display to manipulative gestures in each expertise group, split by the first half versus second half of cued minutes.

Were these representation preferences held throughout problem solving, indicating that experts "saw" different things in their data from the start, or was there a more complex pattern over time? We divided the cued minutes for each participant into early and late minutes. Unpacked by early/late, we see that experts start out the scenario with manipulative gestures but move to display-based gestures (see Fig. 2.11). Thus, experts, like intermediates and novices, begin data analysis thinking about a 3-dimensional brain (even though they are literally seeing 2-D slices of a 3-D brain). With problem solving, experts, unlike intermediates and novices, are better able to move to a more abstract 2-D spatial representation: in the end, their question is not where in the 3-D brain were there regions of activity, but rather how did functional regions in the brain (which are more easily compressed into a single ordinal dimension) differ in their activity levels (by task or by time).

GENERAL DISCUSSION

The goals of this chapter were to draw attention to a major weakness in theorizing in cognitive science (how can we predict representation choice);

provide a new theoretical framing of the issue (by drawing out and contrasting predictions from the three major theoretical camps in cognitive science); and provide some initial examinations of real-world cognition in a complex domain to see how well the various predictions bear out.

Although the evidence is currently from only a two cases and a small number of participants, our data suggest the following directions. First, it appears that the external world (reality and input) does have some influence on internal representation choice. Moreover, it appears that reality primarily matters in novices and early in problem solving. Second, expert representations are best predicted by the match of task goals to neurocomputational constraints—experts appear to exapt particular, existing visual/spatial systems for problem solving on the basis of how well the computational abilities of those systems support the current needs/features of the given task. In particular, we have shown how spatial informational uncertainty is related to the selection of internal visual/spatial representations.

Of all the areas of psychology, research in complex, real-world problem solving seems most removed from all the excitement and breakthroughs in cognitive neuroscience of the last 15 to 20 years. This lack of change in research on higher level cognition is not arbitrary or representative of stubbornness by a particular research community. Instead, it reflects the difficulties in bring neuroscience methodologies to studying something so complex as higher level cognition, which almost by definition, influences the integration of many brain regions and brain systems in complex ways. We hope that the work described in this chapter can show a different way in which neuroscience can bring new insights to the study of higher-level cognition: bringing in theoretical constraints on core components of the problem-solving system based on neuroscience data and theories. We hope that we have also made some progress in convincing researchers of complex cognition that we need to move beyond relying solely on our old theoretical friends of task structure, memory constraints, and embodied cognition to understand complex problem solving.

Caveats

It is important to acknowledge that the current story is just the beginning of the story. Much further empirical work must be done to establish the value of the current story over various alternative explanations of our presented data. As we argued in the beginning of the chapter, the measurement problem for internal representations is a very difficult one. Consequently, we do not know for sure that gestures cleanly correspond to internal representations. Instead, the representations that we observed might only correspond to a subset of the representations that the problem-solvers were entertaining, and perhaps the subset that was easiest to communicate to the listener. Moreover, the act of communication may drive representation choice more than the basic task itself, and the pragmatics of spatial communication by gesture may be important here. Further work with other measures of internal representations, in addition to collecting more data from more participants and in more domains, should be done to strongly validate the story that we are telling about our data.

Contributions of Different Perspectives—Building the Computational Story. What have the different perspectives contributed to our current understanding of how problem-solvers choose internal representations? We argue that each perspective has built on the previous, elaborating the computational story of cognition. The symbolic perspective began by showing us that computational rather than physical properties per se matter—the structure of the problem space matters much more than the particular physical device with which we interact. The embodied cognitive perspective has shown us that many of our computations are performed on external objects or are grounded in knowledge about the world, so input and reality matters in specifying the nature of the computations. Finally, the neurocomputational perspective has shown us that our choice of representations and their computational properties are strongly influenced by our neurobiology. Thus, a complete computational account of problem solving in a domain includes the task, the environment, and the computational abilities of the problem-solver.

Back to Uncertainty in Data Analysis

Linking back to data analysis and uncertainty themes in this volume, our work suggests that uncertainty has perhaps more roles in problem solving that others have discussed. First, it is an object in itself to detect. Uncertainty varies across situations, and the problem-solver needs to be able to detect the situations in which uncertainty levels are especially high. It is this role of uncertainty that much work in statistics lies (including the work in this volume). Second, uncertainty is an object to problem solve about. When one moves into real problem-solving applications, uncertainty has valence (i.e., it is bad for problem solving), and the problem-solver must engage in activities to reduce uncertainty. The work by Trickett et al. in this volume discusses this aspect of uncertainty. Third, uncertainty is an object that influences basic representation choice, and that basic representation choice will influence many other aspects of problem solving. It is this third role that has perhaps not been discussed previously, although we suspect it maybe an interesting lens even in basic statistics course problem solving.

ACKNOWLEDGMENT

Work on this project was supported by grants Grant N00014-02-1-0113 and N00014-03-1-0061 to the first author from the Office of Naval Research.

REFERENCES

Altmann, E. M., & Trafton, J. G. (2002). Memory for goals: An activation-based model. *Cognitive Science, 26*, 39–83.

Anderson, J. R. (1990). *The adaptive character of thought.* Hillsdale, NJ: Lawrence Erlbaum Associates.

Anderson, J. R., Bothell, D., Byrne, M. D., Douglass, S., & LeBiere, C. (2004). An integrated theory of the mind. *Psychological Review, 111(4)*, 1036–1060.

Anderson, J. R., & Lebiere, C. (1998). *Atomic components of thought.* Mahwah, NJ: Lawrence Erlbaum Associates.

Barsalou, L. W. (1999). Perceptual symbol systems. *Behavioral & Brain Sciences, 22(4)*, 577–660.

Broadbent, D. E. (1957). A mechanical model for human attention and immediate memory. *Psychological Review, 64,* 205–215.

Chi, M. T. H., Feltovich, P. J., & Glaser, R. (1981). Categorization and representation of physics problems by experts and novices. *Cognitive Science, 5*, 121–152.

Dietrich, E., & Markman, A. B. (2000). Cognitive dynamics: Computation and representation regained. In E. Dietrich & A. B. Markman (Eds.), *Cognitive dynamics* (pp. 5–30). Mahwah, NJ: Lawrence Erlbaum Associates.

Ehret, B. D., Gray, W. D., & Kirschenbaum, S. S. (2000). Contending with complexity: Developing and using a scaled world in applied cognitive research. *Human Factors, 42(1)*, 8–23.

Fu, W.-T., & Gray, W. D. (2004). Resolving the paradox of the active user: Stable suboptimal performance in interactive tasks. *Cognitive Science, 28(6)*.

Gibson, J. J. (1979). *The ecological approach to visual perception.* Boston: Houghton Mifflin.

Gobet, F., & Simon, H. A. (1996). Recall of random and distorted chess positions: Implications for the theory of expertise. *Memory & Cognition, 24(4)*, 493–503.

Gould, S. J., & Vrba, E. S. (1982). Exaptation—a missing term in the science of form. *Paleobiology, 8*, 4–15.

Gray, W. D., John, B. E., & Atwood, M. E. (1993). Project ernestine: Validating goms for predicting and explaining real-world task performance. *Human Computer Interaction, 8(3)*, 237–309.

Harrison, A. M., & Schunn, C. D. (2002, August). ACT-R/S: A computational and neurologically inspired model of spatial reasoning. *Proceedings of the 24th Annual Meeting of the Cognitive Science Society*, Fairfax, VA.

Hubel, D. H., & Wiesel, T. N. (1962). Receptive fields, binocular interaction and functional architecture in the cat's visual cortex. *Journal of Physiology, 160*, 106–154.

Hutchins, E. (1995a). *Cognition in the wild.* Cambridge, MA: MIT Press.

Hutchins, E. (1995b). How a cockpit remembers its speeds. *Cognitive Science, 19(3)*, 265–288.

Just, M. A., & Carpenter, P. A. (1976a). Eye fixations and cognitive processes. *Cognitive Psychology, 8(4)*, 441–480.

Just, M. A., & Carpenter, P. A. (1976b). The role of eye-fixation research in cognitive psychology. *Behavior Research Methods, Instruments, & Computers, 8(2)*, 139–143.

Kaplan, C. A., & Simon, H. A. (1990). In search of insight. *Cognitive Psychology, 22,* 374–419.

Kieras, D. E., & Meyer, D. E. (1997). An overview of the epic architecture for cognition and performance with application to human–computer interaction. *Human–Computer Interaction, 12*(4), 391–438.

Klahr, D., & Dunbar, K. (1988). Dual space search during scientific reasoning. *Cognitive Science, 12,* 1–48.

Kosslyn, S. M. (1994). *Image and brain: The resolution of the imagery debate.* Cambridge. MA: MIT Press.

Kosslyn, S. M., Ball, T. M., & Reiser, B. J. (1978). Visual images preserve metric spatial information: Evidence from studies of image scanning. *Journal of Experimental Psychology: Human Perception and Performance, 4,* 46–60.

Kosslyn, S. M., Pascual-Leone, A., Felican, O., Camposano, S., Keenan, J. P., Thompson, W. L., et al. (1999). The role of area 17 in visual imagery: Convergent evidence from pet and RTMS. *Science, 284*(April 2), 167–170.

Kosslyn, S. M., Pinker, S., Smith, G., & Shwartz, S. P. (1979). On the demystification of mental imagery. *Behavioral and Brain Science, 2,* 535–548.

Kosslyn, S. M., Thompson, W. L., Kim, I. J., & Alpert, N. M. (1995). Topographical representations of mental images in primary visual cortex. *Nature, 378*(Nov 30), 496–498.

Kotovsky, K., Hayes, J. R., & Simon, H. A. (1985). Why are some problems hard? Evidence from tower of hanoi. *Cognitive Psychology, 17*(2), 248–294.

Larkin, J. H., McDermott, J., Simon, D., & Simon, H. (1980). Expert and novice performance in solving physics problems. *Science, 208,* 140–156.

Larkin, J. H., & Simon, H. A. (1987). Why a diagram is (sometimes) worth 10,000 words. *Cognitive Science, 4,* 317–345.

Lovett, M. C., & Schunn, C. D. (1999). Task representations, strategy variability and base-rate neglect. *Journal of Experimental Psychology: General, 128*(2), 107–130.

Markman, A. B. (1999). *Knowledge representation.* Mahwah, NJ: Lawrence Erlbaum Associates.

McNeill, D. (1992). *Hand and mind: What gestures reveal about thought.* Chicago, IL: University of Chicago Press.

Neisser, U. (1976). *Cognition and reality: Principles and implications of cognitive psychology.* San Francisco: W. H. Freeman.

Newell, A. (1990). *Unified theories of cognition.* Cambridge, MA: Harvard University Press.

Perkins, D. N. (1994). Insight in minds and genes. In R. S. Sternberg & J. E. Davidson (Eds.), *The nature of insight.* Cambridge, MA: MIT Press.

Previc, F. H. (1998). The neuropsychology of 3-d space. *Psychological Bulletin, 124*(2), 123–164.

Pylyshyn, Z. W. (1973). What the mind's eye tells the mind's brain: A critique of mental imagery. *Psychological Bulletin, 80,* 1–24.

Pylyshyn, Z. W. (1981). The imagery debate: Analogue media versus tacit knowledge. *Psychological Review, 88,* 16–45.

Pylyshyn, Z. W. (1994). Some primitive mechanisms of spatial attention. *Cognition, 50*(1–3), 363–384.

Pylyshyn, Z. W. (2002). Mental imagery: In search of a theory. *Behavioral and Brain Science, 25*(2), 157–182.

Scaife, M., & Rogers, Y. (1996). External cognition: How do graphical representations work? *International Journal of Human–Computer Studies, 45*(2), 185–213.

Schunn, C. D., & Klahr, D. (1996). *The problem of problem spaces: When and how to go beyond a 2-space model of scientific discovery.* Paper presented at the The 18th Annual Conference of the Cognitive Science Society, San Diego, CA.

Schunn, C. D., & Klahr, D. (2000). Discovery processes in a more complex task. In D. Klahr (Ed.), *Exploring science: The cognition and development of discovery processes*. Cambridge, MA: MIT Press.

Simon, H. A. (1956). Rational choice and the structure of the environment. *Psychological Review, 63*, 129–138.

Suchman, L. A. (1987). *Plans and situated action: The problem of human–machine communication*. New York: Cambridge University Press.

Tabachneck-Schijf, H. J. M., Leonardo, A. M., & Simon, H. A. (1997). Camera: A computational model of multiple representations. *Cognitive Science, 21*(3), 305–350.

Treisman, A. M. (1969). Strategies and models of selective attention. *Psychological Review, 76*(3), 282–299.

Ungerleider, L. G., & Mishkin, M. (1982). Two cortical visual systems. In D. J. Ingle, M. A. Goodale & R. J. W. Mansfield (Eds.), *Analysis of visual behavior* (pp. 549–586). Cambridge, MA: MIT Press.

Wolfe, J. M. (1994). Guided search 2.0: A revised model of visual search. *Psychonomic Bulletin and Review, 1*(2), 202–238.

3

"I Don't Know What's Going On There": The Use of Spatial Transformations to Deal With and Resolve Uncertainty in Complex Visualizations

Susan Bell Trickett
George Mason University

J. Gregory Trafton
Naval Research Laboratory

Lelyn Saner
Christian D. Schunn
University of Pittsburgh

Imagine a meteorologist preparing a weather forecast. In addition to years of experience and a vast store of domain knowledge, the forecaster has access to satellite images, to computer-generated weather models and programs to display them in a variety of ways, and to an assortment of special-purpose tools that provide additional task-relevant data. There is no shortage of data, yet despite this array of resources, the task remains very challenging. One source of complexity is the uncertainty inherent in these data, uncertainty that takes many forms. Why are two weather models making different predictions? Are the models based on many observations or just a few? Are there enough observations in a given model to trust it? Is one model more reliable than another in certain circumstances, and if so, what are they? Which one, if either, should be believed? How long ago were these data collected? How have things changed since the data were originally displayed? What is the real location of this front, and how is it affected by other changing variables, such as wind direction and speed, which may also have changed?

To complicate matters further, the uncertainty in the data is not explicitly represented; rather, the visualizations indicate that the data *are* exactly as they *appear*. The visualizations thus invite the forecaster to map uncertain data to certain values, yet to do so would most likely lead to erroneous predictions. How does he or she manage this incongruity, in order to develop the most accurate forecast possible?

This example illustrates the basic question we investigate in this chapter: How do people, especially experts, deal with uncertainty in highly spatial domains, when the data are inherently uncertain but the tools actually *display* very little uncertainty? Experts in many domains depend on complex visualizations that use spatial representations of data, in areas as diverse as military operations (e.g., testing and evaluation of electronic warfare systems and of techniques to counter antiship missile threats, mission rehearsal prior to combat), geosciences (e.g., weather analysis and forecasting, geology, environmental science, oceanography) and scientific visualization (e.g., neuroscience, computational fluid dynamics, molecular biology, medical research and practice). In each of these examples—and there are many more we could cite—the practitioner must contend with uncertainty in the data. We first examine how uncertainty affects operations in three representative domains, submarine operations (military), meteorology (geoscience), and fMRI research (scientific visualization), in which dealing with uncertainty is a critical component of the task. We then investigate how experts in two of these domains, meteorology and fMRI, manage uncertainty as they perform problem-solving activities and make decisions as part of their regular task performance.

The sources of uncertainty in these three domains are many and varied. Uncertainty is inherent in the submarine world due to the nature of the primary sensory system, passive sonar. The causes of uncertainty are the ocean environment (the physics of sound transmission through ocean water, interactions with the bottom, wave action, noise caused by ocean creatures and ships, etc.), the under-determined nature of target motion analysis (TMA) from bearings-only measurements, and the unpredictability of human actions and intentions (both unintentional and intentional deception). These problems have become even more critical with the emphasis on operations in the crowded and noisy littoral regions, and uncertainty is the primary cause of error and delayed action. In meteorology, as outlined above, there is considerable uncertainty in Meteorology and Oceanography (METOC) data, both in observations and models. Weather models are based on underlying assumptions that may or may not be accurate, and they may depend on unreliable or sparsely sampled observations to make their predictions; satellite images do not portray current conditions, but rather show "truth" as it was some time in the recent past; weather-related variables are depicted as having absolute values or locations, whereas in reality, only approximations can be displayed. Likewise, in fMRI, several factors contribute to an overall high level of uncertainty. Irrelevant areas of the brain may be activated by subjects' off-task thoughts. The spatial resolution of the display itself is considerably coarser than neurons or even assemblies of neurons. The measurements themselves can be systematically biased by a variety of factors (e.g., the closeness to the skull, deformations in areas near the nasal passages due to breathing). In addition, the processes of neurons themselves are thought to be stochastic and the neuronal processes happen at a faster pace than the temporal resolution of fMRI. Moreover, to deal with the measurement noise, the analysis of the data typically averages data across several seconds of time or across many trials.

Despite the many sources of uncertainty in these domains, the visualizations often do not explicitly display the uncertainty, but may rather present data in a much less ambiguous fashion than is congruent with reality. For example, Figure 3.1 shows examples of three typical different visualizations of fMRI data. Moving counterclockwise, from the top, they show the degree of activation, indicated with a color scale superimposed over a gray-scale structural brain image in three different planar slices and a surface cortex map; a graph of the number of activated voxels in an area as a function of various condition manipulations; and a table of the number of activated voxels in different brain areas (Regions of Interest) as a function of different conditions. Note the lack of uncertainty represented in the display. For example, in the first visualization, the lit areas signifying neural activity are clearly bounded, and even the different colors are unambiguously discrete. Thus the visualization suggests a precision in the mapping between location in the brain and level of neural activity that, in fact, is unlikely to reflect the actual activity within the brain.

Similarly, Figure 3.2 shows some visualizations used in passive sonar: Above, a waterfall diagram shows the angle of various noise sources across the horizontal axis over time across the vertical axis; and below, a table shows the target motion analysis solutions for six different algorithms. Note the range of the differences in the solutions for the different solutions in the tabular display, and the lack of guidance for interpreting those differences. Of the five displayed variables (Range, Bearing, Course, Speed, and Brg Rate ("Bearing Rate"), only Bearing has the same value in each solution. Moreover, the other values differ greatly. Range, for example, varies from a low value of 1,059 to a high of 2,043, Course from 210 to 357, and Speed from

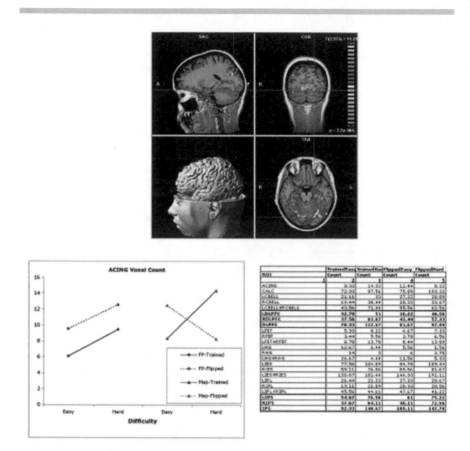

Figure 3.1   Example of visualizations of fMRI data.

62 to 100. Combining these different values into a composite representation of the other submarine compounds those differences, as five completely different scenarios are created. Yet the AO must make a decision about what action to take based on this uncertain information.

Finally, Figure 3.3 shows a typical meteorological chart, displaying not only land masses, but also multiple weather-related variables in relation to those masses. Variables represented include sea height, wind speed, and wind direction. Again, precise values and locations are indicated by wind barbs, alpha-numeric symbols, and defining lines. However, these representations mask a great deal of uncertainty attributable to ranges of values and the dynamic nature of the systems, as well as the questionable trustworthiness and accuracy of the data. Similar mismatches between the implicit certainty

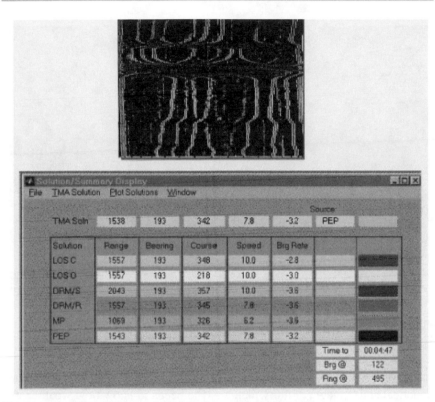

Figure 3.2 Visualizations used in submarine operations.

of the displayed data and the actual uncertainty of those data exist in the submarine domain, because of both the dynamic nature of the data and the many sources of noise in the ocean environment as the data are collected.

The incongruity between the uncertainty inherent in the data and the *lack* of uncertainty explicit in the display presents a serious problem in each of these domains. One of the most time-critical and uncertain events for a submarine is a "close encounter" with another vessel. In such a case the Approach Officer (AO), who is responsible for "fighting the ship" in a hostile encounter, has a very short time in which to assess the evidence (e.g., is the ship friendly or hostile) and take action. As a result, the AO must make safety-critical decisions under extreme uncertainty. Meteorologists must prepare a forecast while contending with inexact information and conflicting model predictions. Weather forecasts are prepared for a customer; inaccurate forecasts can have serious consequences, whether the customer is a Navy

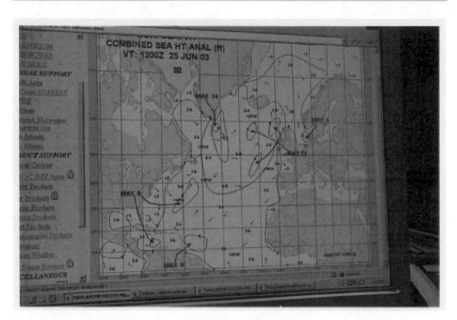

Figure 3.3   Example of meteorological visualization.

pilot who needs detailed flight weather information for the next several hours, a tactical and strategic military planner who needs to know how weather will affect decisions being made for missions, or the general public, who may need to take precautions against severe weather conditions. Results from fMRI and other scientific research are used to inform further research and are often applied to treatments or other problem solutions. fMRI research proceeds along a different timescale from either submarine operations or meteorology; consequently, erroneous results may take weeks, months or even years to be identified and corrected, and may have a significant, negative impact on continuing research.

How do experts think with data and compensate for uncertainty in such uncertain domains? Most studies of decision-making in situations of uncertainty have focused on people's responses to different gambles based on various probable outcomes. In such studies, the level of risk—or uncertainty—is explicitly manipulated by offering participants the opportunity to win money by placing bets with different probabilities of winning and losing. Extensive work in this area has shown that people respond to this type of uncertainty by relying on heuristics rather than, for example, mathematically calculating the likelihood of gain versus loss (e.g., Tversky & Kahneman, 1974).

However, there are several differences between these tasks and those just described that make it unlikely that similar strategies will be used. First, the stakes are much higher, in that the outcome for the experts has real-world implications, as opposed to simply affecting the results of a laboratory study. Second, the tasks themselves explicitly involve the analysis of large amounts of complex data, some of which is uncertain, rather than a simple choice between two constrained options; furthermore, the goal is not to reach a single decision to take one action rather than another, but rather a deeper understanding of a whole set of circumstances, which may itself inform a decision to be taken later on. Third, the information is presented spatially, rather than mathematically; consequently, it is likely that experts will use a spatial strategy to resolve the uncertainty. Three factors have been identified that play an important role in understanding how experts handle uncertainty: First, complex, spatial domains are rife with uncertainty; second, that uncertainty is often not explicitly displayed; and third, disregarding that uncertainty is likely to have harmful consequences. When uncertainty is not explicitly displayed, the expert must add his or her own understanding of uncertainty to the visualization itself, in order to be able to generate useful solutions to the task at hand.

The challenge for experts working in spatial domains such as those discussed above is thus not only to weigh the implications of explicit uncertainty, such as the potential risks given specific odds (although this may be a part of the task). In addition, the experts must develop a means of locating areas of uncertainty and re-evaluating the data in accordance with their revised understanding of the likely accuracy of the representation. Consequently, when a visualization displays information that the expert believes to actually be uncertain, in order to use the data, we propose that the expert must modify his or her internal representation to account for that uncertainty. For example, the submarine operator may need to mentally adjust the bearing of a submarine located on radar, in order to represent it as a range rather than an exact angle. In meteorology, the forecaster may need to mentally add information, such as the range of wind speed, or an updated location of a front, to account for likely changes since the data were originally collected and displayed. In fMRI, the researcher may find it necessary to delete an area of activation from his or her mental representation of the data, determining it to be noise rather than viable data. The expert can then use the modified internal representation of the data, which more accurately reflects the external state of affairs, in order to reason and problem-solve about the situation represented in the external visualization.

Constructing and modifying internal representations takes place by mental processes we call "spatial transformations." Spatial transformations are cognitive operations that a person performs on an internal representation (e.g., a mental image) or an external visualization (e.g., a computer-generated image).[1] Sample spatial transformations are creating a mental image, modifying that mental image by adding or deleting features, mental rotation (Shepard & Metzler, 1971), mentally moving an object, animating a static image (Hegarty, 1992), making comparisons between different views (Kosslyn, Sukel, & Bly, 1999; Trafton, Trickett, & Mintz, 2005), and anything else a person *mentally* does to a visualization in order to understand it or facilitate problem-solving. Spatial transformations may be used in all types of visual-spatial tasks, and thus represent a general problem-solving strategy in this area.

Thus experts viewing unambiguous displays of uncertain data must modify their representation of the data, and spatial transformations are a means by which such mental modifications occur. For example, a meteorologist faced with different weather models making different predictions must somehow resolve those differences in order to construct a single representation of the data. This might be done, for example, by averaging, reconciling, justifying one model over another, creating a composite, or some other means that involves mentally modifying the representation. We hypothesize that when people are more uncertain while working with complex data visualizations, they will perform more spatial transformations than when they are certain. In other words, although spatial transformations may be part of the visual problem-solving toolkit, they are particularly important for resolving uncertainty in complex visual displays.

In order to investigate this hypothesis, we conducted two studies of experts performing their regular tasks. Study 1 presents a re-analysis of previously collected ex-vivo data (Trafton et al., 2000) of a meteorologist preparing a weather brief. It is an initial examination of the relationship between uncertainty and the use of spatial transformations. Study 2 is an *in vivo* study of meteorologists making a forecast and fMRI researchers conducting their own research, designed to elaborate and expand the results of the first study.

STUDY 1

To explore whether expert meteorologists perform more spatial transformations when uncertain, we re-analyzed one expert forecaster from previously collected data (Trafton et al., 2000). The forecaster was an expert Naval meteorological forecaster with 16 years of forecasting experience; in the past year he had made approximately 600 forecasts. The forecaster worked with a

---

[1]If the visualization is external, the operation is not literally performed on the external representation, but rather on the internal model of the external representation.

technician and had access to a "regional center," typically staffed with experienced forecasters who are there to provide assistance as well as specialized visualizations.

Procedure

The forecaster's task was to prepare a written brief for an airplane flown from an aircraft carrier to a destination 12 hours in the future (the destination was Whidbey Island, Washington State). The brief was to cover the entire round trip and the forecaster was asked to provide specific weather information for departure, en-route, destination and alternate airfields. In order to do this, the forecaster had to determine detailed qualitative and quantitative information about the weather conditions. This task was a very familiar one for the forecaster. The forecaster was given 2 hours to finish his task, though it took him less than 50 minutes. Further details of the procedure can be found in Trafton et al., 2000.

Coding Scheme

The forecaster's utterances were transcribed and coded using standard protocol analysis techniques (Ericsson & Simon, 1993). We used a purely syntactic approach to coding uncertainty; hedge words like "probably," "sort of," and explicit verbalizations of uncertainty ("We'll have to see if we agree with that or not") were coded as "uncertain utterances." We also extracted approximately 20% of the forecaster's verbalizations that did not have any uncertainty to use as a control. Spatial transformations were coded for each utterance as well. Table 3.1 shows examples of uncertain/certain utterances as well as spatial transformations.

RESULTS AND DISCUSSION

What is the relationship between uncertainty and spatial cognition? If an expert needs to mentally manipulate a complex visualization in order to understand the uncertainty, we would expect more spatial transformations during the uncertain utterances than the certain utterances. In fact, this is exactly what we found, $\chi^2(1) = 4.1$, $p < .05$. As Figure 3.4 suggests, when the forecaster was uncertain, he performed about twice as many spatial transformations as when he was certain. Said another way, spatial transformations may be associated in this case with factors other than uncertainty, but about 50% of all the spatial transformations are specifically related to uncertainty.

TABLE 3.1
Examples of Certain and Uncertain Utterances
(Indications of Uncertainty in Bold)

Utterance	Code	Spatial Transformations (ST)
Nogaps [a mathematical model] has some precipitation over the Vancouver/Canada border (while viewing a visualization)	Certain	No ST
This is valid today	Certain	No ST
Possibly some rain over Port Angeles	Uncertain	No ST
And then uh, at Port Angeles, there's gonna be some rain up at the north, and if that **sort of** sneaks down, we **could see** a little bit of restriction of visibility, but only down to 5 miles at the worst	Uncertain	ST: mentally moving rain [sneaks down]
I don't think the uh front's gonna get to Whidbey Island [in 12 hours], but it **should be** sitting **right about** over Port Angeles **right around** 0Z this evening	Uncertain	ST: mentally moving front/ animation

STUDY 2

The results of Study 1 suggest that the forecaster was often mentally manipulating the visualizations in order to understand the uncertainty inherent in the domain. However, there are several obvious shortcomings to this study. First, only one forecaster was examined, and these findings could be idiosyncratic to this forecaster. Second, the grain size (sometimes several complete thoughts) was quite large in the utterances examined and the large size of these utterances may have confounded the coding.[2] Also, the task itself was constructed specifically for the purposes of the experiment. In other words, although the participant was a true expert performing a task typical of his daily work, the

---

[2]This was a deliberate feature of Study 1, because it was necessary to see both certainty or lack thereof and the spatial transformation in the same utterance.

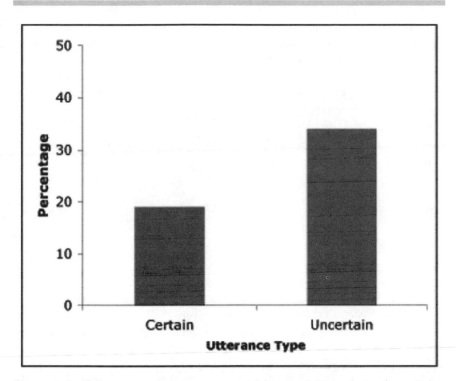

Figure 3.4   Percentage of utterances containing spatial transformations during certain and uncertain utterances.

task was not entirely naturalistic, and it is possible that the slightly artificial nature of this experiment affected the experts' behavior and thus their handling of uncertainty. For example, being asked to perform a constructed task might have made the experts somewhat eager to "get the forecast right" and therefore less likely to express their uncertainty.

In addition to these shortcomings, the coding scheme itself may have biased the results. The syntactic nature of the coding scheme for uncertainty captured uncertainty well at a local or immediate level; that is, within the utterance the verbal expressions of uncertainty were most likely an accurate reflection of the forecasters' uncertainty at a given moment about a specific piece of data. However, the coding scheme may not have captured uncertainty at a more global level—for example, if a forecaster was uncertain about the specific location of a front, that uncertainty might have been expressed in only one utterance, but continued in the forecaster's mind for a much longer period. In such a case, the forecaster might gather additional *certain* data in order to try to resolve the uncertainty. Such utterances would be coded as *certain*, when the forecaster's state of mind was, in fact, *uncertain*. Furthermore, the degree of certainty and the use of spatial transformations could not be independently assessed in this dataset.

In order to eliminate these possible sources of bias, and to improve the generalizability of our results, we conducted a second experiment to further investigate the relationship between uncertainty and the use of spatial transformations, and added a second domain. Study 2 was a true *in vivo* study (Dunbar, 1995, 1997), involving both meteorologists and fMRI researchers conducting their own research.

METHOD

Participants

Participants were two fMRI researchers and two meteorologists. The fMRI researchers had conducted 3 or 4 studies and had an average of approximately 3 years experience in fMRI research. They were thus considered near-experts (see Schunn's chapter in this volume for additional descriptions of these researchers). The meteorologists had many years experience (more than 10 years each) working as Navy forecasters, and were thus experts in this domain.

Procedure

The experiment took place at the participant's regular work location, and all participants had access to all the tools, visualizations, and computer equipment that they usually employed. All participants agreed to be videotaped during the session. Participants working alone were trained to give talk-aloud verbal protocols (Ericsson & Simon, 1993). All participants were instructed to carry out their work as though no camera were present and without explanation to the experimenter. It is important to emphasize that all participants were performing their usual tasks in the manner in which they typically did so, without interruption from the experimenter.

Although the participants performed the task, the experimenter made note of "interesting events." Interesting events consisted of any event that seemed to pique the participant's interest, major changes in the computer display, such as a new visualization or application, an event that spurred a burst of participant activity, and the like. In other words, "interesting events" were those that struck the experimenter, in this online coding, as nonroutine and worthy of further probing.

After the task was completed, the experimenter showed the participant a one-minute segment of the video surrounding the "interesting event"; we refer to these video segments as *interesting minutes.* For each interesting minute, after reviewing the videotape, the experimenter asked the participant "What did you know and what did you not know at this point?" Participants' responses to these questions were also recorded on videotape.

Coding

All utterances, from both the *in vivo* data and the interview data, were transcribed and segmented according to complete thought. For the *in vivo* data, all spatial transformations for the interesting minutes were identified, as described in Study 1. For the interview data, a second, independent coder (from a different lab) coded each utterance as *certain* or *uncertain*, using the same criteria as in Study 1. The difference between the uncertainty coding for the two experiments was that in Study 1, the coding scheme was applied to the *in vivo* data, whereas in Study 2, it was applied to the interview data. Based on the percentage of uncertain utterances in each interview minute, the corresponding *in vivo* minute was coded as *certain* (when fewer than 10% of the utterances were uncertain), *mixed* (when 10 to 20% of the utterances were uncertain), or *uncertain* (when more than 20% of the utterances were uncertain).

The participants' retrospective utterances about their task performance provide an independent measure of their uncertainty during problem solving, and thus address the concern just discussed about possible bias in the uncertainty coding in the first study. It is important to emphasize that the coder for the *in vivo* data did not have access to the interview minutes, or to any coding associated with those minutes. Likewise, the coder of the interview minutes did not have access to the *in vivo* data or the spatial transformation coding associated with it. Thus the two coding schemes were applied completely independently of one another, further precluding possible coding bias in the association between uncertainty and spatial transformations.

RESULTS AND DISCUSSION

Quantitative Analysis

Of the 19 interesting minutes, 5 were coded as certain, 3 as mixed, and 11 as uncertain, thus confirming the large amount of uncertainty practitioners in these domains must contend with. Participants used least spatial transformations in

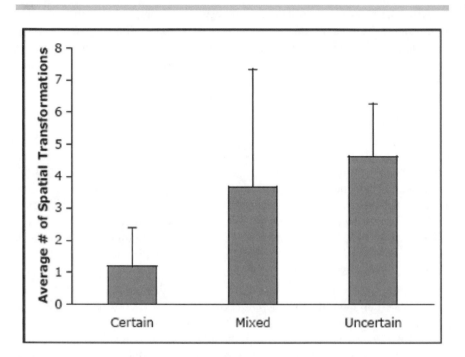

Figure 3.5   Average numbers of spatial transformations used in certain, mixed, and uncertain interesting minutes.

the certain minutes, more in the mixed minutes, and most in the uncertain minutes, and this difference was significant, $\chi^2 (1) = 20.85$, $p < .01$. Figure 3.5 clearly shows the increase in the use of spatial transformations that accompanies the shift from greater certainty to greater uncertainty. These results support our basic hypothesis, that people will use more spatial transformations when they are uncertain than when they are certain.

One possible explanation for this increased use of spatial transformations is that it is part of a pattern of generally increased activity that occurred during uncertainty. That is, perhaps the participants were simply doing more things, or thinking more, when they were uncertain than when they were certain. In order to test this possibility, we examined the number of interface actions the scientists took in the certain and uncertain minutes. Interface actions were defined as manipulations of displayed data, and included closing visualizations and opening new ones, adjusting images (e.g., zooming in to enlarge them), opening and closing windows, etc. in order to advance an understanding of the data. As

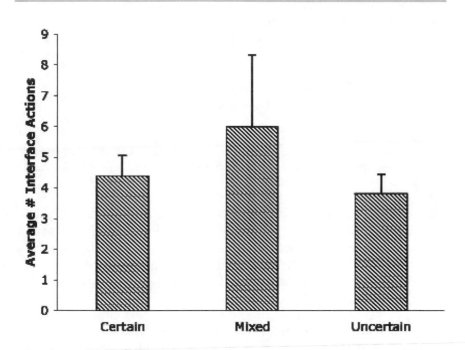

Figure 3.6 Average number of interface actions in certain, mixed, and uncertain interesting minutes.

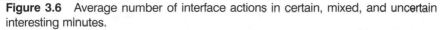

Figure 3.6 shows, the number of interface actions was *not* related to the certainty/ uncertainty coding. Participants used about the same number of interface actions (3.8 compared with 4.4) when they were uncertain as when they were certain, with a slightly increased use of interface actions when their uncertainty level was mixed. The lack of obvious linear increase shown in Figure 3.6 strongly suggests that these practitioners' general level of activity was independent of their level of uncertainty. It certainly indicates that there is no reason to suspect that participants were conducting more interface actions when uncertain than when they were certain.

Qualitative Analysis

We hypothesized that people would use more spatial transformations when they were uncertain than when they were certain, and this hypothesis was supported. We further proposed that spatial transformations would provide a means for practitioners to project their own knowledge—or suspicions—of uncertainty onto the external display, thereby constructing a more accurate internal representation of the data. Experts would then be able to work with this projected, internal representation of uncertainty in order to carry out the task at hand.

There are many instances of this type of process in these data. For example, consider the following extract from the protocol of one meteorologist using the visualization in Figure 3.3:

> You also have a 12 max 14—winds are not supporting that. The next chart has it moving down further to the south. There is a low coming off the coast that is probably getting around, so I would move it further to the south. And that just supports what I said about ours, OK.

The meteorologist's overall goal in this section was to determine whether or not a high seas warning is warranted. First, the meteorologist extracts information about the wave height from the chart (*You also have a 12 max 14*), but then she realizes that there is a mismatch between this information and another source of relevant information, wind speed and direction (*winds are not supporting that*). (The meteorologist had earlier commented that what drives the seas is the winds.) This conflict between two sources of information gives rise to uncertainty on her part. She consults a third source of information in memory—a chart she had looked at previously—and comparing this information with the location of the specific wave height in the current visualization realizes the charts are suggesting two different locations for the "12 max 14." Which location should she use to inform her forecast? With all this information in mind, the forecaster then introduces a fourth data source, an area of low pressure. The interesting thing about this low is that it is not represented on the visualization. In other words, the meteorologist first mentally creates the low (*there is a low coming off the coast*) and then—also mentally—moves it around to position it in relation to the other data already in mind (*that is probably getting around*). She then uses the implications of this new internal representation to mentally relocate the area of "12 max 14" wave height (*so I would move it further to the south*). Inspecting this revision, she is able to resolve the uncertainty (*And that just supports what I said about ours, OK*), because, the more southerly location makes better sense given the spatial transformations she has performed. Spatial transformations thus allow the meteorologist to confirm the uncertainty (comparison between currently displayed and remembered data), to introduce relevant information that is not displayed (the low), to manipulate that information in relation to the displayed data (moving the low), to use domain knowledge to project the implications of these manipulations (relocate the "12 max 14"), and finally to evaluate the results.

Similar examples of the way spatial transformations function are found in the fMRI data. At one point, one of the fMRI researchers expressed some uncertainty about the pattern of activation on the display:

> They're all decreasing below baseline, but it's still hard to know what decreases in activation mean, so I don't know what's going on there. I'll see if Jane knows. I don't think anybody really knows what decreases really mean. … So punish looks like it's a little bit higher, but that's probably not significant, and it looks like [these two] are the same. [Pause] That is—ah! If that's really postcentral gyrus that would make sense—they're hitting a button in both cases.

This entire episode takes place in a context of uncertainty. The researcher begins by reading off information (*They're all decreasing below baseline*), but then acknowledges that that information isn't especially useful in terms of understanding brain functioning, because it is uninterpretable (*I don't think anybody really knows what decreases really mean*). He continues to try to read off information, comparing activation in two conditions (*punish looks like it's a little bit higher*) and interpreting what it might mean (*but that's probably not significant*). Unfortunately, the experiment doesn't seem to have worked (*it looks like these two are the same*). He seems to feel a significant amount of confusion about what the data are saying, because this was an experimental manipulation in which significant differences in activation between conditions were predicted. Then he appears to have an insight (*that is—ah!*) and proceeds to perform a spatial transformation of the data, by positing the area of activation is actually in an adjacent region of the brain (*if that's really postcentral gyrus, that would make sense*). In other words, if the display is not really showing what it purports to, but the area of activation is, in fact, the postcentral gyrus, the pattern of activity "would make sense." The researcher further projects the participants' actions onto the representation (*they're hitting a button in both cases*), a supposition that would account for the lack of difference between the conditions. The uncertainty and confusion can thus be resolved

These two examples are typical of the kind of problem-solving behavior demonstrated during the uncertain minutes: the experts used the visualizations as an initial source of data but then mentally manipulated the visualization in order to accommodate and resolve their uncertainty about what the data really represented. Comparing this behavior with their use of the visualizations during the certain minutes further highlights the role of spatial transformations during uncertainty. Consider this excerpt from one of the certain minutes in the fMRI domain:

Now we're going to do a contrast of areas that are active for words but have, really compare the contrast between the two. Ah, there we go. Now that's what I like to see; it makes a lot more sense. You can see, this is, this is, um, this is beautiful. This is exactly what you want to see for this type of data. You see a trend going right up the um, right here, [these] coordinates—left is right[3]—so right along the right ventral visual pathway, you see this nice stream of activation.

In contrast to the two examples discussed earlier, in this instance the researcher's expectations about differences in activation patterns for the experimental conditions are clearly met. He announces the particular comparison he is going to make, and the data are displayed as he has predicted. His utterances consist entirely of either reading off information from the display (e.g., *You see a trend going right up the um, right here; right along the right ventral visual pathway, you see this nice stream of activation)* or of exclamations of satisfaction (e.g., *this is beautiful; it makes a lot more sense*). There is no uncertainty in his interpretation of the data, and there are no spatial transformations. Perhaps because his expectations have been met, he has no reason to be anything other than certain about the accuracy of the display.

GENERAL DISCUSSION AND CONCLUSION

We conducted two studies to investigate our hypothesis that people using complex visualizations would use more spatial transformations when they are uncertain about the visualization than when they are certain. The results of both studies support this hypothesis. Study 1 provided an in-depth examination of the protocol of a single expert preparing a weather brief, using an online measure of uncertainty. Study 2 provided an extension of Study 1 by expanding the number of domains and participants, and by developing independent coding schemes for uncertainty and spatial transformations. Furthermore, the results of Study 2 showed that participants were not merely engaged in greater general problem-solving activity as uncertainty increased, as the number of interface actions was unrelated to their level of uncertainty.

One caveat to the results of our two studies is that the data are correlational, and consequently, we are unable at this time to conclude that uncertainty causes the experts to use spatial transformations. Nonetheless, given their contrasting behavior when participants were more certain, we do believe that the use of spatial transformations is a strategy by which experts deal with,

---

[3]The comment "left is right" is not a spatial transformation but rather refers to the fact that the left side of the graph represents the right side of the brain; in other words, it describes the mapping of graph to data.

and in some cases resolve, uncertainty in spatial domains. Although it is possible that a spatial strategy could be used in nonspatial domains, such as the likely responses to different gambles based on various probable outcomes discussed earlier in this chapter, we think it unlikely, in fact, that this is the case. Our main point is that in spatial domains, when experts must handle uncertainty, they use spatial transformations to do so.

Specifically, we propose that because the participants were experts or near-experts, they had significant domain knowledge as well as the ability to recognize a large number of patterns in their given domain. Thus, they are aware (through training) that whereas the data appear certain, there are in fact many reasons to doubt its seeming precision and lack of ambiguity. Furthermore, their pattern-recognition capacities (developed from experience) can help guide them to identify those instances when they should doubt the data and make necessary modifications. They make these modifications by means of spatial transformations (mental manipulations) of the displayed data, by mentally creating or deleting data points, mentally moving objects around, mentally animating data, mentally projecting stored memories of past experiences, and the like. The modified representation—now internal—becomes a new resource with which to reason about the data. This internal representation can itself be further modified by additional spatial transformations, as new information is obtained. Thus, in long chains of reasoning, a complex dialogue between the external and internal visualizations may evolve, in which each can be updated until the expert is satisfied that he or she has enough information to reach a conclusion or to make a decision. In contrast, when they are certain about the data, experts use only the external visualization as a source of information, focusing their problem-solving activity on reading off data values or other relevant types of information. When the data are considered reliable and sufficient, no further action is required.

How do our results mesh with the results of other research presented in this volume? Several researchers address issues of reasoning about uncertainty; however, the majority of those papers concentrate on uncertainty as the statistical notion of variability and error. In contrast, the research presented in our chapter focuses primarily on reasoning with visual data, rather than quantitative or statistical data. Whereas it is true that participants in these other studies used or even created graphical representations of statistical uncertainty, they did so mostly in order to represent, manipulate, and understand numerical variability. This use is consistent with the general use of graphs in modern statistics as a tool to understand numbers rather than as a means to examine real underlying effects in the data.

Although variability and error are indeed factors for our experts, there are many more varied sources of uncertainty in the data that they must address—visual uncertainty (e.g., "I'm not sure if my area is being masked by this whole temporal area"), uncertainty about whether the data are complete or accurate (e.g., "I would move [the low] further to the south"), uncertainty about whether the data are outdated (e.g., "I'm somehow having to run off an old model, which is frustrating"), interpretive uncertainty ("It's still hard to know what decreases in activation mean ... I don't think anyone really knows what decreases in activation mean"), and even uncertainty about whether the data in question represent the correct view (e.g., " ... [he made] design files, but I think I told him to do it the wrong way")—to name a few.

The different areas of focus (visual versus quantitative) raise important questions about the reasons for that divergence. Does the difference arise simply from what the individual researchers chose to examine, or does it reflect a genuine difference in an understanding of what data analysis is really about? In other words, to what extent does data analysis, in the sense of interpreting statistical concepts, capture the nature of "thinking with data"?

Statistical reasoning is, in fact, a crucial component of thinking with data. For many people, it is also a difficult process because it requires an understanding of concepts of uncertainty (variability and error), in order for useful interpretations to be constructed. However, we propose that statistical representations of uncertainty are just one of many aspects of uncertainty in thinking with data, and that the full complexity of what constitutes uncertainty when thinking with data might be masked in some experimental settings.

One important factor that may contribute some insight to this issue is the *in vivo* nature of our study. Not only were our participants asked to do tasks that they regularly perform, but they also had access to a wide range of data and analysis tools. Their problem-solving goal was internally motivated. In contrast, the other studies were conducted in a classroom setting with its attendant requirements to complete certain structured learning objectives prior to moving onto another unit of study. The participants were also engaged in problem-solving activities, but their motivation may have been external rather than internal. "Thinking with data" may necessarily mean different things in these different settings, one naturalistic and the other instructional.

A second difference in our study that may be relevant is the fact that our participants were experts with many years of experience and a great deal of accumulated domain knowledge, in contrast to either children learning both the content and the methodology or college students working on an abstract task. As we noted above, we believe that an integral part of our participants' response to uncertainty was initially *recognizing* that uncertainty existed in the data. The large number of patterns stored in memory from prior experience, and the ability to recognize and interpret them, were instrumental in discerning uncertainty, even when it was not explicitly portrayed. Novices and those working in abstract domains cannot rely on pattern recognition mechanisms to help identify areas of uncertainty; nor do they necessarily have the requisite training to understand at a general level the uncertainty inherent in any empirical data (due to measurement error, problems with experimental design, and so on). Thus, it is not surprising that in addition to performing more complex tasks, the experts were more aware of the potential for multiple sources of uncertainty in the data, many of which were not explicitly represented. We suggest that this awareness and ability to exploit it are important factors, specifically in dealing with uncertainty, and more generally in thinking with data. However, how such awareness develops remains an open question.

The issues raised by the differences in these two approaches to data analysis are important as we think more broadly about what it means to "think with data." Are the processes the same regardless of the situation? Or does this, in fact, represent two qualitatively different tasks for experts and novices, or in real-world science as opposed to a laboratory or instructional setting, or in formal science rather than everyday or informal reasoning? A next step to investigate these issues further would be to study how novices in a domain (with some years of formal training and thus the requisite domain knowledge) handle uncertainty.

REFERENCES

Dunbar, K. (1995). How scientists really reason: Scientific reasoning in real-world laboratories. In R. J. Sternberg & J. E. Davidson (Eds.), *The nature of insight* (pp. 365–395). Cambridge, MA: MIT Press.

Dunbar, K. (1997). How scientists think: On-line creativity and conceptual change in science. In T. B. Ward & S. M. Smith (Eds.), *Creative thought: An investigation of conceptual structures and processes* (pp. 461–493). Washington, DC, USA: American Psychological Association.

Ericsson, K. A., & Simon, H. A. (1993). *Protocol analysis: Verbal reports as data.* (2nd ed.). Cambridge, MA: MIT Press.

Hegarty, M. (1992). Mental animation: Inferring motion from static displays of mechanical systems. *Journal of Experimental Psychology: Learning, Memory and Cognition, 18*(5), 1084–1102.

Kosslyn, S. M., Sukel, K. E., & Bly, B. M. (1999). Squinting with the mind's eye: Effects of stimulus resolution on imaginal and perceptual comparisons. *Memory and Cognition, 27*(2), 276–287.

Shepard, R., & Metzler, J. (1971). Mental rotation of three-dimensional objects. *Science, 171*, 701–703.

Trafton, J. G., Trickett, S. B., & Mintz, F. E. (2005). Connecting internal and external representations: Spatial transformations of scientific visualizations. *Foundations of Science, 10*, 89–106.

Trafton, J. G., Trickett, S. B., & Mintz, F. E. (in press). Overlaying images: Spatial transformations of complex visualizations. *Foundations of Science.*

Tversky, A., & Kahneman, D. (1974). Judgment under uncertainty: Heuristics and biases. *Science, 185*, 1124–1131.

4

Students' Conceptual Understanding of the Standard Deviation

Robert C. delMas
University of Minnesota

Yan Liu
National Institute of Education, Singapore

Garfield and Ahlgren (1988) argued that little research has been done on how students come to understand statistical concepts. Mathews and Clark (1997) interviewed eight college students enrolled in an introductory statistics course and found that although all were highly successful in the course, none of the students demonstrated a conceptual understanding of the introductory level material. One area of statistical instruction that has received very little attention is students' understanding of variability (Reading & Shaughnessy, 2004; Shaughnessy, 1997). This is the case despite the central role the concept plays in statistics (Hoerl & Snee, 2001; Moore, 1990; Snee, 1990) and an apparent conceptual gap in students' understanding of variability (Shaughnessy, 1997). An understanding of statistical variation is needed to understand advanced concepts such as the nature of sampling distributions, inference, and p-values (Chance, delMas, & Garfield, 2004; delMas, Garfield, & Chance, 1999; Saldahna & Thompson, 2002; Thompson, Saldahna, & Liu, 2004).

Investigations into students' understanding of sampling variability (Reading & Shaughnessy, 2004) and instructional approaches that affect this understanding (Meletiou-Mavrotheris & Lee, 2002) have been conducted.

Reading and Shaughnessy (2004) present evidence of different levels of sophistication in elementary and secondary students' reasoning about sample variation. Meletiou-Mavrotheris and Lee (2002) found that an instructional design that emphasized statistical variation and statistical process produced a better understanding of the standard deviation, among other concepts, in a group of undergraduates. They were also better at taking both center and spread into account when reasoning about sampling variation in comparison to findings from earlier studies (e.g., Shaughnessy, Watson, Moritz, & Reading, 1999). Garfield, delMas, and Chance (this volume) found that undergraduates developed better understanding of similarities and differences among standard measures of variability through activities based on design principles outlined by Cobb and McClaine (2004). Lehrer and Schauble (this volume) documented elementary school students "invention" of measures of variability through design experiments that promoted agency and modeling through students' direct production of measurements, and methods for representing distributions of the measurements. However, little is still known about students' understanding of measures of variation, how this understanding develops, or how students might apply their understanding to make comparisons of variation between two or more distributions. The main purpose of the current study was to gain a better picture of the different ways that students understand the standard deviation as they participated in guided interactions with a computer tool designed to promote and support a conceptual understanding of the standard deviation.

A CONCEPTUAL ANALYSIS OF STANDARD DEVIATION

In order to have a working understanding of standard deviation, a student needs to coordinate several underlying statistical concepts from which the concept of standard deviation is constructed. Distribution is one of these fundamental concepts. Essentially, an understanding of distribution requires a conception of a variable and the accumulating frequency of its possible values. Therefore, a visual or graphical understanding of distribution involves the coordination of values and density. Such coordination allows the student to consider a question such as "What proportion of the distribution lies inclusively between the values of 4 and 7?"

A second fundamental concept is that of the average, defined as the arithmetic mean. A conceptual understanding of the standard deviation requires more than the knowledge of a procedure for calculating the mean. Imagery that metaphorically considers the mean to behave like a self-adjusting fulcrum on a balance comes close to the necessary conception. Such imagery supports the development of the third foundational concept, that is, deviation from the mean. It is through the coordination of distribution (as represented by the coordination of value and frequency) and deviation (as distance from the mean) that a dynamic conception of the standard deviation is derived as the relative density of values about the mean. A student who possesses this understanding can anticipate how the possible values of a variable and their respective frequencies will, independently and jointly, affect the standard deviation.

RESEARCH DESIGN

Participants

The participants were 12 students registered in an introductory statistics course at a large Midwest research university in the United States during the spring 2003 term. Neither author was an instructor for the course. At the start of this study, the course had covered distributions, methods for constructing graphs, measures of center, and measures of variability. With respect to the standard deviation, students had participated in an activity exploring factors that affect the size of the standard deviation. Students compared nine pairs of graphs to determine which one had a larger standard deviation. Students worked together, identified characteristics of the graphs thought to affect the size of the standard deviation, recorded their predictions, and received feedback. The goal of the activity was to help students see that the size of the standard deviation is related to how values are spread out and away from the mean

Research Materials

A computer application was written in Java and compiled for the Macintosh computer. The program was based on design principles for creating conceptually enhanced software (delMas, 1997; Nickerson, 1995; Snir, Smith, & Grosslight, 1995). Conceptually enhanced software facilitates the development of conceptual understanding by accommodating students' current levels of understanding, providing familiar models and representations, supporting exploration by promoting the frequent generation and testing of predictions, providing clear feedback, and drawing students' attention to aspects of a situation or problem that can be easily dismissed or not observed under normal conditions (Chin & Brewer, 1993; Posner, Strike, Hewson, & Gerzog, 1982; Roth & Anderson, 1988).

Students interacted with the software during an interview conducted by the first author. A digital video camera was used to capture their utterances and gestures. The computer program wrote data to a separate file to capture students' actions and choices, which were time stamped so that they could be coordinated with the digital video recording.

Nature of the Interview

Each student participated in a 1-hour interview. The interview consisted of two main parts: the exploration phase and the testing phase. The exploration phase was designed to help students learn about factors that affect the standard deviation. Each student was presented with five different sets of bars (see Fig. 4.1), one set at a time. For each set of bars, the first task asked a student to find an arrangement that produced the largest possible value for the standard deviation, followed by the task of finding a second arrangement that produced the same value. When a bar was moved into the graphing area, the bar became divided into segments with each segment representing one value, and the value of the deviation from the mean printed within each segment. The third through fifth tasks required three different arrangements that each produced the smallest value for the standard deviation. Each set of bars along with the five tasks comprised a "game."

Students used a button labeled "Check" to determine if an arrangement met the stated criterion for a task. Students were asked to describe what they were thinking, doing, or attending to before checking. In addition, the interviewer asked students to state why they thought an arrangement did or did not meet a criterion once feedback was received. The interviewer also posed questions or created additional bar arrangements to clarify a student's reasoning as needed. Conceptual change can be facilitated through a combination of discovery learning and direct instruction (e.g., Burbules & Linn, 1988) and by drawing students' attention to relevant aspects that might be neglected (e.g., Hardiman, Pollatsek, & Well, 1986). A mean-centered conception of the standard deviation was promoted by drawing attention to the values of deviations from the mean, by asking students how hypothetical movements of the bars would affect the mean, and by the interviewer modeling reasoning of how the distribution of not just the values, but of the deviations from the mean affect the values of the mean and the standard deviation.

The testing phase was designed to assess students' understanding of factors that influence the standard deviation. Students were asked to answer 10 test questions where each test presented a pair of histograms (see Fig. 4.2). For each pair of histograms, the average and standard deviation were displayed for

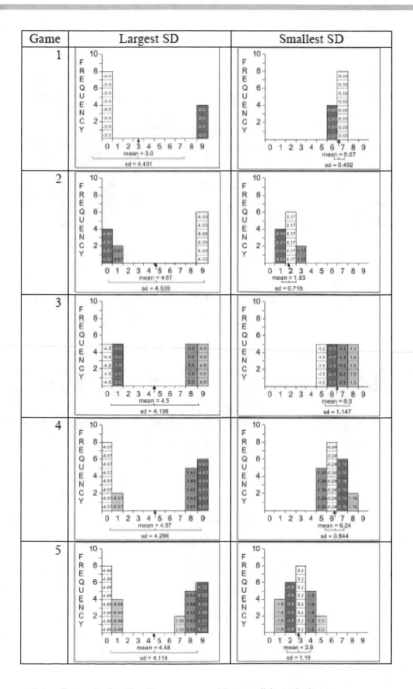

Figure 4.1 Bar sets for the five games with possible solutions.

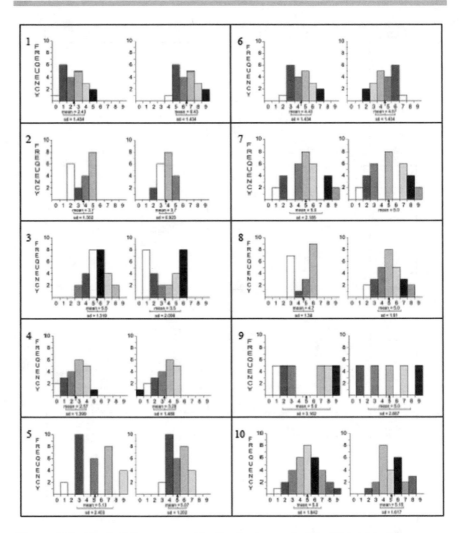

Figure 4.2   Ten test items presented in the second part of the interview.

the graph on the left, but only the average was displayed for the graph on the right. The students were asked to make judgments on whether the standard deviation for the graph on the right was smaller than, larger than, or the same as the graph on the left. Students were asked to provide justifications for their response choice to each test item.

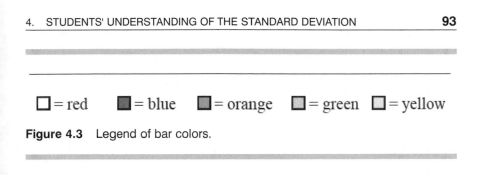

□ = red   ■ = blue   ■ = orange   ■ = green   □ = yellow

Figure 4.3   Legend of bar colors.

RESULTS

Exploratory Phase

The analysis of the exploratory phase focuses on the justifications students presented when asked why they expected an arrangement to satisfy a task criterion. Although some students appeared to start the interview with a fairly sophisticated understanding of factors that affect the standard deviation and how these factors work together, most students started with a very simple, rule-oriented approach that focused on a single factor that affects the size of the standard deviation. The following sections describe the development of students' arrangements and justifications for each task across the five games. Figures of students' bar arrangements are presented to illustrate excerpts from student transcripts. Each bar in the software program was presented in a different color, however, the bars presented in the figures are in gray tones.

Figure 4.3 presents a legend for the bar colors. Table 4.1 presents counts of the different types of justifications students presented for bar arrangements made during the five tasks of each game. Video excerpts that illustrate many of the justifications can be found in delMas and Liu (2003).

Task 1: Largest Standard Deviation

Game 1, Two Bars of Unequal Frequency.   The two-bar set of the first game required only that students place the bars as far apart as possible to produce the largest standard deviation, which the majority of the students did. However, there were slight differences in the justifications that students provided for the arrangements.

Statements that an arrangement should produce the largest possible standard deviation if the values are placed as far away from each other as possible, without mention of distance from the mean, were labeled as Far-Away-Value. This was the most common justification given during Task 1 of the first game when students were asked why an arrangement would have the largest standard deviation.

TABLE 4.1

Number of Students Who Provided Evidence of Each Justification During the Five Tasks for Each Game

	Game 1		Game 2		Game 3		Game 4		Game 5	
	Justification	Count	Justification	Count	Justification	Count	Justification	Count	Justification	Count
Task 1 **Largest SD**	Far Away	10	Far Away	7	Far Away	12	Balance	9	Balance	9
	(Mean	4)	(Mean	1)	(Mean	4)	Far Away	8	Far Away	5
	Range	1	Equal Spread Out	7	Balance	7	(Mean	4)	(Mean	3)
	Big Mean	1	(Order	3)	Mean in Middle	3	Mean in Middle	3	Guess & Check	5
	Bell Shaped	1	Balance	5	Equal Spread Out	1	Guess & Check	6		
	Mean Middle	1	Mean in Middle	1	Guess & Check	2				
	Contiguous	1	Guess & Check	8						
	Guess & Check	4								
Task 2 **Largest SD**	Mirror Image	12	Mirror Image	12	Mirror Image	11	Mirror Image	12	Mirror Image	12
	Far Away	1	Far Away	1			Mean in Middle	1		
	Guess & Check	1								
Task 3 **Smallest SD**	Contiguous	12	Contiguous	11	Contiguous	12	Contiguous	7	Bell Shaped	7
	Location	2	(Order	9)	Mean in Middle	2	(Order	1)	More in Middle	3
	Mean Middle	1	More in Middle	5	Location	1	More in Middle	9	(Mean	2)
	Guess & Check	1	(Mean	4)	Balance	1	(Mean	6)	Guess & Check	4
			Balance	2	More in Middle	1	Bell Shaped	2		
			Location	1	(Mean	1)	Balance	1)		
			Mean in Middle	1	Guess & Check	1	Guess & Check	7		
			Bell Shaped	1						
			Guess & Check	7						
Task 4 **Smallest SD**	Mirror Image	8	Mirror Image	9	Mirror Image	8	Mirror Image	5	Mirror Image	5
	Location	5	Location	4	Location	4	Location	7	Location	7
	Contiguous	2					Guess & Check	1		
Task 5 **Smallest SD**	Mirror Image	8	Mirror Image	6	Mirror Image	4	Mirror Image	7	Mirror Image	5
	Location	5	Location	8	Location	10	Location	6	Location	7
	Contiguous	2	More in Middle	1					Balance	1

Note. *Labels and values in parentheses represent subcategories of justification.

94

In contrast, in the Far-Away-Mean justification, a student stated that the largest standard deviation was obtained by placing the values as far away from the mean as possible. This demonstrated an understanding or awareness of deviation from the mean, which is one of the characteristics that needs to be coordinated with frequency to develop a full understanding of the relationship between distribution and the standard deviation. Only 4 of the 12 students referenced the mean during Task 1 of the first game. Carl provided a clear expression of this rule in the first game, although he was not sure that it was entirely correct.

> Carl: Well ... um ...what I know about standard deviation is, um, given a mean, the more numbers away, the more numbers as far away as possible from the mean, is that increases the standard deviation. So, I tried to make the mean, um, in between both of them, and then have them as far away from the mean as possible. But I don't, yeah, I don't know if that's right or not, but, yeah.

Only one student, Troy, expressed the idea that a bell-shaped distribution will have a smaller standard deviation relative to a "more spread out" distribution. This was made in the context of a Far Away-Value justification.

> Troy: Well, because there's a huge gap, a big gap in the middle there, um, so it's, um, I mean I remember from class that it was the, if they are more, more spread out, or I think that the deviation was higher. Um, like if, uh, if it's like, I remember also if it was peaked, you know like a pyramid or a bell, the smaller the standard deviation. But if it's like, I don't know, I guess kind of like a U-shape or something like that it's a bigger standard deviation.

Game 2, Three Bars of Unequal Frequency. The three-bar set of the second game provided a challenge to the students and produced more revealing information regarding students' initial understanding of standard deviation.

In the Equally Spread Out justification, the student believed that the largest standard deviation occurred when the bars were spread out across the entire range of the number line with equal spacing between the bars. Slightly more than half of the students produced an initial arrangement that qualified as the Equally Spread Out approach. This strategy may have resulted from the class activity on exploring factors that affect the size of the standard deviation described earlier in the section on participants. Students may have translated "spread out away from the mean" to mean "equally spread out." This may be a natural interpretation of the word "spread," in that the term may connote acts of spreading (e.g., spreading a pad of butter on a piece of bread; "spreading out" in the sense of sharing equally among individuals).

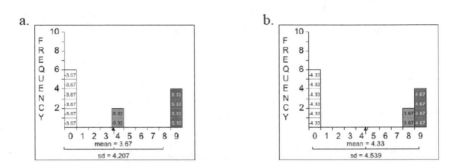

Figure 4.4   Nancy's arrangements for the largest standard deviation in Game 2.

Students using this strategy typically placed one bar above a value of 0, one above 9, and then placed the third bar above 4 or 5. Some students using this approach realized that the third bar could not be placed with equal distance between the lowest and highest positions, so they moved the third bar back and forth between values of 4 and 5 to see which placement produced the larger standard deviation. Nancy provided an example of this strategy. She first created the arrangement in Figure 4.4a when asked to produce the largest standard deviation in Game 2, followed by the arrangement in Figure 4.4b. The interviewer then asked her to describe her thinking.

Nancy: Well, at first I had the biggest bar ... I just put the biggest bar because it was the first one on there. And I just put it somewhere. And then, at first I was just going to put the blue bar and then the orange bar, um, as far as, you know, just have them kind of equally spread out. But then I thought, maybe if I got the orange bar closer to the mean, there's less data on the orange bar, so, er, um, yeah, there's less data there.

Intv: There's fewer values.

Nancy: Fewer values, yeah. So, I wanted to put that closer to the mean than the blue bar because the blue bar has more, more data.

Intv: Mm hmm.

Nancy: So, and then, I didn't know if I put the orange bar right on top of the mean, or if I put it over here by the blue bar, how much of a difference that would make. But I figured the more spread out it would be the bigger the deviation would be, so.

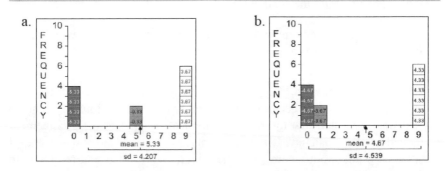

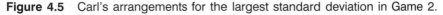

Figure 4.5 Carl's arrangements for the largest standard deviation in Game 2.

Intv: Okay, so by having it kind of evenly spaced here, is that what you're thinking as being more spread out?

Nancy: Yeah. Yeah. Having, like, as much space as I can get in between the values.

Once these students found that the Equally Spread Out arrangement did not produce the largest standard deviation, they typically moved the bars around and observed the standard deviation value, which is referred to as Guess-and-Check behavior. When students finally found a qualifying arrangement for the largest standard deviation, their justifications tended to use a version of the Far Away rule or a new rule that emerged during Game 2 that is labeled Balance.

In Game 2, Carl was trying to arrange three bars to produce the largest possible standard deviation. He first used an Equally Spread Out approach (see Fig. 4.5a) and then appeared frustrated that it did not produce the intended result. The interviewer intervened, trying to help him extend the Far Away—Mean rule he had used in Game 1 to the new situation. With this support, Carl successfully produced the distribution in Figure 4.5b. The interviewer then asked Carl to explain why he thought the arrangement resulted in the largest standard deviation.

Carl: Because ... basically because I have the most amount of numbers possible away from the mean. Um, because if I were ... say I have two bars that are bigger than the one smaller bar,

Intv: Mm hmm.

Carl: If I were to switch these two around.

Intv: The blue and the orange one?

Carl: The blue and the orange. The standard deviation would be smaller then because there's more of the numbers closer to the mean. So, yeah.

Carl did not automatically apply the Far Away—Mean rule to the three bar situation, but he readily accommodated the new situation into the scheme once it was suggested that the rule was applicable and that his arrangement contained an inconsistency. It is interesting to note that Carl's statement, "I didn't even think about where I put the middle bar," which is a reference to the orange bar with a frequency of two, is similar to Nancy's statement that she didn't know how the placement of the orange bar would affect the standard deviation. The program provided feedback to both students that the placement of the short bar was not inconsequential. Carl seemed to have incorporated this feedback into his scheme of the standard deviation ("the most amount of numbers away from the mean").

With the Balance strategy, the bars are arranged so that near equal amounts of values are placed above and below the mean. Typically, the bars were arranged in a recognizable order; descending, in terms of relative height, inward from the opposite extremes of the number scale to produce the largest standard deviation. Mary provides an example of a Balance justification for this type of arrangement in which she notes how the densities of values at each end of the number scale affect the location of the mean, the size of deviations from the mean, and the density of deviations from the mean, which affect the size of the standard deviation.

Mary: Because, and just with a frequency bar of six over at the high-end, um, it makes it so that the mean can stay more towards the middle. Because if you put too much frequency at one end it kind of makes the mean, the mean kind of follows it. Or, I, so I think that this kind of makes it, evens it out so that it, it can be, um, more frequency away from the mean to get the highest standard deviation.

Mary's explanation contained a line of thinking that started to emerge during the second game. She noted that having near-equal amounts of values at both ends of the horizontal scale moved the mean towards the middle of the number line, and reasoned that this produced large numbers of high deviations from the mean, which resulted in a large standard deviation. Arranging the bars in order to place the mean in the perceived middle of a distribution was labeled as the Mean in the Middle strategy.

It was also during the first task in Game 2 that one of the students, Alice, first displayed a coordination of the effects of the values, frequencies, and deviations from the mean on the value of the standard deviation. Alice made the same arrangement as in Figure 4.4b to produce the largest standard deviation in Game 2. The interviewer observed that Alice had moved the blue bar (frequency of 4) next to the red bar (frequency of 6) at one point and asked what she had noticed. She stated that the standard deviation became smaller. The interviewer asked why she thought this happened.

> Alice: Because, um, it's going to move, I think, um, the mean this way [towards the lower end of the number scale]. Yeah. Towards, you know, where more of the values are. So then the deviation there, it's going to be a deviation for more of the numbers are going to be smaller and then there's just a few over here that are going to be further away.

Alice knew that the location of the mean moved toward the larger mass of data, that this caused the deviations in both the red bar and the blue bar to get smaller, which resulted in a larger number of smaller deviations that were not counterbalanced by the two large deviations of the yellow bar, with an overall outcome of a smaller deviation. This demonstrated an ability to coordinate the effects of the deviations and frequencies on the size of the standard deviation.

Game 3, Four Bars of Equal Frequency. The third game presented a four-bar set where all the bars were of equal frequency. This was intended to reduce the complexity of the task in anticipation of the fourth game which presented a four-bar set with bars of different frequencies. Most students did not have difficulty with this task, producing a balanced distribution with two bars at opposite ends of the scale for the largest standard deviation and a contiguous, uniform distribution for the smallest standard deviation. A Far Away justification was given by all the students, with slightly over half noting the balance of the arrangement, and only a few stating that the distribution placed the value as far as possible from the mean.

Game 4, Four Bars of Unequal Frequency. The four bars of unequal frequency in the fourth game proved to be even more complex and challenging to the students. Most of the students initially displayed Guess and Check behavior for the first task in Game 4. They first moved pairs of bars to opposite ends of the number scale, then moved the bars and noted the changes in the standard deviation. For example, Jane seemed to think that the tallest bar needed to be at one end and all the other bars at the other end. To test her conjecture, she first placed the tallest bar at the high end of the scale and the other three bars at the low end (see Fig. 4.6a). She then moved the shortest bar toward the tallest, which resulted in a slightly smaller standard deviation, then went back to the arrangement in Figure 4.6a. She then made the distribution

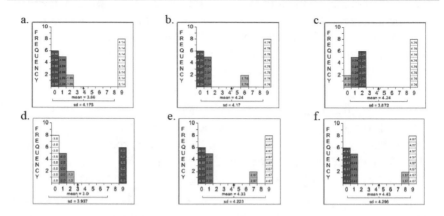

Figure 4.6 Jane's sequence of bar movements to produce a mirror image for Task 2 in Game 4.

in Figure 4.6c, and again returned to Figure 4.6a. Jane next tried the configuration in Figure 4.6d, then went back to Figure 4.6a, checked to see if it met the criterion, and found out that it did not. At this point the interviewer intervened by pointing out how close the mean was to the three bars on the far left, and pointing out that there were 11 values on the left and 8 values on the right. While the interviewer was talking, Jane moved the shortest bar incrementally to the right, one value at a time, apparently observing the change in the standard deviation. The standard deviation became greater than 4.175 once the shortest bar took on values of 7 (see Fig. 4.6e). Her final arrangement is shown in Figure 4.6f. The interviewer asked "You see where the mean is?," to which Jane replied "It's more in the middle." She stated "I think that one would work better," checked it, and found that it did produce the largest standard deviation.

In general, students' conception of the standard deviation at the start of Game 4 did not enable them to go directly to an optimal arrangement. Most appeared to have an understanding that bars needed to be placed at opposite ends of the horizontal scale, and that about equal numbers of values were needed at each end, but they did not demonstrate an understanding of how to maximize the relative density of deviations away from the mean, or an awareness of how this would affect the standard deviation.

Only two students, Carl and Nancy, produced the largest standard deviation with their first bar arrangement. Carl used a combination of Balance and Far Away to justify his arrangement.

Carl: Because, um, though they're different numbers, I'm trying to get, um, the highest amount of numbers away from each other as possible. So, if one's ten and one's eleven, there's an odd number, so one side is automatically going to have ten or eleven. So now it's just a matter of, um, trying to put them as far apart as possible.

Nancy primarily used a Balance statement as justification, but demonstrated a richer understanding on questioning by the interviewer.

Intv: Um, if we switch the positions of the blue and orange bars, and switch them, we'd still have eleven values on the high end, so would the standard deviation stay the same?

Nancy: Um, I don't think so because this one with six would be closer to the mean. More values would be closer to the mean.

Intv: Okay. And what would that do to the standard deviation?

Nancy: It would make it smaller.

It is inferred that Nancy considered the simultaneous effect that bar movement had on both the mean and the deviations of some of the values, and recognized the combined effect of those changes on the size of the standard deviation.

Several other students demonstrated conceptual coordination in their explanations. For example, Alice produced the same graph as in Figure 4.6f and justified why it produced the largest standard deviation with a combination of Balance and Far Away—Mean statements:

Alice: Because, again I wanted to kind of keep the same values on both ends to kind of get the mean to fall in the center. And then, that way they'd both be as far away from the mean as possible. And I think if you put the two middle bars together, then the two, like the largest and the smallest one, you'll get about the same value.

The interviewer followed this statement with a hypothetical question:

Intv: OK. So if we were to switch positions—No, I don't want you to do it, but just think about it. If we were to switch positions of the orange bar [frequency of 5] and the green bar [frequency of 2], what do you think would happen to the standard deviation?

Alice: It would get pulled towards the orange and the red bar. Because there is more frequency over there than on the other two. Because they aren't pulling the mean that much more over.

Intv: OK. What do you think would happen to the standard deviation, then?

Alice: I think it would get smaller.

Similar to Nancy's explanation in the previous section, Alice appeared to coordinate the simultaneous effects of hypothetical bar movements on the value and location of the mean, the size of deviations from the mean, and the resulting effect on the relative size of the standard deviation.

Game 5, Five Bars Of Unequal Frequency. The fifth game presented another challenge with five bars all representing different frequencies.

Of those who started with a Balance plus Far Away approach, only two students, Alice and Linda, produced an optimum arrangement on their first try. This might have been somewhat due to chance. An arrangement that resulted in the largest standard deviation was not obvious because there were several arrangements that appeared balanced and produced a large standard deviation. This resulted in some Guess and Check behavior by the remaining students before they found an arrangement that met the criterion.

Alex, Carl, Jane, Nancy, and Troy tried only one or two other distributions before producing and checking an arrangement with the largest standard deviation. Adam, Jeff, Lora, Mary, and Mona went back and forth between numerous configurations, checking various arrangements before settling on an optimal arrangement. Jeff presented the most Guess and Check behavior, creating seven distinct distributions, often going back to previous arrangements several times. Jeff actually produced an optimal arrangement prior to testing a distribution with a standard deviation that was slightly lower than the largest value, created the optimal arrangement a second time but did not check it, then rearranged the bars ten more times before recreating the optimal arrangement and testing it. Jeff did not demonstrate an understanding of the relative distribution of deviations about the mean, and seemed to have difficulty recalling previous arrangements and the value of the standard deviation. These latter students appeared to know the general pattern that produced the largest standard deviation, but relied on memory and testing multiple versions of the pattern to produce an optimal arrangement.

Task 2: Second Arrangement for the Largest Standard Deviation

For each of the games, a mirror image of the arrangement produced for Task 1 was required to produce a second arrangement of the bars that also resulted in the maximum value of the standard deviation. In Game 1, some students were confused by the task because they did not consider the mirror image to be a "different" arrangement. In these cases, the interviewer indicated that a new arrangement was considered "different" as long as at least one bar was not in the same location when compared to the previous arrangement. All students eventually produced a mirror image arrangement to satisfy the Task 2 criterion in Game 1. Some students expressed this approach as "swapping" or "switching" the position of the bars, whereas others stated that the arrangement was "flip-flopped." Ten of the students immediately produced a mirror image for Task 2 in Game 2. Mary was uncertain that a mirror image would satisfy the criterion, but tested out the arrangement and found that it did. Adam was unique in that he made sixty-five bar movements before producing a mirror image arrangement in Game 2. All of the students' initial arrangements for Task 2 in Game 3 were a mirror image. However, in Game 4, Adam produced three different arrangements before creating a mirror image, whereas all other students produced a mirror image on their first try. By Game 5, all students immediately produced a mirror image.

Troy proposed the Big Mean idea during Task 2 of the first game. Troy was the only student who initially believed that a distribution with a higher mean would have a larger standard deviation. At the end of the Task 1, Troy wondered what would happen if the position of the bars were switched around. The interviewer asked Troy to hold onto that question for the second task. The following is the interchange that took place prior to Troy actually rearranging the bar positions.

Intv: So, before you move anything, uh, it's interesting that you brought it up. What do you think will happen if you switch the positions of the bars? What do you think will happen to the standard deviation?

Troy: Uh, might be lower, I'm thinking.

Intv: OK.

Troy: Oh, it's the same.

Intv: It's the same. Mm hmm.

Troy: And the mean is different, too, so.

Intv: Uh huh.

Troy: I was thinking that if the mean was, I knew the mean was going to be smaller. I thought that would make the standard deviation smaller, but

Intv: Hmm. Any particular reason why, or reasons why you would think having a smaller mean would also, would affect the standard deviation that way, make it a smaller standard deviation?

Troy: Um, I don't know, just the, just that it's a smaller number by itself, I guess, you know.

Troy's reasoning seemed to be primarily one of association: If the mean gets lower, the standard deviation will get lower. Although he appeared to have an understanding of how value and frequency affect the mean, he had not coordinated these changes with changes in the standard deviation.

Task 3: Smallest Standard Deviation

Game 1, Two Bars of Unequal Frequency. In Game 1, all of the students readily made a distribution that met the Task 3 criterion by placing the two bars next to each other. This approach was labeled "Contiguous." Most of the students justified contiguous arrangements by simply stating that placing the bars as close together as possible resulted in the smallest standard deviation. However, none of the students stated that a contiguous arrangement produced the smallest deviations from the mean.

Game 2, Three Bars of Unequal Frequency. All of the students placed the three bars contiguous to each other as their first attempt to produce the smallest possible standard deviation. However, ten of the students placed the bars in ascending or descending order according to frequency as either their first or second configuration (see the examples in Fig. 4.7). Four of the students started with a U-shaped distribution (with the shortest bar in the middle), and two of these students (Jane and Linda) tested the U-shaped distribution before moving to an ascending or descending order arrangement. These arrangements indicated that most of the students did not understand how the relative frequencies of deviations from the mean related to the size of the standard deviation at this stage in the interview.

All of the students produced a contiguous arrangement with the tallest bar in the middle. Two of the students, Alex and Carl, did this on their first attempt. Several others proceeded from their initial ordered distributions to check out almost every possible contiguous configuration before settling on an optimum arrangement. For example, Lora, Mary, and Mona rearranged the bars seven to eight times before checking a bell-shaped distribution that met the criterion. These students appeared to be operating in a Guess and Check

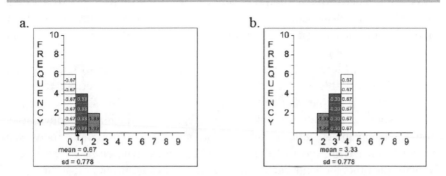

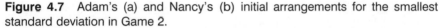

Figure 4.7 Adam's (a) and Nancy's (b) initial arrangements for the smallest standard deviation in Game 2.

manner, working with only the idea that the bars had to be next to each other. This represented an extreme in that others changed the arrangements only two to three times before meeting the criterion. Common progressions among these latter students were from U-shaped, to ordered, to tallest bar in the middle (Jane, Linda, Jeff, and Troy), or from ordered to tallest bar in the middle (Adam and Nancy).

The most common justification for why a configuration met the criterion of the smallest standard deviation in Game 2 was labeled More in the Middle. This was often expressed as having the tallest bar in the middle so that a lot or most of the values are close to the mean. These students mentioned that the mean ended up close to the bar with the tallest frequency. This may have represented the beginning stages of coordinating the effects of frequency, value, and possibly deviation on the size of the standard deviation.

Troy had stated during the first game that bell-shaped distributions tended to have smaller standard deviations. This idea seemed to guide his expectation that a descending order arrangement would produce the smallest standard deviation.

Troy: Um, no gaps in between the bars. And they are kind of, there's kind of a half of a curve there, or bell, or pyramid, or whatever. Those are typically, have smaller, uh, standard deviations.

After checking and finding that the arrangement did not meet the criterion, he made an arrangement with the tallest bar in the center.

Troy: OK. Now it's like, um, you know, you could say that's a complete kind of a bell instead of a half of one.

This produced a distribution that met the criterion, reinforcing Troy's idea that bell-shaped distributions tend to have smaller standard deviations than other distribution shapes. No other students made a Bell-Shaped justification at this stage of the interview.

Carl made a More in the Middle statement during Task 3 of Game 2 that indicated he was able to coordinate the effects of the values and the frequencies represented by the bars on the value of the mean. Carl also appeared to display some coordination between the effects of frequency and deviations from the mean and the value of the standard deviation, although his focus was primarily on having most of the values (the tallest bar) close to the mean. None of the other students demonstrated this type of coordination at this stage of the interview.

Game 3, Four Bars of Equal Frequency. All of the students immediately placed the four bars next to each other. All of the students noted the contiguity of the arrangement that produced the smallest standard deviation. Two students noted that the arrangement placed the mean in the middle of the four bars.

Game 4, Four Bars of Unequal Frequency. For the task of producing the smallest standard deviation, students tended to produce contiguous distributions with the tallest bar in the perceived center (Contiguous and More in the Middle), with only one student, Mona, creating an initial arrangement that was ordered. Mona clearly did not proceed from the notion that most of the values should have small deviations from the mean to minimize the standard deviation. She started with a Contiguous-Descending order arrangement, produced two U-shaped distributions, then went back to her original arrangement and checked if it met the criterion. The interviewer asked, "Do you have as many values as you possibly can real close to the mean?" She then moved the bars into an arrangement with the tallest bar in the middle and stated, "I don't know why I just made that different. I don't know how to explain it … I'm guessing because the top bar's even closer to the—no it's not. No it's not, because it's the mean. Well, yes it is." It appears she noticed that the tallest bar was close to the mean. After this, she made two U-shaped configurations again before settling on an optimal arrangement.

Alice was another student who did not seem to operate from a More in the Middle strategy. She rearranged the bars 12 times before settling on an optimal configuration, and some of her arrangements were U-shaped with at least one of the taller bars to the outside and one of the shorter bars in the middle.

The other students appeared to have learned that an ascending or descending order was not optimal. The Tall in the Middle and More in the Middle rules were offered by three fourths of the students as justifications, with six

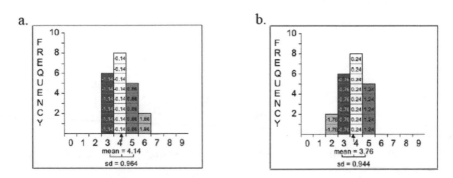

Figure 4.8   Carl's arrangements for the smallest standard deviation in Game 4.

students referencing the position of the mean relative to the bar or bars with the highest frequencies. Most of the initial arrangements did not meet the criterion, which resulted in Guess and Check behavior to fine tune the arrangement. Five of the students made only two different configurations (see Fig. 4.8), but switched between the two repeatedly, apparently checking which one produced the smaller standard deviation.

When a student produced a somewhat bell-shaped distribution that was not optimal and was not certain of how to proceed, the interviewer typically asked the student to describe the shape of the arrangement that was being tested, most of which were somewhat symmetric and bell-shaped. The interviewer asked if the bars could be arranged to produce an even more bell-shaped or symmetric distribution. This usually resulted in the student finding an optimal arrangement of the bars.

Game 5, Five Bars of Unequal Frequency.   All but one student produced the arrangement in Figure 4.9a or Figure 4.9b (or the mirror images of these arrangements) as their first distribution for the smallest standard deviation in Game 5. Both configurations consist of the tallest bar in the middle with the next two tallest bars to either side. This tendency toward an alternating or bell-shaped pattern may have resulted from the interviewer's questions and modeling of the bell-shaped strategy during Game 4. Alex and Lora actually produced an arrangement like Figure 4.10a for their first distribution and checked it without making additional arrangements. All of the other students alternated two or three times primarily between arrangements like those in Figure 4.10a and Figure 4.10b. Students tended to note the bell-shape and symmetry in their explanations for why the distribution met the criterion.

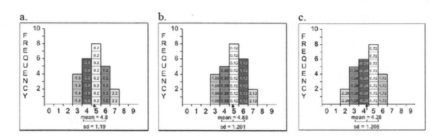

Figure 4.9 Students' initial arrangements for the smallest standard deviation in Game 5.

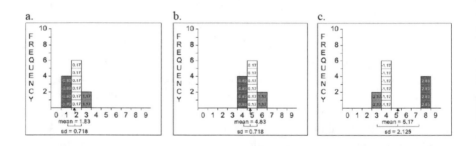

Figure 4.10 Testing Jeff's understanding of the Mirror Image strategy.

Tasks 4 and 5: New Arrangements, Smallest Standard Deviation

Unlike the arrangements that produced the largest standard deviation, there were many possibilities for arrangements that could produce the smallest standard deviation. Distributions that met the criterion resulted from either switching the positions of the two bars (Mirror Image), or moving all the bars an equal distance along the horizontal axis (an approach labeled "Location"), or a combination of both. Many students commented that the contiguity of the bars was related to the size of the standard deviation, but that the location of the bars did not matter.

During Game 2, the interviewer used Task 5 to see if a student could use the strategy that was not used for Task 4. For example, Jeff produced the distribution in Figure 4.10a for Task 3, then moved the bars over to produce Figure 4.10b for Task 4. The interviewer intervened for Task 5 by moving the tallest and shortest bar to the positions indicated in Figure 4.10c, and then asked Jeff to move the third bar to meet the criterion. Jeff did this readily by sliding the mid-height bar next to the tallest.

All students used the Mirror Image and Location strategies for the fourth and fifth tasks in Game 3. Similarly, all but three of the students immediately used either the Mirror Image or Location strategies for Task 4 in Game 4. Jane, Jeff, and Nancy each rearranged the bars five to seven times before producing a second arrangement with the smallest standard deviation. Jeff readily produced a mirror image of the distribution to complete the fifth task. Jane and Nancy both needed support from the interviewer to create a mirror image of the arrangement in the fourth task.

In Game 5, all of the students readily produced a mirror image or moved an arrangement to a new location to produce second and third distributions with the smallest standard deviation. At this stage, all students appeared to understand that the value of the standard deviation was conserved by these transformations.

Summary of Exploratory Phase Justifications

By the end of the exploratory phase, all of the students appeared to understand that the mirror image of a distribution conserved the value of the standard deviation. They also demonstrated the understanding that the relative, and not the absolute, location of the bars determined the standard deviation. Only one student, Troy, appeared to have a prior belief that the location of the mean was directly related to the size of the standard deviation, but he readily used mirror images and moved distributions to new locations to produce arrangements with the same standard deviation by Game 3.

Early on, students' arrangements and justifications indicated an understanding that a large number of values needed to cluster around the mean to produce a relatively small standard deviation, whereas larger numbers of values needed to be placed far from the mean, in both directions, to produce a relatively large standard deviation. Students' justifications became more complex as the number of bars increased. More students made references to the distribution of values relative to the mean, indicating an awareness of deviation. Many presented both Balance and Far Away arguments to justify a distribution for the largest standard deviation, or combined Contiguity and More in the Middle justifications for why a distribution should have the smallest standard deviation. This is consistent with a model of conceptual learning whereby changes in problem representation ability lead to better procedural understanding, which in turn furthers understanding of the concept under study (Rittle-Johnson, Siegler, & Alibali, 2001). Initial representations of the problem may have set the goal of predicting the value of the standard deviation and looking for a factor that would differentiate between smaller and larger values of the statistic. Feedback on erroneous bar arrangements, along with support from the interviewer, may have promoted reformulation of the problem to take into account deviations from the mean, and the density of these deviations about the mean. Even so, only a few students provided justifications that partially resembled a fully coordinated conception of how frequency and deviation from the mean combine to influence the magnitude of the standard deviation by the end of the exploratory phase.

Test Characteristics and Students' Strategies

Table 4.2 presents the justifications students used in their responses to the 10 test items. Students' justifications for their responses tended to be similar to those identified during the exploratory phase, and tended to reflect relevant characteristics of the graphs. For example, all students indicated that the two graphs had the same standard deviation for the first test item, noting that the arrangements were the same but in different locations. Most of the students' justifications for Test Items 2 and 3 were More in the Middle statements, although Test Item 3 also prompted Far Away justifications, probably because the graph on the right was U-shaped. For Test Item 6, students recognized that one graph was the mirror image of the other and that the standard deviations were the same. Almost all of the students gave a Mirror Image justification for their choice in Item 6.

Students found Test Item 4 a little more difficult than the first three tests. Most noted that the only difference between the two graphs was the placement of the black (shortest bar). Only about half of the students provided a justification for their responses, which tended to be either that the graph on the left was more bell-shaped, or that it had more values in the middle or around the mean compared to the graph on the right. A few students stated that the left-hand graph was more skewed.

The difficulty with Test Item 4 may have resulted from the nature of the tasks. The tasks required solutions that had some degree of symmetry and did not require students to produce skewed distributions, although skewed distributions were often generated and checked before an optimal distribution was found for the third task. The arrangements produced for the largest standard deviation were U-shaped, with a large gap through the middle, whereas the optimal arrangements for the smallest distribution were bell- or mound-shaped. This experience during the exploratory phase probably facilitated the comparison in Test Items 2 and 3, but did not necessarily provide experience directly related to the comparison needed to solve Item 4. Nonetheless, the majority of the students answered Item 4 correctly.

TABLE 4.2.

**Number of Students Who Used Each Justification
to Explain Choices During the Testing Phase***

Test	Justification	Count
1	Location	12
2	More in Middle	9
	Bell Shape	3
	Range	1
	Contiguous	1
3	More in Middle	6
	Far Away	4
	(Mean	2)
	(Value	1)
	Bell Shape	2
	Contiguous	1
4	Bell	3
	More in Middle	3
	Balance	1
5	Contiguous	7
	Mean in Middle	1
	More in Middle	1
	Equal Spread Out	1
	Range	1
6	Mirror Image	11
	Mean in Middle	1
7	Contiguous	7
	More in Middle	5
	Far Away-Mean	5
	Mean in Middle	1
	Range	1
8	Calculation	7
	More in Middle	4
	Mean in Middle	4
	Bell Shape	4
	More Values	4
	Range	2
	Contiguous	2
9	More in Middle	6
	Mean in Middle	3
	Far Away-Mean	3
	Calculation	2
	Contiguous	2
10	Calculation	9
	Range	4
	More in Middle	2
	More Values	2
	Mean in Middle	1
	Bell Shape	4
	Frequency	1

Note.   * Labels and values in parentheses represent subcategories of justifications.

Test Item 5 provided the first test of sensitivity to gaps between the bars. Almost all of the students' justifications for Test Item 5 involved statements of contiguity. Two students, Adam and Jeff, appeared to ignore the gaps between bars in the left-hand graph and responded that the two graphs would have the same standard deviation, suggesting that shape was the main feature they considered in their decisions and an insensitivity to spread or deviation from the mean.

Test 7 also tested students' understanding of how gaps affected the standard deviation, although in a more subtle way. All students answered Test 7 correctly, arguing that Contiguity and More Values in the Middle would produce a smaller standard deviation in the left-hand distribution. Test 9 challenged the misconception that having the bars evenly or equally spaced produces a large standard deviation. All students answered Test 9 correctly and offered justifications similar to those used in Test 7.

Test Items 8 and 10 were designed to challenge the idea that a perfectly symmetric, bell-shaped distribution always has the smaller standard deviation. For test item 8, all but one student (Linda) incorrectly indicated that the graph on the right would have a smaller standard deviation. Students noted that there were more bars or values in the graph on the right, or that it had a larger range, but still selected the smaller option as an answer. Students tended to note the bell-shape or the perception that more values were in the middle of the right-hand distribution compared to the one on the left as reasons for their responses.

After checking their answers to Item 8 and finding out it was incorrect, the interviewer attempted to guide the students' attention to the ambiguity that stemmed from a comparison of characteristics between the two graphs. The interviewer suggested that ambiguous situations might require the calculation of the standard deviations, and demonstrated how the information provided by the program could be used to do so.

When students came to Test 10, they were more likely to note the difference in the number of bars or values between the two graphs and resort to calculating the standard deviation for the graph on the right. Nine of the students came to a correct decision predominantly through calculation. Two of the students (Troy and Jane) initially predicted the graph on the right to have a larger standard deviation, noted the discrepancy in range or number of values, calculated the standard deviation, and changed their choice. Three students (Jeff, Lora, and Linda) did not perform calculations and incorrectly responded that the right-hand graph would have a larger standard deviation. Because Linda correctly answered Test Item 8, she did not receive the same guidance from the interviewer as the other students, which may account for her incorrect response on Item 10.

DISCUSSION

The ensemble of justifications, strategies, and conceptions found in this study indicate that students in an introductory statistics course form a variety of ideas as they are first learning about the standard deviation. Some of these ideas, such as the Contiguous, Range, Mean in the Middle, and Far Away-Values justifications, capture some relevant aspects of variation and the standard deviation, but may represent a cursory and fragmented level of understanding. Others such as the Far Away-Mean, Balance, More Values in the Middle, and Bell-Shaped justifications, represent much closer approximations to an integrated understanding. There are still other ideas, notably the prevalent Equally Spread Out and the idiosyncratic Big Mean justifications, which are inconsistent with a coherent conception of the standard deviation. Some students also demonstrated an ability to coordinate the effects of several operations on the value of the standard deviation, an indication of a more integrated conception.

Students' explanations during the testing phase, however, were usually based on finding a single distinguishing characteristic between the two distributions. This suggests that the students tended to take a rule-based, pattern recognition approach when comparing distributions. If this is the case, two questions need to be addressed. What type of experiences are required to move students from a rule-based approach to a more integrated understanding that can be generalized to a variety of contexts? In addition to the interactive experience presented in the current study, do students need additional support to reflect on the relationships between the different factors and to attend to and coordinate the related changes?

A pattern-recognition, rule-based approach is consistent with a goal of finding the right answer by noting characteristics that differentiate one distribution from another and noting the correspondence with the size of the standard deviation. This orientation was supported by the design of the software. Is there a way to modify the task so that there is less emphasis on a correct solution and more emphasis on exploring the relationships among the factors that affect the standard deviation? One possibility is to modify the software so that the mean and standard deviation are not automatically revealed. This might promote reflection and result in less Guess and Check behavior.

The interviewer attempted to extend students' conceptual understanding by trying to draw their attention to relevant aspects of the distributions, and by modeling the desired conceptual understanding. The software was designed to help students identify factors that affect the standard deviation. The software and interview were not designed with the promotion of model building in mind. A model eliciting approach may be more likely to produce the "system-as-a-whole" thinking (Lesh & Carmona, 2003) that is needed for a fully coordinated conception of the standard deviation, and to allow students to develop a more integrated representational system (Lehrer & Schauble, 2003), rather than a collection of separate and potentially conflicting rules.

Several changes to the program could be introduced to support model building and study how it affects understanding of the standard deviation. The software currently draws attention to a single bar rather than visually emphasizing how characteristics change simultaneously. A second display above the graphing area of the histogram that presents horizontal deviation bars colored to match the corresponding vertical frequency bar colors may facilitate coordination of simultaneous changes in values, the mean, deviations, and the standard deviation. In addition, the interview protocol could be modified to elicit conjectures from students about how changes to arrangements will affect the value of the mean and deviations, and how these changes subsequently affect the standard deviation, to promote a coordination of the concepts. This contrasts with the current protocol where the interviewer modeled the thinking and reasoning for the student rather than supporting students to produce their own conjectures and test their implications.

REFERENCES

Burbules, N. C., & Linn, M. C. (1988). Response to contradiction: Scientific reasoning during adolescence. *Journal of Educational Psychology, 80*, 67–75.

Chance, B., delMas, R., & Garfield, J. (2004). Reasoning about sampling distributions. In D. Ben-Zvi & J. Garfield (Eds.), *The challenge of developing statistical literacy, reasoning, and thinking* (pp. 295–323). Dordrecht, The Netherlands: Kluwer.

Chin, C. A., & Brewer, W. F. (1993). The role of anomalous data in knowledge acquisition: A theoretical framework and implications for science instruction. *Review of Educational Research, 63*(1), 1–49.

Cobb, P., & McClain, K. (2004). Principles for instructional design in developing statistical reasoning. In D. Ben-Zvi & J. Garfield (Eds.), *The challenge of developing statistical literacy, reasoning, and thinking* (pp. 375–395). Dordrecht, The Netherlands: Kluwer.

delMas, R. (1997). A framework for the development of software for teaching statistical concepts. In J. B. Garfield & G. Burril (Eds.), *Research on the role of technology in teaching and learning statistics: Proceedings of the 1996 International Association of Statistics Education (IASE) Round Table Conference* (pp. 85–99). Voorburg, The Netherlands: International Statistical Institute.

delMas, R., Garfield, J., & Chance, B. (1999). A model of classroom research in action: Developing simulation activities to improve students' statistical reasoning. *Journal of Statistics Education, 7* (3). Retrieved January 8, 2007, from http://www.amstat.org/publications/jse/

delMas, R., & Liu, Y. (2003). Exploring students' understanding of statistical variation. In L., Carl (Ed.), *Reasoning about variability: Proceedings of the Third International Research Forum On Statistical Reasoning, Literacy, and Reasoning* (on CD at http://www.cst.cmich.edu/users/lee1c/SRTL3/). Mount Pleasant, MI: Central Michigan University.

Garfield, J., & Ahlgren, A. (1988). Difficulties in learning basic concepts in statistics: Implications for research. *Journal for Research in Mathematics Education. 19*, 44–63.

Hardiman, P., Pollatsek, A., & Well, A. D. (1986). Learning to understand the balance beam. *Cognition and Instruction, 3*, 63–86.

Hoerl, R., & Snee, R. D. (2001). *Statistical thinking: Improving business performance.* Duxbury Press.

Lehrer, R., & Schauble, L. (2003). Origins and evolution of model-based reasoning in mathematics and science. *Beyond constructivism: Models and modeling perspectives on mathematics problem solving, learning, and teaching* (pp. 59–70). Mahwah, NJ: Lawrence Erlbaum Associates.

Lesh, R., & Carmona, G. (2003). Piagetian conceptual systems and models for mathematizing everyday experiences. In R. Lesh & H. M. Doerr (Eds.) *Beyond constructivism: Models and modeling perspectives on mathematics problem solving, learning, and teaching* (pp. 71–96). Mahwah, NJ: Lawrence Erlbaum Associates.

Mathews, D., & Clark, J. (1997). *Successful students' conceptions of mean, standard deviation, and the Central Limit Theorem.* Paper presented at the Midwest Conference on Teaching Statistics, Oshkosh, WI.

Meletiou-Mavrotheris, M., & Lee, C. (2002). Teaching students the stochastic nature of statistical concepts in an introductory statistics course. *Statistics Education Research Journal, 1*(2), 22–37. Retrieved January 8, 2007 from http://fehps.une.edu.au/serj

Moore, D. S. (1999, April). Uncertainty. In L. Steen (Ed.), *On the shoulders of giants.* (pp. 95–138) Washington, DC: National Academy Press.

Nickerson, R. S. (1995). Can technology help teach for understanding? In D. N. Perkins, J. L. Schwartz, M. M. West, & M. S. Wiske (Eds.), *Software goes to school: Teaching for understanding with new technologies* (pp. 7–22). New York: Oxford University Press.

Posner, G. J., Strike, K. A., Hewson, P. W., & Gertzog, W. A. (1982). Accommodation of a scientific conception: Toward a theory of conceptual change. *Science Education, 66*(2), 211–227.

Reading, C., & Shaughnessy, J. M. (2004). Reasoning about variation. In D. Ben-Zvi & J. Garfield (Eds.), *The challenge of developing statistical literacy, reasoning, and thinking* (pp. 201–226). Dordrecht, The Netherlands: Kluwer.

Rittle-Johnson, B., Siegler, R. S., & Alibali, M. W. (2001). Developing conceptual understanding and procedural skill in mathematics: An iterative process. *Journal of Educational Psychology, 93*(2), 346–362.

Roth, K., & Anderson, C. (1988). Promoting conceptual change learning from science textbooks. In P. Ramsden (Ed.), *Improving learning: New perspectives* (pp. 109–141). London: Kogan Page.

Saldahna, L. A., & Thompson, P. W. (2002). Conceptions of sample and their relationship to statistical inference. *Educational Studies in Mathematics, 51*(3), 257–270.

Shaughnessy, J. M. (1997). Missed opportunities in research on the teaching and learning of data and chance. In F. Bidulph & K. Carr (Eds.), *Proceedings of the Twentieth Annual Conference of the Mathematics Education Research Group of Australasia* (pp. 6–22). Rotorua, NZ: University of Waikata.

Shaughnessy, J. M., Watson, J., Moritz, J., & Reading, C. (1999, April). School mathematics students' acknowledgment of statistical variation. For the NCTM Research Precession Symposium: *There's More to Life than Centers.* Paper presented at the 77th Annual National Council of Teachers of Mathematics (NCTM) Conference, San Francisco, CA.

Snee, R. (1990). Statistical thinking and its contribution to quality. *The American Statistician, 44*, 116–121.

Snir, J., Smith, C., & Grosslight, L. (1995). Conceptually enhanced simulations: A computer tool for science teaching. In D. N. Perkins, J. L. Schwartz, M. M. West, &

M. S. Wiske (Eds). *Software goes to school: Teaching for understanding with new technologies* (pp. 106–129). New York: Oxford University Press.

Thompson, P. W., Saldahna, L. A., & Liu, Y. (2004, April). *Why statistical inference is hard to understand.* Paper presented at the Annual Meetings of the American Educational Research Association, San Diego, CA.

5

Using Students' Informal Notions of Variability to Develop an Understanding of Formal Measures of Variability

Joan Garfield
Robert C. delMas
University of Minnesota

Beth Chance
California Polytechnic State University-San Luis Obispo

Understanding and reasoning about variability is viewed by statisticians as the core component of statistical thinking (e.g., Hoerl & Snee, 2001; Moore, 1990; Snee, 1990), which, in turn, is the goal of most statistics instruction. Statisticians have a "complex relationship" with variability: in various circumstances they attempt to minimize it, maximize it, estimate it, or simply analyze it (Gould, 2004). Wild and Pfannkuch (1999) developed a model of statistical thinking, based on an empirical study of how statisticians solve problems, which confirms that understanding and reasoning about variability is a key aspect of statistical thinking. They describe how statisticians distinguish between explained and unexplained variation, trying to model and find meaning in explained variation.

When statisticians look at one or more data sets, they often appraise and compare the variability informally and then formally, looking at appropriate graphs and descriptive measures. They look at both the center of a distribution as well as the spread from the center, often referring to more than one representation of the data to lead to better interpretations. Statisticians are also likely to consider sources of variability, including the statistical and measurement processes by which the data were collected. These are all aspects of the way statisticians think, and the way that many teachers of statistics would like their students to think, even in introductory college classes.

RESEARCH ON REASONING ABOUT VARIABILITY

Current research demonstrates that it is extremely difficult for students to reason about variability and that we are just beginning to learn how reasoning about variability develops (see Garfield & Ben-Zvi, 2005). In a teaching experiment involving nurses, Noss, Pozzi, and Hoyles (1999) described a clash between people's intuitions about variation and what they are taught about this concept. Shaughnessy, Watson, Moritz, and Reading (1999) pointed out the lack of research on this topic, and since this chapter, many researchers are increasingly focusing on students' reasoning about variability in different contexts. These contexts include understanding the variability of data (Ben-Zvi, 2004; Konold & Pollatsek, 2002), variability as represented in distributions (Bakker, 2004), in bivariate relationships (Cobb, McClain, & Gravemeijer, 2003; Rubin & Hammerman, 2003), in comparing groups (Biehler, 2001; Lehrer & Schauble, 2002; Makar & Confrey, 2005), in probability contexts (Reading & Shaughnessy, 2004), in understanding measures such as the standard deviation (delMas & Liu, this book), and in sampling (Chance, delMas, & Garfield, 2004; Watson, 2004).

What is clear from these studies is that understanding variability has both informal and formal aspects, from understanding that data vary (e.g., differences in data values) to understanding and interpreting formal measures of variability (e.g., range, interquartile range, and standard deviation). What is also clear is the interconnectedness of variability to concepts of distribution and center (Cobb, Confri, deSessa, Lehrer, & Schuable, 2003). To make the concept even more complex, variability may sometimes be desired and of interest, and sometimes be considered error or noise (Gould, 2004; Konold et al., 2002). From the emerging research it appears that it is difficult to help students move from informal to formal notions of variability, and to see variability as a fundamental idea underlying statistics. It is also difficult for students to recognize the different "faces" of variability, such as overall spread, clustering to the center, or relative deviations from an expectation (e.g., a measure of center or an expected model).

An inconsistent use of terminology is noticeable in the surveyed research studies. Although some use "variability" and "variation" interchangeably, others distinguish between the meanings of these two words. Reading and Shaughnessy (2004) suggest the following distinctions: variation is a noun describing the act of varying, whereas variability is a noun form of the adjective "variable," meaning that something is likely to vary or change. They suggest that variability refers to the characteristic of the entity that is observable, and that variation refers to the describing or measuring of that characteristic.

TEACHING AND LEARNING ABOUT VARIABILITY
IN COLLEGE CLASSES

It appears that many students who complete college statistics classes are unable to understand many basic statistical concepts. Central among these concepts is variability, which has been studied by Mathews and Clark (1997) and later Clark, Kraut, Mathews, and Wimbish (2003), who found that students who received "A" grades in statistics classes were unable to explain the mean, other than as a formula, and had no understanding of the standard deviation. Garfield (2003) found that even students in introductory classes that were using reform textbooks, good activities, and high-quality technology, had significant difficulty reasoning about different aspects of variability, such as representing variability in graphs, comparing groups, and comparing the degree of variability across groups. Lehrer and Schauble (2002) argued that students are given few, if any, conceptual tools with which to reason about variability. In fact, students still appear to learn statistics as a set of tools and techniques, do not see connections among the ideas, and are not able to understand the fundamental ideas that are required for statistical thinking (e.g., Cobb & McClain, 2004; Pfannkuch & Wild, 2004).

Noticeably lacking in the current research literature are studies of how to best impact the learning of college students who are typically introduced to variability in a unit of descriptive statistics, following units of graphing univariate data and measures of center. Measures of variability (or spread) are then introduced, and students learn to calculate and briefly interpret them. Typically, only the formal notion of variability as measured by three different statistics (i.e., the range, interquartile range, and standard deviation) is taught. Students often do not hear the term *variability* stressed again until a unit on sampling, where they are to recognize that the variability of sample means decreases as sample size increases. When students are introduced to statistical inference, variability is then treated as a nuisance parameter because estimating the mean becomes the problem of importance (Gould, 2004). Given this typical introduction in textbooks and class discussion, it is not surprising that few students actually develop an understanding of this important concept. Good activities and software tools designed to promote an understanding of variability do exist. However, they are typically added to a lesson or given as an assignment instead of being integrated into a plan of teaching, and their impact on student understanding has not been subjected to systematic study. So although there have been positive changes in introductory statistics classes, they still fall short of giving students the experiences they need to develop statistical thinking and a deep understanding of key statistical concepts.

There are several explanations for why current introductory college statistics courses have not yet had a larger impact on students' ability to develop statistical reasoning and thinking. Although these reasons relate to general course outcomes, they apply to students' inability to understand and reason about the core concept of variability and how it relates to all topics in an introductory college course. These reasons include:

- Most college courses still teach the same progression of content and emphasize the development of too many skills and procedures (Pfannkuch & Wild, 2004). Many instructors are also reluctant (or feel restricted by the departments they serve) to reduce the number of techniques covered in an introductory course.

- Many instructors still believe that students learn most effectively through lectures and textbook reading. They do not embrace constructivist views of learning, and do not believe in the power of problem solving and activities to help students construct knowledge. In addition, it is very difficult for teachers to know what students are actually learning because student learning of statistics is still typically evaluated through tests that have students produce computations and follow procedures, rather than think or reason statistically.

- Many instructors, although using high quality materials and technological tools, may take a "black box" approach, assuming that simply using the materials and tools (e.g., in class demonstrations) will somehow magically develop students' statistical thinking. They do not know how to take full advantage of the technological tools nor how to design activities to ensure sufficient engagement with the technology to impact students' understanding.

- College teachers tend to work in isolation, teaching their courses without examining their teaching or student learning other than reviewing course evaluations.

A different approach to teaching introductory college statistics is needed, one that will help students develop a deep understanding of the core statistical ideas, understand how concepts are connected, and build their statistical thinking. Rather than present material in a logical fashion, as most textbooks and courses do, a mechanism was needed to help create a new and innovative approach to teaching the concept of variability.

In searching for a mechanism to allow us to develop a new teaching approach, we learned about Japanese Lesson Study and how it enabled teachers to work together to design innovative, unique, "research lessons" to help elementary school students achieve important learning goals in science and mathematics (see Stigler & Hiebert, 1999). We wondered if this method could also be used with college teachers, to design one or more research lessons to help students learn important statistical concepts, and in particular, to help them reason about variability.

This chapter describes what we learned about Japanese Lesson Study and how we adapted the Japanese Lesson Study process to guide a classroom teaching experiment that could be used to develop students' reasoning about variability. In our adaptation of Japanese Lesson Study as a teaching experiment, extensive assessment data was gathered to determine the misconceptions as well as aspects of correct understanding students had, in several classes, including those where the teaching experiment took place. Based on the assessments and the first version of the lesson that was taught and observed, we designed a sequence of two lessons that utilize student's intuitive ideas of variability to develop more formal notions of variability. These two research lessons were collaboratively developed, taught, observed, and evaluated.

METHODOLOGY: THE TEACHING EXPERIMENTS

This section briefly describes the method of Japanese Lesson Study that served as a basis for our teaching experiment and why we were intrigued by its potential for our needs. We then discuss the constraints involved in conducting a teaching experiment in a college statistics class and describe the nature and context of the course we used for our study. We describe the development of our first research lesson, using principles of instructional design in mathematics education, and what we learned from this experience as well as from the students' assessments. We then describe the second pair of research lessons along with assessment data.

Japanese Lesson Study

Japanese Lesson Study (JLS) is a method used by teachers to collaboratively develop "research lessons" that are used by teachers to carefully and systematically study how to achieve a particular learning goal (Hiebert, Morris, & Glass, 2003; Fernandez, Cannon, & Chokshi., 2003). JLS has been studied and written about extensively and is the focus of many new research projects in mathematics and science education (e.g., Fernandez, 2002; Lewis, 2000; Lewis & Tsuchida, 1998). Rather than offer a new technique for teaching students, it offers a mechanism for teachers to systematically investigate and improve their teaching. JLS provides a model for teacher learning and a set of concrete steps that teachers can take, over time, to improve their teaching (Stigler & Hiebert, 1999).

These lessons embody theories about how to help students reach particular learning goals (Hiebert, Gallimore, & Stigler, 2002). They are classroom lessons taught to a regular class of students, but that have special features linked to the research process. According to Lewis and Tsuchida (1998), JLS lessons are focused on important learning goals, carefully planned in collaboration with other teachers, observed by teachers, recorded, discussed, and then revised. They consist of research lessons developed over time by a study group, and contain descriptions of the learning goals, the rationale for the lesson design, descriptions of activities, anticipated responses of students, and suggested responses by the teachers. These lessons may be disseminated widely to other teachers, provide a professional knowledge base for teachers, and thereby contribute to the improvement of teaching and learning.

We decided to try to adapt JLS to college statistics classes as a way to examine and develop students' statistical thinking and reasoning about variability. We saw JLS as a form of design experiment (Cobb, Confrey, diSessa, Lehrer, & Schauble, 2003; The Design-Based Research Collective, 2003) in that JLS can be used to enrich our understanding of students' reasoning and learning (e.g., lesson designs are based on hypothetical learning trajectories and developed through iterative design cycles that compare teacher/researcher conjectures to dense descriptive observations of the learning environment). Our main research question became: Can we construct activities through a JLS process that will engage students, elicit and build on their informal intuitions about variability, and help develop their formal reasoning about variability?

Our JLS group at the University of Minnesota began in September, 2003, and originally consisted of two faculty (Garfield and delMas), one full-time instructor (who coordinates the introductory statistics courses for the department), and four doctoral students who teach their own sections of introductory statistics in the Department of Educational Psychology. These students were pursuing their doctoral degrees in four different areas: mathematics education, learning and cognition, social psychology, and statistics education. One unique feature of this teaching experiment is that the faculty (the primary researchers) and graduate students were all teachers of statistics and had recent experience teaching at the high school or college level. In addition, a research assistant attended meetings to take notes. All sessions were videotaped including the teaching lessons. In the spring semester, the instructor left the group (due to time constraints) and later one of the graduate students dropped out, but we gained another faculty member (Chance) who was visiting on her sabbatical and was conducting a second JLS group with colleagues from a liberal arts colleges in the area. Our first task was to learn enough about JLS to see how we could implement and adapt it in our setting, which involved several important constraints.

Constraints of Conducting Research in College Courses

There is little research conducted in college statistics classes due to many of the same constraints that we faced in our study. Unlike other teaching experiments that may have more time and fewer constraints, this course did have a constraint of having to cover a curriculum that includes descriptive statistics and graphing for univariate and bivariate data, methods of producing and collecting data, probability and probability distributions, sampling and sampling distributions, and statistical inference for one and two sample situations. Therefore, the experiments that took place during class had to be part of the regular class curriculum and not interfere with the syllabus and course structure. Given those constraints, we were fortunate to have one class session set aside during the fall semester and two class sessions reserved during the spring semester for our teaching experiments. These sessions would have typically been used for review or as a day to work on class projects.

Unlike most research studies on the topic of variability, this research took place during class sessions of an upper division introductory college statistics course. In order to understand the context in which the teaching experiment took place, it is important to learn how this introductory class was taught. The course is aimed at liberal arts majors who need a course in quantitative reasoning to fulfill their requirements for a bachelor's degree. This course does not have mathematics prerequisites, so it is often the choice of students who avoid or dislike mathematics. It is a one semester course that meets twice a week, for 75-minute sessions, in a computer lab.

The course was designed around current recommendations for teaching introductory statistics (Cobb 1992; Garfield, Hogg, Schau, & Whittinghill, 2002). The class was not a traditional course where an instructor lectured and students took notes and worked on problems. Instead, students were assigned material to use in preparing for class from a multimedia CD-ROM, *ActivStats* (Velleman, 2003). The CD contained mini-lectures, brief videos of a real-world context for the statistical concepts in that unit, simulation tools or interactive applets, activities using DataDesk software to analyze data, and review/assessment exercises. The book *Active Practice of Statistics* (Moore, 2001) was used along with the CD, primarily as a review of the material and to provide examples, worked out problems, definitions, and homework exercises. Class time was spent discussing material students previewed for that day, followed by hands-on activities and computer labs. Students often worked in groups. The courses used for the teaching experiments fall and spring were taught by two different graduate students who used the same materials and basic instructional method.

Content Presented in Multimedia CD and Textbook

Students learned about measures of variability by studying material on the CD-ROM through the following sequence of topics: data, distributions, summaries of center. At this point they were introduced to measures of spread. Students received the message that it is important to examine and describe distributions in terms of shape, center and spread. Three measures of variability were introduced: the range (difference between highest and lowest values), the interquartile range (IQR) that is the difference between the upper and lower quartiles and represents the spread of the middle half of a data set, and the standard deviation (SD). Two interactive applets were included in the CD, one based on a dotplot, one based on a histogram. Both could be manipulated to visually represent the IQR and SD for a data set. The textbook also defined these measures and showed how they are calculated. It emphasized the need to look at center and spread, and listed properties of the SD (e.g., only use the SD when the mean is an appropriate measure of center, when a distribution is symmetric and unimodal, and the middle 68% of the data is about one SD wide). The description of the instructional materials in the CD and textbook provided a sense of what students would have seen if they prepared for class as instructed. However, many of them most likely skimmed the materials and, at best, might have learned how to compute the measures. The types of homework and quiz questions suggested for student assessment by these materials focused on calculating the summaries and knowing when to use them for different data sets and distributions.

First JLS Group

The group met for 1 hour every other week for 15 weeks. The participants varied from six to eight statistics instructors. We included both novice and experienced teachers, as well as a research assistant to take notes of the discussions on a laptop computer. All meetings were videotaped. Discussions were led and summarized by the first author, who initially prepared background materials and later drafted lesson plans and student handouts to be reviewed by the group.

We began our Lesson Study by reviewing materials about the Lesson Study process (Lewis, 2000) and looking at a sample mathematics lesson plan developed by a JLS group. Some of us had previously viewed videos on JLS that included glimpses of lessons being taught. Following the JLS structure, we began by determining a broad learning goal for students (statistical thinking) and then thinking about how to help students work towards this goal. This led to a discussion and consensus on creating a lesson to develop students' understanding of variability. We began by first discussing our own understanding and all the things that we wanted students to understand about this concept. We asked ourselves: What does it mean for students to understand variability? What would this understanding look like? How would we see or assess it? We agreed that we wanted students to recognize the omnipresence of variability, to be able to understand and interpret measures such as range, IQR, and SD, and to understand how they are represented and related in different graphical representations of data. We also wanted students to understand the concept of no variability, and what to expect if a SD was 0. That led us to discussing the notion of large and small amounts of variability, and how to develop students' ideas from initial notions of "spread" or "spread out" to a more complex understanding of "spread from the center." We had experienced some students' misconceptions of variability such as focusing on the change in heights of bars in a histogram and equating lack of variability with a smooth or uniform distribution. We wanted students to understand variability as a natural phenomenon in the real world and to consider reasons for variability (e.g., measurement error, or individual differences). We also wanted students to reason about the variability of a variable given a description (e.g., scores on an easy test) and be able to draw a graph that represented the predicted variability.

We decided that our main goal for the lessons would be to build on students' informal notions (things vary, how and why things vary) to lead to more formal notions of the standard statistical measures. We focused early Lesson Study discussions on our own notions of different aspects of variability (e.g., comparing groups, variability in samples) and how variability is related to concepts of data, distribution, and center. This led to discussions about what was a reasonable starting point for students' discussions, and decided to begin with the ideas of "a lot" and "a little" variability. We realized that as teachers, we could look at distributions of data and evaluate them in terms of their amount of variability in the data, and when comparing distributions, we would compare not only center but spread. We decided to focus on developing an activity that would lead students to recognize, describe, and justify distributions that show a lot or a little variability. This was motivated by student difficulties that are typically observed later in the course when they encounter sampling distributions and are unable to understand the ideas of decreased variability as sample size increases. We hoped to lead students through an activity that first challenged them to consider and define ideas of a lot and a little variability informally, and then move to using formal measures to compare and describe variability.

After discussions on what we wanted students to understand about variability, we decided to construct a lesson that helped students develop and distinguish between informal and formal ideas of variability. The lesson was based on design principles described by Cobb and McClain (2004). These principles guided us to develop a lesson that would:

- Have students make conjectures about data that can be tested.
- Focus on a central statistical idea.
- Build on the investigative spirit of data analysis.
- Build on the range of data-based arguments that students produce.
- Integrate the use of technological tools that allow students to test their conjectures.
- Promote classroom discourse that includes statistical arguments and sustained exchanges that focus on significant statistical ideas.

First Teaching Experiment

We developed the first lesson over five meetings and taught it in a class during the end of Fall semester (well after this topic had been studied). One of the researchers (Garfield) taught the lesson in one of the undergraduate statistics courses (that was taught by a participating member of the group, who was a graduate student). This first lesson focused on data gathered on graduating seniors at the University of Minnesota. After a brief discussion of the term *variability* and a discussion of what it meant, students were asked to break into groups of three or four to suggest and discuss variables, measured on graduating seniors, that would have a lot or a little variability. They were asked to draw graphs for the variables they chose (without having seen any data, based only on their reasoning) and to explain their reasoning. In a whole-group discussion led by the instructor, the student groups displayed their graphs and discussed their choice of variables, why they thought these variables would have a lot or a little variability, and what type of distribution they expected the variable to have (e.g., one group chose GPA as having the least variability and drew a skewed graph that had mostly high GPAs because these were graduating seniors who must have done well in order to stay in school and graduate). Then, students were instructed to examine and analyze a sample of actual data for graduating seniors (including number of years it took to complete their degree, GPA, number of credits completed, ACT score when admitted, etc.) using the DataDesk software to generate graphs and statistics to compare to their conjectures. A final task was to use the formal measures of variability to describe the variables in the data set.

The lesson was videotaped and members of the JLS group came to watch, observe, and take notes, using an observation/lesson guide prepared in advance. Despite technology problems and not enough time to complete the activity, students were engaged and readily shared their reasoning. The students wrote positive reflections about what they learned. Many said that they felt they had a better appreciation for and understanding of variability based on this single lesson.

Students' discussion and responses, however, revealed that at this point in the course they demonstrated only early levels of distributional thinking and tended to focus on single data points (e.g., outliers) in a distribution. They did not have an understanding of variability other than overall range and differences in values, despite having studied IQR and SD in previous class sessions. The lesson, which was originally intended to help students explore measures of variability, was turned into an exploration of distributions by the students. This suggests that students need to have a strong foundation in distributional thinking (e.g., visually connecting shape and center) before they can isolate and grapple with the complex notion of variability.

Students exhibited expected and unexpected errors in their understanding that were duly noted by the observers, and were then discussed in the debriefing session. For example, one group of students reasoned that GPA (of the graduating seniors) would have the most variability, because they thought that there were so many possible values, due to the extremes of the measurement scale (0 and 4). We noted that many students described good reasons for drawing skewed or symmetric distributions. Unfortunately, we ran out of time and did not get to the second part of the lesson where students were to consider formal measures of variability (e.g., range, IQR and SD).

We learned many lessons from the development, teaching, and evaluation of this first lesson. The first four items in the following list refer to our use of JLS and the fifth was a general result of the teaching experiment. We learned that:

- The JLS format provided a useful structure for creating unique, high quality lessons. We recognized that the collaboratively produced lessons included features that were more creative and completely thought through than any of us would have produced as individuals. We also recognized that we would not have individually generated all the good student discussion prompts, nor would we have been able to predict so many possible student responses or places where things might have gone astray, as we could in a group.
- It was sometimes tempting to think about "teaching" in the lesson, particularly drawing on ways we have approached this material in the past (because we all teach statistics). It was a challenge to think of ways to actively engage students in discovery and discussion.
- Through our discussions, our own understanding of variability deepened and improved, even though some of us have taught this topic for more than 20 years. For example, we became aware of the fact that measures of variability alone are not so useful for describing or comparing groups of data. By struggling with the set of box-plots we planned to give our students we saw how difficult it is to assign labels of "a little" or "a lot" of variability when comparing data sets, because our own perceptions differed, causing us to explain and defend our arguments.
- Anticipating students' possible responses and errors, a standard component of the JLS process of developing lessons, was particularly enlightening. We made a point of doing this as the date approached to try the lesson in the classroom, which often led to last minute changes. We noted that in planning a lecture, instructors typically do not anticipate student responses and reactions, or think about how to respond to them.
- Finally, having students compare variables measured on different scales was confusing, and we needed to find a data set where variables were measured in the same units and on the same scale.

Assessments of Student Reasoning About Variability

We administered a test to students in all sections of the introductory course, to gather some baseline data for comparing students who experienced the research lesson. A draft version of the Comprehensive Assessment of Outcomes in Statistics (CAOS) test (Garfield, delMas, & Chance, 2003) was given to students early in the semester after they had formally "covered" the topics of data, distribution, center, and spread. The test was also given in two other introductory statistics courses, one for lower division students in a different college at the university, and one offered for beginning graduate

3. Match each histogram to one of the following descriptions:

_____a. A set of quiz scores where the quiz was very easy.

_____b. A set of average daily temperatures for Minneapolis in September

_____c. The last digit of phone numbers sampled from a phone book

_____d. The ages of a random sample of graduating seniors at a local college

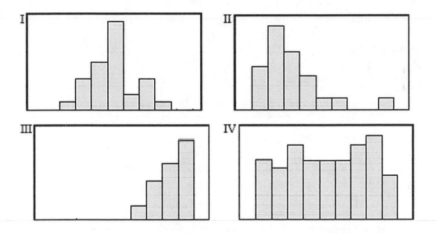

5. Compare the variability of the following histograms. Which has the higher SD and why?

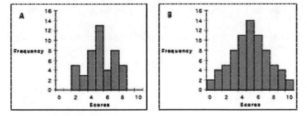

   a. A because it is more spread out
   b. A because it is bumpier
   c. *B because it is more spread out
   d. B because it is bumpier

8. Shown below is a histogram of sale prices (in $10,000 increments) for a random sample of houses in a suburb of a major metropolitan area. Which of the following measures are best for summarizing this distribution?

(Continued)

Informal and Formal Reasoning about Variability

a. Mean and standard deviation

b. Median and Range

c. Mean and Range

*d. Median and Interquartile Range

9. The following two graphs represent amount spent on a pair of jeans, one for a sample of high school girls and one for a sample of high school boys. Which of the following do you think presents the best comparison of the two graphs?

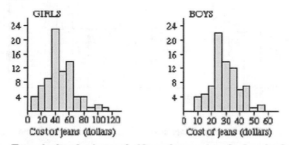

a. The graphs show that in general, girls spend more on jeans than boys, but the values are about the same for both groups.

*b. Although the average amount spent on jeans is higher for girls, there is more variability in the amount spent by girls than by boys.

c. Some girls spent a lot on jeans and some spent a little, but there are some boys who spent more on a pair of jeans than some girls.

d. On average, boys spend about the same on a pair of jeans as girls, and the variability is about the same in both distributions.

Informal and Formal Reasoning about Variability

The boxplots below display annual incomes (in units of 10,000) for households in two cities.

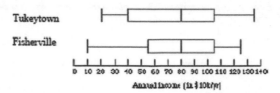

(Continued)

			Both are	Impossible
	Tukeytown	Fisherville	About Equal	to Tell
11. Which city would you expect to have a greater standard deviation in income?	A*	B	C	D

15. The following histograms display hypothetical test scores on a scale of 1-9 for 3 different statistics classes. Among Classes A, B, and C, order them from the lowest to highest standard deviation.

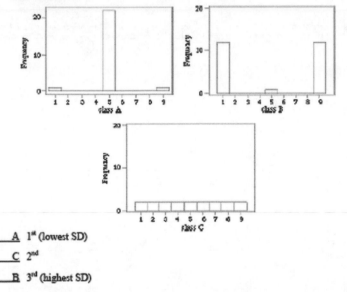

__A__ 1st (lowest SD)

__C__ 2nd

__B__ 3rd (highest SD)

Figure 5.1   Variability Assessment Items included in Pre- and Post-Tests

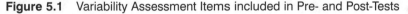

students who had not previously studied statistics, to determine if results were consistent across the different courses, instructors, types of students and materials used. Based on the results, the test was slightly modified and administered again at the end of the course. A subset of items from this test along with a summary of post-test responses are included in Figure 5.1 and Table 5.1, respectively. In the table of results, students in both sections of 3264 are grouped together because there was no difference in their pattern of responses, and we considered this baseline data before investigating the impact of the research lessons.

The analysis of the test data revealed some good aspects of student understanding of variability as well as some misconceptions, with many results consistent across all sections of the course. We found that most students were

TABLE 5.1
Post-Test Summary of Variability Items (Correct Responses in Bold)

Item	Response	1454 (n = 111)[a]		3264 (n = 29)[b]		5261(n = 41)[c]		Total (n = 181)	
		n	%	n	%	n	%	n	%
3a	A	8	7.2	2	6.9	3	7.3	13	7.2
	B	2	1.8	2	6.9	2	4.9	6	3.3
	C	**77**	**69.4**	**21**	**72.4**	**34**	**82.9**	**132**	**72.9**
	D	24	21.6	4	13.8	2	4.9	30	16.6
3b	A	36	32.4	5	17.2	9	22	50	27.6
	B	28	25.2	8	27.6	9	22	45	24.9
	C	3	2.7	3	10.3	1	2.4	7	3.9
	D	**44**	**39.6**	**13**	**44.8**	**22**	**53.7**	**79**	**43.6**
3c	**A**	**39**	**35.1**	**15**	**51.7**	**17**	**42.5**	**71**	**39.4**
	B	36	32.4	4	13.8	6	15	46	25.6
	C	12	10.8	1	3.4	1	2.5	14	7.8
	D	24	21.6	9	31	16	40	49	27.2
3d	A	29	26.1	7	24.1	12	30	48	26.7
	B	**43**	**38.7**	**14**	**48.3**	**23**	**57.5**	**80**	**44.4**
	C	19	17.1	5	17.2	4	10	28	15.6
	D	20	18	3	10.3	1	2.5	24	13.3
5	A	11	9.8	1	3.4	0	0	12	6.6
	B	**78**	**69.6**	**18**	**62.1**	**22**	**53.7**	**118**	**64.8**
	C	18	16.1	9	31	17	41.5	44	24.2
	D	5	4.5	1	3.4	2	4.9	8	4.4
6	A	11	9.8	2	6.9	2	5.1	15	8.3
	B	23	20.5	6	20.7	4	10.3	33	18.3
	C	**74**	**66.1**	**21**	**72.4**	**33**	**84.6**	**128**	**71.1**
	D	4	3.6	0	0	0	0	4	2.2
8	**A**	**27**	**24.1**	**6**	**20.7**	**3**	**7.5**	**36**	**19.9**
	B	8	7.1	5	17.2	10	25	23	12.7
	C	22	19.6	3	10.3	8	20.0	33	18.2

(Continued)

TABLE 5.1 (Continued)

Post-Test Summary of Variability Items (Correct Responses in Bold)

Item	Response	1454 (n = 111)[a]		3264 (n = 29)[b]		5261 (n = 41)[c]		Total (n = 181)	
		n	%	n	%	n	%	n	%
9	D	55	49.1	15	51.7	19	47.5	89	49.2
	A	21	18.8	4	13.8	3	7.3	28	15.4
	B	**77**	**68.8**	**23**	**79.3**	**33**	**80.5**	**133**	**73.1**
	C	9	8	1	3.4	4	9.8	14	7.7
	D	5	4.5	1	3.4	1	2.4	7	3.8
11	**A**	**73**	**65.2**	**13**	**46.4**	**32**	**78**	**118**	**65.2**
	B	20	17.9	5	17.9	7	17.1	32	17.7
	C	19	17	10	35.7	2	4.9	31	17.1
	D	0	0	0	0	0	0	0	0
15a	A	35	31.3	11	37.9	26	63.4	72	39.6
	B	10	8.9	0	0	3	73	13	7.1
	C	**67**	**59.8**	**18**	**62.1**	**12**	**29.3**	**97**	**53.3**
15b	A	28	25	4	13.8	6	14.6	38	20.9
	B	**54**	**48.2**	**21**	**72.4**	**17**	**41.5**	**92**	**50.5**
	C	30	26.8	4	13.8	18	43.9	52	28.6
15c	A	49	43.8	14	48.3	9	22	72	39.6
	B	**48**	**42.9**	**8**	**27.6**	**21**	**51.2**	**77**	**42.3**
	C	15	13.4	7	24.1	11	26.8	33	18.1

Note. [a]1454: Introductory statistics course for lower division students

[b]3264: Introductory statistics course for upper division undergraduate students

[c]5261: Introductory statistics course for beginning graduate students

able to correctly visualize a distribution of easy quiz scores (Item 3a), but expected a distribution of last digits of a phone number to be normally distributed, rather than have a more uniform shape (Item 3d). When asked to select which of two histograms would have a higher standard deviation, most students picked the correct graphs and reason (Item 6). Most students also correctly picked the median and IQR as appropriate summary measures for a skewed-looking histogram. A majority of students also considered variability as well as center when comparing two groups of data (costs of jeans for boys and girls, in Item 9). One item asked students to compare two box-plots, and determine which one might have a higher standard deviation (when both had the same range and one had a larger IQR as revealed by a wider box). Less than half of the students in the target class (the upper division course) gave the correct response, which was much less than the response in the other two courses. In Item 15, students were asked to rank order three histograms in terms of the size of their standard deviations. Here, two thirds of the students picked the flat, rectangular distribution as having the smallest standard deviation, rather than the unimodal graph with a tall bar in the center. About half of these students also incorrectly identified the graph with the tall bar in the middle as having the most variability, perhaps focusing on the fact that the height of this bar was so different from the others.

We found very low correlations between subscales of the test that measured different aspects of reasoning about variability (e.g., representing variability in graphs and recognizing variability in comparing groups). We also noted moderate levels of internal consistency (as measured by the alpha coefficient). These results indicate that students were not connecting the basic idea of variability across topics, something we had hoped to change. The assessment results were fairly consistent from pretest to post-test.

Our examination of the assessment data gathered at the end of the fall semester surprised us when we saw how poorly students performed on the seemingly simple tasks that asked them to rank a set of three histograms in terms of the size of the standard deviation, or to compare which of two box-plots corresponded to the largest standard deviation. A stubborn misconception that appears difficult to overcome is that flat, uniform distributions have little variability and a small standard deviation, when the larger spread of the bars along the x axis actually indicates a lot of variability. Students seem to equate the smoothness of the graph (gradual, usually monotonic changes in bar heights) with little or no variability in the data. This may indicate that they do not associate the "variability" of a distribution solely with the distribution of the values, or they confuse variation in frequency (i.e., bar heights) with variation in value. It also seems inconsistent with the intuitive idea that variability means different data values, which are represented in this flat histogram. We used the information learned from the assessments in the fall to help us revise and restructure the lesson for the spring.

The Second Lesson

During the spring semester, we decided to change the data set to data gathered from the students on the first day of class, and to focus on variables all measured on the same scale. We ended up designing a revised lesson that looked at variability of time in minutes spent each day on activities such as studying, cell phone use, Internet use, eating, exercising, traveling to school, and so on. The first part of the lesson again asked students to think about the variables without looking at them, to choose variables that they expected to have a lot or a little variability, to draw graphs of these variables, and to explain their reasoning and the criteria they used. After a class discussion where students presented their graphs and explained their reasoning, students analyzed the data using DataDesk to see if their conjectures were supported.

Students experienced two class sessions on variability prior to the teaching experiment. The first included activities using box-plots and the five-number summary to compare data-sets gathered on two brands of raisins and how far students travel each day. In a second class session on this topic, students went through the process of calculating a standard deviation and completed an activity that challenged them to estimate and compare standard deviations for multiple pairs of histograms. In a third class, there was a review of measures of center and measures of spread and a quiz was administered.

During the teaching of the new lesson, the JLS group members observed and took notes and the session was also videotaped. Some of us listened carefully to an individual group as they discussed the problem. We noted that the students appeared to be using some aspects of statistical thinking as they discussed the data values, reasoned about outliers, and speculated about how particular questions had been asked on the survey. They did not just treat these data as numbers, but were engaged in thinking about the variables as real data with a meaningful context. However, they seemed to only focus on matching the computer generated graphs to their hypothetical graphs, and were not able to focus on the measures of variability, nor to compare them for the different variables. We found that students tended to focus on outliers, and wanted to eliminate them from the data sets to make the distributions look "more normal." They all felt that the computer results confirmed their conjectures and they seemed to only focus on overall range and shape, and not on spread about the middle (IQR) or from the center (SD).

At the end of the lesson, students were asked to think about some other variables that they could measure about themselves on a daily basis and examine over a period of a month. They were asked to suggest a variable that they thought would have a little variability and one that would have a lot of variability, and write their conjectures down on their worksheets. We were looking for answers that showed students had a reasonable idea of what it means to have very little variability, and were pleased to find most students responded with appropriate examples such as:

- Hours spent in class. I have a pretty regular schedule.
- Time to get to class because it's almost the same everyday.
- Sleep. Pretty much similar amount.
- Number of shirts I wear per day. I only wear between 1–2 shirts per day.
- Time spent in class. I spend about the same amount of time in class each day.
- Showers—because one is taken twice a day, every day.

When asked for examples of variables that would show a lot of variability, students responded:

- Hours spent at work. I have a pretty irregular work schedule.
- Studying, depending on work and assignments.
- Amount of e-mail messages received. It depends how actively you use your e-mail.
- Time spent on my computer per day. Some days my class load is a lot so time spent on it is high, where other days it is all book work.
- Spending time w/my friends varies a lot because sometimes I have a lot of stuff to do, school-related.
- Exercise. Because I tend to start off good but slack off towards the end of the week.
- Driving—I have an erratic schedule and driving is something that I do often, but sometimes FAR and sometimes NEAR (I never know).

Students were also asked to respond to the following question: "How did seeing the actual summary statistics for these two variables affect your thinking about variability? In particular, how did it affect or change your thinking about the meaning of 'a lot' or 'a little' variability?" The responses were generally unclear. Students did not seem to have used the summary statistics as we had anticipated, relying more on the computer generated graphs to compare to their hypothetical graphs. Some of their responses included:

- Variability isn't necessarily a lot of data but how the data is distributed.
- That you can recognize that by looking at a graph (histogram)

- A picture helps you to actually see variability. I didn't really change my thinking of variability much though. Outliers you can see though.
- Summary statistics showed me the S.D. which clearly showed on avg. how much the data varied from the mean.
- Actual summary statistics didn't change my thinking at all. I believe I pretty much nailed it.

Students were also asked to describe the criteria they would use in the future to evaluate the amount of variability shown in a graph. In some cases, students tried to use their fragmented statistical knowledge to produce incoherent answers such as: "look at the shape, center and spread and evaluate the data taken. There will be a small standard deviation, as well as a normal distribution." Some tried to relate shape to variability, but focused on whether it is symmetrical or skewed as a way of evaluating variability. Perhaps they were trying to explain that outliers found in skewed distributions would influence some measures of variability. Many students referred to looking at the range of the data and a few mentioned looking at the standard deviation or at both range and SD to see if they were small. The IQR was never mentioned, perhaps because it is associated most with box-plots, and most students had generated histograms of data.

Several students mentioned the impact of outliers and that they would increase variability. So, a graph without outliers would be more likely to have a small amount of variability. This focus obscured the idea of clustering in the center as an aspect of low variability. Some students expected a unimodal distribution using good reasoning. For example, one wrote: "little variability would mean a population having less difference, mostly a unimodal" and another wrote: "whether it is unimodal + has no outliers." A few students seemed to have a sense of both clustering to the middle and range, as two aspects of variability. For example: "if things are clumped together without a huge range" and "whether or not data clusters on around the mean if it does, low variability. If lots of outliers → high variability."

A final question asked students to define "a lot" of variability. Some mentioned there would be a large range and standard deviation (again, ignoring the IQR). Several mentioned skewness, again apparently linking skewness to outliers. A few students mentioned that they would expect a graph to not be unimodal, or to be bimodal or multimodal. This seemed to be a good response if students were envisioning spread away from the center of a distribution. A typical response was "a lot of variability is when the data is spread out and there are many outliers." One thoughtful response was "It is comparative, so you have to look at several graphs to get an idea." We agreed that the notion of a lot or a little begs a comparison to another data set.

We felt that this revised lesson went fairly well, that students seemed to be struggling with the concept and some were moving from informal notions of range to more sophisticated notions of modality and clumping balanced with range and outliers.

The Third Lesson

Based on the end point of this second lesson, we developed a second part, our third lesson, to be implemented the last week of classes. After many discussions about the task of choosing one variable with the most variability and one with the least variability, the Lesson Study group examined the data sets and compared the three statistics (range, interquartile range, and standard deviation) for the variables. Each measure of variability produced a different rank ordering of these time variables from lowest to highest variability. We decided to present this complex task to students, because it would require them to consider the shapes of the distributions, the various graphs and measures, and the presence of outliers to make their decisions. The lesson that was developed (see Fig. 5.2 for the student worksheet) began by asking students to revisit the set of variables by examining their box-plots, histograms, and summary statistics in order to select the one with the most and the one with the least variability. Students worked in small groups and recorded the criteria they used to make these decisions. They were informed that the outliers were real data values and not errors, so they would not discard them. Students used good reasoning to make their choices. All but one group selected travel time as having the least variability because it had both the smallest SD and range. Only one group reasoned that a different variable, time communicating with parents, had the smallest variability because it had the smallest IQR. This group's impressive justification was that the range and SD were not appropriate summaries for travel times due to the skewness and outliers in that distribution. When selecting a variable with the most variability, students narrowed the debate to three of the variables (studying, Internet use, and eating). Again, one group had more insightful arguments for the distribution that had the largest spread (IQR), in contrast to groups that did not acknowledge how outliers inflated measures of spread such as range and SD.

The last part of the activity asked students to focus on two variables that had essentially the same SD, but one variable had a higher range and the other had a higher IQR. We asked students to explain the inconsistency. Many seemed to struggle with this task, going back over what they had learned about each measure. However, a large group discussion identified how the distribution of the variable with the smaller IQR and larger range could lead

Group Member Names:

Data: From First day survey given to students in EPSY 3264 Spring 2004

Variables	**Average number of minute** per day spent:
Study	Studying
Sleep	Sleeping
Travel	Travelling to school
Eating	Eating meals and snacks.
Internet	On the internet
Exercise	Exercising
Parents	Communicating with your parents by email, phone, or in person

FIRST TASK: Identify a variable with the least variability

1. Using the attached sheets which contain boxplots, histograms, and summary statistics for the variables listed above, discuss and identify which variable has the **strongest** evidence that the variable has the **SMALLEST amount of variability**. Be sure to identify the characteristics of the distributions and the criteria your group is using to make your decision.

2. Assign a recorder and have the recorder write in the space below the evidence and criteria the group used to decide why the identified variable has the **SMALLEST variability**.

SECOND TASK: Identify a variable with the most variability

3. Repeat this process to discuss and identify which variable has the **strongest** evidence that the variable has the **LARGEST amount of variability**. Again, have the recorder write down the evidence and criteria the group used to decide why the identified variable has the **LARGEST variablity**.

THIRD TASK: Comparing the measures of variability

Now, look at **graphs** and **statistics** for the two variables **EATING** and **STUDY**. They both have about the same value for the standard deviation. However, one of the variables has a larger Range, while the other has a larger IQR.

In your group, discuss and jot down answers to the following questions:

- How is it that both variables can have the same value for one measure of variability (the standard deviation), but have values that are in opposite directions for the other two measures (IQR and Range)?
- How is this related to what each measure represents about the variability in the distributions?
- Why don't all three measures confirm that the two distributions have the same variability, or that one distribution has more variability that the other?

[Graphs included in original are omitted here for space considerations.]

Figure 5.2   Student Worksheet for the Third Lesson

to a similar SD as the variable with a smaller range but larger IQR. Finally, the instructor led a discussion about what each measure conveys about variability in a distribution, what each measure doesn't indicate, and when to use each measure. Students seemed to be engaged in the discussion, although they struggled to reconcile the differences in the measures and to identify what each one represents. This final discussion seemed an important part of the lesson, in that it built on the previous discussions and exposed students to a deeper understanding of the measures and the concepts.

RESULTS: POST-LESSON ASSESSMENT

At the end of spring semester, the same assessment was given as at the end of the fall semester. The results were compared to those of the fall classes, with particular attention paid to the items that assessed the concept of variability and comparisons of variability using different graphical representations. On the set of items where students had to match histograms to variables (Item 3), performance in the spring was comparable to or somewhat better than the fall performance. In particular, students in the spring were better at matching the rectangular-shaped histogram to the description of a variable that was based on random digits (47% selected the correct answer). A higher percentage (47%) selected the correct histogram when asked which had a higher standard deviation and why (Item 5). The most striking improvement in scores was for Item 9, where students were asked to compare two histograms that differed in both the center and the amount of variability. Ninety-four percent of the students picked the correct interpretation that noted differences in both center and variability. Students also performed better on Item 15 where they were asked to rank order three histograms based on the size of the standard deviation. About half of the students picked the correct order, compared to about 25% of the students on the post-test in fall semester. A noticeable number of students still wanted to pick the rectangular distribution (class C) to have the smallest SD but fewer picked this option than in the fall. It was disappointing to note that the percentage of students who picked a box-plot that would most likely have a greater standard deviation in a pair of box-plots (Item 11) was lower than expected (41%) and lower than some classes in the fall. In addition to data gathered on this assessment, the instructor for this class noted improved explanations and discussion related to variability on student projects turned in at the end of the class. Students appeared to be better able to describe and compare variability for two sets of data collected in the project.

DISCUSSION

It is perhaps surprising to note that despite multiple lessons on measures of variability, most students did not demonstrate a conceptual understanding of these ideas until the end of the course. It seemed to require repeated engagement and reinforcement with these seemingly elementary ideas and measures throughout the course, which is not typical for this topic. Usually after the IQR and Range are introduced early in a course, they are abandoned for the SD that is used from that point on.

We found that students initially tended to focus on the idea of range (overall spread) and individual points (outliers) and were not focusing on where most of the data were (clumping in the center), which is similar to the results reported by delMas and Liu (this volume). Recent research on reasoning about distribution confirms that students tend to see data sets as individual values and not as an entity or aggregate of values (e.g., Ben-Zvi & Arcavi, 2001). It was very difficult to help the students develop the concept of variability as spread from the center, which takes into account central clustering as well as endpoints. After completing several activities, homework, and several class sessions on this topic, students did not seem to understand what IQR and SD represent nor how they relate to ideas of center and distribution.

In addition to (or perhaps instead of) the formal class sessions on these measures, we needed to include two additional lessons where students made and tested conjectures, and reasoned about measures of variability and the fuzzy notion of "a lot" and "a little" variability. By the final discussion of what each measure tells us, and what each doesn't tell us, students seemed to be developing an appreciation for the complexity of the idea of variability, the differences between each measure, and when they are most and least useful. Although we noticed some improvement on assessment items compared to students in the fall, the overall assessment results indicated that students had a long way to go to be able to express and apply an understanding of variability in different problem contexts. General theories of learning suggest that students' developing ideas (in this case, of variability) need to be frequently revisited and reinforced, otherwise they will quickly disappear.

We believe that it is important to connect the intuitive knowledge students have about variability to the new ideas they are learning and to connect their less sophisticated strategies to more sophisticated reasoning. Theories of conceptual change expect students to move from less to more elaborate and sophisticated conceptions by applying and extending their understanding to a wide array of situations (e.g., Piaget, 2001). Of special importance are situations where the production of correct reasoning or solutions requires modifications to students' intuitive ideas (Chin & Brewer, 1993). We are currently envisioning the following hypothetical learning trajectory for developing this type of reasoning:

- Begin with students' basic understanding that data vary.
- Investigate why measurements vary and processes that lead to variation in data.
- Examine graphical representations of variability; use graphs to compare the variability of more than one data set.
- Focus on the bumps and clumps that appear in some graphs, and what they indicate about variability in the middle of a data set.
- Promote awareness of both the overall spread and where the majority of the data are distributed.
- Examine measures of center and how measures of variability are based on spread from the center, recognizing how measures of variability are most informative in the context of a measure of center.
- Determine relative characteristics (e.g., resistance) of different measures of variability for different types of distributions, and when it makes sense to use particular measures as summaries of variability for particular distributions.

CONCLUSIONS AND IMPLICATIONS

Variability is the most fundamental aspect of statistical reasoning and yet possibly the most difficult concept for students to understand and apply. Although most teachers and texts emphasize computation and procedural approaches to this concept (e.g., how to compute each measure of variability and when it is appropriate to use them), most students proceed through their statistics courses never understanding the idea of variability as spread from the center, nor how the different measures are related to different features of a distribution. It is important that students understand that variability, just like center, represents aspects of a data set as a whole. We found that students do have informal intuitions about variability that may serve as a good foundation for studying the formal measures. The two intuitions are variability is represented by overall spread and by differences in data values (e.g., not all values are the same). However, students tend to focus primarily on outliers, either using outliers as a criteria for a lot of variability or wanting to remove the outliers (instead of looking at the spread of most of the data, or using a resistant measure such as IQR). Developing the more complex notion of variability as the "typical" spread from the center seems to be very difficult, as is using the measures together to make interpretations of variability. We think that the series of two lessons we developed are a good way to help build these notions. The first lesson asked students to consider variables with a lot or a little variability, to draw hypothetical graphs of these variables, and then to compare them to computer-generated statistics and graphs. The second lesson asked them to consider graphs and statistics for the entire set of variables, and to come up with criteria for a lot or a little variability. The part of the activity where they had to explain why two variables could have the same SD but one had a larger Range and the other had a larger IQR led to a fruitful class discussion on the formal measures of variability in terms of what they represent and what information they do not include. By the end of these two lessons, students should have a better understanding of the measures and how they relate to distributions and centers.

One of the challenges in teaching statistics is motivating students to engage in reasoning about complex and challenging concepts. We are convinced that context has an important effect on student reasoning. If they understand and care about the data, they will be more likely to engage in statistical reasoning and in struggling to make sense. Teachers need to find problems and contexts that are motivating, interesting, and relevant to students' lives (Doerr & English, 2003). Although our data were relevant, we realized that our problem was not, a challenge discussed by Lehrer and Schauble (this volume). Asking students to select or rank variables according to variability is not a practical or everyday task, like ranking restaurants (e.g., Doerr & English, 2003). It was difficult for our LS group to develop a real problem context to motivate our activity, so we chose to use interesting data and were pleased to see that students were engaged. Nevertheless, the activity may have been better if a real context (e.g., monitoring blood pressure or identifying a problematic manufacturing process) were used. We were trying to help students develop a model of variability: what it means, what it looks like, what affects it. We will next look to the modeling research in mathematics education (e.g., Lehrer & Romberg, 1996; Lehrer & Schauble, this volume) for more insights on how to help students develop models with carefully designed model-eliciting activities.

A final note relates to the process of developing the lessons for this teaching experiment. We learned that LS is an extremely effective way to help statistics teachers focus on important learning goals, to create new approaches that enable students to construct knowledge, and to break away from focusing on traditional topics and sequences. Building on design principles of Cobb and McClain (2004), we now have a working model for a research lesson that incorporates student immersion in real data and use of technology, and that is able to engage students to reflect on key ideas. By constructing and observing the teaching of the research lessons we were excited by the noticeable differences between these classes and a more typical college statistics class. We believe that Lesson Study can be used to work towards the goal of a revised, pared down curriculum for introductory college courses, one of the recommendations in a draft set of guidelines developed by a project supported by the American Statistical Association (Franklin and Garfield, in press). JLS also appears to offer a way to use a constructivist approach to learning to help develop students' reasoning about variability, resulting in improved statistical thinking. We hope to continue elements of JLS as we conduct more teaching experiments in the college statistics classroom in future years.

ACKNOWLEDGMENTS

The authors wish to acknowledge the contributions of several graduate students who participated in this project as teachers or research assistants: Panayiota Kendeou, Sharon Lane-Getaz, Agnes Kiss, Kei Lee, Ann Ooms, and Brenda Tiefenbruck.

REFERENCES

Bakker, A. (2004). Learning to reason about distributions. In D. Ben-Zvi & J. Garfield (Eds.), *The challenge of developing statistical literacy, reasoning, and thinking* (pp. 147–168). Dordrecht, The Netherlands: Kluwer.

Ben-Zvi, D. (2004). Reasoning about data analysis. In D. Ben-Zvi & J. Garfield (Eds.), *The challenge of developing statistical literacy, reasoning, and thinking* (pp. 121–146). Dordrecht, The Netherlands: Kluwer.

Biehler, R. (2001). Students' difficulties in practicing computer-supported data analysis: Some hypothetical generalizations form results of two exploratory studies. In C. Reading (Ed.), *Background readings for SRTL–2* (pp. 169–190). Armidale, NSW, Australia: University of New England.

Chance, B., delMas, R., & Garfield, J. (2004). Reasoning about sampling distributions. In D. Ben-Zvi & J. Garfield (Eds.), *The challenge of developing statistical literacy, reasoning, and thinking* (pp. 295–324). Dordrecht, The Netherlands: Kluwer.

Chin, C. A., & Brewer, W. F. (1993). The role of anomalous data in knowledge acquisition: A theoretical framework and implications for science instruction. *Review of Educational Research, 63*(1), 1–49.

Clark, J. M., Kraut, G., Mathews, D., & Wimbish, J. (2003). *The "fundamental theorem" of statistics: Classifying student understanding of basic statistical concepts.* Unpublished manuscript.

Cobb, G. (1992). Teaching statistics. In L. A. Steen (Ed.), *Heeding the call for change: Suggestions for curricular action* (pp. 375–396). Washington, DC: Mathematical Association of America.

Cobb, P., Confrey, J., diSessa, A., Lehrer, R., & Schauble, L. (2003). *Educational Researcher, 32*(1), 9–13.

Cobb, P., & McClain, K. (2004). Principles for instructional design in developing statistical reasoning. In D. Ben-Zvi & J. Garfield (Eds.), *The challenge of developing statistical literacy, reasoning, and thinking* (pp. 375–396). Dordrecht, The Netherlands: Kluwer.

Cobb, P., McClain, K., & Gravemeijer, K. (2003). Learning about statistical covariation. *Cognition and Instruction 21*(1), 1–78.

delMas, R., & Liu, Y. (2003, July). Exploring students' understanding of statistical variation. Proceedings of the Third International Conference on Statistical Reasoning, Thinking, and Learning (SRTL–3), University of Nebraska, Lincoln.

Doerr, H., & English, L. (2003). A modeling perspective on students' mathematical reasoning about data. *Journal for Research in Mathematics Education, 34*(2), 110–136.

Fernandez, C. (2002). Learning from Japanese approaches to professional development: The case of lesson study. *Journal of Teacher Education, 53*(5), 390–405.

Fernandez, C., Cannon, J., & Chokshi, S. (2003). A U.S.–Japan lesson study collaboration reveals critical lenses for examining practice. *Teaching and Teacher Education, 19*(2), 171–185.

Franklin, C. & Garfield, J. (2006). The GAISE Project: Developing Statistics Education Guidelines for Pre K–12 and College Courses. In G. Burrill (Ed.), *Thinking and reasoning with data and chance: 2006 NCTM Yearbook* (pp. 345–375). Reston, VA: National Council of Teachers of Mathematics.

Garfield, J. (2003). Assessing statistical reasoning. *Statistics Education Research Journal.* 2(1). Retrieved December 2, 2003 from http://www.stat.auckland.ac.nz/~iase/serj/SERJ2(1).pdf

Garfield, J., & Ben-Zvi, D. (2005). A framework for teaching and assessing reasoning about variability. *Statistics Education Research Journal* 4(1), 92–99.

Garfield, J., delMas, R., & Chance, B. (2003, April). *The web-based ARTIST project (Assessment Resource Tools for Improving Statistical Thinking).* Paper presented at AERA, Chicago.

Garfield, J., Hogg, B., Schau, C., & Whittinghill, D. (2002). First courses in statistical sciences: The state of educational reform efforts. *Journal of Statistics Education.* 10(2). Retrieved December 2, 2003, from http://www.amstat.org/publications/jse/v10n2/garfield.html

Gould, R. (2004). Variability: One statistician's view. *Statistics Education Research Journal, 3*(2), 7–16.

Hiebert, J., Gallimore, R., & Stigler, J. W. (2002). A knowledge base for the teaching profession: What would it look like and how can we get one? *Educational Researcher, 31*(5), 3–15.

Hiebert, J., Morris, A. K., & Glass, B. (2003). Learning to teach: An "experiment" model for teaching and teacher preparation in mathematics. *Journal of Mathematics Teacher Education, 66,* 201–222.

Hoerl, R., & Snee, R. D. (2001). *Statistical thinking: Improving business performance.* San Jose, CA: Duxbury Press.

Konold, C., & Pollatsek, A. (2002). Data analysis as the search for signals in noisy processes. *Journal for Research in Mathematics Education, 33*(4), 259–289.

Konold, C., Robinson, A., Khalil, K., Pollatsek, A., Well, A., Wing, R., & Mayr, S. (2002, December). *Students' use of modal clumps to summarize data.* Proceedings of the Sixth International Conference on Teaching Statistics (ICOTS–6). Retrieved December 2, 2003 from http://www.stat.auckland.ac.nz/~iase/ publications.php

Lehrer, R., & Romber, T. (1996). Exploring children's data modeling. *Cognition and Instruction. 14* (1), 69–108

Lehrer, R., & Schauble, L. (2002). *Distribution: A resource for understanding error and natural variation.* Proceedings of the Sixth International Conference on Teaching Statistics (ICOTS–6). Retrieved December 2, 2003 from http://www.stat.auckland.ac.nz/~iase/publications.php

Lewis, C. (2000, April). *Lesson study: The core of Japanese professional development.* Invited address to the Special Interest Group on Research in Mathematics Education, Annual meeting of the American Educational Research Association (AERA), New Orleans.

Lewis, C., & Tsuchida, I. (1998). A lesson is like a swiftly flowing river: How research lessons improve Japanese education. *American Educator,* Winter, 12–17, 50–52.

Makar, K., & Confrey, J. (2004). Secondary teachers' statistical reasoning in comparing two groups. In D. Ben-Zvi & J. Garfield (Eds.) *The challenge of developing statistical literacy, reasoning, and thinking* (pp. 353–374). Dordrecht, The Netherlands: Kluwer.

Mathews, D., & Clark, J. (1997). *Successful students' conceptions of mean, standard deviation, and the Central Limit Theorem.* Paper presented at the Midwest Conference on Teaching Statistics, Oshkosh, WI.

Moore, D. S. (1990). Uncertainty. In L. Steen (Ed.), *On the shoulders of giants* (pp. 95–138). Washington, DC: National Academy Press.

Moore, D. S. (2001). *Active practice of statistics: A text for multimedia learning.* W.H. Freeman and Co.

Noss, R., Pozzi, S., & Hoyles, C. (1999). Touching epistemologies: Meanings of average and variation in nursing practice. *Educational Studies in Mathematics, 40,* 25–51.

Pfannkuch, M., & Wild, C. (2004). Statistical thinking: An historical perspective. In D. Ben-Zvi & J. Garfield (Eds.).*The challenge of developing statistical literacy, reasoning, and thinking* (pp. 17–46). Dordrecht, The Netherlands: Kluwer.

Piaget, J. (2001). *Studies in reflecting abstraction.* (Ed. and trans., Robert L. Campbell). Philadelphia: Taylor and Francis.

Reading, C., & Shaughnessy, J. M. (2004). Reasoning about variation. In D. Ben-Zvi & J. Garfield (Eds.), *The challenge of developing statistical literacy, reasoning, and thinking* (pp. 201–226). Dordrecht, The Netherlands: Kluwer.

Rubin, A., & Hammerman, J. K. (2003, July). *Reasoning in the presence of variability.* Proceedings of the Third International Conference on Statistical Reasoning, Thinking, and Learning (SRTL–3), University of Nebraska, Lincoln.

Rumelhart, D. E., & McClelland, J. L. (1989). The architecture of mind: A connectionist approach. In M. I. Posner (Ed.), *Foundations of cognitive science* (pp. 113–159). Cambridge, MA: MIT Press.

Shaughnessy, J. M., Watson, J., Moritz, J., & Reading, C. (1999, April). *School mathematics students' acknowledgment of statistical variation.* Paper presented at the NCTM Research Presession, San Francisco, CA.

Simon, M. (1995). Reconstructing mathematics pedagogy from a constructivist perspective. *Journal of Research in Mathematics Education, 25*(2), 114–115.

Snee, R. (1990). Statistical thinking and its contribution to quality. *The American Statistician, 44,* 116–121.

The Design-Based Research Collective (2003). Design-based research: An emerging paradigm for educational inquiry. *Educational Researcher, 32*(1), 5–8.

Stigler, J. & Hiebert, J. (1999). *The teaching gap.* New York: The Free Press.

Velleman, P. (2003). *ActivStats CD-ROM, 2003–2004 Edition.* Glenview, IL: Addison Wesley.

Watson, J. M. (2004). Developing reasoning about samples. In D. Ben-Zvi & J. Garfield (Eds.) *The challenge of developing statistical literacy, reasoning, and thinking.* Dordrecht, The Netherlands: Kluwer.

Wild, C. J., & Pfannkuch, M. (1999). Statistical thinking in empirical enquiry. *Statistical Review, 67,* 223–265.

6

Contrasting Emerging Conceptions of Distribution in Contexts of Error and Natural Variation

Richard Lehrer
Leona Schauble
Vanderbilt University

Early investigators in a topic of study often take for granted that the phenomenon of interest is straightforward to identify and characterize. Differing conceptualizations of the field usually come into focus only after some of the initial work has been done and people are in a position to survey the landmarks of the field and note the points of disagreement. This may be our current state of progress in research on variation and uncertainty, which has been widely investigated both by psychologists (e.g., Kahneman, Solvic, & Tversky, 1982; Konold, 1989; Nisbett, Krantz, Jepson, & Kunda, 1983; Nisbett & Ross, 1980) and by educators (Mokros & Russell, 1995; Pollatsek, Lima, & Well, 1981; Strauss & Bichler, 1988). Psychological studies typically concern whether and how participants' informal ways of thinking are consistent with strategies prescribed by a canonical view of concepts like probability, chance, and sample size. Similarly, educational studies tend to focus on how participants learn or think about certain statistics, such as the entailments of the mean of a sample. In this chapter, we describe a somewhat different approach to statistical reasoning, one that emphasizes *data modeling* (Lehrer & Romberg, 1996). As we describe, a data modeling approach focuses on how statistical reasoning is recruited as a way of investigating genuine questions about the world. Data modeling is, in fact, what professionals actually do when they reason statistically (Wild & Pfannkuch, 1999), and moreover, it is central to a wide variety of enterprises, including engineering, politics, medicine, and natural science.

Scientific models, for example, are generated with acute awareness of their entailments for data, and data are recorded and structured as a way of making progress in articulating a scientific model or adjudicating among rival models. This tight relationship between model and data holds generally in domains where inquiry is conducted by inscribing, representing, and mathematizing key aspects of the world (Goodwin, 2000; Kline, 1980; Latour, 1990). Participating in these practices entails adopting a modeling stance, in which the definition and meaning of data are under negotiation, rather than fixed in advance. This dynamic view of the relation between modeling and meaning is in strong contrast to the way that statistics is usually taught, namely, as if statistical reasoning entailed the application of routine procedures to problem templates. Data modeling includes deciding which aspects of the world are relevant to the conceptual model, how best to measure them, how to structure and represent the resulting measures, and then how to make inferences that are situated within and informed by knowledge about the qualities of those measures and representations.

In the first part of the chapter, we explain this conceptualization of the field of statistical reasoning in greater detail and provide illustrations from our 10-year research program in the developmental resources and challenges that young children bring to data modeling. The National Council of Teachers of Mathematics (2000) has advised that foundations for statistical reasoning should be built from the earliest years of education, rather than reserved for high school or university study. Current research with middle and elementary school students suggests that young children possess many conceptual resources that, with thoughtfully designed and implemented instruction, can be bootstrapped toward sophisticated forms of reasoning not typically observed in the early grades (Cobb, McClain, & Gravemeijer, 2003; Lehrer & Schauble, 2002; Petrosino, Lehrer, & Schauble, 2003) Our objective in this first part of the chapter is to "open up" data modeling, exposing what is potentially there to be learned by young students, and in particular, emphasizing parts of the data modeling process that are important educational targets, yet typically overlooked or taken for granted in most educational and psychological portrayals of statistical reasoning.

Our perspective on development is not one that leads us to ask questions like whether children "have" some developmental capability with respect to these components. If there are developmental capabilities that are inherent and related to age in a predictable way, they are not the ones that interest us here. Rather, we understand thinking and reasoning and their development as grounded within contexts that are social and designed, rather than naturally maturing. Thinking is brought into being and supported within contexts that are fashioned by people. Whether or not environments are designed in an intentional way, they generate and shape thinking via norms for the kinds of questions that get pursued, the activities and tasks that structure and focus day to day life, the forms of argument and justification that are considered compelling, and the criteria for a convincing explanation. As researchers and educators, we are interested in understanding the relationships between the long-term development of knowledge and the environments—broadly defined—that enable and support development.

The second part of the chapter focuses more specifically on inference, presenting new findings from studies in which elementary students worked in data modeling contexts with an emphasis on statistical inference. This research, like all of the research described in the chapter, was conducted within a public school district about 15 miles from a Midwestern state university, where we established a long-term research and educational improvement collaboration with elementary and middle school teachers and their administrators. In this collaborative effort, teachers worked in cross-grade teams and as a larger community to pursue data modeling as a thematic approach to improving mathematics and science instruction. Teachers learned to teach new forms of mathematics, such as geometry, data, measure, probability, and algebra, and systematically investigated the development of student thinking in these topics, which remain understudied at the early grades (Lehrer & Schauble, 2002). They explored ways that children could learn to use these new mathematical resources to understand science, especially through the development, evaluation, and revision of models. Although teachers worked with university partners to learn new forms of mathematics and science themselves and to study how their students thought about these ideas, the researchers conducted longitudinal studies of student thinking and learning. Elsewhere (Lehrer & Schauble, in press) we report analyses of the learning data for both students and their teachers in this collaborative research (student learning data were in mathematics and science; teachers' learning data focused on their understanding of student thinking in key topics of mathematics and science). In both groups, there were substantial gains in learning, measured as change over time (across grades) and also (within a grade) as compared to national performance on key items from the National Assessment of Educational Progress and other items developed by researchers working in related fields.

WHAT IS DATA MODELING?

Figure 6.1 identifies the components of data modeling that our research suggests are especially important and also delineates the relationships among these components. The figure illustrates how components of data modeling are tightly interactive, rather than rigidly sequential, a point foregrounded by data modeling approaches to statistics but backgrounded by most educational approaches. Each of the components in the figure represents a nexus of both conceptual challenge that children confront and conceptual resources that children bring to the enterprise of reasoning with and about data. The upper triangular region in the figure prefigures the design of research, a portion of modeling widely studied by other investigators (Klahr, Chen, & Toth, 2001; Kuhn, 1989; Metz, 2004) and therefore, not revisited here. The lower triangular region encompasses analysis, depicted as an interaction among data structures, representations, and models of inference. The empirical emphasis in this chapter is on the role of distribution in supporting inference, but we draw on previous studies to paint a broader portrait of data modeling.

Posing Questions

Although it may seem obvious that data only stand as data in relation to an issue or question, most data and statistics curricula place little or no emphasis on question posing. That may be because it is so widely noted that children are excellent at asking questions, as anyone who has spent time around a 3-year-old can attest. However, children's questions often reflect superficial and ephemeral interests and do not necessarily motivate and sustain the kind of investigation that is needed to push beyond casual curiosity. Moreover, children's questions are not always educationally productive, that is, potentially fruitful from a scientific or mathematical perspective. Indeed, to make sure that work with data is oriented toward fruitful questions, curricula typically sidestep this potential problem by posing the questions that students will investigate. As a result, students may not well understand the grounding for the question they are "investigating." Adults often underestimate the knowledge required to provide context, meaning, and motivation for a question, and as the field of cognitive development has repeatedly demonstrated (i.e., Carey, 1985), adults often are unaware of the many ways that children's content and structure of knowledge in almost any topic can vary from those held by the typical adult. As a result, the implications of a question that are obvious to adults may be invisible to children.

Children's questions about scientific phenomena reliably become more variable, interesting, and scientifically productive as their experience with the

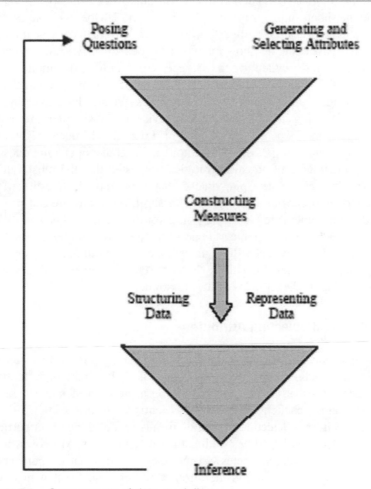

Figure 6.1 Components of data modeling.

phenomenon cumulates (Lehrer, Schauble, Carpenter, & Penner, 2000; Lehrer, Carpenter, Schauble, & Putz, 2000; Lehrer, Schauble, & Petrosino, 2001). For example, when asked to generate questions they would like to investigate about Wisconsin Fast Plants™, third-graders with little personal knowledge of or experience about the plants tended to focus narrowly on their name ("How fast do they grow?") or their height ("How tall do they get?"), the most obvious aspect of growth for many children. Yet, after observing only one life cycle of the plants, their questions expanded dramatically, to include, among others:

"Do the rates of change in height remain constant over the lifespan?" "Do the roots and the shoots of plants grow in the same way?" "Does the volume of the canopy increase in constant proportion over time?" "What is a typical number of buds on a Fast Plant, and how many seeds does a bud typically produce?" Findings like these, which we have repeatedly replicated, emphasize the importance of developing students' initial knowledge about phenomena that will serve as the topic of their data investigations. We also have experimented with ways of helping students develop and revise their own criteria for a good question (Lehrer, Carpenter, Schauble, & Putz, 2000; Lucas, Broderick, Lehrer, & Bohanon, in press). For example, sixth-graders pursuing questions about the functioning of aquatic ecologies suggested that the most valuable questions helped classmates "piggyback," that is, build on the question to generate new ones (Lucas et al., in press). In short, questions are not properly regarded as unproblematic launching points for the more serious work of data analysis. Instead, they are an integral part of the process, framing the kinds and qualities of information that will be investigated and, in turn, being subject to retuning and sometimes dramatic revision by early attempts to find ways of operationalizing the key aspects of the question.

Generating and Selecting Attributes

Carving up events and objects in the world into variables is an important step toward data modeling, but it does not come easily. It is no simple matter to identify attributes that are key for addressing a question of interest; in fact, doing so remains a challenge for working scientists (Stevens & Hall, 1998), as well as for children. Selecting attributes means seeing things in a particular way, as a collection of qualities, rather than intact objects. Moreover, it also means eliminating other attributes—sometimes qualities that are perceptually or otherwise salient—from consideration. Children, and for that matter, all novices to the "modeling game" (Hestenes, 1992) tend to find this deliberate elimination of information to be counterintuitive. For example, first-graders decided to keep track of the growth of flowering amaryllis by cutting out and mounting strips of paper that preserved the heights of the plants at each day of measure. However, the strips looked like stems to the children, who then insisted on coloring all of them green (even though using only a single color made it more difficult to compare the heights of different plants) and adorning each strip with a flower. The idea of representing *heights,* rather than *plants*, emerged only gradually across weeks as the teacher focused activity on the measurement, representation, and comparison of plant heights at different points in the life cycle, and eventually, on patterns of growth across the life cycle (for further details see Lehrer & Schauble, 2002a).

The point of this example is that constructing data involves both the selection and the abstraction of perception. Something spoken is replaced by something written, an event is replaced by a video of that event (the video omits smell, taste, heft, etc.), a sensation of heat is replaced by a pointer reading on a thermometer, and so on. Note that these attributes, in turn, may be further combined and abstracted (several pointer readings are arranged as values in a table or in a graphical display). Deciding *what to observe* is a major accomplishment that takes time and effort. It is informed by questions and often disciplines questions to further specificity and validity.

Measuring

A base of experience with the attributes under consideration is also important for informing critical decisions about measurement. A plan to keep track of changes in the heights of plants needs to be informed by expectations about the rate and endpoints of growth. This knowledge suggests appropriate units of measure (centimeters? meters?) and also informs one's sense about the precision of measure that will be satisfactory. Moreover, knowledge of the phenomenon under investigation is required to inform a group's agreement about *how* to measure so that comparison and aggregation can be supported. Fifth graders argued at length about whether keeping track of plant heights meant measuring from the bottom of the pot (where the roots might be) or from the top of the soil (where the stem becomes visible). When the plants began to grow, they often developed multiple branching stems, necessitating decisions about how to decide which stem to measure, and how to identify it permanently so as to avoid measuring different stems from occasion to occasion. Stems that did not grow "straight up" created consternation and resulted in heated arguments about a "fair way" to measure stems that bent or flopped over as they grew. Similarly, students who had decided to keep records of plant "width" needed to decide what measurement could serve as an index of that attribute, given that the branches did not grow in positions that were directly oppositional from each other, as they had expected (Lehrer & Schauble, 2005).

Similar decisions must be made with other forms of measurement, such as assigning objects or events to constructed categories (Lehrer & Romberg, 1996). In a third-grade class, children collected self-portraits from students in a range of grades and then attempted to identify and characterize important age-related differences in the features of the portraits that were drawn. In other words, they were trying to generate predictive categories. Students readily noticed that the youngest portrait-drawers tended to draw eyes that were perfectly round, and developed the conjecture that eye shape in a picture might predict the age of its author. However, on their first attempt, students generated 23 different categories to describe the eye shapes on the portraits. Indeed, they developed so many categories (as the teacher commented, "A category for every eyeball shape they could possibly find") that their category system was useless. In this case, the measurement system was *too* precise for the goal. After agreeing that 23 categories of eye shapes were not very useful, the students reconsidered the most informative ways to regroup the shapes into categorizes that would best summarize the variability in the portraits (see diPerna, 2002). Participation in the solution of measurement dilemmas like these (as opposed to following procedures on a teacher-generated data sheet) provides a strong grounding in how measurements were developed and what that process means for interpreting variability in measurements, believability of measurements, and change over time in measurements.

Beyond deciding what and how to measure, students frequently need to struggle with the conceptual underpinnings of measurement. Even students who appear proficient with rulers and scales sometimes fail to understand the theory of measure that underlies the routinized procedures they have acquired. These partial understandings often lead to well-documented errors, like failing to properly interpret fractional units or insisting that the length of an object is equivalent to the value on the ruler that is lined up with its end, even though the other end of the object may not be aligned with the ruler's zero-point. The growing literature about young children's understanding and acquisition of a theory of measure provides further details about what is entailed in achieving a solid grasp of this component of data modeling (Lehrer, 2003).

The arrow between "Generating and Selecting Attributes" and "Constructing Measures" in Figure 6.1 is bidirectional, communicating that it is not simply that selecting attributes leads to decisions about how to measure them. Equally important, struggling with issues of how to measure often leads to reconceptualizing the attribute in question (see Lucas et al., 2005). Similarly, both components are intimately involved in the posing of a researchable question, so that decisions about attribute and measure very frequently change the question being investigated, sometimes in subtle and sometimes dramatic ways. Pickering (1995) used the term *mechanic grip* to refer to the challenge of identifying a way to get purchase on events and objects in the world, wrestling them into measurements that are amenable for further analysis. Sometimes, but not always, achieving a mechanic grip includes the further challenge of developing an apparatus that renders these attributes amenable to measurement. The apparatus may be in the form either of a physical instrument or machine or any other way of arranging the world so that it can be effectively studied (as in the staging of an experiment).

Although design of experiments often receives more attention, a premature focus on design may obscure the importance of how, in scientific practice, questions, attributes, and measures often co-originate.

Structuring Data

Structuring and displaying data are intimately related; representational change both reflects and instigates new ways of thinking about the data. The major point for both data structure and data display, however, is that structure is constructed, not inherent. The researcher imposes structure by deciding the focus of the question under investigation and selecting the categories around which to describe and organize the data that are collected.

At the minimum, every data set should include two types of information: an identifier that indexes who or what is being described (a number, a name, a label) and a description of the qualities being studied. However, even with the simplest of data sets, students often have difficulties imposing structure consistently. For example, they tend to overlook the fact that important information that they personally know needs to be explicitly specified in the data set. The converse is also true; they frequently include information that is redundant (for example, a column labeled "boys" and another labeled "girls" rather than a single column labeled "gender"—see Hancock, 1992). The latter example is a manifestation of developing a means to think of data as having a dimensional structure. The cells of spreadsheets assume such constructions, but their form and function are not obvious to students. The left panel of Figure 6.2 displays one kind of structure children imposed on the portrait data referred to previously. The columnar structure signals not dimension, but rather, uncoordinated lists of attributes. In contrast, the structure depicted in the right panel of Figure 6.2 has an attribute-value dimensional structure that assisted children's efforts to develop a workable classification model (Lehrer & Schauble, 2000).

Novices at all ages tend to regard data as answers to specific questions that were conceived in advance, rather than a reusable resource that can be queried with new questions that emerge after the data have been collected. Rather than consulting and possibly restructuring their data to address a new question, novices often tend instead to think of collecting more data (Glaser, Schauble, Raghavan, & Zeitz, 1992). Regarding data as a potential source for new questions assumes a stance toward the data that we refer to as *objectifying* data (Lehrer & Romberg, 1996), that is, mentally stepping away from the cases that the data represent to treat the data as objects in their own right. As one might expect, this perspective is challenging for young students, but it is the perspective that permits one to seek patterns and relationships that were not noticed in the original phenomena. Rather than taking a *case view* of the data, where what is salient is the particular objects being studied (my plant, your plant, his plant with all their unique history and qualities), objectifying the data entails taking an *aggregate view*, in which the data themselves are objects of manipulation, inspection, and conjecture.

Displaying Data

The relationships between data display and data structure are intimate. A data display reflects the structure that the inquirer has imposed on the data, communicating that structure in ways that can support arguments or claims. Typically, students are taught canonical forms of data displays and their proper uses. However, it is easy for this form of instruction to miss the point that the design of data displays needs to be firmly grounded in an intent to communicate, a sense of the likely audience, and a vision of how the display may be interpreted. Students should come to regard data display as a form of argument, not as an inert picture of something.

As one might expect, students are often unaware that viewers may not share the designer's knowledge of either the phenomenon or the display. Indeed, in the absence of continued reminders that the designer must be accountable for the interpretation of his or her display, some students tend to show a preference for novel, artistic, or even arcane design features over those that communicate clearly. Figure 6.3, drawn by 3 fifth-graders working together, represents the heights of 63 Wisconsin Fast Plants™ on the 23rd day of their life cycle. The three students who designed this display had been asked, along with other teams of students in their class, to develop a way that would clearly identify the "typical" height of a plant on its 23rd day of growth and also "how spread out" the data were.

Understanding how much work is involved in helping youngsters understand the key idea of "audience" for a display, the teacher, Mark Rohlfing, asked groups of children to exchange displays. Then, uninitiated students publicly attempted to interpret the displays of the groups who had designed them.

The team given responsibility for interpreting Figure 6.3 gave it a game try, but eventually had to appeal to the design team to figure out their procedures for plotting each of the values on the display. As you might suppose, values are defined on this display as points at the intersection between the axes, and the other symbols on the graph indicate duplicate values and candidate "typical" values. The class was initially attracted to the novelty of the display, which looked quite unlike those generated by other teams. Indeed, this display was awarded the ultimate fifth grade compliment (it was deemed "cool"). However, this initial enthusiasm began to wane as the class turned

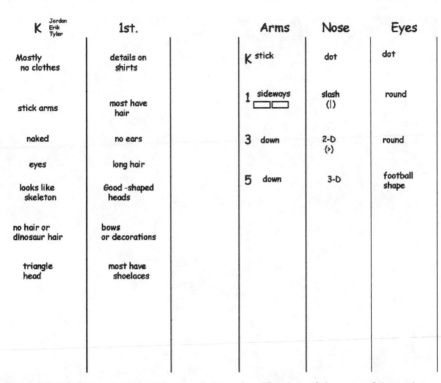

Figure 6.2 Data structures for modeling classification of the age of the artist.

their attention to identifying how the graph communicated the "typical" height of a plant and the "spread of the data." As one student finally concluded, "I don't think, if you weren't the one who made that graph, that you'd have any idea what it shows."

Our collaborating teachers find it helpful to provide students with plenty of practice at switching between the roles of display generator and display interpreter. Without repeated practice in assuming and eventually, coordinating these roles, it is difficult to develop and bring an "audience" perspective to the task of designing a data representation. Although we certainly do not hold the position that students must reinvent every mathematical convention, there are other benefits, as well, to providing repeated opportunities to invent and critique data displays. These experiences make it much more likely that when students encounter conventional data displays, they will be in a better position to consider the intentions of the designer and to understand the communication problems that the conventions were meant to resolve.

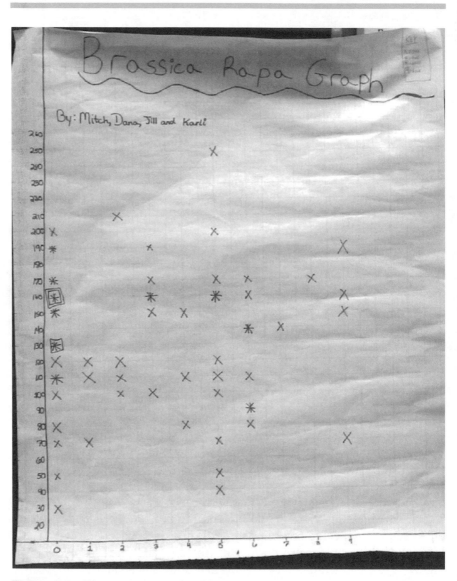

Figure 6.3 Display invented by fifth-grade children to highlight typical plant heights and spread.

In an earlier section, we pointed out that measures and attributes are mutually determined. For students, their resolution creates new challenges of data structure and representation. If one's interest is in describing growth, what is a good way to display the relationship between time of growth and height? And, might the display make evident something important that was not in one's original field of conception? For example, a third-grade class developed a line graph to depict rates of growth for a sample of approximately two dozen Wisconsin Fast Plants.™ The graph had an emergent quality, an "S-shaped" curve that was not observable by looking at plants in the world (Lehrer, Schauble, Carpenter, & Penner, 2000). However, seeing in this way depended on developing a "disciplined perception" (Stevens & Hall, 1998), a firm grounding in a Cartesian system. Moreover, the shape of the curve was determined in light of variation, accounted for by selecting and connecting midpoints of the distributions of plant heights at each of the days of measurement. The midpoints were then connected in intervals that defined piecewise linear segments. This way of representing "typical growth," which was proposed by one of the third-graders, was contentious among the students because some of the midpoints did not correspond to any particular casevalue. Children found it counterintuitive to accept as "typical" a value that did not appear in the original distribution. From an educational perspective, this debate provided a pathway toward the idealization and imagined qualities of the world necessary for adopting a modeling stance. The form of the growth curve was eventually tested in other systems of living organisms, and its replication spurred new questions. For example, why would it be that bacteria populations and plants could be described by the same growth curve? In this case and in others, explanatory models and data models mutually bootstrapped conceptual development (Lehrer & Schauble, 2002b).

Inference

As should now be evident, all of the components in Figure 6.1 are more complex than a simple diagram can easily portray. The final component, inference, is particularly complex. As we demonstrate, it entails not only orchestrating and coordinating all the other components in the figure, but also, sustaining a long chain of logic to support a conclusion. In this section, rather than describing this chain of logic directly, we do so via example, describing two different contexts for introducing students to distribution and inference. These two contexts, which contrasted in conceptually important ways, illustrate well what is difficult for young students in this final component in the Figure 6.1 framework.

The two educational contexts that are the focus of the contrast are measurement and natural variation. In recently completed research studies (Lehrer & Schauble, 2005; Petrosino, Lehrer, & Schauble, 2003) we have used each of these contexts to introduce children in the elementary grades to conceptions of distribution and inference. In each context, thinking about distribution was embedded within a larger cycle of modeling and experiment. Accordingly, we intended that children would come to see distributions as tools for thought—as a practical means to reason about difference in light of variation, and as a guide for interpreting experiments that were not pre-arranged to produce the large effects characteristic of school science. Instead, we wanted children to struggle with the complex question of how you know when two distributions are different, a puzzle that does not come up when differences between experimental conditions are so extreme that the distributions do not overlap at all. In the section that follows, we summarize results obtained from these two design studies, emphasizing their implications for young students' mastery of inference. Thus, the emphasis of this research is on comparing *distributions* of measures, not on the simple forms of categorical inference that have been more widely studied in the literature (i.e., inferences of inclusion and exclusion in which a potential cause does or does not covary with an outcome (c.f., Kuhn, Amsel, & O'Loughlin, 1989; Schauble, 1990). Arguably, comparing distributions is common in the kind of statistical thinking commonly employed in science.

Inference in a Measurement Context. Historically, measurement played a central role in the development of distribution (Porter, 1986). Astronomers measured stellar distances and were disconcerted to find that presumably fixed distances appeared to vary from measure to measure. Yet, the variation in measure was structured, a discovery that set the stage for the invention of (Gaussian) distribution. In previous research with elementary school children, we noted that repeated measures of qualities of matter, such as the mass or volume of objects made of different substances, provoked contest among children: Which of the measures should be used? What was fair? Resolution of these debates revealed that children considered volume and mass to be fixed, and they readily attributed discrepancies in measurements to sources of error, like the tool or method employed to measure (Lehrer, Schauble, Strom & Pligge, 2001; Lehrer, Strom, & Confrey, 2002). For example, third-grade students determined the volume of rectangular prisms by measuring the lengths and finding their products. However, the only way they could think of to find the volume of spheres was to measure the water they displaced. Differences in the relative precision of these two forms of estimate were very visible to children. So, too, were person-to-person differences in measuring the same object. In this light, we conjectured that with appropriate support, children might be in a position to consider the structure of variability inherent in measure. Our approach to introducing distribution relied on several affordances of the measurement context. By affordances, we mean to refer to prospective resources for thinking available to an ideal learner—what Piaget called the epistemic subject.

First, measurement affords *agency*. If measure is framed as activity, rather than as a product, students can mentally simulate the role of agents. As a consequence, foundations of distributional reasoning, such as notions of stochastic (repeated, random) process, have counterparts in distinguishable forms of activity—forms that students can readily identify. For example, stochastic process relies on the construction of *trial* (Horvath & Lehrer, 1998)—the assumption of identity over repeated instances of a process. In measurement, trial finds expression as the repeated activity of a measurer or in the collective activity of a group of measurers acting in concert. Similarly, precision of measure and its effects on the shape of a distribution can be attributed to the activity of a measurer who uses different tools or methods. Our belief that agency is an important resource for learning is grounded in accounts of situated cognition, which underscore the importance of mediated activity (Wertsch, 1998) and of grounded symbolism (Barsalou, 1999).

Second, measurement affords *emergence*. That is, measures of distribution, such as center or spread, can be viewed as emerging from and characterizing the collective activity of agent-measurers. Hence, in this context, a statistic, such as the median or mean, can be viewed literally as a measure of central tendency (Konold & Pollatsek, 2002), and the explanation for such a tendency can be attributed to the notion of a true or fixed value. Similarly, a statistic summarizing the spread of the distribution can be readily interpreted as reflecting tools or methods employed by agent-measurers. Thus, measurement appears to offer promising connections between case and aggregate views of the data. We recognize that much has been made of the prospective problems that emergence poses for theory development (e.g., Resnick, 1997, argues that it is difficult to understand emergence because of a bias toward expecting that structure must be determined by a central controller), but we consider emergence as a resource, rather than as an obstacle.

Third, although each agent is individual, given similar means and tools, agents tend to produce similar measures. "Close, but not identical" is a potential entrée to the idea of *interval*, creating the potential to view measures within the interval as exchangeable. Interval is foundational to the notion of *density,* which transforms data into ordered counts within (ever-decreasing) intervals.

Inference in a Natural Variation Context. Porter (1986) reports that historically, analogies between distributions of physical measures and distribution as descriptors of "the average man" or of other naturally varying events were, at best, strained. The acquisition of a wide grasp of the relationship between these ideas occurred over the course of nearly a century, and its slow diffusion suggests some prospective challenges for instruction. To ground these challenges, consider natural variation in the heights of a collection of plants at any particular day of growth. Distribution readily captures the structure of this variation, but from the perspective of a learner, what challenges does it pose?

The first is the relative *obscurity of a first-person perspective*. In contrast to measurement contexts, a collection of plants seems to invite a third-person point of view, because the activity of plant growth is inherent to the plant. Even if one were to "be a plant," only the result of growth is visible, not the process. Hence, the perspective most readily available is that of the collective (one sees a bunch of plants or perhaps even worse for students, just a batch of measures). Reasoning about cases of natural variation proceeds from the vantage point of the aggregate, in distinct counterpoint to the connection between case and aggregate afforded by measurement contexts.

A second potential obstacle to reasoning in contexts of natural variation is an appropriate interpretation of measures of distribution. What does a concept like "average plant" or "average spread" imply about a collection of plants? What processes might account for these statistics, or for changes in them over the life span of a collection of plants? It is difficult to conceive of these *statistics as emergent qualities of growth* because growth processes are largely invisible and inferred.

Conceiving of a sample of measures as one of a potentially infinite number of samples is not a perspective readily transportable to contexts of natural variation. Indeed, for students, this would probably entail imagining a stochastic process of growing again. Although it may not be difficult to measure again, growing again is costly in time and money, and sometimes is terminally impractical.

Finally, opportunities for identity and the cultivation of interest are central to learning (Boaler, 2000; Carpenter & Lehrer, 1999; Dewey, 1938), but measurement and natural variation contexts may not have equivalent affordances with respect to interest. Distribution has the potential to emerge from the activity of students most readily in contexts of measure. Changes in distributions can be connected in principle to changes in patterns of student activity. As designers of instruction to support student learning, this seems like a pathway for development that can be readily learner-centered (National Research Council, 2000). The prospects for natural variation are less clear. As we describe, one of our goals was to help students come to see distribution as a signature of growth processes. That is, as plants grow through their life cycle, the shape of the distribution of heights of a collection of plants changes, and these shifts are signatures of different processes. Yet, this goal requires knowledge that is not within the immediate grasp of students. Its practicality becomes evident only after one has distribution in hand, with the implication that there are good opportunities for instructional mischief—the "you'll see why later" paradigm of schooling. Of course, there is always a negotiation between existing practices and one's enactment of these practices in any community, including one consisting of learners (Wenger, 1998). Yet, it is important to consider the costs and potential trajectories of such negotiations.

In summary, contexts of measurement and natural variation afford different starting points and trajectories for learning about distribution. Contexts of measurement appear to provide pathways for developing understanding of distribution as mediated by learners' agency. Distribution emerges from students' bodily activity, and qualities of distribution can be mapped readily back into these forms of activity. Contexts of natural variation, in contrast, entail a number of distinct challenges. Although similarities among plants are visible and perhaps suggestive of exchangeability (hence, supporting ideas about interval and density), natural variation does not, for the most part, lend itself to first-person perspective. However, the ubiquity and importance of natural variation suggest that finding ways of supporting student learning has a potential for high return. In the next section, we summarize principles guiding our design of instruction in each context, along with some of the results obtained in classroom design studies.

CLASSROOM DESIGN STUDIES

We conducted two classroom studies, one featuring measurement and the other, natural variation. We first designed instruction to support student learning in the context of measure in a fourth grade class in a public elementary school located in the Midwest (Petrosino, Lehrer, & Schauble, 2003). The instructional design aimed to exploit the affordances of measurement for developing reasoning about distribution that we described earlier. Students then put their knowledge to use by conducting and interpreting experiments about the optimal design for model rockets. The second study was conducted the following year with the same teacher and with many of the same students, now in the fifth grade. This instructional design was aimed at exploring reasoning about distribution in the context of natural variation, with efforts made to support obstacles to student reasoning as they became apparent during the course of the study. Students again put their knowledge to use by conducting and interpreting experiments, this time on factors that affect plant growth. The educational plans for both studies were guided by design heuristics that we developed during the course of the larger encompassing effort aimed at changing teaching and learning of mathematics and science (Lehrer & Schauble, 2000; 2005). Three of these heuristics are especially pertinent here.

Instructional Design Heuristics

Modeling. The first design principle was a commitment to modeling, as outlined in the initial section of this chapter. Hence, there was a focus on educational tasks and activities in which qualities of distribution functioned to describe, summarize, and extend some aspect of an experienced situation, preferably one centered in student activity. Distribution served as a model.

Representational Competence. The second heuristic was a commitment to the development of representational competence (Greeno & Hall, 1997) as an essential constituent of mathematical and scientific learning. To address the development of representational competence, we repeatedly asked students to invent, critique, and revise inscriptions. Decisions about what is worth representing, and why, engage students in a form of self-explanation (Chi & Bassok, 1980). But inscriptions function in the larger world as way to construct argument (in the disciplinary sense), so we also made an effort to create audiences for these inscriptions. Moreover, ideally, we wished to fix the target of representation so that inscriptions become layered or "cascaded" (Latour, 1990). By this, we mean that the products of one inscriptional form (for example, calculated rates of growth) become elements in a new inscriptional form (for example, a graph that depicts changes in growth rates). This kind of reuse and combination of inscriptional forms both elaborates explanation and widens its scope (Lehrer, Schauble, Carpenter & Penner, 2000). Such "circulating reference" (Latour, 1999, p. 24) is also a hallmark of professional practice in sciences: Inscriptions are recruited to argument (Lehrer & Schauble, 2000, 2005). These processes are amplified when students' attention is explicitly focused on developing and articulating criteria for preferring or selecting certain representational forms for particular purposes, a goal that diSessa refers to as *meta-representation* (diSessa, 2002, 2004). For instance, as we briefly described earlier, different student-generated representations of the same set of data foreground different senses of the "shape" of the distribution associated with these data. Thinking about the "shape of the data" can, in turn, initiate closer attention to interval, an important conceptual foundation to distribution.

Measure. Engaging students in the design and development of measures generally leads to closer examination of the nature of the attribute or bundle of attributes being measured. Moreover, engaging in the design of measures opens the possibility of treating attributes as quantities (Thompson, 1994). What is considered an attribute often changes as one considers its measure (Lehrer, Jacobson, et al., 1998). Here our goal was to have students invent ways of measuring qualities of distribution, such as central tendency or spread.

In the remaining sections of the chapter, we summarize highlights from these two coordinated classroom design studies. The purpose is to give a sense of what we mean by inference, the final component in the Figure 6.1 framework. As becomes evident, we consider ideas about distribution and comparing distributions to be key, as, indeed, they are in professional contexts where the goal is to achieve justified inference about uncertain situations.

Measurement Context: Highlights of Design and Lessons Learned

In the fourth grade, we first asked students to use a cardboard "height-o-meter" to measure the height of the school's flagpole (see Petrosino et al., 2003). Students recorded their measurements on 3 x 5 index cards, and their teacher asked them to arrange their cards to show "how you would organize this." The instruction was sufficiently ambiguous to invite multiple solutions, some featuring "middle numbers" and splits of data above and below these values. Other groups constructed "bins" of similar values (e.g., 9's). During classroom discussion, the teacher intervened in two significant ways. First, working with the student groups who generated bins, he ordered the data in whole number intervals from left to right. This arrangement made central tendency evident and highlighted the fact that some values were extreme. This display also set the stage for considering whether or not extreme values were all that likely to recur if the class repeated their measurements. Generally, students attributed extreme values to mistakes—failure to account correctly for one's own height or position in relation to the flagpole in calculating the estimate of the flagpole's height from the reading taken on the height-o-meter. Students agreed that errors like these were less likely to recur, and that they would expect to see instead most of the measurements in the middle of the distribution.

One student, Isaac, explicitly noted that ordered lists did not support the perception of these differences as readily as the display with the bins. As an example, he referred to two measurements on both charts: 13.8 and 15.5 ft. On the ordered list, these values were juxtaposed, but in the bin display, an interval (14) intervened between the "13s" and "15s" bins, making more evident the outlier status of the 15.5 ft. measurement.

Students went on to consider the overall "shape of the data" that resulted from grouping measures by bins (intervals), and several proposed that special attention should be paid to the middle region, where one would find values a "little over" or a "little under" the "real" height of the flagpole. Although qualities of the middle emerged only during consideration of how to "organize" the data, we noted that students had ready recourse to their activity as measurers to explain the resulting symmetry: They reasoned that estimates were as likely to overshoot as to undershoot, and extreme values could be explained in principle by recourse to an imagined process of repeated measure. The notion of bins of data made the idea of interval accessible, and the symmetry visible in this display gave it functional significance.

From this starting point, the instructional design moved on to include invention of a measure of height (a "typical" value, interpreted as a good estimate of the real height) and introduction of a measure of spread that followed from the children's notions of overshooting and undershooting the center value. This "spread number" was the median absolute value of the distances between each measurement and the center. Students then went on to create a distribution of these differences, initially represented as bins of signed differences of "spread." While inspecting this first display, students concluded that under- and overestimates were equally likely, so that although sign was informative about direction of difference from the median, magnitude was a better means for thinking about "how spread out the data were." This discussion led to a display of the distribution of absolute values of difference from the median. It was from this display that students constructed a "spread number," or the median of the absolute values. We put spread number to work by providing different (metal, as opposed to cardboard) tools for measuring the height of the flagpole, and students noted that more precise measurement was accompanied by tighter clusters of difference scores and also by lower spread numbers. Thus, changes in a statistic that described a quality of the distribution that all could see, its spread, were again explained by experienced differences in measurement processes.

In the concluding phase of the study, students repeatedly launched model rockets of different design and measured their apogees with the same tool they had employed to measure the height of the flagpole. Their initial conjecture was that model rockets with pointed nose cones would "cut through the air," so they anticipated that even considering measure variation, pointy nose cones would travel higher than rockets with rounded nose cones. The data from multiple launches and measures of rounded nose cone rockets were pooled, and students, assisted by their teacher, created 3 "superbins," anchored by the median with boundaries determined by the spread number: launches below the median and greater than 1 spread number, launches encompassing the median +/− 1 spread number, and the remainder above the median and 1 spread number. The middle bin approximated a mid-50 conventional split of the data. The teacher asked students to predict the location of the pointed rocket launches within this reference distribution. Students were disconcerted to find that 86% of the launches of the rockets with pointed nose cones fell into the lowest superbin of the reference distribution. Reluctantly, they concluded that the weight of evidence suggested that their conjecture must be wrong.

Post-instructional interviews and related assessments suggested that students' reasoning about experiment generally took into account the need to consider variation when making judgments about effects. Moreover, students were generally adept at predicting how distributions would change, given variations in methods and tools of measure. Despite inevitable glitches, we interpreted the results of this design study as supporting the viability of an approach to distribution and inference via measurement. Measurement afforded agency, and agency allowed students to make sense of emergent qualities of distribution, like symmetry, center, and spread. Sense-making was bootstrapped by efforts to measure (Just how would one measure spread?) and to explain these qualities of distribution (e.g., Just why should a distribution be symmetric?), reflecting our design commitments. Students proved able to deploy this knowledge to reason about experiments that they conducted and also those conducted by others, thinking about measurement distribution as a model for reasoning about potential experimental effects. Designing and comparing systems of representation were threaded throughout the sequence of lessons, again consistent with our design principles. In fact, in spite of the caveats that we described earlier, we felt guardedly optimistic about moving on with these students in the following year to reason about natural variation.

Natural Variation Context: Highlights of Design and Lessons Learned

In the fifth grade, the class, which now consisted of the same teacher and most of the same students, investigated the growth of Wisconsin Fast Plants.™ In the context of these investigations, students wondered about the effects of different levels of light and fertilizer on the heights of plants, and designed two experiments to test their initial conjectures, basically, the more light and/or fertilizer, the taller the plants would grow. They also posed a series of questions about how (individual) plants might change over the lifecycle. As described earlier, students debated how to measure height and employed their previous experience with measure to standardize a method. Some proposed multiple measurements, a lesson apparently learned from the previous year. We first entered into the investigation by introducing a new goal: to design a display that would show "typical" (an explicit bridge to the measurement context) height and how spread out 63 plants were grown under "normal" conditions of light and fertilizer. We designed the task to promote consideration of "shape."

Much to our surprise, students generated many different solutions, including the "coordinate graph" shown in Figure 6.3. Only one of these solutions spontaneously included explicit attention to interval. Our first lesson learned was that we had not done enough to build bridges between measurement and natural variation. Yet as conversation unfolded, we began to realize that perhaps there was no easy bridge. Student conversations made it apparent that meaning of center and spread, so transparent in the measurement context, was entirely obscure in this new context. In fact, students treated the displays as descriptions and did not volunteer any causal mechanisms to account for the shape of the data. Comparing displays did appear to generate a better understanding of how choices made by designers of representations would influence what one could see. Contrasts among case-value plots, representing each plant's height by a scaled length (Fig. 6.4), and "bins" plots (intervals; Fig. 6.5) made these effects clear. How could these different shapes of data be reconciled?

One group of students proposed that the very idea of a typical plant didn't make much sense, but that a better approach might emphasize a "typical area" (referring to a region in the binned display where most of the values clustered). The teacher again played a proactive role, appealing to stochastic process. Seizing on the idea of a typical region, he asked students to consider where they might expect the plant heights to cluster "if we grew them again." This gave some added impetus to the notion of regions or splits of data, rather than point estimates.

In the next phase of instruction, we built on this image of "growing again" by conducting investigations with sampling. First, we put all 63 measurements of plant height taken on the 23rd day of growth and put them into an envelope. Students drew out samples of 21 and frequency displays of the samples. As students expected, plant heights from bins in the middle of the distribution appeared in greater proportions. Using a computer tool developed by diSessa, students investigated the shape of sample medians under different numbers of picks and different numbers of samples. They were initially astonished but readily made sense of the lack of variability in the distributions of the sample medians. However, throughout this activity, some students continued to struggle with its relationships to the world of plants. In particular, a few students continued to reject the idea of an ideal typical plant ("How can a plant height be typical if we see all these heights?" one asked) and struggled with the related notion that sampling can be a way of finding out what might happen if we "grow them again." Although most students accepted this relationship all of the time, and all of them accepted it some of the time, a few raised concerns from time to time about its status as a valid stand-in for nature.

Moving back to the idea of a "typical region," students worked to develop four-point descriptions of their data distributions, delineating medians and quartiles. Hearing one of the researchers refer to the median and quarter-split points as "hinges," students suggested that the data between these points could be conceived as the "doors" of the distribution. Students noted that as the "doors" become narrower (that is, encompassing a smaller portion of the range of the distribution), the density of the data in that quartile increased. Or, as the students put it, "When the doors become skinnier, they get taller." Students sketched the shape of the data distributions as the plants grew, noting how changes in shape reflected different phases of the life cycle. For example, students noticed that shortly after the plant shoots emerged from the ground, the distribution was positively skewed ("Because," as one student pointed out, "you can't get any shorter than 0 mm"). As the plants grew, variability in heights increased (due to different onsets of growth and inherent natural variation), and the distributions became roughly normal. At the end of the life cycle, the distribution was negatively skewed, as all the plants reached an approximately similar final height. These explorations of the "shape of the data" were coordinated with five-point summary, as students considered where the "middle 50" of the data would be during these different lifecycle phases.

The investigated culminated by comparing distributions of height for plants grown under different conditions of light and fertilizer. Students inspected these distributions and, in a class discussion, summarized evidence about which condition resulted in taller plants. The two distributions being compared were not of equal number, so simple counts of values in particular locations were not a compelling argument. Armed with ideas from previous discussions, students quickly generated "evidence" that each found compelling: the tallest plant in the distribution, shortest plant in the distribution, greatest proportion of heights over a proposed cut-point, proportion of values that overlap in the two distributions, location of the upper hinge, lower hinge, or middle 50%—all of these and more were proposed by various students as evidence in support of a particular opinion. Unfortunately, the more they talked, the more students began to realize that different measures led to different conclusions. How could this be resolved?

At this point, students were asked to re-evaluate the location of similar proportions of the distributions, but now also consider what we would expect to see if we grew the plants again. Taking the "spread" of the distributions into

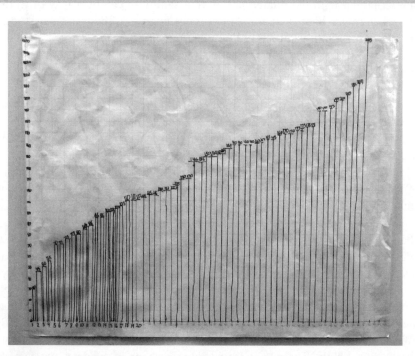

Figure 6.4 Invented display emphasizing value of each case gives one sense of the shape of the data.

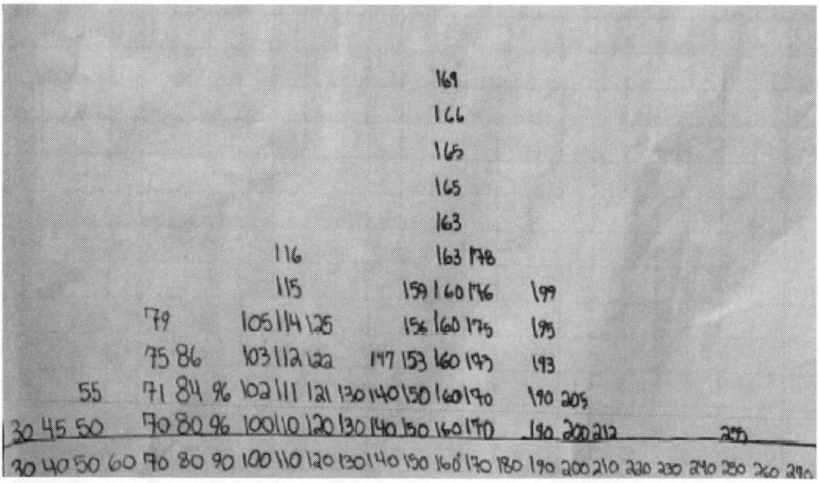

Figure 6.5 Invented display featuring intervals of values gives another sense of the shape of the data.

account, what is the likelihood just by chance alone that these two distributions would differ in the observed ways? This was a step too far for most students, but one marched up to the board to indicate where he would expect the median of one distribution to fall in reference to the other "if the two distributions were really different." He indicated a location within the upper tail of the referent.

As we learned, of the two contexts, natural variation is far more challenging than measurement. The lack of an agent view, relative obscurity of mechanism, and the uncertain status of what a "typical value" means—all these caused difficulties for some students, and sometimes these difficulties resurfaced repeatedly. This does not mean that we consider the enterprise a failure from an educational standpoint. The data from final assessments revealed that students had good intuitions about the shape of a sample based on the shape of a parent population, could make inferences about stage of growth from looking at a distribution of heights, and could appeal to multiple forms of evidence to decide whether two unequal-sized distributions were in fact different. Students even showed some proficiency at generating a distribution that met the constraints of a five-point summary that we proposed (we provided the number of cases, highest and lowest values, median, and the 25% and 75% splits). Regardless, we came away from this experience re-convinced that concepts that are "the same" from a disciplinary perspective may not at all be the same from the viewpoint of a learner. As we and others continue to pursue research in data modeling, understanding the roots of these challenges in particular corners of statistical reasoning (as well as identifying productive foundations for learning) will continue to guide our efforts.

ACKNOWLEDGMENTS

This research was supported by the National Science Foundation, Grant 0337675. The views expressed do not necessarily reflect those of the Foundation. Both authors contributed equally to this work.

REFERENCES

Barsalou, L. W. (1999). Perceptual symbol systems. *Behavioral and Brain Sciences, 22,* 577–660.

Boaler, J. (2000). Mathematics from another world: Traditional communities and the alienation of learners. *Journal of Mathematical Behavior, 18,* 379–397.

Carey, S. (1985). *Conceptual change in childhood.* Cambridge, MA: MIT Press.

Carpenter, T. P., & Lehrer, R. (1999). Teaching and learning mathematics with understanding. In E. Fennema & T. R. Romberg (Eds.), *Mathematics classrooms that promotes understanding* (pp. 19–32). Mahwah, NJ: Lawrence Erlbaum Associates.

Chi, M. T. H., & Bassok, M. (1980). Learning from examples via self-explanations. In L. B. Resnick (Ed.), *Knowing learning and instruction: Essays in honor of Robert Glaser* (pp. 251–282). Hillsdale, NJ: Lawrence Erlbaum Associates.

Cobb, P., McClain, K., & Gravemeijer, K. (2003). Learning about statistical covariation. *Cognition and Instruction, 22*, 1–78.

Dewey, J. (1938). *Experience and education.* New York: Collier Books.

diPerna, E. (2002). Data models of ourselves: Body self-portrait project. In R. Lehrer & L. Schauble (Eds.), *Investigating real data in the classroom* (pp. 81–97). New York: Teachers College Press.

DiSessa, A. A. (2004). Meta-representation: Native competence and targets for instruction. *Cognition and Instruction, 22*, 293–332.

DiSessa, A. A. (2002). Students' criteria for representational adequacy. In K. Gravemeijer, R. Lehrer, B. Van Oers, & L. Verschaffel (Eds.), *Symbolizing, modeling and tool use in mathematics education* (pp. 105–129). Boston: Kluwer.

Glaser, R., Schauble, L., Raghavan, K., & Zeitz, C. (1992). Scientific reasoning across different domains. In E. DeCorte, M. Linn, H. Mandl, & L. Verschaffel, (Eds.), *Computer-based learning environments and problem solving* (pp. 345–371). Berlin: Springer-Verlag.

Goodwin, C. (2000). Practices of color classification. *Mind, Culture, and Activity, 7*, 19–36.

Greeno, J. G., & Hall, R. (1997, January). Practicing representation: Learning with and about representational forms. *Phi Delta Kappa*, 361–367.

Hancock, C., Kaput, J. J., & Goldsmith, L. T. (1992). Authentic inquiry with data: Critical barriers to classroom implementation. *Educational Psychologist, 27*, 337–364.

Hestenes, D. (1992). Modeling games in the Newtonian world. *American Journal of Physics, 60*, 732–748.

Horvath, J. K., & Lehrer, R. (1988). A model-based perspective on the development of children's understanding of chance and uncertainty. In S. P. LaJoie (Ed.), *Reflections on statistics: Agendas for learning, teaching, and assessment in K–12* (pp. 121–148). Mahwah, NJ: Lawrence Erlbaum Associates.

Kahneman, D., Slovic, P., & Tversky, A. (Eds.). (1982), *Judgment under uncertainty: Heuristics and biases.* New York: Cambridge University Press.

Klahr, D., Chen, Z., & Toth, E. E. (2001). Cognitive development and science education: Ships passing in the night or beacons of mutual illumination? In S. M. Carver & D. Klahr (Eds.), *Cognition and Instruction: 25 years of progress.* (pp. 75–120). Mahwah, NJ: Lawrence Erlbaum Associates.

Kline, M. (1980). *Mathematics. The loss of certainty.* Oxford: Oxford University Press.

Konold, C. (1989). Informal conceptions of probability. *Cognition and Instruction, 6*, 59–98.

Konold, C., & Pollatsek, A. (2002). Data analysis as the search for signals in noisy processes. *Journal for Research in Mathematics Education, 33*, 259–289.

Kuhn, D., Amsel, E., & O'Loughlin, M. (1988). *The development of scientific thinking skills.* San Diego: Academic Press.

Latour, B. (1990). Drawing things together. In M. Lynch & S. Woolgar (Eds.), *Representation in scientific practice* (pp. 19–68). Cambridge, MA: MIT Press.

Lehrer, R. (2003). Developing understanding of measurement. In J. Kilpatrick, W. G. Martin, & D. E. Schifter (Eds.), *A research companion to principles and standards for school mathematics* (pp.179–192). Reston, VA: National Council of Teachers of Mathematics.

Lehrer, R., Carpenter, S., Schauble, L., & Putz, A. (2000). Designing classrooms that support inquiry. In J. Minstrell & E. V. Zee (Eds.), *Inquiring into inquiry learning and teaching in science* (pp. 80–99). Washington, DC: American Association for the Advancement of Science.

Lehrer, R., Jacobson, C., Thoyre, G., Kemeny, V., Strom, D., Horvath, J., Gance, S., & Koehler, M. (1998). Developing understanding of geometry and space in the primary grades. In R. Lehrer & D. Chasan (Eds.), *Designing learning environments for developing understanding of geometry and space* (pp. 169–200). Mahwah, NJ: Lawrence Erlbaum Associates.

Lehrer, R., & Romberg, T. (1996). Exploring children's data modeling. *Cognition and Instruction:* 14(1), 69–108.

Lehrer, R., & Schauble, L., Carpenter S., & Penner, D. E. (2000). Modeling in mathematics and science. In R. Glaser (Ed.), *Advances in instructional psychology* (Vol. 5.; pp.101–159). Mahwah, NJ: Lawrence Erlbaum Associates.

Lehrer, R., & Schauble, L. (2001). Reconsidering the role of experiment in science education. In K. Crowley, S. Schunn, & T. Okada (Eds.), *Designing for science: Implications from everyday, classroom, and professional settings* (pp. 251–278). Mahwah, NJ: Lawrence Erlbaum Associates.

Lehrer, R., & Schauble, L. (2002a). Symbolic communication in mathematics and science: Co-constituting inscription and thought. In E. D. Amsel & J. Byrnes (Eds.), *Language, literacy and cognitive development. The development and consequences communication.* (pp. 167–192). Mahwah, NJ: Lawrence Erlbaum Associates.

Lehrer, R., & Schauble, L. (2002b). Inventing data structures for representational purposes: Elementary grade students' classification models. *Mathematical Thinking and Learning, 2,* 49–72.

Lehrer, R., & Schauble, L. (2005). Developing modeling and argument in elementary grades. In T. A. Romberg, T. P. Carpenter, & I F. Dremock (Eds.), *Understanding mathematics and science matters.* Mahwah, NJ: Lawrence Erlbaum Associates.

Lehrer, R., Schauble, L., & Petrosino, A. (2001). Reconsidering the role of experiment in science education. In K. Crowley, C. Schunn, & T. Okada (Eds.), Designing for science. Implications from everyday, classroom, and professional settings (pp. 251–278). Mahwah, NJ: Lawrence Erlbaum Associates.

Lehrer, R., Schauble, L., Strom, D., & Pligge, M. (2001). Similarity of form and substance: Modeling material kind. In D. Klahr & S. Carver (Eds.), *Cognition and instruction: 25 years of progress* (pp. 39–74). Mahwah, NJ: Lawrence Erlbaum Associates.

Lehrer, R., Schauble, L., & Penner, D.E. (2000). The inter-related development of inscriptions and conceptual understanding. In P. Cobb, E, Yackel, & K. McClain (Eds.), *Symbolizing and communication in mathematics classrooms: Perspectives on discourse, tools, and instructional design* (pp. 325–360). Mahwah, NJ: Lawrence Erlbaum Associates.

Lehrer, R., Strom, D., & Confrey, J. (2002). Grounding metaphors and inscriptional resonance: Children's emerging understanding of mathematical similarity. Cognition and Instruction, 20, 359–398.

Lucas, D., Broderick, N., Lehrer, R. & Bohanon, R. (2005). Making the grounds of scientific inquiry visible in the classroom. *Science Scope, 29*(3), 39–42.

Metz, K. E. (2004). Children's understanding of scientific inquiry: Their conceptualization of uncertainty in investigations of their own design. *Cognition and Instruction, 22,* 219–290.

Mokros, J., & Russell, S. J, (1995). Children's concepts of average and representativeness. *Journal for Research in Mathematics Education, 26,* 20–39.

National Council of Teachers of Mathematics (2000). *Principles and standards for school mathematics.* Reston, VA: Author.

National Research Council. (2000). *How people learn.* Washington, DC: National Academy Press.

Nisbett, R. E., Krantz, D. H., Jepson, C., & Kunda, A. (1983). The use of statistical heuristics in everyday inductive reasoning. *Psychological Review, 90,* 339–363.

Nisbett, R., & Ross, L. (1980). *Human inference: Strategies and shortcomings of social judgment.* Englewood Cliffs, NJ: Prentice Hall.

Petrosino, A., Lehrer, R., & Schauble, L. (2003). Structuring error and experimental variation as distribution in the fourth grade. *Mathematical Thinking and Learning, 5,* 131–156.

Pickering, A. (1995). *The mangle of practice. Time, agency, and science.* Chicago: University of Chicago Press.

Pollatsek, A., Lima, S., & Well, A. (1981). Concept of computation: Students' understanding of the mean. *Educational Studies in Mathematics, 12,* 191–204.

Porter, T. M. (1986). *The rise of statistical thinking 1820–1900.* Princeton, NJ: Princeton University Press.

Resnick, M. (1994). *Turtles, termites, and traffic jams.* Cambridge, MA: MIT Press.

Schauble, L. (1990). Belief revision in children: The role of prior knowledge and strategies for generating evidence. *Journal of Experimental Child Psychology, 49,* 31–57.

Strauss, S., & Bichler, E. (1988). The development of children's concepts of the arithmetic average. *Journal for Research in Mathematics Education 19,* 64–80.

Stevens, R., & Hall, R. (1998). Disciplined perception: Learning to see in technoscience. In M. Lampert & M. L. Blunk (Eds.), *Talking mathematics* (pp. 107–149). Cambridge, UK: Cambridge University Press.

Thompson, P. W. (1994). The development of the concept of speed and its relationship to concepts of rate. In G. Harel & J. Confrey (Eds.), *The development of multiplicative reasoning in the learning of mathematics.* (pp. 179–234). Albany, NY: SUNY Press.

Wenger, E. (1998). *Communities of practice: Learning, meaning, and identity.* Cambridge, UK: Cambridge University Press.

Wertsh, J. V. (1998). *Mind as action.* New York, NY: Oxford University Press.

Wild, C. J., & Pfannkuch, M. (1999). Statistical thinking in empirical inquiry. *International Statistical Review, 67,* 223–265.

7

Discussion of Part I: Variation in the Meaning and Learning of Variation

Gaea Leinhardt
University of Pittsburgh

Jorge Larreamendy-Joerns
Universidad de los Andes, Colombia

FROM THE PAST

In his characteristically obscure style, Parmenides of Elea, one of the most influential pre-Socratic philosophers, argued 25 centuries ago against the common-sensical belief of the physical world as a reality of plurality and change. In the poem *On Nature*, his only surviving work, Parmenides asserted that what exists

> Is completed
> From every direction like the bulk of a well-rounded sphere,
> Everywhere from the center equally matched; for it must not be any larger
> Or any smaller here or there;
> For neither is there what-is-not, which could stop it from reaching
> Its like; nor is there a way in which what-is could be
> More here and less there, since it all inviolably is
> For equal to itself from every direction it lies uniformly within limits.
> (Parmenides, fragment VIII, 42–49, trans. 1984)

The fragment evokes the familiar image of the sphere as a representation of perfection, seamlessness, and unity, and advances the argument that variation gets in the way of knowing and is, in some sense, messy. Parmenides' cryptic demonstration, and to no less extent Pythagoras' fascination with numbers and geometry, instituted very early in the history of Western thought our longing for essences and stability. It is not coincidental that Plato decided to devote one of his most complex and intriguing dialogues to issues concerning Parmenides' philosophy. Parmenides played a crucial role in the development of Plato's theory of forms, whose standard doctrine can be found in the *Phaedo* and the *Republic,* and according to which eternal, unchanging, qualities or principles exist independently of the changing world of phenomena. It is worth noticing that in the economy of both Parmenides' and Plato's arguments, variation was a perceptual primitive in that it was immediately apprehended by the senses. However, it was also deemed a barrier to true understanding (hence, to philosophy) and was to be transcended.

Parmenides, as well other members of the Eleatic school and Plato himself, had Heraclitus in their sight when they focused their arguments. Heraclitus embraced the idea of irreducible change and variation as core constituents of reality: "As they step into the same rivers, different and still different waters flow upon them" (Heraclitus, fragment XII, trans. 1987). Heraclitus' fragments are far from the formal rigor of Parmenides and the late Plato. They are oracular in style, sometimes witty, and lead occasionally to a paradoxical state that is close to the spirit of his more substantive claims. But it takes an appreciation of the enlightening perplexity that oracles were meant to provoke in devotees to realize that for Heraclitus the changing and variable quality of reality was far from being a matter of immediate perception. On the contrary, for Heraclitus the apprehension of change and difference was an accomplishment. Thus, in a sense, we are even: Neither the permanence and ideality of true forms, nor the transient nature of experience are self-evident to the human mind.

Cognitive science does not take side in this argument. Foundational works in cognitive science (Bruner, Goodnow, & Austin, 1956; Simon & Gregg, 1967; Simon & Lea, 1974) show that those cognitive entities, concepts, that transcend the flux of reality are momentous achievements, both developmentally and computationally speaking. In fact, computational algorithms and psychologically plausible models of pattern recognition have been and continue to be a Holy Grail in cognitive science. Thus, we fully concur with Parmenides and Plato that knowing implies going beyond ephemeral reality. Yet, we do not support the corollary that variation is unproblematic or to be "gotten beyond."

The chapters of this section of the 33rd Carnegie Symposium strongly suggest that there is nothing self-evident about the notions of variation and uncertainty. In a narrow sense, the chapters present us with empirical research dealing with how people reason about and understand concepts, such as standard deviation, error, distribution, and measurement resolution that are critical to the practice of statistics. In a broader sense, however, the chapters provide evidence that the understanding of variation is cognitively challenging and that such understanding plays a crucial role in making sound inferences from data and in the practice of science. The chapters take on the issue of variation in the realm of statistics and measurement (broadly conceived). This is a fortunate choice, in our view, because statistics as a discipline has been central in mediating, in the context of modern science, the dispute between what we might call the Parmenidian and the Heraclitean views.

Statistics is concerned with securing sound inferences from data. At a descriptive level, the issue at stake is finding indexes that are maximally informative of the distributional properties of a batch of data. This suggests a need to talk about measures of center and spread. Exploratory Data Analysis aims simultaneously at the recognition of patterns and at the inscription of variation (Tukey, 1977). At an inferential level, the issue at stake is estimation, namely, the relationship between the behavior of a statistic with respect to the behavior of a population parameter. Securing sound inferences from data also requires that we add the practice of modeling. Modeling is the formalization of the behavior of variables as a function of other variables. In statistical modeling, variation acquires an epistemic duplicity that is crucial for scientific inquiry: Variation is split between accounted variance and error. Thus, at the center of statistics as a disciplinary practice lies variation with its two faces: an object of inquiry and something to be explained away.

The theme of variation as error was crucial to the advancement of physical sciences and to the historical emergence of statistics as an autonomous discipline. According to Stigler (1986), concerns about variation resulting from imperfections of measurement instruments and methods played a central role in the development of mathematical statistics in astronomy in the 18th and early 19th centuries. For example, Thomas Simpson attempted in1740 a first demonstration of the method of taking the mean of astronomical observations to "diminish the errors arising from the imperfections of instruments and of the organ of sense." Calculating the mean of several observations was by then a method universally followed by astronomers to reach legitimate conclusions. The use of such a method was preceded by a period in which the legitimacy and trustworthiness of observations and scientific discoveries depended heavily on the authority of the observer or the superiority of one's telescopes (Helden, 1994). Statistics was recognized as one way to discern true values from discrepant observations. Simpson was the first to provide a probabilistic analysis of the advantages of the mean relative to single observations, by focusing on the error distributions, rather than on the distribution of actual observations (Stigler, 1986).

Nearly 60 years later, Adrien Marie Legendre published *Nouvelle Methodes pour La Détermination des Orbites des Cometes* [New Methods for the Determination of the Orbits of Comets] (1805), where he presented the method of least squares in order to minimize errors about the estimate of true values. Legendre was interested in determining the parabolic path of comets from observations taken at equal intervals. Legendre developed what is currently called a mathematical optimization technique for fitting a specified model to the observed data. The true value of quantities (i.e., the true path of the comet) could be then distinguished from fallible, error-containing measures. This use of statistics to track down the truth is manifest in Legendre's own words: "By this method [least squares], a kind of equilibrium is established among the errors which, because it prevents the extremes from dominating, is appropriate for revealing the state of the system which most nearly approaches the truth" (cited in Stigler, 1986, p. 13).

A conceptualization of types of errors grew parallel to the development of mathematical treatments of variation. One example is the work of the American mathematician William Chauvenet, who in 1871 distinguished between constant or regular errors, on the one hand, and irregular or accidental errors, on the other. The former refer to variations that are attributable to "any determinate law" (refraction, aberration, systematic effects of instruments, and 'personal equations') and that can be safely removed (mathematically or materially) when they are properly understood. The latter constitute variations "governed by no fixed law connecting them with the circumstances of the observations, and therefore, never subjected *a priori* to computation" (Chauvenet, 1871, p. 471). According to Chauvenet, the aim of the method of least square was "the restriction of the effect of irregular errors within the narrowest limits according to the theory of probabilities, and, at the same time, to determine from the observations themselves the errors to which out results are probably liable." (Chauvenet, 1871, p. 472).

Variation, however, is not only a proxy for error (regular or otherwise), but also a subject of inquiry, as when change and difference become interesting in and of themselves. Research in astronomy and biology (two disciplines that have been key to the development of statistics) illustrate this meaning. For example, Stigler (1986) recounts in his *History of Statistics* the quest of Jacques Cassini in 1740 to document the lack of uniform change in the obliquity of the ecliptic (e.g., the angle between the axis of rotation of the Earth and the ecliptic plane in which the Earth rotates around the Sun). He was faced with a complex problem of pattern detection within variation, where some variation might represent true differences, while other variation was probably noise. Cassini compared observations made over 2,000 years with values found by linear interpolation. Cassini assessed the internal consistency of adjacent observations to rule out the possibility of error. He also evaluated the plausibility of variation by looking at the differences between interpolations and observations that Cassini himself considered being valid. The issue for Cassini was not only to weed out error, but also to find a particular form of variation between observations and interpolations consistent with theoretical expectations about changes over time in the obliquity of the ecliptic.

In contrast to the treatment of variation in astronomy, in evolutionary biology variation is part and parcel of the core theory. Biology is concerned with the invariant principles, processes, and structures of living organisms. Unity is found, among others, in the universal genetic code shared by organisms, in the architectural features underlying taxa, and in the simple yet powerful explanatory algorithms of evolutionary theory. Yet, as a discipline, biology also aims to document the diversity and complex interaction of living forms at different levels of organization, a goal that is deeply rooted in the tradition of natural history (Brooks & McLennan, 2002; Futuyma, 1998; Gould, 2002a,). According to Gould (2002b),

> the Darwinian principle of natural selection yields temporal change—"evolution" in the biological definition—by a twofold process of generating copious and undirected variation within a population, and then passing only a biased (selected) portion of this variation to the next generation. In this manner, the variation within a population at any moment can be converted into differences in mean values (such as average size or average braininess) among successive populations through time. For this fundamental reason, we call such theories of change "variation" as opposed to more conventional, and more direct, models of "transformational" change imposed by natural laws that mandate a particular trajectory based on inherent, and therefore predictable, properties of substances and environments. (Gould, 2002b, p. 247).

The idea of variation both as differences among specimens in a population or a sample (or between species in a clade), and as difference of population or sample means over time was essential to Fisher's development of the procedures for analysis of variance. For example, in his classical analysis of the different species of irises (*setosa*, *versicolor*, and *virginica*), Fisher (1936) was interested in documenting the hypothesis that the species *Iris versicolor* was a hybrid of the two other species. He developed a compound measure of four discrete traits (sepal length, sepal width, petal length, and petal width) and partitioned variance between species and within species on those variables. For Fisher, variation was clearly not an error, for different measures within and between Iris species were an expression of biological diversity. As Fisher argued, variation between means indicated taxonomic difference and the degree of overlap of distributions hinted at taxonomic relatedness. Fisher's analysis of the use of multiple measures in taxonomic problems marks a significant event in the advancement of statistics and biology. But more importantly, it constitutes a reminder that the development (and understanding) of statistical procedures goes in tandem with the treatment of substantive issues in science.

The Legendre and Fisher examples illustrate the use of statistics in the service of specific disciplinary queries. However, when he wrote the 1936 article for *Annals of Eugenics*, Fisher was not truly writing as a biologist; he was writing as an applied mathematician, who had a solution that could be applied to a problem. Similarly, Tukey (1977) in considering statistics as the systematic study of not so easily seen patterns contributed the important notion of a "batch" and its description as an entity in and of itself. Long before Tukey, statisticians treated assemblages of numbers as entities in and of themselves. But it was Tukey who emphasized that, with the use of language and intuitive representations such as stem-and-leaf displays and box-and-whisker plots, we can see specific aspects of variation. So, in a sense, Tukey restituted, through visualization, the immediacy of variation that had been laboriously formalized since the 19th century. Of course, the risk in looking at data as an object is that the characteristics of the display become ends in themselves, and the not altogether common-sensical notion that groups of numbers are of themselves objects and playthings becomes assumed. It should also be remembered that these presentational systems were in some ways rebellions to the least squares approach precisely because the social science data that Tukey dealt with was not always so well behaved as the astronomical data that was in the origin of Legendre's and Gauss' work.

TO THE PRESENT

The discussion up to this point has not simply been a desire to scratch an historical itch. Rather, it has been to point out that the ideas with which this symposium is grappling have a lengthy history that bespeaks both an importance and a subtlety. We take from this excursion the idea that variation can be seen as error, as an integral part of the phenomena to be explained (in fact, an explanatory attribute), and an inherent aspect of data. We take from the lessons of the past the notion that some ideas surrounding variation are harder than others to grasp, represent, and make use of. We turn now to considering the set of chapters in light of these two issues: What is variation? What is hard about learning and understanding it? Each of the chapters in this session made many contributions and we start with those. We think the chapters are united in their attempts to come to grips with these fundamental ideas and in doing so link well to the work that has gone on before.

Contributions

Garfield, delMas, and Chance, and delMas and Liu build on a detailed analysis of students' understanding of measures of center and spread. They document both in the context of a single activity and through a series of classroom lessons the challenges that distributional thinking poses to students. For example, the authors show that when comparing distributions, students often focus on single features (e.g., shape) or on single sets of descriptive statistics (e.g., mean, standard deviation), at the expense of a more integrated understanding, where multiple features or measures are brought to bear. To go beyond the idea of variation as a "nuisance parameter," only secondary to measures of center, Garfield and colleagues recommend encouraging students to think of variation as a natural phenomenon and to conjecture about consider reasons for variability.

Masnick, Klahr, and Morris examine, from a developmental point of view, the role of conceptual expectations in the understanding of variation. Building on Hon's (1989) taxonomy of errors and following the tradition of Chauvenet, the authors explicitly connect the issue of variation to the broader problem of experimental error and show that children have powerful intuitions about variation that can be built on. The result is a complex picture of the factors that influence children's intuitions about the meaning of variability. Their analyses suggest that children's sensitivity to variation and to the distinction between true variation and variation resulting from experimental error depends on their conceptual expectations about the plausibility of values. When reasoning about well-understood phenomena (e.g., ramps), children are sensitive to sources of error and are reasonably confident about their predictions. The situation is reversed in poorly understood domains (e.g., pendulum), where the children's misconceptions get in the way of a careful examination of data. Interestingly, Masnick and colleagues show that in the absence of strong expectations, both children and adults pay increased attention to patterns in the data. Taken together, these results suggest that the meaning that is attributed to variation is a complex function of theoretical expectations, the salience of patterns in the data, and the understanding of the logic underlying experimental work.

Lehrer and Schauble broaden further the context of variation, including not only the logic of experimentation, but also the full range of modeling practices. Variation is not only a formal attribute of data, but also an issue that becomes apparent in activities such as question posing, selection of relevant variables, construction of measures, development of data structures and representations, and inference making. In our view, Lehrer and Schauble make two major contributions to the discussion. First, they remind us that statistical reasoning is recruited as a way to investigate genuine, meaningful questions. In that sense, statistical concepts and procedures make sense only within an extended logic of inquiry. Inquiry here does not simply mean posing interesting research questions, and then attacking them through unproblematic, ready-made tools. Inquiry involves argumentation and negotiation all the way through the practice of modeling. Lehrer and Schauble take pains in showing us that there is nothing trivial or self-explanatory about crafting a researchable question, "carving up events and objects in the world into variables," deciding on the protocol of measurements, shaping data structures, judging the rhetorical and informational power of representations, and making sound conclusions. These practices are problematic not because of the inexperience of learners, but because they do not rest on natural or indisputable logic, but stem from social agreement.

A second contribution of Lehrer and Schauble rests with the emphasis on how thinking is "brought into being and supported within contexts that are fashioned by people." This perspective is manifest both in their general approach to the study of statistical reasoning and in their analysis of specific cognitive challenges. For example, Lehrer and Schauble explain in terms of agency the difference between understanding variation in measurement contexts and understanding it as a natural occurrence. Measurement contexts (e.g., flagpole activity) afford framing variation as a result of stochastic processes of measurement. This meaning of variation is close to the problems of measurement in astronomy that Legendre investigated. Lehrer and Schauble claim that seeing variation from a first-person perspective, as the result of one's repeated activity, constitutes an affordance for understanding. This affordance is, however, not readily available for natural variation, in which case the opacity of the genetic mechanisms responsible for variation make variation at the aggregate level more salient (i.e., variation across members of a population). At a more general level, a situated perspective on thinking requires that research on statistical reasoning be conducted in enriched contexts and under conditions of engagement that go beyond what is traditional in laboratory studies. These requirements depart from research in which statistical reasoning is studied by asking individual subjects to answer questions or solve problems with relatively little social and artifactual support.

Trickett et al. and Schunn et al. add to the discussion by exploring how mature science practitioners deal with uncertainty in complex domains. Uncertainty is associated with inherent intractability of phenomena and limited resolution of measurement and visualization. The authors examine how experts choose representations as a function of the task environment and neurocomputational constraints, and how they engage in cognitive actions to reduce uncertainty.

What is Variation?

Taken as a whole the chapters differ in the ways in which they define or consider variation. The difference is reflected in formalizations, representations, and instructional stances toward the concept. The range of idea seems to move from variation as a form of error to be minimized and understood within the framework of a research enterprise to one in which variation is a source of uncertainty with which the scientist must come to grips. In the next section we take on the first of our two issues: What is variation?

Two different emphases on variation are represented in the chapters. The first is the idea of variation as error and as an epiphenomenon of measurement. This perspective suggests that, although error is an idealized concept and errors cannot be known exactly, in principle the value of a known error could be applied as a correction to the observed measures, thus decreasing variation. Errors, as Masnick and colleagues argue, are not limited to matters of measurement, but involve issues of design, execution, and interpretation. Once errors are weeded out, we are left with systematic variation, that is, with variation that points to real differences. Thus, in this emphasis, variation is to be expected, yet explained away, except when it points to systematic differences. The idea of variation as error from the true estimate is clearly represented in the work of Masnick et al., Lehrer and Schauble (in what they call context of measurement), Garfield, delMas, and Chance, and delMas and Liu.

DelMas and Liu, however, take a more syntactic approach, treating variation as an object and defining it with respect to the center of a statistical distribution. In this context, variation is given a more mathematical meaning. In their study, emphasis is not placed on the identification of sources of error (because data is not driven by theoretical considerations), but on the statistical means to describe variation and represent it. Students play with histograms and compare the standard deviations of different distributions. The focus is on how the measure is affected by spread from the center and density. Although the activity allows students to address misconceptions and counter potentially deceptive features of histograms with respect to the spread of data, the estimation of variation does not support further content-related inferences because data is not connected to any particular inquiry.

The second emphasis is the idea of variation as a constitutive feature of a domain. This meaning is tipped off in the work of Lehrer and Schauble, in which the difference between variation resulting from measurement and natural variation is built into the instructional design. Although, to our knowledge, the students' experiment with Fast Plants™ was not designed to deal primarily with issues of biological diversity, the students were sensitive to natural variation as an irreducible and meaningful phenomenon. Some of them even problematized the idea of an "average plant" and devised corresponding representations.

Schunn et al. and Trickett et al. privilege the idea of variation as uncertainty. Uncertainty is seen both as an objective property of complex causal systems in the real word and as the result of informational limitations of the representational artifacts used in the experimental task. In either case, understanding uncertainty, defined as a range of values or attributes that can reasonably be ascribed to the phenomenon of interest, is critical for expert problem solving. The authors report *in vivo* and *ex vivo* research with experts who recognize uncertainty as a starting point and set themselves to differentiate signal from noise. The experts know from the onset that the representations they are operating on are incomplete and limited, and choose gestural representations and engage in spatial transformations to decrease uncertainty.

One particularly valuable aspect of the studies of expert performance in weather forecast, submarine navigation, and fMRI is that they show how representations are problematic artifacts in that they do not depict uncertainty, even when uncertainty really matters. The studies show experts wrestling with representations and being fully aware of the complexity and low error tolerance of their domain of inquiry. In that sense, these experts are not only thinking with data, but also data, that is, deciding what counts as evidence. In attempting both to consider uncertainty and estimate its scope, experts bring a wealth of knowledge to bear, from their awareness of the limitations in the resolution of visual imagery and the incompleteness or obsolescence of information to their recognition of gaps in the causal models that guide reasoning. This problematic character of representations and reasoning about what counts as data in the light of research queries and judgments of plausibility is also present in the classroom activity reported by Lehrer and Schauble, in which children struggle to design data representations that may address their questions and match their intuitions.

Learning and Understanding Variation

If we move from the meaning of variation to what is hard about learning it and understanding it, we see three major themes in the chapters. The first theme is that, for students to learn and understand variation, they need to have access to intuitions, theories, or circumstances that make variation in the data more or less plausible. This constitutes a kind of constrained expectation, which is akin to the external assessment of data and variation that Cassini undertook with the astronomical observations of the ecliptic. In other words, students need to make meaning of variation not only as a mathematical feature, but also as an expected (or unlikely) outcome. This theme is explicitly addressed in the chapters of Masnick et al., Schunn et al., Trickett et al., Garfield et al., and Lehrer and Schauble.

Yet, Masnick et al., Lehrer and Schauble, and Trickett et al., go beyond the general prescription that variation is to be understood in the context of meaningful queries with respect to which students' prior knowledge can be brought to bear. They claim further that knowledge of the likely mechanisms (or, more generally, causes) responsible for variation in the data is crucial for learning and understanding. Masnick and colleagues argue for an expanded understanding of error within the logic of experimentation. In turn, Lehrer and Schauble underscore the role of practices (e.g., stochastic measurement) and the effect of domain-specific processes (e.g., mutation and sexual recombination) that respectively produce and underlie variation. Finally, Trickett and colleagues show, with no instructional pretense, that expert understanding of uncertainty and variation is anchored in an understanding of the factors and variables that fail to show up in the visual representations of data.

Somewhat subsidiary to the first theme is the idea that learning and understanding variation necessitates an awareness of what it is that is varying, that is, a sense of a difference in magnitude along a dimension. This theme draws attention to the issue that defining a variable is not trivial. The work of Lehrer and Schauble is particularly relevant to this point because it foregrounds the idea that prior to the inscription of variation through representations, students (and scientists) need to slice events into discrete events, amenable to quantification and computation. In so doing, Lehrer and Schauble debunk the immediacy of data and show that there is a long road between observations, quantifications, and counts (which are the entities on which statistics operates). In that sense, as Pickering (1993) argues, inscriptions are not simple acts of recording, but consequential epistemological moves.

The third and final theme is the idea that understanding and learning variation requires attention to the formal properties of data. That is what is referred to when Garfield, delMas, and Chance, and delMas and Liu talk about the challenge of distributional thinking, or about how the notion of variation stands on top of the notion of center, or about how students should learn not only computational procedures but also the conditions under which measures of center and spread are maximally informative. Thinking about inscribed data, once removed from the meaning and anecdotes of inquiry, with the assistance of the formal apparatus of statistics, is a part of the modeling process that Lehrer and Schauble refer to, and one in which students appropriate, by virtue of their learning, the accumulated knowledge of statistics as a discipline.

Jointly, the chapters suggest that understanding and learning variation can build on children's and students' questions and intuitions. The instructional challenge is to design conditions of inquiry and supporting environments so that the nature and location of intuitions are refined and advance towards more canonical and formalized representations. Emphasis should be placed on the development of authentic and rich environments that permit students to explore the multiple meanings of variation within a single effort. Students should also engage in interpretation under ambiguous circumstances, and come to understand variation not simply as a mathematical feature but as something that helps to bracket the strength of claims. For these purposes, as delMas and Liu suggest, computer environments hold the promise of enhanced representational and interactive capabilities. But computer environments cannot be assumed to be effective learning tools if variation is not connected to substantive issues in a domain of inquiry or if there is a disconnect between the practice of statistics and the substantiation of claims. The risk here is simply teaching the multiple ways of representing variation without considering the function they serve (Lovett, 2001; Lovett & Greenhouse, 2000).

The research programs of Kahneman (2002) and Nisbett (Nisbett, Krantz, Jepson, & Kunda, 1983) on the use of statistical heuristics in everyday reasoning and in the intuitive meaning of variation are an indication that issues surrounding probability and variation have been central to cognitive science for some time. The chapters of this 33rd Carnegie Symposium give us a fresh take on the matter. We have a myriad of research conditions: children with and without instruction, contrasts of high knowledge and low knowledge situations, responses to technological interventions, and centrality of issues of representation. We have design experiments with students pursuing authentic questions, developing their own inscriptions, and attempting calculations on their own. We have design experiments at the college level built around the Japanese lesson study model, and research with experts in naturalist conditions. These chapters represent some good uses of both traditional cognitive science and more embedded sociocultural approaches to understanding the domain to be studied and to be taught. But, most importantly, the chapters show us that variation and uncertainty are productive notions in the sense that they invite students to consider subtleties that matter and from which inferences can achieve a more secure grounding.

In resurrecting the voices from the past, both ancient Greek and enlightenment-era European, we sought to ground the core issues with which this Symposium and the six chapters were engaged. Specifically, we wanted to remind readers and authors alike of the intricate and multiple meanings of variation, as well as the non-obvious aspects of understanding them. We also wanted to emphasize the significant roles played out in scientific inquiry by astronomy and biology, which have been the touchstones of these different meanings. The grounded understandings of both the demands of learning and the resources available for learning so powerfully discussed by Kahneman (2002) have been well advanced by the chapters in this symposium.

REFERENCES

Brooks D. R., & McLennan, D. A. (2002). *The nature of diversity: An evolutionary voyage of discovery*. Toronto: University of Toronto Press.

Bruner, J., Goodnow, J., & Austin, A. (1956). *A study of thinking*. New York: Wiley.

Chauvenet, W. (1871). *Manual of spherical and practical astronomy: Theory and use of astronomical instruments* (Vol. II). Philadelphia, PA: Lipponcott & Co.

Fisher, R. A. (1936). The use of multiple measurements in taxonomic problems. *Annals of Eugenics, 7*, 179–188.

Funkhouser, H. G. (1937). Historical development of graphical representation of statistical data. *Osiris, 3*, 269–404.

Futuyma, D. J. (1998). Wherefore and whither the naturalist? *The American Naturalist, 151*(1), 1–6.

Gould, S. J. (2002a). *The structure of evolutionary theory*. Cambridge, MA: The Belknap Press of Harvard University Press.

Gould, S. J. (2002b). What does the dreaded "E" word mean anyway? In S. J. Gould (Ed.), *I have landed: The end of a beginning in natural history* (pp. 241–256). New York: Harmony Books.

Helden, A. v. (1994). Telescopes and authority from Galileo to Cassini. *Osiris, 9*, 8–29,

Heraclitus. (trans. 1987). *Fragments* (a text and translation with a commentary by T. M. Robinson). Toronto: University of Toronto Press.

Kahneman, D. (2002). Maps of bounded rationality: A perspective on intuitive judgment and choice. *Nobel Prize Lecture, December 8, 2002*.

Lovett, M. (2001). A collaborative convergence on studying reasoning processes: A case study in statistics. In D. Klahr & S. Carver (Eds.), *Cognition and Instruction: 25 years of progress* (pp. 347–384). Mahwah, NJ: Lawrence Erlbaum Associates.

Lovett, M., & Greenhouse, J. (2000). Applying cognitive theory to statistics instruction. *The American Statistician, 54*(3), 196–206.

Nisbett, R. E., Krantz, D. H., Jepson, C., & Kunda, Z. (1983). The use of statistical heuristics in everyday inductive reasoning. *Psychological Review, 90*(4), 339–363.

Parmenides of Elea. (trans. 1984). *Fragments* (a text and translation with an introduction by David Gallop). Toronto: University of Toronto Press.

Pickering, A. (1993). The mangle of practice: Agency and emergence in the sociology of science. *American Journal of Sociology, 99*, 3, 559–589.

Simon, H. A., & Gregg, L. W. (1967). Process models and stochastic theories of simple concept formation. *Journal of Mathematical Psychology, 4*, 246–276.

Simon, H. A., & Lea, G. (1974). Problem solving and rule induction: A unified view. In L. W. Gregg (Ed.), *Knowledge and cognition* (pp. 105–128). Hillsdale, NJ: Lawrence Erlbaum Associates.

Stigler, S. (1986). *The history of statistics: The measurement of uncertainty before 1900*. Cambridge, MA: Belknap Press.

Tukey, J. W. (1977). *Exploratory data analysis*. Reading, MA: Addison-Wesley.

II

Statistical Reasoning and Data Analysis

8

Do Naïve Theories Ever Go Away? Using Brain and Behavior to Understand Changes in Concepts

Kevin N. Dunbar
Jonathan A. Fugelsang
Courtney Stein
Dartmouth College

Many of the major revolutions in the history of science can be thought of as changes in the conceptual understanding of the world (Dunbar & Fugelsang, 2005a, 2005b; Nersessian, 1998; Thagard, 1992, 2003). In addition to entire fields in science, individual students and scientists can be seen to change their conceptual structures as they acquire new information, whether it be theoretical, methodological, or empirical, in a scientific field. Understanding this conceptual change, both within individuals and within scientific fields, is thus central to our understanding of science, science education, and the scientific mind. The acquisition of new theories and data are clearly at the heart of conceptual change, but what methods can we use to determine what happens when conceptual change occurs, and how can we use this knowledge to better inform the educational system? One approach has been to couch our understanding of concepts and conceptual structures in terms of changes in symbolic representations using the techniques, models, and theories of cognitive science. Many of the excellent chapters in this volume pursue this approach (e.g., Klahr, this volume); however, following our previous work integrating naturalistic research and cognitive models (Dunbar, 1995; Blanchette & Dunbar, 2001; Fugelsang, Stein, Green, & Dunbar, 2004) we use converging methods to understand conceptual change. A combination of traditional cognitive methods and contemporary brain imaging techniques are used to determine how new concepts are acquired, how theory and data are combined, and what happens when conceptual change occurs.

THEORY, DATA, AND CONCEPTUAL CHANGE

Since Thomas Kuhn's *Structure of Scientific Revolutions* (Kuhn, 1962) most researchers distinguish between minor and major changes in a concept (Chi, 1992; Thagard, 1992). Minor changes in a concept are thought to consist of additions or deletions of links to knowledge, whereas major changes (known as conceptual change) are thought to consist of widespread restructuring of knowledge around new principles. As Chi and Roscoe (2002) point out, minor changes are often easy to achieve as they involve a simple change such as classifying an insect as a type of animal, rather than as a unique entity. However, major changes in a concept require not just the addition or deletion of a feature, but the reorganization of the relations both between features of a conceptual structure and between different conceptual structures. This widespread reorganization both within and between conceptual structures is a complex process that is thought to be extremely difficult to achieve. Students in fields such as biology, physics, and chemistry often develop many faulty theories of the world (commonly referred to as *misconceptions*) that are very resistant to change. Put another way, conceptual change in science is notoriously difficult to achieve and is a key problem for our educational system.

   Using naturalistic observations of scientist during lab meetings (a method we have termed *in vivo* cognition; Dunbar, 1995) we have been able to observe conceptual change first-hand. A major conceptual shift was found to occur after a group of immunologists obtained a series of unexpected findings, which forced the scientists to propose a new concept in immunology. This new concept, in turn, forced changes in other concepts (Dunbar, 2001). Using a more traditional cognitive experimental approach, termed *in vitro* cognition, we (Dunbar & Fugelsang, 2005b; Fugelsang et al., 2004) found that subjects also underwent conceptual changes analogous to those seen with scientists (Dunbar, 1995). However, not all changes in a concept are major conceptual changes. In fact minor changes in a concept are the norm and major conceptual changes appear to be quite rare. The factors at the root of this major conceptual change view have been difficult to determine, though there have been a number of studies developmentally (Carey, 1985; Chi, 1992; Chi & Roscoe, 2002), in the history of science (Nersessian, 1998; Thagard, 1992), and in physics education (Clement, 1982; Mestre, 1991) that give detailed accounts of the changes in knowledge representation that occur while people switch from one way of representing knowledge to another.

Although there have been numerous theoretical and applied accounts of the nature of conceptual change (e.g., Limón & Mason, 2002; Kalman, Rohar, & Wells, 2004), relatively little is known of the mechanisms that underlie the different types of conceptual change, what educational interventions really foster conceptual change, what is the role of data and theory in conceptual change, and how brain based mechanisms might constrain when and how conceptual change occurs. Here, we outline three different ways we have been investigating conceptual change, each of which highlight an important feature of the way that peoples' theories change, or for that matter, do not change. We begin with an investigation of the way students conceptualize the causes of the seasons.

CONCEPTUAL CHANGE AND THE CAUSES OF THE SEASONS

One area where students have great difficulty in acquiring new concepts is in understanding the causes of the different seasons. Many children, and even more importantly many adults, believe that the reason for the Earth's seasons is the distance between the earth and the sun at different times during the year. The two most commonly held explanations that students offer are: (1) physical proximity—that the earth is physically closer to the sun at different times of the year, and (2) hemispheric proximity—that one hemisphere is closer to the sun at different times of the year. Many of us believe that the earth travels around the sun in an exaggerated elliptical orbit, and frequently science textbooks display the path of the earths' orbit in this manner (e.g., in the *DK Oxford Illustrated American Dictionary,* 1998, p. 743). However, the earth's orbit around the sun is basically circular. In fact, the earth is slightly closer to the sun in the winter! However, even when this is explained to adults, they still believe that there is something about the distance between the earth and the sun that causes the seasons.

Much research over the last 20 years has revealed that even physics students have misconceptions *regarding the causes of the seasons. In the famous documentary* A Private Universe (Schneps & Sadler, 1988) 23 students, faculty, and staff at the Harvard University commencement ceremony were asked why it is hotter in the summer than in the winter, with all but two saying it is because the earth is closer to the sun in the summer than in the winter. These results were found for varying levels of education, from those students with no science background to those who had taken classes in planetary motion. Current research in our laboratory has demonstrated that Harvard is no exception. Like the Harvard students, undergraduates at Dartmouth College have strong misconceptions about seasonal change (Stein & Dunbar, 2003). Furthermore, research in the private Universe project has routinely found that students, and even teachers believe that the seasons are caused solely by the distance of the earth from the sun. Given that this concept is taught throughout elementary school, middle school, and high school it is important to determine how pervasive this conception of the seasons is and how easy or difficult it is to change concepts of seasonal change.

Before beginning on the task, we asked undergraduate students to write out an explanation for why the earth has different seasons. After completing their written descriptions, students were asked a series of multiple-choice questions to assess any misconceptions they might have about why the earth has different seasons. They were then presented with a series of trials in which they were shown a month corresponding to each of the four seasons and then presented with a picture of a globe with two spots marked on it. One spot was always located between 23.5 degrees North to 23.5 degrees South of the equator, whereas the other was always located outside of this range in the opposite hemisphere. Participants were asked to choose which of the two locations represented the shortest distance between the earth and the sun. After the first set of trials, participants were shown a video explaining why we have seasons (http://kids.msfc.nasa.gov/earth/seasons/EarthSeasons.asp). The video demonstrates how the orbit of the earth is, essentially, circular, and how the tilt of the earth influences the seasons. After watching the video, students completed another set of trials and answered the multiple-choice questions again. They were then given the opportunity to adjust their written descriptions of why the earth has different seasons (participants were provided with a blue pen when writing their original descriptions and a red pen when making any changes at the end of the study). Thus we were able to compare students' answers before they watched the video with their answers after they watched the video.

Let us first consider students' initial answers to the questionnaire. Our results indicate that 94% of participants have misconceptions about seasonal change, with the majority falling into the category of hemispheric proximity. Data from the task also indicates participants are taking into account the tilt of the earth's axis when making their decisions (overall accuracy was about 75%). Turning now to the effect of the NASA video on students' answers, we found that the short video intervention designed to address these misconceptions helped only with simple information regarding the shape of the earth's orbit around the sun, but had little effect on student's ability to integrate new information about how the angle of the suns' rays effect the different seasons. Before the intervention, only 25% of participants answered correctly regarding the shape of the earth's orbit around the sun compared to 75% after the intervention. However, only *one* student (2%) changed their answer from the incorrect (hemispheric proximity) answer to the correct answer regarding the reason for seasonal change. In addition, only 25% of the students added information about the angle of the suns' rays to their written descriptions after completing the task. Based on the changes to their written descriptions, we would have expected participants to have higher accuracy scores after watching the video, however, there was no change in accuracy scores after the intervention.

Why did the video, which was supposed to address the misconceptions, have a no significant effect on students? Interestingly both students' responses and their explanations, indicate that they did not encode the relevant information that was inconsistent with their theory. The key source of the students' difficulty is that they fail to integrate different sources of information correctly. In this situation they need to know that the orbit of the earth around the sun is basically circular and that the axis of the earth determines the angle of the suns' rays as they hit the earth. The students do take the axis into account and are willing to accept that the shape of the orbit is nearly circular, but fail to incorporate how this influences the angle of the suns' rays and therefore believe that the seasons are caused by the Northern hemisphere being closer to the sun in July than in January. Thus, students merely modify their old theory rather than engage in the reorganization of knowledge that is necessary for conceptual change.

Our work on the seasons illustrates the difficulty of achieving conceptual change. Even when students are presented with information inconsistent with their views, they maintain their incorrect theories. Why is it so difficult to change concepts in the face of new information? Another line of research on causal thinking that we have been conducting provides many clues and insights into why it is so difficult to achieve conceptual change. Below we discuss two studies that investigate these questions. In the first experiment (Fugelsang & Dunbar, 2005) we investigate what happens when students encounter data that are either consistent or inconsistent with their theory. In the second experiment, we investigate the degree to which students' theories are modifiable if given a preponderance of disconfirming data. We use fMRI to answer these questions and argue that these studies have important implications both for educational theory and educational practice.

USING fMRI TO INVESTIGATE THE EFFECTS
OF DATA ON PEOPLES' THEORIES

Why is conceptual change so hard to achieve and what types of information are needed to foster this change? Our research on the seasons reported in the previous section demonstrates that even when students are given precise information about a theory, their theories do not change. One frequent approach to this problem is to present students with data that are inconsistent with their theories. The assumption is that by presenting students with anomalies they will realize that their original theory is incorrect and will then reorganize (restructure) their knowledge eliminating naïve theories. The use of anomalies has therefore been central to proposals for a constructivist education (e.g., Baker & Piburn, 1997; Mortimer & Machado, 2000). How can we determine what has happened when a student acquires a new scientific concept? The approach that we take here is to look at the recruitment of specialized neural circuits in the brain and ask what networks are involved when people are given data that are inconsistent or consistent with their theory. Because cognitive neuroscientists have identified the major brain areas involved in memory, learning, attention, and reasoning (see Gazzaniga, 2004, for a comprehensive account of what is known about the brain in these topics), it is now possible to understand the types of cognitive and neural changes that occur in educationally relevant learning. In the next section we provide an overview of our recent findings on conceptual change in science.

We (Fugelsang & Dunbar, 2005) used fMRI to investigate changes in concepts. We gave students data that were either consistent or inconsistent with a theory related to the effectiveness of drugs designed to relieve symptoms of depression. We also varied how plausible the theory was by presenting participants with a brief introductory statement that contained either (1) a direct plausible causal mechanism of action linking a red pill to a mood outcome, or (2) no direct causal mechanism of action linking a red pill to a mood outcome. Participants were then provided with data in a trial-by-trial format where they viewed multiple trials of data for each type of drug. These data were either *consistent* with their theory or *inconsistent* with their theory. After seeing 20 trials of data the participants were then asked how likely it was that the given drug was effective, that is, that it caused a reduction in patients' symptoms of depression. Note that this experimental procedure for studying participants' causal reasoning from data closely resembles that discussed in Danks (this volume).

We used two measures of conceptual change. First, we examined changed in participant's ratings of how causally relevant a variable was, and second, we examined changes that occurred in the brain as a function of theory and data consistency. Specifically, we were interested in the degree to which theory and data consistency modulates the recruitment of brain networks typically associated with learning (i.e., the caudate and parahippocampal gyrus) or areas commonly thought to be indicative of error detection and response inhibition (i.e., anterior cingulate cortex and dorsolateral prefrontal cortex). We propose that dissociations of brain-based measures of learning and inhibition may serve as a useful index of the degree to which participants are updating their representations in the face of new information.

We found that when people were given data that were consistent with their preferred theories, areas thought to be involved with learning (i.e., caudate and parahippocampal gyrus) showed increased levels of activation relative to baseline. However, when participants were presented with data that were inconsistent with their preferred theory the anterior cingulate, precuneus and dorsolateral prefrontal cortex showed increased levels of activation. The anterior cingulate is thought to be a region of the brain associated with error detection and conflict monitoring whereas the dorsolateral prefrontal cortex is thought to be one of the prime regions involved in effortful processing and working memory. These results indicate that when data are consistent with a theory, then minor changes in concepts are achieved through standard learning structures.

This experiment also demonstrates one of the reasons why conceptual change is so difficult: When people receive information that is inconsistent with their preferred theory learning does not easily occur. In a related study we sought to gain more information on the mechanisms underlying minor conceptual change by increasing the number of learning trials that a participant is exposed to and by tracking both behavioral and brain-based changes as a function of the number of data trials. Using this approach, we could see whether there is a differential rate of learning for plausible as opposed to implausible theories. What we found is that, as in the previous experiment, data that were inconsistent with a plausible theory did not preferentially activate learning mechanisms. Surprisingly, even after 96 trials of data we saw no increased levels of activation in learning associated areas. Furthermore, regions associated with error detection and response inhibition continued to be recruited throughout the data accumulation phase of the experiment. These results indicate that even minor conceptual changes are difficult to obtain. Both the behavioral data and the fMRI data are consistent with this interpretation.

How should we interpret the anterior cingulate activation? There are two main views of the primary role of the anterior cingulate in cognition. One view is that it is an area of the brain that notes unusual events or errors in the environment. The other view is that the anterior cingulate is involved in inhibiting responses. Either of these two views indicates that in our experiment, participants are treating data that are inconsistent with their plausible theories in ways that are different from consistent information. From the perspective of science education these data clearly show that just presenting students with anomalies will *not* produce conceptual change. What the results of these two experiments show is that prior belief in a theory influences the interpretation of data in a highly specific way. Specifically, data inconsistent with one's expectations are treated as errors and thus not easily incorporated into one's knowledge representation.

INVESTIGATING MAJOR CONCEPTUAL CHANGE

In our next study we examined the brain basis of major conceptual change by studying students who have had undergone a conceptual change with students who have not undergone a conceptual change. We also wanted to present students with information that was consistent or inconsistent with their current representation of a concept. From our previous study (Fugelsang & Dunbar, 2005) we knew that information inconsistent with a theoretical perspective should reliably recruit neural tissue in the anterior cingulate cortex, and that we could thus use this activation as an index of conceptual change. Here, we examined students that had taken no high school or college-level physics courses and compared them to students who had taken at least five college-level physics courses. Students were the same in all other respects having equal SAT scores, ages, and an equal distribution of genders.

We chose physics as a domain because physics concepts such as Newtonian conceptions of mechanics are very difficult for students to acquire. This issue has been the focus of much research in the physics education and cognitive science communities (Clement, 1982; diSessa, 1993; Hammer, 1996; McCloskey, Washburn, & Felch, 1983; Mestre, 1991; Reddish & Steinberg, 1999). On the basis of more than 20 years of research it is now known that students possess a knowledge of physics concepts that is quite different from that being taught in physics courses, and that students tenaciously hold on to their original views despite empirical demonstrations and theoretical expositions of the correct views. Many people hold erroneous beliefs about motion similar to a medieval "Impetus" theory (McCloskey, Caramazza, & Green, 1980). Furthermore, students appear to maintain "Impetus" notions even after one or two courses in physics (e.g., Kozhevnikov & Hegarty, 2001). Thus, it is only after extensive learning that there is a conceptual shift from "Impetus" theories of motion to "Newtonian" scientific theories.

We showed students movies of two balls falling and asked the students to press a key if this was the way that the balls should fall in a frictionless environment, or to press another key if the balls were falling in a way that was inconsistent with what they would expect. Subjects saw the two balls falling at the same rate or at a different rate. The balls could be of the same size (both large or both small), or could be of different sizes (one large and one small). We were particularly interested in comparing what we call "Newtonian" movies, where two balls of unequal size fall at the same rate, with "Impetus" movies in which the bigger ball fell at a faster rate than the smaller ball. The "Newtonian" movies are consistent with "Newtonian" mechanics where balls of different mass fall at the same rate. Thus, for these movies we expected the physics students to regard the movies as normal. We expected the physics students to classify the "Impetus" movies in which the bigger movie falls faster than the smaller movie as abnormal. Conversely, we expected the nonphysics students to classify the "Newtonian" movies as abnormal and the "Impetus" movies as normal. We were interested in whether the brain activation patterns for the two different types of movies would interact with students' background.

The fMRI data indicates that physics students had made the conceptual leap from a naïve "Impetus" view of physics to a "Newtonian" theory. First, when the physics students saw the "Impetus" movies (with the bigger balls falling faster than the smaller balls), the anterior cingulate showed increased activation relative to baseline. Thus, the physics students appeared to be regarding the "Impetus" movie as erroneous, whereas the nonphysics students saw the "Newtonian" movie as erroneous. Conversely, when the nonphysics students saw the two balls falling at the same rate regardless of size, the anterior cingulate showed increased activation, indicating that they regarded these movies as strange or erroneous thus resulting in response conflict.

The results of our physics study parallel those of our work on complex causal thinking: Information that is inconsistent with a currently held theory activates areas of the brain that are associated with error detection. What is interesting here is that half of our non-physics students correctly judged that two balls falling at the same rate is natural and thus gave normatively correct answers. However, these same students who gave normatively correct answers still showed relatively greater activation in the anterior cingulate cortex when they saw two balls of different mass falling at the same rate. This result indicates that despite giving the correct answer, brain imaging data reveals that the students had not undergone the deep conceptual change needed to produce the correct answer for the right reasons. One hypothesis that we have about the difference between the behavioral responses and the imaging data is that many students can give the right answer without truly understanding why. The imaging data allows us to gain a greater depth in understanding what students know. Activation in other brain sites, such as the medial prefrontal cortex also track students' understanding of concepts in physics. Thus, a key goal in our current research program is to understand the networks of brain sites that are involved in conceptual change.

ASSESSING THEORY, DATA, AND CONCEPTUAL CHANGE

Across three studies that have explored both varying amounts of experience with a theory and varying amounts of data consistent or inconsistent with a theory, we see that one's naïve theory can readily be invoked. These results have important implications for many types of educational interventions and for theories of what happens when we educate our students. The standard theory is that by presenting students with either large amounts of data, key anomalies, or new theories we can induce students to abandon their old theories and reorganize their knowledge. Many educational theorists see this conceptual reorganization as being *the* key goal of education and see conceptual change as so complete that students will not even be able to conceptualize their old theories following a conceptual change (Kuhn's notion of incommensurability). Yet the results of the experiments reported in this chapter indicate that even when conceptual change appears to have taken place, students still have access to the old naïve theories and that these theories appear to be actively inhibited rather than reorganized and absorbed into the new theory.

IS EDUCATIONAL NEUROSCIENCE "A BRIDGE TOO FAR"?

Whether knowledge of brain functions and learning can be used to benefit education has been a topic of great controversy over the past decade (see Petitto & Dunbar, in press; Fitzpatrick, 2005 for an overview of the controversy). Some have argued that studies in neuroscience are so far removed from educational practice that they have little relevance to education (e.g., Bruer, 1998, 2002, 2003). This has spurred an understandable worry in the education community that research on brain function is not relevant to education. Making inferences from brain imaging data to education is notoriously difficult. As Bruer (2002) has argued, many claims have been dubious. Often neuroscientists have extrapolated from a small sample using a non-educationally relevant task, which as Bruer has argued, is fraught with difficulties. We have attempted to avoid many of these problems in a number of different ways. First, we are using educationally relevant tasks rather than a vaguely analogous task. Our physics task is the topic of explicit instruction in almost every school in the country. Our complex causal thinking task is similar to many mechanisms that are taught in schools and the types of consistent and inconsistent information are the same as that used in most science curricula. We need to ask what does functional brain imaging work tell us that educators don't already know, cognitive theories don't already tell us, or standard, and less expensive, cognitive methodologies already tell us? Functional brain imaging can allow us to grasp a deeper understating of the mechanisms that underlie learning. In so doing, these methodologies can help us better develop teaching techniques and curricula that facilitate and promote better learning.

It is important to note that the very same criticisms that have been made of Cognitive Neuroscience have been made of Cognitive Psychology. In fact there is an entire literature devoted to criticizing cognitive psychology that uses exactly the same arguments that Bruer raises against Educational Neuroscience (see Cole, 1988; Dunbar & Blanchette, 2001; Gibson, 1968; Neisser, 1982; Suchman, 1988). Where does this leave us? One way of framing the issue is in terms of there being a correct level of analysis for education. Here, Bruer attempts the classic reductionist approach of boiling everything down to cognition. An alternative approach is to use converging evidence from multiple disciplines to answer important questions in education. Rather than proposing one level as basic, educators use knowledge from disciplines as diverse as sociology, cognitive psychology, neuroscience, and even molecular biology that together constrain the types of models and theories that researchers propose to understand educational issues. This is precisely the methodology we adopt when attempting to understand the important issue of what happens when students evolve theories of scientific phenomena. Cognitive Psychology is the appropriate level of analysis to solve many problems in education. Cognitive Neuroscience provides us with another level of analysis that when used together with traditional cognitive approaches, can provide us with a deeper understanding of learning and education.

REFERENCES

American Association for the Advancement of Science. (1989). *Science for all Americans: Summary, project 2061*. Washington, DC: AAAS Books.

Baker, D. R., & Piburn, M. D. (1997). *Constructing science in middle and secondary school classrooms*. Needham Heights, MA: Allyn & Bacon.

Baker, L. M., & Dunbar, K. (2001). Experimental design heuristics for scientific discovery: The use of baseline and known controls. *International Journal of Human Computer Studies, 53*, 335–349.

Blanchette, I., & Dunbar, K. (2001). Analogy use in naturalistic settings: The influence of audience, emotion, and goals. *Memory & Cognition, 29*, 730-735.

Bruer, J. (1998). The brain and child development: Time for some critical thinking. *Public Health Reports, 113*, 388–397.

Bruer, J. (2002). Avoiding the pediatrician's error: How neuroscientists can help educators (and themselves). *Nature Neuroscience, 5*, 1031–1033.

Bruer, J. (2003). *At the current time, might it be better to encourage research in NeuroLearning (a basic science) rather than NeuroEducation (an applied science)?*

Published abstracts of the session commemorating the 400th anniversary of the Foundation of the Pontifical Academy of Sciences. Vatican City: Pontifical Academy of Sciences.

Carey, S. (1985). *Conceptual change in childhood*. Cambridge, MA: MIT Press.

Cole, M. (1996). *Cultural psychology*: A once and future discipline. Cambridge, MA: Belknap/Harvard. University Press.

Cole, M. (1988). Cross-cultural research in the socio-historical tradition. *Human Development, 31*, 147-157.

Chi, M. T. H. (1992). Conceptual change within and across ontological categories" Examples from learning and discovery in science. In R. Giere (Ed.), *Cognitive models of science: Minnesota Studies in the philosophy of science* (pp. 129–186). Minneapolis: University of Minnesota Press.

Chi, M. T. H., & Roscoe, R. D. (2002). The processes and challenges of conceptual change. In M. Limon & L. Mason (Eds). *Reconsidering conceptual change: Issues in theory and practice* (pp. 3–27). The Netherlands: Kluwer.

Clement, J. (1982). Students' preconceptions in introductory mechanics. *American Journal of Physics, 50*, 66–71.

Cole, M. (1996). *Cultural psychology: A once and future discipline*. Cambridge, MA: Belknap/Harvard University Press.

diSessa, A. (1993). Towards an epistemology of physics. *Cognition and Instruction, 10*, 105–225.

DK Oxford Illustrated American Dictionary. New York: Dorling Kindersley Publishing.

Dunbar, K. (1995). How scientists really reason: Scientific reasoning in real-world laboratories. In R. J. Sternberg & J. E. Davidson (Eds.), *The nature of insight* (pp. 365–395). Cambridge, MA: MIT Press.

Dunbar, K. (2001). What scientific thinking reveals about the nature of cognition. In K. Crowley, C. D. Schunn, & T. Okada, (Eds.), *Designing for science: Implications from everyday, classroom, and professional settings* (pp. 313–334). Hillsdale, NJ: Lawrence Erlbaum Associates.

Dunbar, K., & Blanchette, I. (2001). The invivo/invitro approach to cognition: The case of analogy. *Trends in Cognitive Sciences, 5*, 334–339.

Dunbar, K., & Fugelsang, J. (2005a). Scientific thinking and reasoning. In K. Holyoak & R. Morrison (Eds.), *Cambridge handbook of thinking & reasoning* (pp. 705–725). New York: Cambridge University Press.

Dunbar, K., & Fugelsang, J. (2005b). Causal thinking in science: How scientists and students interpret the unexpected. In M. E. Gorman, R. D. Tweney, D. Gooding, & A. Kincannon (Eds.), *Scientific and technical thinking* (pp. 57–79). Mahwah, NJ: Lawrence Erlbaum Associates.

Fitzpatrick, S. (2005). Brain imaging and the *"Cognitive Paparazzi:" Viewing snapshots of mental life out of context*. Paper presented at the AAAS Annual Meeting, Washington, DC.

Fugelsang, J., & Dunbar, K. (2005). Brain-based mechanisms underlying complex causal thinking. *Neuropsychologia, 48*, 1204–1213.

Fugelsang, J., Stein, C., Green, A., & Dunbar, K. (2004). Theory and data interactions of the scientific mind: Evidence from the molecular and the cognitive laboratory. *Canadian Journal of Experimental Psychology, 58,* 132–141.

Galili, I., & Bar, V. (1992). Motion implies force: Where to expect vestiges of the misconception? *International Journal of Science Education, 14*, 63–81.

Gazzaniga, M. S. (2004). *The cognitive neurosciences III: Third edition*. Cambridge MA: MIT Press.

Gibson, J. J. (1966). *The senses considered as perceptual systems*. Boston, MA: Houghton Mifflin.

Gibson, J. J. (1968). What gives rise to the perception of motion? *Psychological Review, 75*(4), 335–346.

Goswami, U. (2004). Neuroscience and education. *British Journal of Educational Psychology, 74*(1), 1–14.

Hammer, D. (1996). Misconceptions or *p*-prims: How may alternative perspectives of cognitive structure influence instructional perceptions and intentions? *Journal of the Learning Sciences, 5*(2), 97–127.

Kalman, C. S., Rohar, S., & Wells, D. (2004). Enhancing conceptual change using argumentative essays. *American Journal of Physics, 72,* 715–717.

Keil, F. C. (1999). Conceptual change. In R. Wilson & F. Keil (Eds.), *The MIT encyclopedia of cognitive science.* Cambridge, MA: MIT Press.

Kozhevnikov, M., & Hegarty, M. A. (2001). Impetus beliefs as default heuristics: Dissociation between explicit and implicit knowledge about motion. *Psychonomic Bulletin & Review, 8,* 439–453.

Kuhn, T. (1962). *The structure of scientific revolutions.* Chicago: University of Chicago Press.

Limon, M., & Mason, L. (Eds.). *Reframing the process of conceptual change.* Amsterdam: Kluwer.

McCloskey, M., Caramazza, A., & Green, B. (1980). Curvilinear motion in the absence of external forces: naive beliefs about the motion of objects. *Science, 210,* 1139–1141.

McCloskey, M., Washburn, A., & Felch, L. (1983). Intuitive physics: The straight-down belief and its origin. *Journal of Experimental Psychology: Learning, Memory, and Cognition, 9,* 636–649.

McDermott, L. C., & Redish, L. (1999). Research letter on physics education research. *American Journal of Physics, 67,* 755.

Mestre, J. P. (1991). Learning and instruction in pre-college physical science. *Physics Today, 44,* 56–62.

Mortimer, E. F., & Machado, A. H. (2000). Anomalies and conflicts in classroom discourse. *Science Education, 84,* 429–444.

Neisser, U. (1982). Memory: What are the important questions? *In memory observed.* New York: Freeman.

Nersessian, N. J. (1998). Conceptual change. In W. Bechtel & G. Graham (Eds.), *A companion to cognitive science* (pp. 155–166). Malden, MA: Blackwell.

Nersessian, N. (1998). Kuhn and the cognitive revolution. *Configurations, 6,* 87–120.

Petitto, L. A., & Dunbar, K. N. (in press). New findings from educational neuroscience on bilingual brains, scientific brains, and the educated mind. In K. Fischer & T. Kazir (Eds.), *Building usable knowledge in mind, brain, & education.* New York: Cambridge University Press.

Redish, E. F., & Steinberg, R. N. (1999). Teaching physics: Figuring out what works. *Physics Today, 52,* 24–30.

Schneps, M., & Sadler, P. (1988). *A private universe* [film]. Pyramid Films.

Stein, C., & Dunbar, K. (2003, October). *Approaches to changing basic knowledge misconceptions: When the solution becomes the problem.* Poster presented at the third biennial meeting of the Cognitive Development Society, Park City, UT.

Suchman, L. (1988). *Plans and situated actions: The problem of human/machine communication.* Cambridge, UK: Cambridge University Press.

Thagard, P. (1992). *Conceptual revolutions.* Princeton, NJ: Princeton University Press.

Thagard, P. (2003). Conceptual change. In L. Nadel (Ed.), *Encyclopedia of cognitive science* (vol. 1; pp. 666–670). London: Macmillan.

9

Intricacies of Statistical Inference and Teachers' Understandings of Them

Patrick W. Thompson
Arizona State University

Yan Liu
National Institute of Education, Singapore

Luis A. Saldanha
Portland State University

Hypothesis testing has an odd logic. We collect a sample, calculate a statistic, and produce a probability of obtaining it or a more extreme value. From a naïve perspective, the probability of that sample is 1. It happened. This is not unlike picking an item from a container with items in unknown proportions and then asking about the probability of picking the item you picked. Of course, to sophisticates of the subject this is silly. They know that a probability statement about a sample's statistic is not really about that sample. It is about the process of collecting sample statistics from a population of values having an assumed distribution.[1] Velleman (1997) addresses a related issue nicely when he asks and answers his own question, "Where is the randomness?" in regard to a confidence interval. He says,

---

[1] This itself is a sophisticated description. We do not simply collect statistics, as if they were there to collect. We collect samples and calculate statistics from them. But to a sophisticate of the subject, the process is collapsed into collecting statistics.

> When constructing confidence intervals keep in mind that the confidence interval is the random quantity whereas the population parameter is fixed and unchanging. Interpretations of confidence intervals should reflect this distinction. When we say, "with 90% confidence, $63.5 = \mu = 65.5$," we do not mean that "90% of the time μ will be between 63.5 and 65.5," but rather that in the long run, 90% of the intervals we compute from independently drawn samples will include the true mean. (Velleman, 1997, p. 185)

Velleman's explanation clarifies that "90% confidence" is not a claim about a specific interval, but rather is a claim about the *method* by which such intervals are produced. Similar conceptions are at the foundation of hypothesis testing, except that hypothesis testing draws on the logic of indirect argument. We assume that all possible values of the test statistic are distributed somehow, centered at the population parameter, and gauge whether the value we obtained is sufficiently unusual relative to those assumptions that it puts them in doubt. If so, then we conclude that our assumptions are faulty.

It would seem from the previous discussion that to conceive of sampling as a stochastic process is key in all of statistical inference. A number of studies have shown that a focus on understanding sampling stochastically is more complex than it appears. In an important series of studies, delMas and colleagues (Chance, delMas, & Garfield, in press; delMas, Garfield, & Chance, 1999, 2004) found that even with intense instructional support using computer simulations, a relatively low percentage of students attained a moderate understanding of sampling distributions. They summarized:

> Students appeared to confuse the idea that large samples resemble the population with the idea that a distribution of sample means from large samples will resemble a normal distribution. They also demonstrated a tendency to think that as sample size increased, the distribution of sample means would look MORE like the population, confusing the Law of Large Numbers with the Central Limit Theorem. What they seemed to observe and learn in class quickly disappeared when completing the post-test items. In addition, when solving contextual items, many students did not appear to understand that the variability among sample means is less than the variability in the population, or that the variability among sample means decreases as sample size increases. Although these results were surprising, they led us to reconsider the complexities involved in learning to reason about sampling distributions. (delMas et al., 2004, pp. 18–19)

DelMas et al. also (2004) noted that had they assessed students' understanding only during instruction, based on students' work and their close engagement with ideas, they would have drawn a very different conclusion. As they indicated in their summary, during instruction students seemed to rethink their naïve conceptions of sampling and distribution and showed apparent progress in developing coherent understandings. The post-instruction assessment indicates that they came to rely on instructional supports during class without dramatic changes in their original understandings. delMas et al.'s results are consistent with Dunbar's (this volume) theory that major conceptual change is difficult when students cannot assimilate current experience to existing ways of thinking.

An additional consideration in understanding why "take a sample" is hard to understand stochastically, and thus why students find it so difficult to learn ideas of sampling distribution and statistical inference, is that one must distinguish between variability among individuals in a sample, variability among individuals in the sampled population, and variability among statistics calculated from samples drawn from it (Rubin, Bruce, & Tenney, 1991; Saldanha & Thompson, 2002; Thompson, Saldanha, & Liu, 2004; Well, Pollatsek, & Boyce, 1990). Although the idea of stochastic process is clearly entailed in both notions of variability, to understand sampling as a stochastic process is far more complex than to understand selection as a stochastic process. A well-developed sense of variability among values of a statistic also entails the coordination of understandings of samples as items in themselves and of samples as composed of individuals from a population (Saldanha & Thompson, 2002; Thompson et al., 2004) and it entails the understanding that repeatedly collecting samples has the result that the values of a statistic are distributed somehow within a range of possibilities (Horvath & Lehrer, 1998; Konold & Pollatsek, 2002). Moreover, to understand sampling as a stochastic process is problematic because of its fundamental reliance on randomness, which is known to be troublesome for people at all ages (Batanero & Serrano, 1999; Falk & Konold, 1994, 1997; Metz, 1998).[2]

We came to appreciate the complexities of well-formed concepts of sample and statistical inference through two teaching experiments with high school students on the ideas of distributions of sample statistics and margin of error (Saldanha & Thompson, 2002; Thompson & Saldanha, 2000; Thompson et al., 2004). Results from both teaching experiments were consistent with other findings in regard to students' difficulties (delMas et al., 1999, 2004; Earley, 2001, 2004). However, due to constructivist teaching experiments' focus on obtaining data that supports conceptual analysis (Glasersfeld, 1972, 1995; Steffe, 1996; Thompson, 2000) and modeling (Steffe, 1991; Steffe & Thompson, 2000) we were able to dissect students' reasoning to suggest a model of well-formed concepts of sample and sampling.

---

[2]Studies by Schwartz and colleagues and by Watson examine students' understanding of sample, but without attending to the stochastic nature of "take a sample" (Schwartz, Goldman, Vye, & Barron, 1998; Watson, 2001, 2002; Watson & Moritz, 2000).

The model addresses both why students have difficulty with the ideas of sample and distributions of sample statistics and proposes conceptions that, at this moment, seem to support competent reasoning about distributions of sample statistics and margin of error. Those students who reasoned flexibly about distributions of sample statistics and margin of error had what we called a *multiplicative conception of sample* (Saldanha & Thompson, 2002; Thompson & Saldanha, 2000). This is a conception composed of a scheme of related ideas: a hierarchical image of sample that allowed students to conceive a collection of samples so that the samples in it were simultaneously items in a collection and composed of other items; sampling as a stochastic process (hence entailing an image of variability among samples); and the idea that each sample had an associated statistic that therefore varied as samples varied. Moreover, these students had a *bounded* sense of variation that entailed two aspects: a quasi-proportional relationship between samples and population, which therefore translated into a sense of bounded variation in their statistics, and a sense that extreme variation was less likely than small variations. All this seemed to support their anticipation of a *distribution* of sample statistics that was independent of (i.e., underlay) particular ways of displaying it. We note also that students who had difficulty during the course and with the interview questions seemed to break down in one or more of these areas.

We developed the outline of this model as a result of a 9-day teaching experiment (TE1) with 27 junior and senior high school students enrolled in a non-AP, semester-long statistics course (Saldanha & Thompson, 2002; Thompson & Saldanha, 2000). We then designed an 18-day teaching experiment (TE2), conducted the following year, that involved 8 students (one 10th-grader, three 11th-graders, and four seniors) in a non-AP year-long statistics course. TE2 focused on supporting students' development of the various aspects of a multiplicative conception of sample. The short story of TE2 is that even armed with the insights just discussed, our efforts to support the students in TE2 in building the components of a multiplicative conception of sample were fraught with periods of backtracking to patch together things that went wrong in students' understandings, and even when we were successful at helping them build the "parts," they found it extremely difficult to coordinate them. Two examples: We addressed students' persistent difficulties in TE1 in distinguishing reliably between samples and individuals when both ideas were present in a discussion or situation by giving greater emphasis to activities of hand sampling in TE2. However, students in TE2 still found it difficult to maintain that distinction and revealed their difficulty in a wide variety of settings. Second, we focused explicitly on the idea of distributions of sample statistics as being created through the stochastic process "take a sample," yet students' understandings remained fragile throughout the teaching experiment. We refer readers to (Saldanha, 2004; Saldanha & Thompson, 2002; Thompson & Saldanha, 2000; Thompson et al., 2004) for more complete descriptions of these teaching experiments' instruction and analyses.

TEACHERS' UNDERSTANDINGS OF CONCEPTS ASSOCIATED WITH STATISTICAL INFERENCE

With our tentative understandings of why statistical inference is hard for students to learn as background, we were interested in what teachers understood of the issues we found to be crucial in students' understandings and the extent to which they saw them as pedagogical issues in teaching probability and statistical inference. To this end, we designed a 2-week summer workshop/seminar for high school teachers. The seminar was advertised as "an opportunity to learn about issues involved in teaching and learning probability and statistics with understanding and about what constitutes a profound understanding of probability and statistics." Of 12 applicants we selected eight who met our criteria—having taken coursework in statistics and probability and currently teaching, having taught, or preparing to teach high school statistics either as a stand-alone course or as a unit within another course. Participating teachers received a stipend equivalent to ½ month's salary. The research team prepared for the seminar by meeting weekly for 8 months to devise a set of issues that would be addressed in it, selecting video segments and student work from prior teaching experiments to use in seminar discussions, and preparing teacher activities.

Table 9.1 presents demographic information on the eight selected teachers. None of the teachers had extensive coursework in statistics. All had at least a BA in mathematics or mathematics education. Statistics backgrounds varied between self-study (statistics and probability through regression analysis) to an undergraduate sequence in mathematical statistics. Two teachers (Linda and Betty) had experience in statistics applications. Linda taught operations research at a Navy Nuclear Power school and Betty was trained in and taught the Ford Motor Company FAMS statistical quality control high school curriculum.

We interviewed each teacher three times: Prior to the seminar about his or her understandings of sampling, variability, and the law of large numbers (Appendix I); at the end of the first week on statistical inference (Appendix II); and at the end of Week 2 on probability and stochastic reasoning. This chapter focuses on Week 1, in which issues of inference were prominent.

The seminar lasted 2 weeks in June 2001, with the last day of each week devoted to individual interviews. Each session began at 9:00 a.m. and ended

TABLE 9.1
Demographic Information on Seminar Participants

Teacher	Years Teaching	Degree	Stat Background	Taught
John	3	MS Applied Math	2 courses math stat	AP Calc, AP Stat
Nicole	24	MAT Math	Regression anal (self study)	AP Calc, Units in stat
Sarah	28	BA Math Ed	Ed research, test & meas	Pre-calc, Units in stat
Betty	9	BA Math Ed	Ed research, FAMS training	Alg 2, Prob & Stat
Lucy	2	BA Math, BA Ed	Intro stat, AP Stat training	Alg 2, Units in stat
Linda	9	MS Math	2 courses math stat	Calc, Units in stat
Henry	7	BS Math Ed, M.Ed.		AP Calc, AP Stat
Alice	21	BA Math	1 sem math stat, bus stat	Calc hon, Units in stat

at 3:00 p.m., with 60 minutes for lunch. An overview of topics is given in Table 9.2. All sessions were led by a high school AP statistics teacher (Terry) who had collaborated in the seminar design throughout the planning period.

PRE-SEMINAR INTERVIEWS

The pre-seminar interviews were designed to reveal teachers' understandings of sampling as a stochastic process and of sampling variability. They were asked to read an excerpt from chapter 4 of Moore's *Basic Practice of Statistics*. In it Moore develops the ideas of parameter estimation by sampling, sampling distributions, and the central limit theorem. Table 9.3 lists summaries of what the teachers thought the chapter was about and what were the important ideas in it. Only John and Henry saw that the excerpt was clearly about sampling distributions, although Henry gave greater importance to the central limit theorem. The other teachers saw less organization than John, focusing more on smaller ideas as if they were a list of topics.

Questions 6, 8, and 11 turned out to be the most revealing of teachers' understandings. Question 6 asked what was varying with regard to the statement, "Buying several securities rather than just one reduces the variability of the return on investments." Moore intended the statement to be understood as about average return on collections of stocks at the end of a fixed period of

TABLE 9.2
Overview of Seminar Topics

Week	Monday	Tuesday	Wednesday	Thursday	Friday
June 11–June 15	• Data, samples, and polls • "Is this result unusual?": Concrete foundations for inference and hypothesis testing	• Statistical unusualness • Statistical accuracy • Distributions of sample statistics	• Margin of error • Putting it all together	• Students' understandings of distributions of sample statistics • Analysis of textbook treatments of sampling distributions	• Interviews
June 18–June 22	• Textbook analysis of probability intro • Probabilistic versus nonprobabilistic situations	• Conditional probability • Contingency tables and conditional probability • Students' difficulties with conditional probability	• More conditional probability • Uses of notation	• Analysis of textbook definitions of probability • Data analysis: Measures of association	• Interviews

TABLE 9.3
What the Chapter Was About and Important Ideas in It

Teacher	Response
John	Sampling distributions. Everything else hangs off of it.
Nicole	Law of large numbers, central limit theorem, mean remains the same but standard deviation changes as you take larger samples
Sarah	Statistics versus parameters; mean and standard deviation; effect of sample size on a sample's distribution
Lucy	Statistic versus parameter; central limit theorem, law of large numbers
Betty	Population versus sample; distributing the data shows how the deviation can affect the mean and standard deviation; law of large numbers; central limit theorem
Linda	Population distribution versus sampling distribution; overall picture of sample and mean; what a mean is; problems can be solved with formulas
Henry	Didn't answer Question 1. Instead commented on quality of the text's prose and presentation Important ideas are: Distributions; mean and standard deviation; central limit theorem
Alice	Random sampling; parameter versus statistic; central limit theorem

time, and to mean that, for a given period of time, the distribution of average returns on collections of, say, 10 stocks, over that time period will be less variable than will the distribution of returns on the population of individual stocks from which they are formed. However, every teacher initially interpreted the statement as saying that the average rate of return on a collection of stocks will vary less over time from its original price than will the return on any of the individual stocks in it.[3] Only John, after some probing, reconsidered his answer to say that the variability occurred from "investment to investment."

Question 8 repeated a sentence fragment from Moore's text, "The fact that averages of several observations are less variable ..." and asked teachers to interpret it. Table 9.4 shows that only John interpreted the statement distributionally, saying that the averages will cluster more tightly around the population mean than will individual measurements. Linda said that the averages of the samples, speaking of more than one average, would be closer to the true mean than the individual measurements. The remaining teachers all said that when you average the measurements you would get a result that is closer to the "true mean" than the individual measurements that make up the average.

---

[3]We realize that another way of examining variability is by computing the variance of a stock's value from its running average rate of return (which is the exponent of an exponential function), but Moore's point still remains that the comparison is between a distribution of average rates of return for collections and a distribution of average rates of return for individual stocks.

TABLE 9.4
Teachers Interpretations Of 8a, "Average Will Be Less Variable"

John	Means of samples (collections of measurements) will cluster more tightly around the population mean than will individual measurements
Nicole	The average will be closer to the mean
Sarah	If you average your data it will be closer to the true average of total population
Lucy	Difference between population mean and sample mean will be less than the difference between individual measurements and the population mean
Betty	Compute running averages as you select a sample and the running averages will be closer to the true mean
Linda	The averages of samples will be closer to the true mean than will individual measures.
Henry	Larger the sample the closer will be the average to the true mean.
Alice	Difference between true mean and calculated average will be less than between true mean and individual measurements.

Question 8b stated:

The author also says,
It is common practice to repeat a careful measurement several times and report the average of the results.
Does this mean that if I take one measurement of an object's weight, and if you take 4 measurements of its weight and calculate their average, then your average will be more accurate than my measurement? (Explain.)

Table 9.5 shows that several teachers were more sensitive to issues of variability in answering Question 8b than in answering 8a, although none of them referred to a distribution of averages. John said that this statement applies only to the long run—that in the long run the average would be closer. Nicole and Sarah said that it should be true theoretically, but the thing you are measuring might change during the measurement process. Lucy, Linda, Henry, and Alice said that it could or should be, but it might not. Only Betty said that the average would definitely be closer to the true measurement.

In question 11, Moore misstated the Law of Large Numbers, saying that necessarily becomes closer to μ as the sample size increases. Table 9.6 shows that only John noticed this, saying that he disagreed with the statement, that it should say that if they repeated their sampling, Luis would "have the better estimate" (but was unclear about what that would mean). Nicole, Betty, Linda, and Alice interpreted the statement as written. Sarah and Henry initially interpreted it as written, and then qualified their interpretation to say

TABLE 9.5
Teachers' Responses To 8b, "Accuracy Of 1 Measurement
Versus Average Of 4 Measurements"

John	Statement by itself tells us nothing. If we assume this is repeated, then in the long run I will get a good estimate of the actual mean, and you won't.
Nicole	Theoretically, the average of my four measurements should be closer than your one. But also need to measure many times because the thing you are measuring (e.g., air quality) can change over short periods of time.
Sarah	Probably not. Many variables undefined – measuring instrument, time of day, age of person. (Fix them?) Then theoretically, yes, but actually might not.
Lucy	Depends. I pick 4 you pick one. Your one could be closer than any of my four.
Betty	Yes.
Linda	Not necessarily. But you minimize the chance of being wrong by measuring it more times. Less chance of being close when measuring only once (but cannot articulate "less chance").
Henry	Could be. Also, measuring four times gives greater chance to detect measurement error.
Alice	Probably should be, but I don't know whether it would be.

TABLE 9.6
Teachers' Interpretations of Moore's Law of Large Numbers

John	If you go by Moore, then Luis. But I disagree—cannot stop there. Must resample. A sample of size 100 should be closer than a sample of size 10.
Nicole	Sounds like a limit.
Sarah	Take a larger sample size and you'll get closer to the mean. (Like a limit?) Like a reality. More times than not it should be closer.
Lucy	Larger sample more likely to be closer than smaller sample. (Likely?) Could be farther but probably closer.
Betty	Take the average of many samples and you'll be closer to the mean than an individual score.
Linda	The more observations the closer the sample mean is to the population mean.
Henry	The more observations and the more samples, the better is the representation of the population. To get the true average you would have to repeat sampling. The larger the sample increases the likelihood that you will be getting the true average.
Alice	As the number of observations increase, calculating a running average, the closer the average is to the population average.

TABLE 9.7
Teachers' Responses to Accuracies of Yan's Sample
of 50 and Luis' Sample of 100

John	Objected to just one sample. Said repeated sampling is necessary (but did not talk about distribution of sample means). "Larger sample is better estimate."
Nicole	Both samples are random? (Yes.) Luis is closer.
Sarah	Based on Moore's statement it should be closer. But most of the time the larger sample should be closer.
Lucy	Luis, most likely. Most of the time the larger sample will have a closer mean, but there can be variability.
Betty	According to this the larger should be closer. But the average of those two would be closer to the true height than either one of your averages.
Linda	Luis. (For sure?) Not for sure ... probably. Probably need more observations to be sure Luis' is closer, but I don't know how many women there are in Nashville to know how many observations you need.
Henry	They both could be just as accurate. You're looking for a breaking point (1/10 the population size) to be sure.
Alice	According to the LLN, the sample of 100 is closer. (Okay with this?) Yes. But the LLN says you should keep going.

"the likelihood is increased" that the sample mean is closer to μ with increased sample size, although Henry confounded number of samples with sample size. John and Lucy said that the statement said that means of larger samples "should" be closer to μ than means of smaller samples. Sarah, Henry, and Lucy did not think that their interpretations were in conflict with Moore's statement. It is worth noting that, in this question none of the teachers interpreted the Law of Large Numbers distributionally, in the sense that means of larger samples will cluster more tightly around the population mean than would means of smaller samples.

Question 11b asked teachers to compare the accuracies of Yan's sample of Size 50 and Luis' sample of Size 100. By Moore's s Law of Large Numbers, Luis' sample would be necessarily closer. By the standard Law of Large Numbers, we could say only that Luis' sample is "more likely" to be closer, meaning that a larger proportion of all samples of Size 100 would be within a given range of the population mean than all samples of Size 50. Table 9.7 shows that only Nicole stated flatly that Luis' sample mean would be closer to the population mean than Yan's. Sarah, Betty, and Alice conditioned their response on Moore's wording. Each teacher responded consistently with their response to 11b when asked the follow-up question, whether they would say the same thing if Luis' sample was of Size 52,

The pre-interviews suggest that, like students in our teaching experiments, the teachers, with the exception of John, were predisposed to think in terms of individual samples and not in terms of collections of samples, and thus distributions of samples statistics were not a construct by which they could form arguments. "Likelihood" of a sample statistic being close to a population parameter was a property of individual samples and not of a distribution of sample statistics. Moreover, when asked to consider what was varying when comparing investments in collections of stocks versus individual stocks, they thought of a single collection of stocks in comparison to individual stocks in it. Only John came to see, after our probing questions, that it was a collection of collections that were less variable than individual stocks. Finally, only John and Linda referred to collections of averages when explaining what "the average will be less variable" meant, and although Linda referred to "averages" in the plural, it was not clear that she had a distribution in mind.

THE SEMINAR

As seen from Table 9.2, the seminar's first week was devoted to issues of understanding and teaching statistical inference. It might seem odd that we covered inference before probability. We did this for two reasons. First, our focus on inference was highly informal, never drawing on technical understandings of probability, and emphasizing the idea of distribution. Second, the idea of distribution would be central to our sessions on probability, too, and we hoped to avoid any carry-over effect that might have happened had we covered probability before inference.

The seminars were conducted in a free-discussion format. Terry began each session with pre-planned activities and a "guide" for discussions we hoped would happen, but the discussions often strayed from the central point and most of the time those digressions were important enough that Terry would see where they went. Terry would then nudge the discussions back to the current main point. For the purposes of this chapter we first focus on teachers' discussions of *unusualness* during the first three days of the seminar. This idea turned out to be especially slippery for teachers, each expressing confusion at various times. We focused on unusualness for several reasons. First, as already mentioned, the logic of hypothesis testing is that one rejects a null hypothesis whenever an observed sample is judged to be sufficiently unusual (improbable, rare) in light of it. This logic demands that we assume the sample statistic of interest has some underlying distribution, for without assuming a distribution we have no way to gauge any sample's rarity. This assumption is made *independently* of the sample. It is like a policy decision: "If, according to our assumptions, we judge that samples like the one observed occur less than $x\%$ of the time (i.e., are sufficiently unusual), then our sampling procedure was not random, it was biased, or values of the sample statistic are not distributed as we presumed." Second, we observed in high school teaching experiments (Saldanha, 2004; Saldanha & Thompson, 2002; Thompson & Saldanha, 2000; Thompson et al., 2004) that students had a powerful sense of "unusual" as meaning simply that the observed result is surprising, where "surprising" meant differing substantially from what they anticipated. By this meaning, if one has no prior expectation about what a result should be, then no result is unusual. Because students made theoretical commitments regarding distributions of outcomes infrequently, their attempts to apply the logic of hypothesis testing often became a meaningless exercise.

We begin with an episode from Day 3 of the seminar. We started the day by engaging the teachers in discussion of the following question, adapted from Konold (1994).

> Ephram works at a theater, taking tickets for one movie per night at a theater that holds 250 people. The town has 30,000 people. He estimates that he knows 300 of them by name. Ephram noticed that he often saw at least two people he knew. Is it in fact unusual that at least two people Ephram knows attend the movie he shows, or could people be coming because he is there?

The teachers first gave intuitive answers. All said it would not be unusual for Ephram to see two people he knows. Subsequent discussion focused on the method for investigating the question, and it revealed that only one teacher, Alice, had a conception of unusualness that was grounded in a scheme of distribution of sample statistics. She proposed, as the method of investigating the question, "Each night record how many he knew out of the 250 and keep track of it over a long period of time," which suggested that she had conceived of "Ephram sees x people he knows" as a random event and would evaluate the likelihood of outcomes "Ephram sees at least two people he knows" against the distribution of a large number of possible outcomes.

Other teachers had various conceptions of unusualness. Three teachers, Sarah, Linda, and Betty stated flatly that something is unusual if it is unexpected, and expectations are made on the basis of personal experience. John's conception of unusualness was also subjective and nonstochastic. He justified his intuitive answer by reasoning that Ephram knows 300 people out of 30,000 people in his town, so for every 100 people, he knows 1 person. On any given night he should know 2.5 people out of 250 people who come to the theatre, given that this 250 people is a representative sample of 30,000 in his town. John employed what we call the *proportionality heuristic*: evaluating the likelihood of a sample statistic by comparing it against the population proportion or a statistic of a larger sample. He did not conceptualize a scheme of repeated sampling that would allow him to quantify unusualness. Henry's conception of unusualness was somewhat stochastic, albeit nonstandard. He defined unusualness as, "Something is unusual if I'm doing it less than 50% of the time." The ensuing discussion revealed that the teachers, with exception of Alice, had a subjective conception of unusualness, and this conception did not support their thinking in hypothesis testing.

The second major idea was the logic of hypothesis testing, which is similar to that of proof by contradiction. In proof by contradiction, we establish a statement given certain conditions by assuming its negation and then bringing that assumption into conflict with an implication of it or with an accepted fact. We then conclude that the statement is true under the given conditions because its negation is untenable. In hypothesis testing, we test the plausibility of H_1 by assuming a rival, complementary hypothesis, H_0, and then examining the likelihood of obtaining results similar to what actually occurred given that H_0 is true. A small chance of results like what actually occurred with H_0 being true casts doubt on the plausibility of H_0 and in turn suggests the viability of H_1.

To understand the teachers' understanding of the logic of hypothesis testing, we engaged them in a discussion of the following task:

> Assume that sampling procedures are acceptable and that a sample is collected having 60% favoring Pepsi. Argue for or against this conclusion: *This sample suggests that there are more people in the sampled population who prefer Pepsi than prefer Coca Cola.*

This question was accompanied by a list of 135 simulated samples of Size 100 taken from a population that was split 50–50 in their preference for Coca Cola or Pepsi. Four of the 135 sample statistics exceeded 60%.

Three teachers, Lucy, John, and Henry, said that the statement *there were more people in the sampled population who prefer Pepsi than prefer Coca Cola* was false. They based their claim on the evidence that only 2.96% of the simulated samples had 60% or more favoring Pepsi. Their logic seemed to have been: If the population was indeed unevenly split, with more Pepsi drinkers than Coke drinkers, then you would expect to get samples like the one obtained (60% Pepsi drinkers) more frequently than 2.96% of the time. The rarity of such samples suggested that the population was *not* unevenly split. They seemed to understand the list as containing *actual* sample proportions. This puzzled us because in nearly the same breath they spoke both that there should be more samples above 60% if that was the actual break and of the simulation of drawing from a population split 50–50.

Terry, the seminar leader, pushed the teachers to explain the tension between (1) we actually got a sample of which 60% preferred Pepsi, and

(2) the sample's occurrence is rare under the assumption that the population is evenly split. Henry suggested that the sample was not randomly chosen. John suggested that the assumption of 50–50 split was not valid.

One teacher, Linda, insisted that the assumption should not be rejected on the basis of one sample. Her argument was that no matter how rare a sample is, it *can* occur, thus its occurrence cannot be used against any assumption. (We called this the "OJ" argument.) Her opposition to rejecting the assumption of evenly split population (H_0) rested on her commitment to the null hypothesis and her concern for whether the null hypothesis had been proven false. Linda said she would reject H_0 only if there was overwhelming evidence against it, and she therefore opposed "rejecting the null on the basis of one sample." She instead proposed to take more samples to see whether H_0 was right or wrong. Linda reasoned that, because any rare sample could, theoretically, occur, one sample cannot provide overwhelming evidence. Linda's concern for establishing the truth or falsity of a null hypothesis is inconsistent with the idea of a decision rule. A decision rule does not tell us whether the null hypothesis in any one context is right or wrong. Rather, it tells us that if we apply the decision rule consistently, then we can anticipate, over the long run, rejecting H_0 inappropriately a small percent of the time.

In sum, the discussion and interviews from this seminar revealed a spectrum of choices that the teachers made when facing the question, "Do we reject a null hypothesis when a sample is unusual in light of it?" illustrates the structure of that spectrum.

This figure (Fig. 9.1) captures the varieties of choices the teachers made when a small *p-value* was found. Decisions 1–3 are likely to be made by people who are committed to the null hypothesis, meaning they must have evidence against it to abandon it, whereas people who are committed to the alternative hypothesis would reject the null on the basis of a small p-value. The results of the discussion suggested that most of the teachers exhibited a commitment to the null hypothesis (the initial assumption that the population was evenly split), whereas in standard hypothesis testing, one's commitment is to the alternative hypothesis. That is, it is the alternative hypothesis that one suspects is true, and the logic of hypothesis testing provides a conservative method for confirming it.

Towards the end of the discussion, Pat proposed a way of thinking about observed events that led Henry and John to eventually concur with him that the data suggested that the chance of getting samples of 60% or more was sufficiently rare so as to reject the assumption that the population was evenly split. In this discussion (see Fig. 9.2), Pat proposed an analogy between taking a sample and flipping a pen.

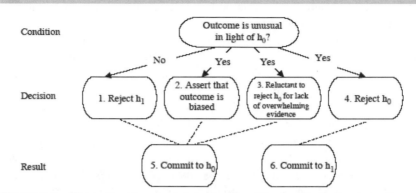

Figure 9.1   Theoretical framework for teachers' logic of hypothesis testing.

In this rather extended exchange, Pat again highlighted the logic of hypothesis testing: When a sample occurs, and the likelihood of the sample's occurrence is rare under a given assumption, we conclude that either (1) the assumption is right, but the sample is not randomly chosen; or (2) the sample is randomly chosen, so the given assumption is not warranted. Pat expressed one variation of this logic: If (1) a sample occurred, (2) the likelihood of the sample's occurrence is rare under a given assumption, and (3) the sample is randomly chosen, then we conclude that the given assumption is not valid. The discussion ended with John and Henry agreeing explicitly with the logic of hypothesis testing and the others at least suppressing any disagreement.

We asked this question in the first end-of-week interview to see the extent to which the teachers had internalized the logic of hypothesis testing.

> The Metro Tech Alumni Association surveyed 20 randomly selected graduates of Metro Tech, asking them if they were satisfied with the education that Metro gave them. Only 60% of the graduates said they were very satisfied. However, the administration claims that more than 80% of all graduates are very satisfied. Do you believe the administration? Can you test their claim?

This interview question presents a typical hypothesis testing scenario: There was a stated claim about a population parameter, namely that 80% of all graduates of Metro Tech were very satisfied with the education that Metro gave them. A random sample of 20 graduates found that only 60% of them said they were satisfied. The implied question was, "Are samples like or more extreme than 60% sufficiently rare, assuming the administration's claim, to reject that claim?"

All the teachers noticed the large difference between 60% and 80%, and they believed the small sample size was the reason for it. They had different

1.	Pat	Suppose I tell you that while you were talking, I flipped my pen and it landed on its tip and stayed there.
2.	John	I will say do that 1000 more times, and I'll bet you it won't happen once.
3.	Pat	Well. I'm not going to do that. But I'm asking you, do you believe it?
4.	Linda	Sure.
5.	Betty	Sure, there is a chance that could happen.
6.	Pat	Do you believe it?
7.	Sarah	Which tip?
		(Terry &Alice Laugh.)
8.	Pat	The pointy tip.
9.	Sarah	No.
10.	Henry	Do I believe you? If I know nothing about you, I would not believe you. But if I have a personal relationship with you, and I know that you have a tendency to tell the truth, an I know that it could happen, it'd be rare but it could happen, I might have a tendency tc believe you. But if you have a equal likelihood of lying to me, then I would say that I don't believe you.
11.	Pat	Why not?
12.	Henry	Because it's very rare, very very rare.
13.	John	It's a little different from this situation.
14.	Pat	How can we talk about one instance? You are making an inference about what I do ove the long run.
15.	Henry	It could happen.
16.	Pat	It could happen
17.	John	But the difference is this: if you tell me you flip a coin 10 times, all 10 times it came up with heads, I don't believe you. But if you tell me 6 times it came up with the heads, then I could believe you. Because getting 6 heads is a lot more likely than getting 10 heads.
18.	Pat	Now, the point is that there is an implied, you are using a tacit decision rule. You are discounting a claim using a tacit decision. That tacit decision rule has to do with how rare, how frequently would you expect this thing that I claim happening could happen. See, essentially, you are saying, I know that really could happen, but my decision is to say, I don't believe it. I imagine the relative frequency to be exceeding a certain threshold.
19.	Pat:	Now, suppose that you look at my pen, and it is landing on its tip, then what would you say?
20.	Henry:	I would have to investigate the pen, the wire. I still would doubt it.
21.	Pat :	Oh, no, you are looking at it.
22.	Henry:	I have to investigate, seeing is not validity.
23.	John:	We haven't been told, maybe some of the constraints of the experiment were left out.
24.	Pat:	All right. In other words, you assumed the way it worked. You are saying it couldn't have worked the way you assumed it would. Something is different.
25.	Henry:	Something is different. My assumption was wrong.
26.	Pat:	Yeah, so then what you are doing is that, saying that, "Gee, this happened. But I thougl I know the way these things work. And if they in fact work the way I assume they do, this will be extremely rare, and if it does happen, then probably it doesn't work the way I assume it works." See there is reverse logic to it?
27.	Henry :	Right.
28.	Pat:	Do you all see now that what that entails is hypothesis testing?
29.	John:	Yeah.
30.	Pat :	So we're deciding whether or not to reject the null hypothesis. [Pat explicitly points ou the equivalence of "the initial assumption" and "the null hypothesis".]
31.	John :	Right.
32.	Henry:	In which we would have.
33.	Terry:	I probably would. 2.9%, that's pretty unlikely.

Figure 9.2   Extended excerpt of discussion.

opinions about whether they believed the administration's claim. Nicole and Betty said they did not believe it. Betty believed that there need to have more samples to back up the claim. Henry, Linda, Alice, and Sarah said they believed the claim. Henry, Linda, and Alice based their choice on their belief that despite the sample results being 60%, the population percent being 80% was still *possible*. Sarah, however, did not think that 80% was a claim about the population percent. Rather, she thought it was a sample result, and it was self-evident to her that two samples should produce different results. John and Lucy were hesitant in making a decision, with Lucy leaning towards not believing the administration because the claimed figure was much bigger than the sample result. In short, we see strong evidence of teachers employing a nondistributional way of thinking about the scenario, and this opened each of them to using a logic of evidence rather than a logic of hypothesis testing.

When asked how they would test the administration's claim, only Henry proposed to use hypothesis testing. The methods other teachers proposed fall into the following categories:

1. Take many more samples of Size 20 from the population of graduates (John, Nicole, Sarah, Alice).
2. Take a larger sample from the population of graduates (Alice).
3. Take one or a few more samples of Size 20 from the population of graduates (Lucy, Betty).
4. Survey the entire population (Linda).

In sum, teachers' responses on this interview question suggested that they did not employ spontaneously the method of hypothesis testing for the situation. Instead, 7 of 8 teachers proposed methods of investigation that presumed that they would have access to the population, and none of these methods were well-defined policies that would allow one to make consistent judgment. This led to our conjecture that even though the teachers might have understood the logic of hypothesis testing at the end of the seminar, they did not understand its functionality. In other words, they did not know the types (or models) of questions that hypothesis testing was created for, and how hypothesis testing became a particularly useful tool for answering these types of questions.

Overall, the results revealed that the majority of teachers embraced conceptions of probability and logic of hypothesis testing that will support not using it in ways that its inventors intended. Only one teacher conceptualized unusualness within a scheme of repeated sampling, and thus the others did not incorporate the idea of a distribution of sample statistics in their thinking of statistical inference. Most of the teachers did not understand the logic of hypothesis testing, or if they understood it they thought it was irrelevant to settle competing claims about a population parameter. This was revealed in the nonconventional decisions they made when a collected sample fell into the category of "unusual" in light of an assumption. These decisions revealed their commitment to a logic of evidence, as distinct from a logic of hypothesis testing, in examining the viability of the null hypothesis. Beyond the complexity of hypothesis testing as a concept, we conjecture that part of teachers' difficulties was due to their commitment to evidence-based, as in legal, argumentation with regard to accepting or rejecting a claim. Thus, even when they came to understand the logic of hypothesis testing, that logic itself was not relevant to making decisions about viability of claims. This conjecture was supported by the interview data where only one teacher proposed hypothesis testing as the method of investigation.

CONCLUSIONS AND IMPLICATIONS

The results of our intervention revealed that teachers' difficulty in understanding and employing statistical inference came in part from their compartmentalized knowledge of probability and of statistical inference. That is, their conceptions of probability (or unusualness) were not grounded in the conception of distribution, and thus did not support thinking about distributions of sample statistics and the probabilities (i.e., proportions of values) that a statistic is in a particular range. The implication of this result is that instructions on probability and on statistical inference must be designed with the principal purpose that it helps one understand probability statistically and to understand statistics probabilistically. This purpose might be achieved by designing instruction so that teachers develop the capacity and orientation to think in terms of *distributions of sample statistics*, which hopefully would have the salutary effect of supporting a stochastic, distributional conception of probability, and lead to their inclusion of distributions of sample statistics in their understanding of statistical inference. We suspect that teachers who value distributional reasoning in probability and who imagine a statistic as having a distribution of values will be better positioned to help students reason probabilistically about statistical claims.

We also learned that part of the teachers' difficulties in understanding hypothesis testing was a result of their logic of argumentation, namely the belief that rejecting a null hypothesis means to prove it is wrong. The implication of this result is that understanding hypothesis testing entails a substantial departure from teachers' prior experience and their established beliefs in regard to reasoning about data. To confront these hidden beliefs, we could, for example, design activities according to the framework in Figure 9.1 to have teachers consider the implications of each choice they might make in regard to claims and evidence. In having teachers reflect on the tacit beliefs behind nonconventional choices, we might help them come to internalize the logic of hypothesis testing so that it becomes, for them, a natural way of thinking.

Finally, we note that although these teachers' difficulties with hypothesis testing resembled those had by high school students, they differed in important respects. Both groups held logics of argumentation that resembled a legal argument, but students had greater difficulty forming an image of "take a sample" as a stochastic process. The teachers understood a table of sample outcomes (one that we had also used with students) as portraying a distribution more readily than did students, yet the two groups applied similar types of reasoning when judging the viability of claims about the population. This suggests to us that the problem of helping teachers help students understand statistical inference is doubly difficult. Not only must teachers understand students' difficulties and ways they might overcome them, they must adjust their own understandings to support a logic of argumentation that is alien to them.

ACKNOWLEDGMENTS

Research reported in this chapter was supported by National Science Foundation Grants No. REC-9811879 and EHR-0353470. Any conclusions or recommendations stated here are those of the authors and do not necessarily reflect official positions of NSF.

REFERENCES

Batanero, C., & Serrano, L. (1999). The meaning of randomness for secondary school students. *Journal for Research in Mathematics Education, 30*(5), 558–567.

Chance, B. L., delMas, R. C., & Garfield, J. (in press). Reasoning about sampling distributions. In D. Ben-Zvi & J. Garfield (Eds.), *The challenge of developing statistical literacy, reasoning, and thinking*. Dordrecht, The Netherlands: Kluwer.

delMas, R. C., Garfield, J., & Chance, B. L. (1999, April). *Exploring the role of computer simulations in developing understanding of sampling distributions*. Paper presented at the Annual Meeting of the American Educational Research Association. Montreal, Canada.

delMas, R. C., Garfield, J., & Chance, B. L. (2004, April). *Using assessment to study the development of students' reasoning about sampling distributions*. Paper presented at the annual meeting of the American Educational Research Association. San Diego, CA.

Earley, M. A. (2001). *Investigating the development of knowledge structures in introductory statistics*. Unpublished doctoral dissertation, University of Toledo, Toledo, OH.

Earley, M. A. (2004). *Overcoming the complexity of the sampling distribution concept in introductory statistics courses*. San Diego, CA: Annual Meeting of the American Educational Research Association.

Falk, R., & Konold, C. C. (1994). Random means hard to digest. *Focus on Learning Problems in Mathematics, 16*(1), 2–12.

Falk, R., & Konold, C. C. (1997). Making sense of randomness: Implicit encoding as a basis for judgment. *Psychological Review, 104*, 301–318.

Glasersfeld, E. v. (1972). Semantic analysis of verbs in terms of conceptual situations. *Linguistics, 94*, 90–107.

Glasersfeld, E. v. (1995). *Radical constructivism: A way of knowing and learning.* London: Falmer Press.

Horvath, J. K., & Lehrer, R. (1998). A model-based perspective on the development of children's understanding of chance and uncertainty. In S. P. Lojoie (Ed.), *Reflections on statistics: Learning, teaching, and assessment in grades K–12* (pp. 121–148). Mahwah, NJ: Lawrence Erlbaum Associates.

Konold, C. C. (1994). *Datascope user manual.* Palo Alto, CA: Intellimation.

Konold, C. C., & Pollatsek, A. (2002). Data Analysis as the search for signals in noisy processes. *Journal for Research in Mathematics Education, 33*(4), 259–289.

Metz, K. E. (1998). Emergent understanding and attribution of randomness: Comparative analysis of the reasoning of primary grade children and undergraduates. *Cognition and Instruction, 16*(3), 285–365.

Rubin, A., Bruce, B., & Tenney, Y. (1991). Learning about sampling: Trouble at the core of statistics. In D. Vere-Jones (Ed.), *Proceedings of the third International Conference on Teaching Statistics* (vol. 1; pp. 314–319). Dunedin, New Zealand: ISI Publications in Statistical Education.

Saldanha, L. A. (2004). *"Is this sample unusual?": An investigation of students exploring connections between sampling distributions and statistical inference.* Unpublished doctoral dissertation, Vanderbilt University, Nashville, TN.

Saldanha, L. A., & Thompson, P. W. (2002). Conceptions of sample and their relationship to statistical inference. *Educational Studies in Mathematics, 51*(3), 257–270.

Schwartz, D. L., Goldman, S. R., Vye, N. J., & Barron, B. J. (1998). Aligning everyday and mathematical reasoning: The case of sampling assumptions. In S. P. Lojoie (Ed.), *Reflections on statistics: Learning, teaching, and assessment in grades K–12* (pp. 233–274). Mahwah, NJ: Lawrence Erlbaum Associates.

Steffe, L. P. (1991). The constructivist teaching experiment: Illustrations and implications. In E. von Glasersfeld (Ed.), *Radical constructivism in mathematics education* (pp. 177–194). Dordrecht, The Netherlands: Kluwer.

Steffe, L. P. (1996). Radical constructivism: A way of knowing and learning [Review of the same title, by Ernst von Glasersfeld]. *Zentralblatt für Didaktik der Mathematik* [International reviews on Mathematical Education], *96*(6), 202–204.

Steffe, L. P., & Thompson, P. W. (2000). Teaching experiment methodology: Underlying principles and essential elements. In R. Lesh & A. E. Kelly (Eds.), *Research design in mathematics and science education* (pp. 267–307). Mahwah, NJ: Lawrence Erlbaum Associates.

Thompson, P. W. (2000). Radical constructivism: Reflections and directions. In L. P. Steffe & P. W. Thompson (Eds.), *Radical constructivism in action: Building on the pioneering work of Ernst von Glasersfeld* (pp. 412–448). London: Falmer Press.

Thompson, P. W., & Saldanha, L. A. (2000). Conceptual issues in understanding sampling distributions and margins of error. In M. Fernandez (Ed.), *Proceedings of the 22nd Annual meeting of the International Group for the Psychology of Mathematics Education.* Athens, GA: University of Georgia.

Thompson, P. W., Saldanha, L. A., & Liu, Y. (2004). *Why statistical inference is hard to understand.* San Diego, CA: Annual Meeting of the American Educational Research Association.

Velleman, P. F. (1997). *Data desk statistics guide.* Ithaca, NY: Data Description, Inc.

Watson, J. M. (2001). Longitudinal development of inferential reasoning by school students. *Educational Studies in Mathematics, 47*(3), 337–372.

Watson, J. M. (2002). Inferential reasoning and the influence of cognitive conflict. *Educational Studies in Mathematics, 51*(3), 225–256.

Watson, J. M., & Moritz, J. B. (2000). Developing concepts of sampling. *Journal for Research in Mathematics Education, 31*(1), 44–70.

Well, A. D., Pollatsek, A., & Boyce, S. J. (1990). Understanding the effects of sample size on the variability of the mean. *Journal of Organizational Behavior and Human Decision Processes, 47*, 289–312.

APPENDIX I: PRE-SEMINAR INTERVIEW

Prelude

I am going to ask you some questions that are based on the reading we asked you to do. Please do not think that we expect you to be able to respond immediately with answers to them or to have mastered the ideas they address. Rather, we need to have a sense of what you understand about these ideas ahead of the workshop so that we can determine how your thinking and understandings were influenced by participating in it.

So, please answer these questions to the best of your ability, but also be assured that we are not judging your answers.

General Questions

(Teachers were given an excerpt from Moore's *Basic Practice of Statistics* on samples, sample means, and variability of the sample mean.)

1. What was this excerpt about?
2. What are your impressions of it?
3. What, in your opinion, are the important ideas in it?
4. What in this excerpt would you anticipate that students might have trouble with?
5. Are there any parts of the excerpt that, in your opinion, are problematic?

Particular Questions

6. On page 292 in Example 4.23 the author says,

   "Buying several securities rather than just one reduces the variability of the return on investment.

What is varying that its variability is reduced?

7. Please interpret the histogram on page 292. What is it showing?
8. On page 295, Example 4.24, the author says,

> The fact that averages of several observations are less variable …

a. What might this mean?
b. The author also says,

> It is common practice to repeat a careful measurement several times and report the average of the results.

Does this mean that if I take one measurement of an object's weight and you take 4 measurements of its weight and calculate their average, then your average will be more accurate than my measurement? (Explain.)

9. On page 294, the author says,

> "The sampling distribution of $\overline{X}$ is the distribution of the values of $\overline{X}$ in all possible samples of the same size from the population.

Could you please explain what this is talking about?

10. Problem 4.81 on page 301 makes these statements:
   a. The distribution of annual returns on common stocks is roughly symmetric, but extreme observations are more frequent than in a normal distribution
   b. Because the distribution is not strongly non-normal, the mean return over even a moderate number of years is close to normal.
   c. In the long run, annual real returns on common stocks have varied with mean about 9% and standard deviation about 28%
   d. Andrew plans to retire in 45 years and is considering investing in stocks
   e. What is the probability (assuming that the past pattern of variation continues) that the mean annual return on common stocks over the next 45 years will exceed 15%?

Please interpret these statements.

11. Here is the author's statement of the *Law of Large Numbers*:

> Draw observations at random from any population with finite $\overline{X}$ mean μ. As the number of observations drawn increases, the mean the observed values gets closer and closer to μ.

a. Please explain what this statement says.

b. Assume we are sampling from the females in Nashville, TN and that we calculate a sample's mean height.

—Yan collected a random sample of 50 females and calculated their mean height.
—Luis collected a random sample of 100 females and calculated their mean height.
—Whose mean height is closer to the population mean (i.e., the mean height of all girls in the population)?

c. *If answer to (b) is "Luis"*: Suppose Luis' sample contains 52 females. Would you say the same thing?

APPENDIX II: MIDSEMINAR INTERVIEW

Question 1

The Metro Tech Alumni Association surveyed 20 randomly selected graduates of Metro Tech, asking them to if they were satisfied with the education that Metro gave them. Only 61% of the graduates said they were very satisfied. However, the administration claims that more than 80% of all graduates are very satisfied

Do you believe the administration? Can you test their claim?

Question 2

A Harris poll of 535 people, held prior to Timothy McVeigh's execution, reported that 73% of U.S. citizens supported the death penalty. Harris reported that this poll had a margin of error of ±5%.

Please interpret "±5%. How might they have determined this? How could they test their claim of "± 5%"?

Question 3

Here is a partial data display of information gathered by the US News and World Report in 1997 on the country's top colleges. [The data table included in the original question is omitted here, but it included for each college measures such as *Reputation Rating*, *Retention*, and *Graduation Rate*.]

Different collegiate associations, such as NCAA conferences, were interested in developing a measure of overall association stature (you can probably guess which ones were for or against this!).

Dr. Robert Horness of Colgate University thought that the formula *mean (Reputation Rating) mean (Brand Value Rating) might be useful in this regard.*

A new association of 23 schools announced a score of 1,300 on the Horness scale. Is that good?

(Let the teacher give an initial response. If s/he says something equivalent to "I need to see the distribution of measures," then use Fathom to produce a histogram.

Question 4

Mrs. Smithey conducted a computer simulation of collecting 100 samples of Size 25 from a population having 32% with characteristic X. A student wondered out loud what the point of doing the simulation is when you already know the answer!

Please comment. What is the purpose of using a simulation to make collections of sample statistics?

Question 5

Which of each pair is the more fundamental idea:
   Equation or Function
   Sampling Distribution or Distribution of Sample Statistics
   Parameter or Statistic

10

Middle School Students' Use of Appropriate and Inappropriate Evidence in Writing Scientific Explanations

Katherine L. McNeill
Boston College

Joseph Krajcik
University of Michigan

The National Research Council (1996) and the American Association for the Advancement of Science (1993) call for scientific literacy for all. All students need knowledge of scientific concepts and inquiry practices required for personal decision making, participation in societal and cultural affairs, and economic productivity. Science education should support students' development toward competent participation in a science infused world (McGinn & Roth, 1999). This type of participation should be obtainable for all students, not just those who are educated for scientific professions. Consequently, we are interested in supporting all students in learning scientific concepts and inquiry practices.

By scientific inquiry practices, we mean the multiple ways of knowing which scientists use to study the natural world (National Research Council, 1996). Key scientific inquiry practices called for by national standards documents include asking questions, designing experiments, analyzing data, and constructing explanations (American Association for the Advancement of Science, 1993; National Research Council, 1996). In this study, we focus on analyzing data and constructing explanations. These practices are essential not only for scientists, but for all individuals. On a daily basis, individuals need to evaluate scientific data provided to them in written form such as newspapers and magazines as well spoken through television and radio. Citizens need to be able to evaluate that data to determine whether the claims being made based on the data and reasoning are valid. This type of data evaluation, like other scientific inquiry practices, is dependent both on a general understanding of how to evaluate data as well as an understanding of the science content.

In this study, we explore when students use appropriate evidence and when they use inappropriate evidence to support their claims. Our work focuses on an 8-week project-based chemistry curriculum designed to support seventh-grade students in using evidence and constructing scientific explanations. We examine the characteristics of these students' explanations, their understanding of the content knowledge, and the assessment tasks to unpack what may be influencing students' use of evidence.

OUR INSTRUCTIONAL MODEL
FOR SCIENTIFIC EXPLANATIONS

In our work, we examine how students construct scientific explanations using evidence. We use a specific instructional model for evidence-based scientific explanations as a tool for both classroom practice and research. We provide both teachers and students with this model to make the typically implicit framework of explanation, explicit to both teachers and students.

Our instructional model for scientific explanation uses an adapted version of Toulmin's (1958) model of argumentation and builds off previous science educators' research on students' construction of scientific explanations and arguments (Bell & Linn, 2000; Jiménez-Aleixandre, Rodríguez, & Duschl, 2000; Lee & Songer, 2004; Sandoval, 2003; Zembal-Saul, Munford, Crawford, Friedrichsen, & Land, 2002). Our explanation framework includes three components: a claim (similar to Toulmin's claim), evidence (similar to Toulmin's data), and reasoning (a combination of Toulmin's warrants and backing). The claim makes an assertion or conclusion that addresses the original question or problem. The evidence supports the student's claim using scientific data. This data can come from an investigation that students complete or from another source, such as observations, reading material, or archived data. The data need to be both appropriate and sufficient to support the claim. Appropriate data are relevant to the question or problem and relate to the given claim. Data are sufficient when they include the necessary quantity to convince someone of a claim. The reasoning is a justification that links the claim and evidence and shows why the data counts as evidence to support the claim by using the appropriate scientific principles.

Kuhn argues (1993) that argument, or in our case scientific explanation, is a form of thinking that transcends the particular content to which it refers. Students can construct scientific explanations across different content areas. Although an explanation model, such as Toulmin's, can be used to assess the structure of an explanation, it cannot determine the scientific accuracy of the explanation (Driver, Newton, & Osborne, 2000). Instead, both the domain general explanation framework and the domain-specific context of the assessment task determine the correctness of the explanation. Consequently, in both teaching students about explanation and assessing students' construction of explanations we embed the scientific inquiry practice in a specific context.

STUDENT DIFFICULTIES CONSTRUCTING EXPLANATIONS

Prior research in science classrooms suggests that students have difficulty constructing high-quality scientific explanations where they articulate and defend their claims (Sadler, 2004). For example, students have difficulty understanding what counts as evidence (Sadler, 2004) and using appropriate evidence (Sandoval, 2003; Sandoval & Reiser, 1997). Instead, students will draw on data that do not support their claim. Consequently, we are interested in whether students use appropriate evidence to support their claim or if they draw on evidence that is not relevant.

Students' claims also do not necessarily relate to their *evidence*. Instead, students often rely on their personal views instead of evidence to draw conclusions (Hogan & Maglienti, 2001). Students have a particularly difficult time reasoning from primary data, especially when measurement error plays an important role (Kanari & Millar, 2004). Students can recognize variation in data and use characteristics of data in their reasoning, but their ability to draw final conclusions from that data can depend on the context. Masnick, Klahr, and Morris (this volume) concluded that young students who poorly understood the context of the investigation had difficulty interpreting data, particularly when the interpretation of that data contradicted their prior beliefs. Students will likely discount data if the data contradicts their current theory (Chinn & Brewer, 2001) and they will only consider data if they can come up with a mechanism for the pattern of data (Koslowski, 1996). When students evaluate data, more general reasoning strategies interact with domain-specific knowledge (Chinn & Brewer, 2001). Whether students use appropriate and inappropriate evidence may depend on their prior understanding of a particular content area or task.

Students also have difficulty providing the backing, or what we refer to as *reasoning*, for why they chose the evidence (Bell & Linn, 2000) in their written explanations. Other researchers have shown that during classroom discourse, discussions tend to be dominated by claims with little backing to support their claims (Jiménez-Aleixandre, Rodríguez & Duschl, 2000). Our previous work supports these ideas. We found that middle school students' had the most difficulty with the reasoning component of scientific explanations (McNeill, Lizotte, Krajcik, & Marx, 2006; McNeill et al., 2003). Although students' reasoning improved over the course of the 6–8 week instructional unit, it was consistently of lower quality than their claims or evidence. Students' reasoning often just linked their claim and evidence and less frequently articulated the scientific principles that allowed them to make that connection.

Similar to students' ability to evaluate and use data, providing accurate reasoning is related to students understanding of the content. Students with stronger content knowledge provide stronger reasoning in their scientific explanations (McNeill et al., 2006). Previous research with students has found that their success at completing scientific inquiry practices is highly dependent on their understanding of both the content and the scientific inquiry practices (Metz, 2000). Both domain- specific and general reasoning are essential for students' effective evaluation of data and construction of scientific explanations.

Although previous work has shown that students have difficulty with components of scientific explanations, there has been little research unpacking exactly when students have difficulty or why they have difficulty. In this chapter, we address the following research question: What difficulties do middle school students have using evidence and reasoning when constructing scientific explanations? How does content area influence students' use of evidence and reasoning? Furthermore, we attempt to unpack what may be causing these student difficulties.

INSTRUCTIONAL CONTEXT

Our Model of Learning

Our work is rooted in social constructivist learning theories that argue that understanding is contextualized and a function of social interactions with others (Blumenfeld, Marx, Patrick, Krajcik, & Soloway, 1997; Driver, Asoko, Leach, Mortimer, & Scott, 1994; Singer, Marx, Krajcik, & Chambers, 2000). Our model of learning stems from five important features: *active construction*, *situated cognition, community, discourse,* and *cognitive tools* (Rivet & Krajcik, 2004; Singer et al., 2000). *Active construction* of knowledge states that students create new knowledge and understanding based on what they already know and believe. This knowledge includes not only content knowledge, but also knowledge students have acquired because of their social roles connected with race, class, gender and their cultural and ethnic affiliations (Bransford, Brown, & Cocking, 2000). *Situated cognition* recognizes that learning is a social process and students make meaning through their interactions with other people, tools, and the environment (Lave & Wenger, 1991). Within the classroom, these interactions occur in a *community* of practice where students learn to learn from their teacher, peers, and other resources (Brown et al., 1993). Science has its own special *discourse* and that language is the primary means for communicating scientific knowledge (Lemke, 1990). Students need to learn how to talk using scientific discourse and not just talk about science. Scientific discourse does not just mean scientific words, but it includes different ways of knowing in science, such as asking questions, designing experiments, and constructing explanations (Driver et al., 1994). Another important component of the classroom environment is *cognitive tools*. Cognitive tools provide supporting structures to students that act as intellectual partners to extend performance and learning (Solomon, Perkins, & Globerson, 1991). Cognitive tools can range from computer software that allows students to create complex representations to written instructional scaffolds that encourage students to include evidence in their explanations. In all cases, they allow students to function at a level beyond their own independent cognitive abilities to engage in complex problem solving.

Learning-Goals-Driven Design Model

To engage middle school students in developing a deep understanding of science content and scientific inquiry practices, we developed a seventh-grade chemistry unit, "How Can I Make New Stuff From Old Stuff?" (referred to as "Stuff") that sustains students in learning over a 6- to 8-week period (McNeill et al., 2004). We designed the *Stuff* unit using a *learning-goals-driven design* process, based on the backwards design model of Wiggins and McTighe (1998). The central focus is to identify learning goals and derive *learning performances* that illustrate how students should use the scientific content and practices in real tasks (Reiser, Krajcik, Moje, & Marx, 2003). *Learning performances* reflect the reasoning tasks we want students to be able to do with scientific knowledge. Learning performances reformulate a scientific content standard in terms of scientific practices that *use* that content, such as students being able to define terms, describe phenomena, use models to explain patterns in data, construct scientific explanations, or test hypotheses. The articulated learning performances serve as guides for designing activities and assessments. We developed learning performance by crossing a content specific standard with a scientific inquiry practice standard. Table 10.1 gives an example.

TABLE 10.1
Developing Learning Performances

Content Standard	Scientific Practice Standard	Learning Performance
When substances interact to form new substances, the elements composing them combine in new ways. In such recombinations, the properties of the new combinations may be very different from those of the old (AAAS, 1990, p. 47).	Develop ... explanations ... using evidence. (NRC, 1996, A: 1/4, 5-8) Think critically and logically to make the relationships between evidence and explanation. (NRC 1996, A: 1/5, 5-8)	Students construct scientific explanations stating a claim whether a chemical reaction occurred, evidence in the form of properties, and reasoning that a chemical reaction is a process in which old substances interact to form new substances with different properties than the old substances.

Description of Stuff Unit

Stuff engages students in the study of substances and properties, the nature of chemical reactions, and the conservation of matter. In the *Stuff* unit, we contextualized the concepts and scientific inquiry in real-world experience by focusing on making soap from fat or lard and sodium hydroxide (making new stuff from old stuff). Students complete a number of investigations where they revisit soap and fat throughout the unit. These cycles help students delve deeper into the key learning goals including both target science content and the scientific inquiry practices such as the analysis of data and construction of scientific explanations.

Initially, students explore two unknowns (soap and fat) to introduce the concepts of substance and property. In order to develop students understanding of properties, they investigate solubility, melting point, and density for soap and fat. Next, students explore a number of chemical reactions by observing macroscopic phenomena, including making soap from fat. Finally, students build on their understandings by exploring what happens to mass during chemical reactions. Throughout the unit, students alternate between exploring the macroscopic phenomena and using molecular models to explain the phenomena. The unit ends with testing the properties of their homemade soap to determine whether or not they created a new substance.

Supporting Students' Understanding of Scientific Explanations

To support students' construction of scientific explanation we embedded several strategies into our instructional unit including: making the rationale behind explanation explicit, modeling how to construct explanations, providing students with opportunities to engage in explanation construction, and including written scaffolds on students' investigation sheets.

Revealing the tacit framework of scientific explanation can facilitate students' explanation construction (Reiser et al., 2001). We accomplish this through both written scaffolds in the instructional sheets and encouraging teacher practices that help students understand this framework. Initially, teachers introduce the framework for scientific explanation during a focal lesson where they discuss the importance of explanation construction and define the three components of scientific explanation. In our previous work, we have found that when teachers discuss the rationale behind scientific explanations, that students construct stronger explanations (Lizotte, McNeill, & Krajcik, 2004).

Also, during the focal lesson teachers model how to construct an explanation. Teacher modeling of scientific inquiry practices can result in more effective learning environments (Crawford, 2000; Tabak & Reiser, 1997). Specifically, for scientific explanation modeling can help students engage in this practice (Lizotte, McNeill, & Krajcik, 2004). After the initial focal lesson, we encourage teachers to continue modeling explanation construction throughout the unit. The student readers also include both strong and weak examples of scientific explanations for the teacher and students to critique.

In order for students to learn how to evaluate data, they need numerous opportunities to evaluate rich, complex models of data (Chinn & Brewer, 2001; Lehrer & Schauble, 2002). We assume that students also need numerous opportunities to engage in scientific explanations. Over the course of the unit, students construct at least 10 explanations.

Written scaffolds embedded in student materials can scaffold students' development of scientific inquiry practices, modeling, and metacognitive skills and knowledge (White & Frederiksen, 1998). Our work builds off of this research on written scaffolds as well as our previous research where we found that fading written scaffolds resulted in students constructing stronger explanations (McNeill et al., 2006). We provide scaffolds in the student investigation sheets that initially define the three components of scientific explanations (i.e., claim, evidence, and reasoning) and then fade over time.

METHOD

Participants

For this study, we report findings from teachers in urban and suburban sites in the Midwest that enacted the *Stuff* unit. Teachers and students in the urban site came from a large urban district implementing reform-based curricula. The teachers and students were predominately African American with the

TABLE 10.2
Participants from the 2003–2004 School Year

| | 2003–2004 School Year | | |
Site	Urban	Suburban	Total
Schools	7	1	8
Teachers	7	3	10
Classrooms	29	5	34
Students	955	79	1034

students coming from lower to lower-middle income families. The teachers and students from the suburban site were from an independent middle school in a large college town also involved in implementing reform-based curricula. The teachers and the majority of the students were Caucasian with the students coming from middle to upper-middle income families. It was the second time for three teachers in the urban school and for the three teachers in the suburban site enacting the *Stuff* unit. All teachers completed lessons necessary for the study, with the time of enactment ranging from 5 ½ weeks to 8 weeks. Table 10.2 shows the breakdown of teachers, classroom and students in the two sites for the 2003–2004 school year.

Assessment Data

All students completed identical pre- and post-test measures that included 15 multiple-choice items and 4 open-ended responses. Only students who completed all parts of the test were included in the analysis. Due to high absenteeism and mobility in the urban schools, a number of students did not complete both the pre- and post-tests. Consequently, our analysis only includes 700 of the students.

Multiple-choice responses were scored and tallied for a maximum possible score of 15. We developed rubrics to score the 4 open-ended items. Maximum score on the open-ended items was 15. All questions were scored by one rater. We then randomly sampled 20% of the open-ended test items and a second independent rater scored them. For each of the four open-ended test items our estimates of inter-rater reliability were calculated by percent agreements. Our inter-rater agreement was above 93% for each component (i.e., claim, evidence, and reasoning) of each question.

The multiple-choice items covered the three key learning goals of the unit: substance and properties, chemical reactions, and conservation of mass.

Appendix A includes four sample multiple-choice items that align with the substance and properties and chemical reaction learning goals, which are the focus of this analysis. Appendix B includes the open-ended items that asked students to write scientific explanations for these two different content areas. Both items include appropriate evidence (e.g., density and melting point) that should be used to answer the question and inappropriate evidence (e.g., mass and volume) that is not relevant to the particular task.

To assess student understanding of scientific explanation, we developed a *base* rubric to use across different content areas (Harris et al., 2006). We used our base rubrics to develop *specific* rubrics for assessing students on each learning and assessment task for our chemistry unit. Appendix C includes the specific rubrics we used to score the two explanation tasks on the pre- and post-test. The rubric includes the three components of scientific explanation (claim, evidence, and reasoning) and discusses the criteria for different levels of each component. For example, for the highest score for evidence, students need to include appropriate evidence that addresses the particular task, sufficient evidence in that they include enough data to support the claim, and not include any inappropriate evidence. We calculated students' total evidence scores by subtracting the number of appropriate pieces evidence minus one if they included any inappropriate evidence.[1]

We discuss three examples from the substance and property explanation to demonstrate how we used the rubrics to score students' responses. Student A provides an example of a strong explanation.[2]

> Student A: Liquid 1 and 4 are indeed the same substance. Looking at this data, the properties include density, color, and melting point. Mass is not a property. Density, color, and M.P. are all the same for Liquid 1 and 4. Because all of these properties are the same, 1 and 4 are the same substance.

This student provides an accurate claim that Liquid 1 and 4 are the same substance. She provides three pieces of appropriate evidence (density, color, and melting point) and no inappropriate evidence. She also includes the highest level of reasoning because she states that the same substances have the same properties.

---

[1]However, we did not give students negative evidence scores. If they received a zero for appropriate evidence and a one for inappropriate evidence, their total evidence score was still recorded as a zero. Yet we kept track that these students had received a one for inappropriate evidence for other analyses.

[2]Students' original spelling, grammar, and punctuation are intact in this and all future examples.

The second example, Student B, provides an example of a weak explanation.

> Student B: No, the liquids are not the same substance because some are different and some are the same like Liquid 1 and Liquid 4 is just that Liquid 4 has different mass than Liquid 1. Some has color like Liquid 1, Liquid 2, and Liquid 4, they all has no color but Liquid 3 the color is silver. And also Liquid 2, and Liquid 3 has different density than Liquid 1 & 2. Liquids 2 & 3 has different melting point.

This student received zeros for claim, appropriate evidence, and reasoning. The student received a score for inappropriate evidence because he included mass as evidence for determining whether two liquids are the same substance.

The final example, Student C, provides a mixed response. The response includes both correct and incorrect components.

> Student C: Out of the 4 liquids, none of them are alike. They aren't alike because the density of 2 & 3 are different from 1 & 4. The color of Liquid 3 is different from 2, 1, & 4. The mass of 3 & 4 is different from 1 & 2. The melting point of 1 & 4 is different from 2 & 3. In order for these liquids to be the same substances, they must have the same properties.

This student received a zero for claim and evidence, because she did not provide the claim that Liquids 1 and 4 are the same substance or provide any evidence to support why the substances are the same. Student C received a score for inappropriate evidence, because she included mass as important for determining whether two liquids are the same substance. Although the student receives low scores for claim and evidence, she did receive a high score for reasoning. The last sentence includes a correct scientific statement that in order for two substances to be the same, they must have the same properties. This example illustrates how the rubric codes each component independent of the score received on the other two components. Even though Student C was unable to construct an accurate claim or evidence, she did receive credit in her reasoning for having some understanding of the underlying general scientific principle. Consequently, the rubric allows us to tease apart a student's understanding of a particular component, though a drawback is that it does not provide a holistic score of the overall coherence of the explanation.

RESULTS AND DISCUSSION

In this study, we examine when students use appropriate evidence and when they use inappropriate evidence to support their claims. To address this overarching question, our analyses address the following subquestions:

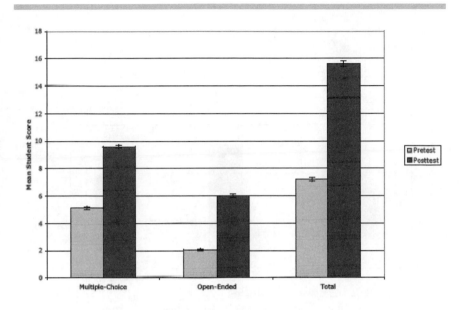

Figure 10.1   Overall student learning gains (n = 700).

1. Do students achieve learning gains for both the science content and the different components of scientific explanations during the unit?
2. What difficulties do middle school students have using appropriate evidence when constructing scientific explanations?
3. How does the content area and task influence students' use of appropriate and inappropriate evidence?

We then explore possible causes for students' use of appropriate and inappropriate evidence.

Student Learning Gains

Before examining students' learning for scientific explanations, we first examined whether students learned the key learning goals addressed in the unit. Figure 10.1 provides the student mean scores for the multiple-choice items, the open-ended questions, and the total test score for the pre- and post-tests. We conducted one-tailed paired t-tests to test the significance of students' learning gains. Students achieved significant learning gains on the multiple-choice, $t(699) = 37.19, p < .001$, open-ended, $t(699) = 33.96, p < .001$, and total test score, $t(699) = 42.85, p < .001$. The effects sizes for student learning for

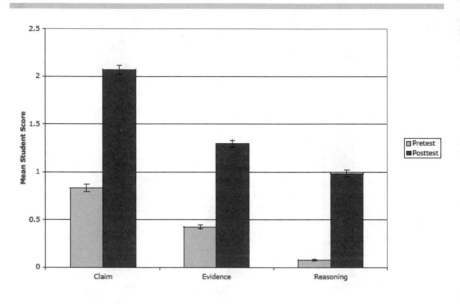

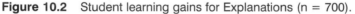

Figure 10.2   Student learning gains for Explanations (n = 700).

the multiple-choice, open-ended and total scores were 1.81, 2.05 and 2.34 respectively.[3] This suggests that students had a much stronger understanding of the content and scientific inquiry practices after the instructional unit.

Next, we examined students' learning for the evidence-based scientific explanations they constructed. Figure 10.2 provides the means for student scores for the different components of scientific explanation. Again, we conducted one-tailed paired t-tests to test the significance of students' learning gains. Students achieved significant learning gains on claim, $t(699) = 23.93$, $p < .001$, evidence, $t(699) = 22.43$, $p < .001$, and reasoning, $t(699) = 25.77$, $p < .001$.

The effect sizes were 1.24 for claim, 1.51 for evidence, and 3.75 for reasoning. Interestingly, in the previous two enactments we found that students' reasoning was consistently much lower than their claims and evidence (McNeill et al., 2006; McNeill et al., 2003). Consequently, we made revisions to the instructional unit and professional development to help both teachers and students with the reasoning component. The results from the present study show that students' reasoning scores had greater learning gains and were closer to their evidence score by the end of the unit than in previous

---

[3]Effect Size was calculated by dividing the difference between post-test and pretest mean scores by the pretest standard deviation.

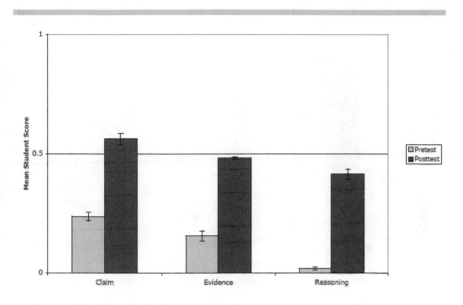

Figure 10.3   Learning gains for substance and property explanations (n = 700).

studies. However, students' evidence and reasoning were still lower than their claim scores and low at an absolute level. These results suggest that providing evidence and reasoning continued to challenge students. Consequently, in this study we further unpack potential causes of these difficulties.

Students' Explanation Scores By Content Area

We examined whether students' learning gains and overall performance for scientific explanations differed by content area. Figures 10.3 and 10.4 provide the breakdown for claim, evidence, and reasoning for two content areas: substance/property and chemical reactions.

For both explanations, students achieved significant learning gains for claim, evidence, and reasoning ($ps < .001$).

Comparing the post-test values for the two explanations shows that students scored higher on the chemical reaction claim than the substance and property claim.[4] Yet they scored lower on the chemical reaction evidence and reasoning. We found these results surprising. We would have predicted that if

---

[4]We weighted students claim, evidence, and reasoning scores so that the maximum score was 1.25 for each component for both the substance and property explanation and the chemical reaction explanation.

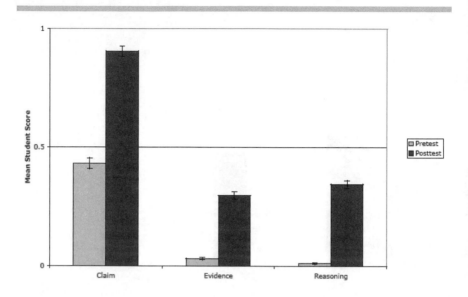

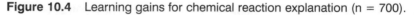

Figure 10.4   Learning gains for chemical reaction explanation (n = 700).

students scored higher on claim, they would also score higher on evidence and reasoning because even though we coded each component independently students use the evidence and reasoning to construct their claims. To further unpack this trend, we examined students' use of both appropriate and inappropriate evidence.

Students' Use of Inappropriate Evidence

We explored whether students used inappropriate evidence in their explanations and whether this differed for the two content areas. In examining students' responses, we found that of the 700 students, 125 provided inappropriate evidence for the substance and property explanation, whereas 184 students provided inappropriate evidence for the chemical reaction explanation (see Table 10.3). This suggests that students were more likely to include inappropriate evidence for the chemical reaction explanation. This is one possible reason for why students' evidence scores were lower for the chemical reaction explanation than the substance and property explanation. The lower total evidence scores might have been a result of this greater use of inappropriate evidence, because we calculated the total evidence score by subtracting the inappropriate evidence from the appropriate evidence.

TABLE 10.3
Students' Use of Inappropriate Evidence in Explanations (n = 700)

			Substance and Property Explanation		
			0^a	1^b	Total
Chemical Reaction	0^a	Count	436	80	516
Explanation		% of Total	62.3%	11.4%	73.7%
	1^b	Count	141	43	184
		% of Total	19.9%	6.4%	26.3%
Total		Count	579	124	703
		% of Total	82.1%	17.9%	100.0%

a.   0 = Student did not use inappropriate evidence
b.   1 = Student did use inappropriate evidence

Table 10.3 shows that 43 students provided inappropriate evidence for both explanations. Overall the majority of students included inappropriate evidence in only one question or the other. For the substance and property explanation, 80 students provided inappropriate evidence that did not for the chemical reaction question, whereas for the chemical reaction question 141 students provided inappropriate evidence that did not on the substance and property question.

Consequently, we examined which students provided inappropriate evidence and which students provided appropriate evidence for the two questions. By exploring students' use of evidence, we hoped to come up with some initial hypothesis of why students provided inappropriate evidence. Such findings would allow us to provide guidance to the field in how to help students provide appropriate evidence.

Substance and Property Explanation.   The substance and property explanation item (Appendix B) includes three pieces of appropriate evidence (density, color, and melting point) and one piece of inappropriate evidence (mass). We were interested in how similar and different students were who included the inappropriate evidence (i.e., mass) in their responses compared to those who did not include inappropriate evidence in terms of their claims, reasoning, and content knowledge. We predicted that students who did not include inappropriate evidence would have stronger claims, reasoning, and content knowledge.

To test whether the students differed, we conducted a two-way analysis of variance (ANOVA) where we split students into four groups based on their use of evidence on the post-test for the substance and property explanation. The four groups consisted of students who used: (1) No appropriate evidence and

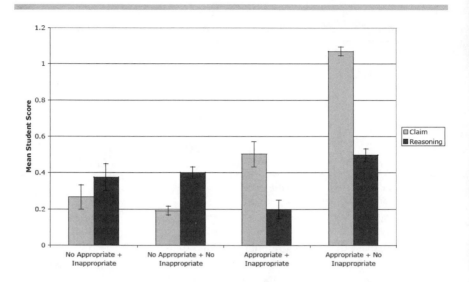

Figure 10.5 Substance and property claim and reasoning scores by students' use of evidence.

inappropriate evidence, (2) No appropriate evidence and no inappropriate evidence, (3) Appropriate evidence and inappropriate evidence, and (4) Appropriate evidence and no inappropriate evidence. The results from the two-way ANOVA for students' post-test claim and reasoning scores by their use of appropriate and inappropriate evidence are shown in Figure 10.5. There is a significant difference in the scores for the four groups of students for claim, F (3, 696) = 191.287, $p < .001$, and reasoning, F (3, 696) = 5.991, $p < .001$.

Students who used appropriate evidence (i.e., density, color, and melting point), but did not use inappropriate evidence (i.e., mass) had the highest claim and reasoning scores. This matches our predictions of what we thought would occur. Even though the rubric scores each component independent of the others, students typically base their claims on their evidence and reasoning. Consequently, we would expect that students with higher claims would also have higher evidence and reasoning scores. For the substance and property item, the use of appropriate evidence appears to be particularly important for constructing the valid claim that Liquids 1 and 4 are the same substance. The two groups of students that used appropriate evidence scored higher than the two groups that did not use appropriate evidence.

We also explored if a relationship existed between students' understanding of the content and their use of appropriate and inappropriate evidence. We used

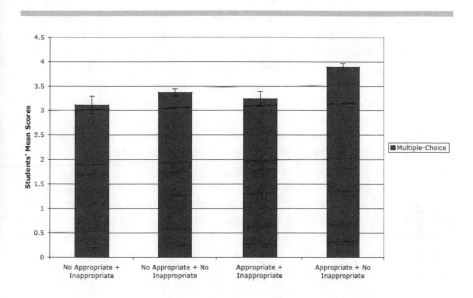

Figure 10.6   Substance and property multiple-choice scores by students' use of evidence.

students' scores on the multiple-choice items on the post-test for the substance and property items as a measure of their understanding of the content. To test whether the four groups of students differed in their understanding of the content, we completed a two-way ANOVA for students' multiple-choice scores by their use of appropriate and inappropriate evidence. Figure 10.6 displays the results from this analysis. A significant difference exists for the four groups of students' multiple-choice scores, $F(3, 696) = 12.947$, $p < .001$. Students who used appropriate evidence, but did not use inappropriate evidence had the highest content score. This suggests a relationship between students' understanding of the content and their ability to use appropriate evidence. Overall, students' scores on the substance/property multiple-choice items were significantly correlated with their substance/property explanations, $rs(700) = 0.26$ for claim, 0.23 for evidence, and 0.35 for reasoning, $ps < .001$. Students who had higher multiple-choice scores in a content area also had higher explanation scores in that area.

Students who have a stronger understanding of the content are more likely to include appropriate evidence and less likely to include inappropriate evidence. Furthermore, students who include appropriate evidence and do not include inappropriate evidence are more likely to construct stronger claims and reasoning.

Chemical Reaction Explanation. We expected to find similar results to the substance and property explanation for the chemical reaction explanation. We predicted that students who did include appropriate evidence and did not include inappropriate evidence would have stronger claims, reasoning, and content knowledge. In this explanation item (Appendix B), there are three pieces of appropriate evidence (density, melting point, and solubility) and two pieces of inappropriate evidence (mass and volume). We categorized students as including inappropriate evidence if they used either or both mass and volume.

Again, we split students into four groups based on their use of evidence: (1) No appropriate evidence and inappropriate evidence, (2) No appropriate evidence and no inappropriate evidence, (3) Appropriate evidence and inappropriate evidence, and (4) Appropriate evidence and no inappropriate evidence. To test whether the four groups differed we completed a two-way ANOVA for students' post-test claim and reasoning scores by their use of appropriate and inappropriate evidence. A significant difference in the scores for the four groups of students exists for claim, $F (3, 696) = 42.979, p < .001$, and reasoning, $F (3, 696) = 7.311, p < .001$ (Fig. 10.7).

The trend for students' claim scores is different than in the substance and property explanation. Although students who included no appropriate and no inappropriate evidence had lower claim scores, the claim scores for the other three groups of students did not differ. Particularly noteworthy is that students who included inappropriate evidence, but no appropriate evidence had similar claim scores to students who included appropriate evidence, but no inappropriate evidence. This suggests that students were able to use inappropriate evidence (i.e., mass and weight) to come up with the correct claim that a chemical reaction did occur. Students reasoning scores were similar to the substance and property explanation. Students who used appropriate evidence, but no inappropriate evidence again provided the strongest reasoning.

We also tested whether the four groups of students differed in their understanding of the content by completing a two-way ANOVA for students' multiple-choice scores by their use of appropriate and inappropriate evidence. Figure 10.8 displays the results from this analysis. There is a significant difference, $F (3, 696) = 29.335, p < .001$. Similar to the substance and property explanation, students who used appropriate evidence, but who did not use inappropriate evidence had higher content knowledge. Again, we also see that students' scores on the chemical reaction multiple-choice items were significantly correlated with their chemical reaction explanations, $rs (700) = 0.23$ for claim, 0.33 for evidence, and 0.29 for reasoning, $ps < .001$.

The reasoning and content analysis showed similar trends across the two explanations, but students' use of appropriate and inappropriate evidence to support their claims varied. Although a relationship existed between using appropriate evidence and creating the correct claim for the substance and

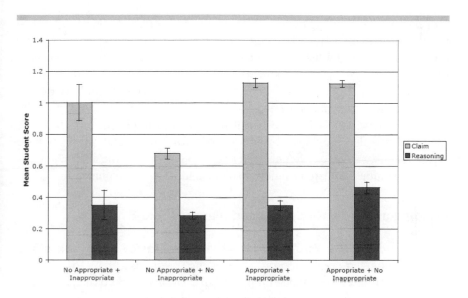

Figure 10.7   Chemical reaction claim and reasoning scores by students' use of evidence.

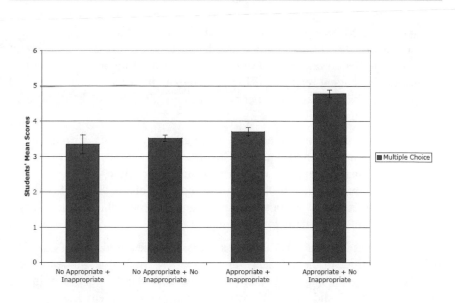

Figure 10.8   Chemical reaction multiple-choice scores by students' use of evidence.

property explanation, that same relationship did not exist for the chemical reaction explanation. For the chemical reaction explanation, students who provided no evidence had lower claim scores, yet students who used inappropriate evidence were just as likely to construct the correct claim as those who use appropriate evidence. In order to investigate what might have caused these students to use inappropriate evidence in the chemical reaction explanation, we reexamined the assessment items and examples of student work. This analysis also provides possible reasons for why overall students have higher claims, yet lower evidence and reasoning scores for the chemical reaction explanation compared to the substance and property explanation.

Exploration of Why Students Used Inappropriate Evidence

Differences in the Wording of the Assessment Task. First we examined why students who used inappropriate evidence were less likely to make the correct claim for the substance property explanation yet more likely to make the correct claim for the chemical reaction explanation. Looking back at these two explanation questions (Appendix B), we realized that for the chemical reaction question students can actually use the inappropriate evidence to make the correct claim. Students can examine the question and see that the mass and volume changed. Consequently, they can claim that a chemical reaction occurred because the mass and/or volume changed from before stirring and heating to after stirring and heating. In this case, we gave them credit for providing the correct claim even though they used incorrect evidence to get there. The student response below is one example of a student who used inappropriate evidence to construct an accurate claim for the chemical reaction explanation.

> Student D: A chemical reaction occured when Carlos stirred and heated butanic acid and butanol. Chemical reaction—is when two or more substances interact to make a new substance. Before the reaction the mass of butanic acid was 9.78 g and the butanol was 8.22. After the reaction the mass of the butanic acid was 1.74 g and the butanol was 2.00 g Therefore a chemical reactions did occur.

This student used the data that the mass changed to determine that a chemical reaction occurred. In the substance and property explanation, students were less likely to use the inappropriate evidence to make the correct claim. In this question, Liquid 1 and Liquid 2 have the same mass, whereas Liquid 1 and Liquid 4 have the same density, color, and melting point. Consequently, a student who focuses on mass is less likely to make an accurate claim. For example, one student responded:

Student E: No. None of the liquid was the same but Liquid 1 and 4 would have been the same substance if their mass was the same.

By including mass, this student decided that Liquids 1 and 4 were not the same substance. The use of inappropriate evidence results in an incorrect claim.

This provides an important lesson for both the design and evaluation of assessment items. It is important to consider the different information that can be used to construct the correct answer for a question. Although we consciously included inappropriate evidence in the assessment items because we were interested in how students would use the evidence, we did not consider that the inappropriate evidence could be used to construct the correct claim for the chemical reaction item. Because the inappropriate evidence was included in an open-ended item, students' written responses offered some insight into their use of the inappropriate evidence. Designers need to be particularly careful when including inappropriate evidence in a multiple-choice item to consider how a student might use the evidence.

Differences in What Counts as Evidence.   The question still remains why students were more likely to include inappropriate evidence in their explanations for chemical reactions (see Table 10.1). One possibility, is again, the wording of the question. For the chemical reaction explanation, students might have known that they were looking for whether "a change" occurred. Because all five measurements (density, melting point, mass, volume, and solubility) changed, students could use all of the measurements to make the claim so they might not have considered the appropriateness of each data point. For the substance and property explanation, students might have known that they were looking for "similar" measurements. In the assessment item, different measurements are the same for different pairs of liquids. Mass and color are the same for Liquids 1 and 2, whereas density, color and melting point are the same for Liquids 1 and 4. This difference may have encouraged students to think more deeply about the appropriateness of each data point for determining whether two liquids are the same substance.

Another possibility is that students' understanding of what counts as evidence for a chemical reaction was not as stronger as their understanding of what counts as evidence for two substances to be the same. Understanding chemical reactions builds off of their understanding of substance and properties and it may be more difficult for students. Students may have understood that mass and/or volume are not properties to differentiate substances yet they still thought they were signs of a chemical reaction. For example, the following are one student's responses to both the substance and property question and the chemical reaction question.

Student G:

Substance and Property: Liquid 1 and 4 are of the same substance. Because all of the properties are the same, color, density, and melting point are the same. Mass is the same, but it does not count.

Chemical Reaction: When the density and the mass changed and went up higher that showed that a chemical reaction occurred.

It is interesting that this student did not think that mass "counted" for determining whether two substances were the same, yet he thought it was important for determining whether a chemical reaction occurred. There were, in fact, 141 students who thought mass and/or volume were important for determining whether a chemical reaction occurred, but did not think that mass was important for determining whether two liquids are the same substance. Perhaps students thought that although mass and volume are not properties, they are still somehow a sign of a chemical reaction. The majority of students, who used mass in their chemical reaction explanations, but not in their substance explanations, did not explicitly articulate why they were making that distinction. However, there were a couple of students who described why they thought it was important to include mass and volume as evidence for the chemical reaction explanation, but not for the substance and property explanation. The following response offers one example.

Student H:

Substance and Property: Liquid 1 and Liquid 4 are the same substances. They have the same density, 0.93 g/cm^3. They are both colorless. They both have the same melting point of -98° C. The only different about them is their mass, but mass is not a property because it varies with sample sizes. The evidence shows that Liquid 1 and Liquid 4 are the same substances because they have the same properties.

Chemical Reaction: A chemical reaction did occur. Evidence of this is that neither of the beginning substances share the same amount of density with either of the end substances. Also, the melting points changed from $-7.9°C$ and $89.5°C$ to $-91.5°C$ and $0.0°C$. Another piece of evidence is that the mass changed from 10.18 cm^3 and 10.15 cm^3 to 2.00 cm^3 and 2.00 cm^3. The solubility also changed. Because the mass and volume decreased so much, I think that gas formed. This data is evidence of a chemical reaction because properties changed.

This suggests that when the student read the data table for the chemical reaction explanation, she thought the differences in mass and volume told her about whether a gas formed. The student interpreted the data for after mixing as the total mass and volume of Layer A and Layer B instead of realizing that the text states that Carlos took a sample of Layer A and Layer B.

Students might have been confused by mass and volume because of the investigations they completed during the unit. Students performed a couple of investigations that included chemical reactions that produced a gas. For example, students combined sodium bicarbonate (baking soda) and calcium chloride (road salt) with a solution of phenol red in a sealed plastic bag and then observed three major changes: temperature change, color change, and the bag inflated with a gas (carbon dioxide).[5] The following transcript is from a classroom discussion of this reaction. The transcript focuses on one group of three students who have just combined the substances in the plastic bag.

S1: Hey stop. Hey it turned yellow.

S2: It is changing colors.

S3: Mrs., Ms., Ms. Hill, it is changing to yellow now.

S1: It turned into yellow.

S2: Come on.

S3: Yeah. It is hot right here. Feel right there.

Teacher: Ok. What else is going on? We need to write down our observations. Yours is starting to get hot? Oh.

S2: There are bubbles. There is a temperature change.

Teacher: What's going on with the bag?

S2: It is shrinking. (pause). It is airing up. I mean.

Teacher: Write down our observations (addressing the whole class).

S3: It looks like—

S2: It is getting cold.

Teacher: Oh. So you are telling me that the color does not turn yellow? (Addressing a different group)

S2: And the bag is blown up.

Teacher: All right, wait we need to be writing this down. It started to bubble.

S2: There is fizz, temperature change (Quietly talking while writing).

Teacher: Wait a minute. Wait these bags are starting to get bigger to me.

S4: Yup. It is starting to be inflated.

Multiple Students: (Laugh.)

Teacher: Oh. I like that word.

---

[5]Although the students do not make this distinction, two different chemical reactions actually occur in this investigation: (1) sodium bicarbonate and calcium chloride form sodium chloride, calcium carbonate, carbon dioxide, and water; and (2) carbon dioxide, water, and phenol red form hydrogen-carbonate ion and altered phenol red. Phenol red is an acid/base indicator and changes from red to yellow because of the altered acidity of the solution.

Both the students and teacher discussed how the bag inflated or got bigger. Students associated this change in size with a chemical reaction. In retrospect, the curriculum did not clearly distinguish between the volume and mass of the chemical reaction as a whole system and the volume and mass of individual substances. Hence, students may have been confused by when mass and volume count as evidence. From their experiences with substances, students may have understood that mass and volume are not properties so they are inappropriate evidence to determine whether two liquids are the same substance. They may also have understood that mass is conserved in a closed system, but can change in an open system. Yet they may have been unclear of the role of mass and volume to determine whether a chemical reaction occurs. Students' responses for the chemical reaction explanation suggest that a number of students thought that a change in mass and volume counted as evidence for a chemical reaction.

CONCLUSION

Students do not typically construct strong explanations where they support their knowledge claims (Sadler, 2004). Yet constructing explanations can be a powerful way for students to actively construct knowledge. By engaging in an instructional unit where students received an explicit framework for scientific explanation, multiple opportunities to construct explanations and support during those learning tasks, students created stronger explanations by the end of the unit. In post-unit assessment tasks, students provided stronger claims and justification for those claims including evidence and reasoning. In contrast to our previous research (McNeill et al., 2006; McNeill et al., 2003), we see that students reasoning scores started to approach their evidence scores by the end of the unit. These improved learning gains for reasoning may be the result of our revisions to the unit in which we made the reasoning component more explicit for students and provided more detailed scaffolds in the student investigation sheets.

Specifically, in this study we examined when students used appropriate evidence and when they used inappropriate evidence. Similar to other research (Sandoval, 2003; Sandoval & Reiser, 1997), we found that students had difficulty including appropriate evidence to support their claims. At the end of the unit, a number of students still included inappropriate evidence in their explanations. We also found that students' ability to construct scientific explanations depended on the context. Students' ability to reason from data depends on the context, particularly in terms of students' prior understanding of the theoretical context (Masnick, Klahr, & Morris, this volume). Both students' understanding of the content knowledge and their understanding of the scientific inquiry practice can influence their ability to complete a practice. Individuals' lack of conceptual understanding can impede their ability to reason in science (Sadler, 2004). For the substance and property as well as the chemical reaction explanations, we found that students with stronger content understanding constructed stronger explanations and were less likely to use inappropriate evidence in their explanations. This suggests that strong content knowledge is important to appropriately take part in scientific inquiry practices such as accurately constructing scientific explanations. Students may be unable to apply their understanding of a scientific inquiry practice to a context without an understanding of the particular science content. In our current research, we are exploring how both domain specific knowledge and general knowledge of scientific explanations influence students' ability to construct scientific explanations, as well as the roles of curriculum scaffolds and teacher practices in students' learning of both types of knowledge.

In this study, we found that students' use of evidence varied for the two different assessment tasks. Specifically, students were more likely to include inappropriate evidence in their explanations for the chemical reaction assessment task. We conjecture that there are two possible causes for students' use of inappropriate evidence for this task: the wording of the assessment task and difficulty knowing what counts as evidence for chemical reactions.

In assessing students' ability to construct explanations or analyze data, it is important to consider what knowledge is needed to accurately answer the assessment task. In constructing the chemical reaction explanation item, we did not consider that the inappropriate evidence could be used to support an accurate claim for the question. Project 2061 has created an analysis procedure for assessment items in which they determine the alignment to a learning goal based on whether the content is both necessary and sufficient to answer the question (Stern & Ahlgren, 2002). In the chemical reaction task, knowing that changes in mass and volume are not always evidence of a chemical reaction (e.g., could be the result of a phase change) was not necessary to construct the correct claim that a chemical reaction occurred. Rather students could believe that changes in mass and volume are evidence of a chemical reaction and actually construct the correct claim. This differed compared to the substance and property item where the mass data suggested that the wrong two liquids were the same substance, Liquids 1 and 2. This suggests that it is important to consider what knowledge is needed to construct the correct claim for an assessment task. Otherwise, an assessment item may not be testing the desired knowledge.

Students' use of inappropriate evidence in the chemical reaction item may also have been influenced by what they thought counted as evidence of a chemical reaction. When interpreting data, people take into consideration whether they can imagine a mechanism that might account for any patterns in the data (Koslowski, 1996). In the chemical reaction task, students may have attempted to come up with a mechanism for the decreasing mass and volume. In their previous experiments in class, they found that when chemical reactions produce gas that a change in mass and volume can occur. Connecting this classroom experience to the change in mass and volume in the chemical reaction assessment task may be why more students used inappropriate data for this task compared to the substance and property task.

Students associated "change" with chemical reactions and they could imagine a plausible mechanism to account for this change. It may be that students had a beginning understanding of chemical reactions that involved change, but had not yet differentiated what does and what does not change in a chemical reaction. Furthermore, understanding chemical reactions builds from an understanding of substance and properties. The chemical reaction assessment task requires more sophisticated thinking and links to other related knowledge structures, because it requires that students first have an understanding of properties and substance. This may make it more difficult for students to understand what counts as evidence for a chemical reaction to occur and may be why more students included inappropriate evidence in their chemical reaction explanation.

By having students construct explanations where they provide not only their claims, but also their evidence and reasoning, we obtained greater insight into student thinking. If this assessment task had been a multiple-choice item or only asked students to state whether a chemical reaction occurred, we could not tell that a number of students were in fact using inappropriate evidence to create the claim. Having students construct scientific explanations can be an important tool to help make students thinking visible for both researchers and teachers. Encouraging students to articulate their evidence and reasoning provides researchers more information about how to revise instructional materials and provides teachers with important formative assessment. Formative assessments allow teachers to use the evidence from the assessment to change their instructional plans to better meet the needs of their students (Black, 2003).

Students' success in using evidence depends on both the content and context of the learning task. In previous iterations of revising the curriculum, we added activities and phenomena to specifically address that mass and volume are not properties and cannot be used to differentiate substances. We have not explicitly addressed why you would not rely on mass and volume to determine whether a chemical reaction occurred. In future revisions of the curriculum, we plan to address this student difficulty. We hope to include greater support during the unit to help students understand what counts as evidence for chemical reactions. Furthermore, we plan to revise the chemical reaction assessment task so that mass and volume can no longer be used to construct the correct claim. Although we plan to continue including inappropriate evidence in our items, we need to think more carefully about how students may use that evidence in their responses and what it means when they include inappropriate evidence.

We also need to continue providing students with practice to both use evidence in their explanations and critique other people's use of evidence in explanation. If our goal is to help students develop competent participation in a science infused world (McGinn & Roth, 1999), success on one learning or assessment task is not sufficient. Analyzing data and using data to support claims is a complex task that varies depending on the context. Students need considerable practice to understand what counts as evidence to support knowledge claims and how that evidence changes depending on the content and context of the task.

ACKNOWLEDGMENTS

The research reported here was supported in part by the National Science Foundation (REC 0101780 and 0227557). Any opinions expressed in this work are those of the authors and do not necessarily represent either those of the funding agency, the University of Michigan, or Boston College.

REFERENCES

American Association for the Advancement of Science. (1993). *Benchmarks for science literacy.* New York: Oxford University Press.

Bell, P., & Linn, M. (2000). Scientific arguments as learning artifacts: Designing for learning from the web with KIE. *International Journal of Science Education, 22 (8),* 797–817.

Black, P. (2003). The importance of everyday assessment. In J. M. Atkin & J. E. Coffey (Eds.), *Everyday assessment in the science classroom* (pp. 1–11). Arlington, VA: NSTA Press.

Blumenfeld, P. C., Marx, R. W., Patrick, H. Krajcik, J., & Soloway, E. (1997). Teaching for understanding. In B. J. Biddle, T. L. Good, & I. F. Goodson (Eds.), *International handbook of teachers and teaching* (pp. 819–878). Dordrecht, The Netherlands: Kluwer.

Bransford, J. D., Brown, A. L., & Cocking, R. R. (Eds.). (2000). *How people learn: Brain, mind, experience, and school.* Washington, DC: National Research Council.

Brown, A. L., Ash, D., Rutherford, M., Nakagawa, K., Gordon, A., & Campione, J. C. (1993). Distributed expertise in the classroom. In G. Salomon (Ed.), *Distributed cognitions: Psychological and educational considerations* (pp. 188–228). Cambridge, UK: Cambridge University Press.

Chinn, C. A., & Brewer, W. F. (2001). Models of data: A theory of how people evaluate data. *Cognition and Instruction, 19,* 323–393.

Crawford, B. A. (2000). Embracing the essence of inquiry: New roles for science teachers. *Journal of Research in Science Teaching, 37*(9), 916–937.

Driver, R., Asoko, H., Leach, J., Mortimer, E., & Scott, P. (1994). Constructing scientific knowledge in the classroom. *Educational Researcher, 23*(7), 5–12.

Driver, R., Newton, P., & Osborne, J. (2000). Establishing the norms of scientific argumentation in classrooms. *Science Education, 84(3),* 287–312.

Harris, C. J., McNeill, K. L., Lizotte, D. L., Marx, R. W., & Krajcik, J. (2006). Usable assessments for teaching science content and inquiry standards. In M. McMahon, P. Simmons, R. Sommers, D., DeBaets, & F. Crowley (Eds.), *Assessment in science: Practical experiences and education research* (pp. 67–88). Arlington, VA: National Science Teachers Association Press.

Hogan, K., & Maglienti, M. (2001). Comparing the epistemological underpinnings of students' and scientists' reasoning about conclusions. *Journal of Research in Science Teaching, 38*(6), 663–687.

Jiménez-Aleixandre, M. P., Rodríguez, A. B., & Duschl, R. A. (2000). "Doing the lesson" or "doing science": Argument in high school genetics. *Science Education, 84,* 757–792.

Kanari, Z., & Millar, R. (2004). Reasoning from data: How students collect and interpret data in science investigations. *Journal of Research in Science Teaching, 31*(7), 748–769.

Koslowski, B. (1996). *Theory and evidence: The development of scientific reasoning.* Cambridge, MA: MIT Press.

Krajcik, J., Blumenfeld, P., Marx, R., & Soloway, E. (2000). Instructional, curricular, and technological supports for inquiry in science classrooms. In J. Minstrell & E. v. Zee (Eds.), *Inquiring into inquiry learning and teaching in science* (pp. 283–315). Washington DC: AAAS.

Kuhn, D. (1993). Science as argument: Implications for teaching and learning scientific thinking. *Science Education, 77,* 319–338.

Lave, J., & Wenger, E. (1991). *Situated learning: Legitimate peripheral participation.* Cambridge, UK: Cambridge University Press.

Lee, H.-S., & Songer, N. B. (2004, April). *Longitudinal knowledge development: Scaffolds for Inquiry.* Paper presented at the annual meeting of the American Educational Research Association, San Diego, CA.

Lehrer, R., & Schauble, L. (Eds.). (2002). *Investigating real data in the classroom: Expanding children's understanding of math and science.* New York: Teachers College Press.

Lemke, J. (1990). *Talking science: Language, learning, and values.* Norwood, NJ: Ablex.

Lizotte, D. J., McNeill, K. L., & Krajcik, J. (2004). Teacher practices that support students' construction of scientific explanations in middle school classrooms. In Y. Kafai, W. Sandoval, N. Enyedy, A. Nixon, & F. Herrera (Eds.), *Proceedings of the sixth international conference of the learning sciences* (pp. 310–317). Mahwah, NJ: Lawrence Erlbaum Associates.

McGinn, M. K., & Roth, W-M. (1999). Preparing students for competent scientific practice: Implications of recent research in science and technology studies. *Educational Researcher, 28*(3), 14–24.

McNeill, K. L., Harris, C. J., Heitzman, M., Lizotte, D. J., Sutherland, L. M., & Krajcik, J. (2004). How can I make new stuff from old stuff? In J. Krajcik & B. J. Reiser (Eds.), *IQWST: Investigating and questioning our world through science and technology* (pp. 1–208). Ann Arbor, MI: University of Michigan.

McNeill, K. L., Lizotte, D. J, Harris, C. J., Scott, L. A., Krajcik, J., & Marx, R. W. (2003, March). *Using backward design to create standards-based middle-school inquiry-oriented chemistry curriculum and assessment materials.* Paper presented at the annual meeting of the National Association for Research in Science Teaching, Philadelphia, PA.

McNeill, K. L., Lizotte, D. J, Krajcik, J., & Marx, R. W. (2006). Supporting students' construction of scientific explanations by fading scaffolds in instructional materials. *The Journal of the Learning Sciences, 15*(2), 153–191.

Metz, K. E. (2000). Young children's inquiry in biology: Building the knowledge bases to empower independent inquiry. In J. Minstrell & E. H. van Zee (eds.), *Inquiry into inquiry learning and teaching in science* (pp. 371–404). Washington, DC: American Association for the Advancement of Science.

National Research Council. (1996). *National science education standards*. Washington, DC: National Academy Press.

Reiser, B. J., Krajcik, J., Moje, E. B., & Marx, R. W. (2003, March). *Design strategies for developing science instructional materials*. Paper presented at the Annual Meeting of the National Association for Research in Science Teaching, Philadelphia, PA.

Reiser, B., Tabak, I., Sandoval, W., Smith, B., Steinmuller, F., & Leone, A. (2001). BGuILE: Strategic and conceptual scaffolds for scientific inquiry in biology classrooms. In S. M. Carver & D. Klahr (Eds.), *Cognition and instruction: Twenty-five years of progress* (pp. 263–305). Mahwah, NJ: Lawrence Erlbaum Associates.

Rivet, A. E., & Krajcik, J. S. (2004). Achieving standards in urban systemic reform: An example of a sixth-grade project-based science curriculum. *Journal of Research in Science Teaching, 41*(7), 669–692.

Sadler, T. D. (2004). Informal reasoning regarding socioscientific issues: A critical review of research. *Journal of Research in Science Teaching, 41*(5), 513–536.

Sandoval, W. (2003). Conceptual and epistemic aspects of students' scientific explanations. *The Journal of the Learning Sciences, 12*(1), 5–51.

Sandoval, W. A. & Reiser, B. (1997, March). *Evolving explanations in high school biology*. Paper presented at the Annual Meeting of the American Educational Research Association. Chicago, IL.

Singer, J., Marx, R., Krajcik, J., & Chambers, J. (2000). Constructing extended inquiry projects: Curriculum materials for science education. *Educational Psychologist, 35*(3), 165–178.

Salomon, G., Perkins, D. N., & Globerson, T. (1991). Partners in cognition: Extending human intelligence with intelligent technologies. *Educational Researcher, 20*(2), 2–9.

Stern, L., & Ahlgren, A. (2002). Analysis of students' assessments in middle school curriculum materials: Aiming precisely at benchmarks and standards. *Journal of Research in Science Teaching, 39*(9), 889–910.

Tabak, I., & Reiser, B. J. (1997). Complementary roles of software-based scaffolding and teacher–student interactions in inquiry learning. In R. Hall, N. Miyake, & N. Enyedy (Eds.), *Proceedings of Computer Support for Collaborative Learning '97* (pp. 289–298). Mahwah, NJ: Lawrence Erlbaum Associates.

Toulmin, S. (1958). *The uses of argument*. Cambridge, UK: Cambridge University Press.

White, B., & Frederiksen, J. (1998). Inquiry, modeling, and metacognition: Making science accessible to all students. *Cognition and Instruction, 16*(1), 3–118.

Wiggins, G., & McTighe, J. (1998). *Understanding by design*. Alexandria, VA: Association for Supervision and Curriculum Development.

Zembal-Saul, C., Munford, D., Crawford, B., Friedrichsen, P. & Land, S. (2002). Scaffolding preservice science teachers' evidence-based arguments during an investigation of natural selection. *Research in Science Education, 32 (4)*, 437–465.

APPENDIX A: SAMPLE MULTIPLE-CHOICE ITEMS

1. To determine if a chemical reaction occurred, you should measure and compare which of the following?
   A. volume of the materials
   B. shape of the products
   C. properties of the substances
   D. mass of the reactants

5. Which of the following is an example of a chemical reaction?
   A. mixing lemonade powder with water
   B. burning marshmallows over a fire
   C. melting butter in a pan
   D. boiling water on a stove

12. A property is
   A. determined by the amount of a substance.
   B. made of one type of substance.
   C. a process to make a new substance.
   D. a characteristic of a substance.

3. A student found two green powders that look the same. He wants to figure out if the two powders are the same or different substances. Which of the following is the best method to use?
   A. Measure the mass, volume, and temperature of each powder and compare.
   B. Combine both green powders and see if there is a chemical reaction.
   C. Mix the 2 green powders together and then test the properties.
   D. Determine the density, solubility, and melting point of each powder and compare.

APPENDIX B: SCIENTIFIC EXPLANATION ITEMS

Substance and Property Explanation

Examine the following data table:

	Density	Color	Mass	Melting Point
Liquid 1	0.93 g/cm³	no color	38 g	–98°C
Liquid 2	0.79 g/cm³	no color	38 g	26°C
Liquid 3	13.6 g/cm³	silver	21 g	–39°C
Liquid 4	0.93 g/cm³	no color	16 g	–98°C

Write a scientific explanation that states whether any of the liquids are the same substance.

Chemical Reaction Explanation

Carlos takes some measurements of two liquids—butanic acid and butanol. Then he stirs the two liquids together and heats them. After stirring and heating the liquids, they form two separate layers—Layer A and Layer B. Carlos uses an eyedropper to get a sample from each layer and takes some measurements of each sample. Here are his results:

		Measurements				
		Density	Melting Point	Mass	Volume	Solubility in water
Before stirring	Butanic acid	0.96 g/cm³	–7.9°C	9.78 g	10.18 cm³	Yes
& heating	Butanol	0.81 g/cm³	–89.5°C	8.22 g	10.15 cm³	Yes
After stirring	Layer A	0.87 g/cm³	–91.5°C	1.74 g	2.00 cm³	No
& heating	Layer B	1.00 g/cm³	0.0°C	2.00 g	2.00 cm³	Yes

Write a scientific explanation that states whether a chemical reaction occurred when Carlos stirred and heated butanic acid and butanol.

APPENDIX C: SPECIFIC RUBRICS

Specific Rubric for Substance and Property Scientific Explanation

Component	Level		
	0	1	2
Claim – A statement or conclusion that answers the original question/problem.	Does not make a claim. or makes an inaccurate claim.	Makes an accurate but incomplete claim.	Makes an accurate and complete claim.
	State none of the liquids are the same or specifies the wrong liquid.	Vague statement, like "some of the liquids are the same."	Explicitly states "Liquids 1 and 4 are the same substance."
	0	**1 & 2**	**3**
Evidence – Scientific data that supports the claim. The data needs to be appropriate and sufficient to support the claim.	Does not provide evidence, or only provides inappropriate evidence (Evidence that does not support claim).	Provides appropriate, but insufficient evidence to support claim, May include some inappropriate evidence.	Provides appropriate and sufficient evidence to support claim.
	Provides inappropriate data, like "the mass is the same" or provides vague evidence, like "the data table is my evidence."	Provides 1 or 2 of the following pieces of evidence: the density, melting point, and color of liquids 1 and 4 are the same. May also include inappropriate evidence, like mass.	Provides all 3 of the following pieces of evidence: the density, melting point, and color of liquids_1 and 4 are the same.
	0	**1, 2 & 3**	**4**
Reasoning – A justification that links the claim and evidence and includes appropriate and sufficient scientific principles to defend the claim.	Does not provide reasoning, or only provides reasoning that does not link evidence to claim.	Repeats evidence and links it to the claim. May include some scientific principles but not sufficient.	Provides accurate and complete reasoning that links evidence to claim. Includes appropriate and sufficient scientific principles.
	Provides an inappropriate reasoning statement like "they are like the fat and soap we used in class" or does not provide any reasoning.	Repeats the density, melting point, and color are the same and states that this shows they are the same substance. Or provides an incomplete generalization about properties, like "mass is not a	Includes a complete generalization that density, melting point, and color are all properties. Same substances have the same properties. Because liquids 1 and 4 have the same properties, they are the same substance.

APPENDIX C: SPECIFIC RUBRICS

Specific Rubric for Chemical Reaction Scientific Explanation

Component	Level			
Claim—	0	1		1
A statement or conclusion that answers the original question/problem.	Does not make a claim, or makes an inaccurate claim	Does not apply to this learning task		Makes an accurate and complete claim.
	to States that a chemical reaction did not occur.			States that a chemical reaction did occur.
Evidence —	0	1 & 2		3
Scientific data that supports the claim. The data needs to be appropriate and sufficient to support the claim.	Does not provide evidence, or only provides inappropriate evidence (Evidence that does not support claim).	Provides appropriate, but insufficient evidence to support claim, May include some inappropriate evidence		Provides appropriate and sufficient evidence to support claim.
	Provides inappropriate data, like "the mass and volume changed" or provides vague evidence, like "the data shows me it is true."	Provides 1 or 2 of the following pieces of evidence: Butanic acid and butanol have different solubilities, melting points, and densities compared to Layer A and Layer B. May also include inappropriate evidence, like mass or volume.		Provides all 3 of the following pieces of evidence: Butanic acid and butanol have different solubilities, melting points, and densities compared to Layer A and Layer B. May also include inappropriate evidence, like mass.
Reasoning –	0	1, 2, 3 & 4		5
A justification that links the claim and evidence and includes appropriate and sufficient scientific principles to defend the claim and evidence.	Does not provide reasoning, or only provides reasoning that does not link evidence to claim.	Repeats evidence and links it to the claim. May include some scientific principles but not sufficient.		Provides accurate and complete reasoning that links evidence to claim. Includes appropriate and sufficient scientific principles.
	Provides an inappropriate reasoning statement like "a chemical reaction did not occur because Layers A and B are not substances," or does not provide any reasoning.	Repeats the solubility, melting point, and density changed, which show a reaction occurred. Or provides either A or B: A. A chemical reaction creates new or dirrerent substances OR B. Different substances have different properties.		Includes a complete generalization that: A. A chemical reaction creates new or different substances AND B. Different substances have different properties.

265

11

Designing a Data Analysis Tool for Learners

Clifford Konold
University of Massachusetts Amherst

In this chapter, I describe ideas underlying the design of a software tool we developed for middle school students (Konold & Miller, 2005). The tool—*TinkerPlots*—allows students to organize data to help them see patterns and trends in data much in the spirit of visualization tools such as *Data Desk* (DataDescription, Inc.). But we also intend teachers and curriculum designers to use it to help students build solid conceptual understandings of what statistics are and how we can use them.

Designers of educational software tools inevitably struggle with the issue of complexity. In general, a simple tool will minimize the time needed to learn it at the expense of range of applications. On the other hand, designing a tool to handle a wide range of applications risks overwhelming students. I contrast the decisions we made regarding complexity when we developed *DataScope* 15 years ago with those we recently made in designing *TinkerPlots*, and describe how our more recent tack has served to increase student engagement at the same time it helps them see critical connections among display types. More generally, I suggest that in the attempt to avoid overwhelming students, too many educational environments managed instead to underwhelm them and thus serve to stifle rather than foster learning.

Before looking at the issue of complexity, I describe more general considerations that influenced our decisions about the basic nature of *TinkerPlots*. These include views about (1) what statistics is and where the practice of statistics might be headed and (2) how to approach designing for student learning.

OVERARCHING DESIGN CONSIDERATIONS

The Growing Role of Statistics

How can we teach statistics so that students better understand it? This was the primary question that 25 years ago motivated me and my colleagues to begin researching the statistical reasoning of undergraduate students. Our assumption was that if we could better understand students' intuitive beliefs, we could design more effective instruction. We researched student reasoning regarding concepts fundamental to the introductory statistics course. These included the concept of probability (Konold, 1989; Konold, Pollatsek, Well, Lohmeier, & Lipson, 1993; randomness (Falk & Konold, 1997); sampling (Pollatsek, Konold, Well, & Lima, 1984); and the Law of Large Numbers (Well, Pollatsek, & Boyce, 1990).

We find ourselves today concerned with a different set of questions. These include:

- What are the core ideas in statistics and data analysis?
- What are the statistical capabilities that today's citizens need, and what will they need 25 years from now?
- How do we start early in young peoples' lives to develop these capabilities?

Three interrelated developments are largely responsible, I believe, for this change of research focus. First, there has been an expansion of our view of statistical practice, a difference often signaled by use of the term *data analysis* in place of *statistics*. Much of the credit for enlarging our vision of how to analyze data goes to John Tukey. His 1977 book, *Exploratory Data Analysis*, in which he advocated that we look past the ends of our inferential noses, was in many ways ahead of its time.

Second, the United States, as have many other countries, has committed itself to introducing data analysis to students beginning as early as the first grade (NCTM, 2000). The reason often given for starting data analysis early in the curriculum is the ubiquity of data and chance in our everyday and professional lives. The objective has become not to teach statistics to a few but to build a data literate citizenry. Given that we never really figured out how to teach statistics well to college undergraduates, this is a daunting, if laudable, undertaking.

Finally, the enhanced capabilities and widespread availability of the computer has spawned a new set of tools and techniques for detecting patterns in massive data sets. These methods, sometimes referred to as "data visualization" and "data mining," take advantage of what our eyes (or ears, Flowers & Hauer, 1992) do exceptionally well. The parody of the statistician as a "number cruncher" is dated. A more fitting term for the modern version might be *plot wringer*.

Because of the ubiquity of data and their critical role across multiple disciplines and institutions, formally trained statisticians are now a thin sliver of those who work with data. Jim Landwehr, who was a candidate for the 2005 President-Elect of the American Statistical Association, made this observation in his ballot statement (http://www.intelliscaninc.com/amstat_90.htm#s02):

> I believe that a statistical problem-solving approach is an important, ingrained component of today's economy and society and will continue to thrive. It is not so obvious to me, however, that the same could be said of "core statistics" as a discipline or "core statisticians" as employees. With our diversity of topics and interests and with their importance to society, we statisticians face the dangers of fragmentation. Statistics can and will be done by people with primary training in other disciplines and with job titles that don't sound anything like "statistician." This is fine and we could not stop it even if we wanted to.

The growing stores of data along with the perception that we now have tools that permit us to efficiently "mine" them is helping to shape a heightened sense of accountability. As patients we view it as our right and obligation to examine the long-term performance of hospitals and individual doctors before submitting ourselves to their care. We expect that their recommendations are based on looking at past success rates of therapies and procedures. And this is not the case just in medicine. We expect nearly all our institutions—government, education, financial, business—to monitor and improve their performance using data. Where data exist, none of us are immune. Among the reasons Red Sox officials gave for firing manager Gracy Little at the end of the 2003 baseball season was his "unwillingness to rely on statistical analysis in making managerial decisions" (Thamel, 2003, p. 3). Public education will likely slip the noose of the No Child Left Behind legislation, but not without putting in place a more reasonable set of expectations and ways of objectively monitoring them. The information age is fast spawning the age of accountability.

It is critical that we consider these trends as we design data analysis tools and curricula for students. Our current efforts at teaching young students about data and chance are still overly influenced by statistical methods and applications of 30 or 50 years ago. This is not to suggest that we lay all bets on guesses about where the field might be headed. But we do need to imagine what skills today's students will likely be using 10 and 25 years from now and for what purposes. At the same time, we need to work harder to understand what the core ideas in statistics are and how to recognize them and their precursors in the reasoning of the 10-year-old. We can assume that these underlying concepts (e.g., covariation and density) will be evolving more slowly than the various methods we might use to think about or represent them (e.g., scatter-plot displays and histograms).

Bottom-Up Versus Top-Down Development

During the past few years, mathematics and science educators have been investigating how students reason about mathematical and scientific concepts and applying what they learn to improve education. This has led to methods of bottom-up instructional design, which takes into account not only where we want students to end up, but also where they are coming from. Earlier approaches, in contrast, emphasized a top-down approach in which the college-level course—taken as the ultimate goal—was progressively stripped down for lower grades. Figures 11.1, 11.2, 11.3, and 11.4 are a characterization of how statistics curriculum materials and tools have been produced and how, in contrast, we approached the design of *TinkerPlots*.

When they began several years ago to design statistics courses for the high school, educators patterned the curricula largely after the introductory college course in statistics, as if they were dropping a short rope down from the college level to students in high school (see Fig. 11.1). When, more recently, educators began developing statistics units for middle and elementary school students, they continued to lower the rope (Fig. 11.2), basically by removing from the college curricula the concepts and skills they considered too difficult for younger students. The objectives and content at a particular level are thus whatever was left over after subjecting the college course to this subtractive process. So grades 3–5 get line graphs and medians, grades 6–8 get scatter-plots and means, and grades 9–12 get regression lines and sampling distributions (see National Council of Teachers of Mathematics, 2000).

Designers of statistics software tools for young students have generally followed the same top-down approach, developing software packages that are fundamentally stripped-down professional tools (Biehler, 1997, p. 169). These programs provide a subset of conventional graph types and are simpler than professional tools only in that they have fewer, and more basic, options. More recently, Cobb, Gravemeijer, and their colleagues at Vanderbilt University and the Freudenthal Institute, have taken a different approach in designing the *Mini Tools* for use in the middle school. They incorporated into the *Mini Tools* a small set of graph types—case-value plots, stacked dot-plots, and scatter-plots. And in large part they decided what to include in the tool by building from a particular theory of mathematics learning and on

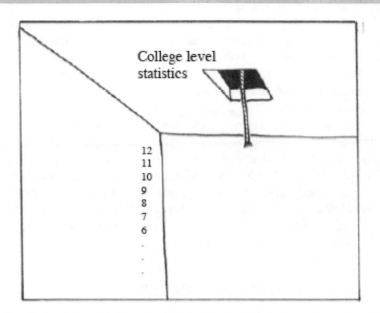

Figure 11.1 A top-down approach to developing tools and curricula for high school based on the college course.

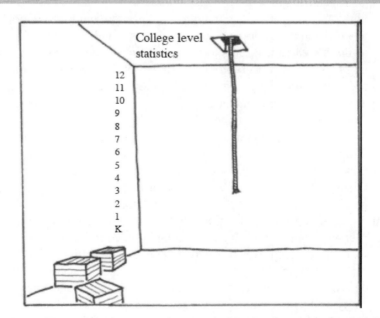

Figure 11.2 The top-down approach extended to development of materials for the lower grades.

research about student reasoning (Bakker, 2002; Cobb, 1999; Cobb, McClain, & Gravemeijer, 2003). In this way, their instructional units and accompanying software take into account not only where instruction should be headed; working from the bottom up, they also attempt to build on how students understand data and how they are prone, before instruction, to use data to support or formulate conjectures (Fig. 11.3).

In designing *TinkerPlots*, we undertook a more radical approach. First we assumed that we did not know quite where K–12 curricula should be headed and that, in any case, there were likely to be many ways for students to get there, a multiplicity of student understandings from which we could productively build up (Fig. 11.4). What held us in check, however, was an additional objective of designing software that was useful to curriculum designers writing materials that meet the NCTM Standards (2000) on data analysis. As I illustrate later, these two objectives pulled us at times in opposite directions, generating a set of tensions some of which were productive.

THE PROBLEM OF COMPLEXITY

Put five statistics educators in a room with the objective of specifying what should be in a data analysis tool intended for young students. The list of essential capabilities they generate is guaranteed to quickly grow to an alarming length. And no matter how many capabilities are built into a tool, teachers and curriculum developers—even students—will still find things they want to do, but cannot. If as a software developer you try to be helpful by including most of what everyone wants in a tool, it becomes so bloated that users then complain they cannot find what they want. Thus when it comes to the question of whether to include lots of features in a software tool, it's generally "damned if you do, damned if you don't."

Biehler (1997) refers to this as the *complexity-of-tool problem*. He suggests that one approach to addressing it is to design tools that become more sophisticated as the user gains expertise. This is just what successful computer games manage to do through a number of means (Gee, 2003), but it is hard to imagine implementing this in an educational software tool. The *Mini Tools* comprise three separate applications that the developers introduce in a specified order according to their understanding of how rudimentary skills in data analysis might develop over instruction. Perhaps the suite of *Mini Tools* is a simple example of the kind of evolving software Biehler had in mind.

In developing *DataScope* 15 years ago, we took a different approach to the complexity problem (Konold, 1995; Konold & Miller, 1994). *DataScope* is data-analysis software intended for students aged 14–17. We conceived of it

Figure 11.3 Using in conjunction a bottom up and top down approach, hoping to hook up in the middle.

Figure 11.4 A diversified bottom-up approach aimed at a moving or ambiguous target.

as a basic set of tools that would allow students to investigate multivariate data sets in the spirit of Exploratory Data Analysis (Tukey, 1977). To combat the complexity problem, we implemented only five basic representations: histograms (and bar graphs), box-plots, scatter-plots, one and two-way tables of frequencies, and tables of descriptive statistics. Our hope was that by limiting student choices, more instructional time could be focused on learning underlying concepts and data inquiry skills.

In many ways, we accomplished our goal with *DataScope*. Students took relatively little time to learn to use it, and it proved sufficiently general to allow them to flexibly explore multivariate data (Konold, 1995). However, one persistent pattern of student use troubled us. To explore a particular question, students would often select the relevant variables and then choose from the menus one of the five display options, often with only a vague idea of what the option they selected would produce. If that display did not seem useful, they would try another, and another, until they found a display that seemed to suit their purposes. If they were preparing an assignment or report, many students generated and printed out every possible display. There are undoubtedly several reasons for this behavior; Biehler (1998) reports similar tendencies among older students using software with considerably more options. However, it seemed clear that the limited number of displays in *DataScope* explained in part this trial-and-error approach, as there was little cost in always trying everything. Had this behavior been prevalent only among novice users, it would have not been of much concern. But, it persisted as students gained experience.

When we were field-testing *DataScope*, I had a fantasy that students would want to work with it outside of class—just for the fun of it, if you will. One day I walked into a class to discover that a student was already there. She had fired up the computer and was so engrossed that she didn't notice me. Trying not to disturb her, I quelled my excitement and tiptoed around her to see what data she was exploring. Alas, it was not the glow of *DataScope* lighting her face, but one of the rather mindless puzzles that early Macs included under the Apple menu. This was the closest I got in the *DataScope* days to realizing my fantasy.

It was this fantasy—of seeing students enjoying using a tool and using it with purpose—that drove many of the basic design decisions in *TinkerPlots*. The result was a tool that in ways is a complete opposite of *DataScope*. Rather than working to reduce the complexity of *TinkerPlots*, we purposely increased it. With rare exceptions, students are extremely enthusiastic with *TinkerPlots* and frequently ask to work with it outside of class. I believe that a big part of *TinkerPlots*' appeal has to do with its complexity. In what follows, I attempt to describe how we managed to build a complex tool that motivates students rather than overwhelms them.

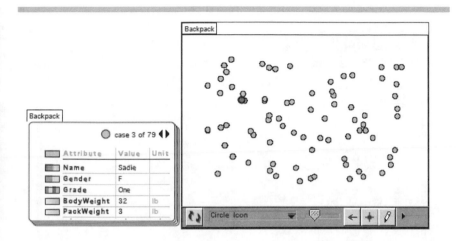

Figure 11.5 Information on 79 students along with their backpack weights displayed in *TinkerPlots*. Each case (student) is represented in a plot window (right) as a case icon. Initially, the case icons appear as shown here, randomly arranged. Clicking the Mix-up button (lower left of the plot window) sends the icons into a new random arrangement. The case highlighted in the plot window belongs to Sadie, whose data appears in the stack of Data Cards on the left.

Constructing Data Displays Using *TinkerPlots*

On first opening the plot window in *TinkerPlots*, individual case icons appear in it haphazardly arranged (see Fig. 11.5). Given the goal of answering a particular question about the data, the immediate problem facing students is how to impose some suitable organization on the case icons. *TinkerPlots* comes with no ready-made displays—no bar graphs, pie charts, or histograms. Instead, students build these and other representations by progressively organizing data icons in the plot window using basic operators including *order*, *stack*, and *separate*.

Figure 11.5 shows data I typically use as part of a first introduction to *TinkerPlots*. I ask the class whether they think students in higher grades carry heavier backpacks than do students in lower grades. I then have them explore this data set to see whether it supports their expectations. Figures 11.6 through 11.8 are a series of screen shots showing one way in which these data might be organized with *TinkerPlots* to answer this question.

In Figure 11.6, the cases have been separated into four bins according to the weight of the backpacks. This separation required first selecting the attribute PackWeight in the Data Cards and then pulling a plot icon to the

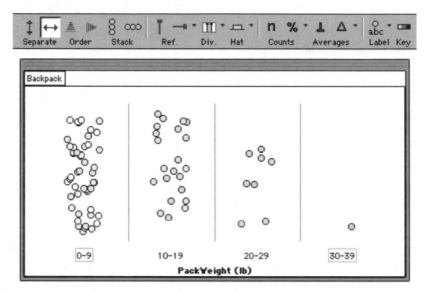

Figure 11.6 Plot icons separated into four bins according to the weight of students' backpacks. Shown above the plot window is a tool bar that includes various plotting options. When one of these buttons is pressed, it appears highlighted (as the horizontal Separate button currently is). Pressing that button again removes the effects of that operation from the plot.

right to form the desired number of bins. To progress to the representation shown in Figure 11.7, the icons were stacked, then separated completely until the case icons appeared over their actual values on a number line. Then the attribute Grade was selected, shown by the fact that the plot icons now appear in various shades of gray (in color, they appear red). With Grade selected, the Grade 5 students were separated vertically from the other grades. If we were to continue pulling out each of the three other grades one by one, we'd then see the distributions of PackWeight for each of the four grades in this data set (grades 1, 3, 5, and 7). We could go on to place *dividers* to indicate where the cases cluster, or to display the location of the means of all four groups (see Rubin, Hammerman, Campbell, & Puttick, [2005] for a description of the various *TinkerPlots* options that novices used to make comparisons between groups).

Making these displays in *TinkerPlots* is considerably more complex than it would be in *DataScope*, *Mini Tools*, *Tabletop*, *Fathom*, or most any professional or educational tool. In almost all of these packages, one would simply specify

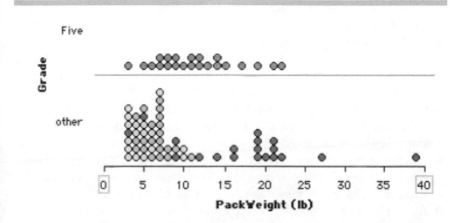

Figure 11.7   Cases have been stacked, then fully separated on the x axis until there are no bins. Then the grade 5 students have been separated out vertically, forming a new y axis. The cases are now colored according to grade, with darker gray (red in the actual program) indicating higher grade levels.

the two attributes and the appropriate graph type (e.g., stacked dot-plot). As we have seen, making such a stacked dot-plot in *TinkerPlots* requires perhaps 10 separate steps. What is important to keep in mind, however, is that the students, particularly when they are just learning the tool, typically do not have in mind a particular graph type they want to make as they organize the data. Rather, they take small steps in *TinkerPlots*, each step motivated by the goal of altering slightly the current display to move closer to their goal—in this case of being able to compare the pack weights of the different grades. Because each of these individual steps is small, it is relatively easy for students to evaluate whether the step is an improvement or not. If it is not a productive move, they can easily backtrack. The fact that with each step the icons animate into their new positions also helps students to determine the nature of, and evaluate, each modification.

There are a number of reasons we designed *TinkerPlots* as a construction set. A primary objective was that by giving students more fundamental choices about how to represent the data, they would develop the sense that they were making their own graphic representation rather than selecting from a set of pre-formed options. When I have students investigate the backpack data with *TinkerPlots*, I give them the task of making a graph that they can use to answer the question posed above. Having a specific task, especially when first learning *TinkerPlots*, is crucial. Without a clear goal, students would have no end to inch toward and thus no basis for evaluating their actions.

After about 30 minutes, most of the students have answered the question to their satisfaction. I then have them walk around the room to observe the displays that other students have made. What they see is an incredible variety, which immediately presents them with the problem of learning how to interpret these different displays, all of which are purportedly showing the same thing. But more importantly, seeing all these different graphs makes it clear to them that *TinkerPlots* is not doing the representational work for them. Rather, they are using it as they might a set of construction blocks to fashion a design of their own making. They are in the driver's seat, which means they have to make thoughtful decisions; mindlessly pressing buttons will most likely give them a poor result. Indeed, it is quite easy in *TinkerPlots* to make cluttered and useless displays.

There are numerous factors that affect the interpretability of a data display (Tufte, 1983). Many of these factors are ordinarily controlled by a software tool. In *TinkerPlots*, we chose to leave some rather fundamental display aspects under direct user control. Figure 11.8 shows the four levels of grade separated out on the *y* axis. But the plot icons are so large that they spill over the bin lines, and any subtle features of the four distributions are obscured. This sort of plot-crowding routinely occurs as students are making various graphs in *TinkerPlots*, and it is up to them to manually control the size of icons, which they quickly learn to do. It is a control they seem to enjoy exercising.

Note, too, in Figure 11.8 that the four levels of grade are not ordered sensibly. The current order resulted from the particular way each group was pulled out of the "other" category visible in Figure 11.7. In creating this data set, we intentionally entered the values of grade as text rather than as numbers so that students would tend initially to get a display like this, with values of grade not in an order ideal for comparing them. The ordering can be quickly changed, however, by dragging axis labels to the desired locations. Once ordered, students can sweep their eyes from bottom to top to evaluate the pattern of differences among the groups without having to continually refer back to the axis labels. In fact, it is this type of ordering from which graphic displays of data derive much of their power.

Leaving such details to the student further increases the complexity of the program. However, taking control of things like icon size, bin size, and the ordering of values on an axis helps students to become explicitly aware of important principles that underlie good data display. Furthermore, leaving these fundamental responsibilities to the student is yet another way of communicating to them that they, and not the software tool, are ultimately in control of what they produce. Finally, these are factors that most students seem to enjoy having direct control over. Part of this satisfaction undoubtedly comes from the fairly direct nature of the control and would be lost if instead we had used dialogue boxes.

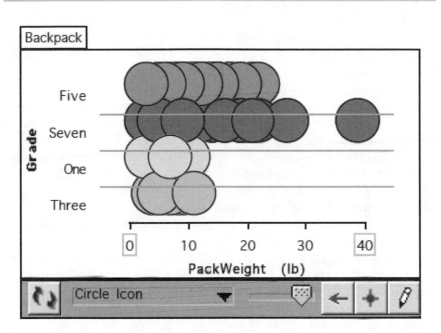

Figure 11.8 The plot icons in this graph are so large they obscure much of the data. Their size is under user control via the slider located on the tool bar below the plot.

Making the Complex Manageable

Certainly, it is not the complexity itself that makes *TinkerPlots* compelling, but the nature of that complexity. Indeed, one of the ways Biehler (1997) suggested to make a complex tool manageable is to build it around a "conceptual structure . . . which supports its piecewise appropriation" (p. 169). We chose the operators *separate*, *order*, and *stack* after having observed how students (and we ourselves) organized data on a table when it was presented as a collection of cards with information about each case on a separate card (Harradine & Konold, 2006). We then worked to implement these operations in the software in a way that would allow students to see the computer operations as akin to what they do when physically arranging real-world objects. This sense—that one already knows what the primary software operators will do—becomes important in building up expectations about how the various operators will interact when they are combined, because it is this ability to combine operators in *TinkerPlots* that makes it complex, and powerful.

Implementing these intuitive operators in the software was harder than we initially expected, however. In our first testable prototype, about half of the representations that students would make by combining operators were non-sensical. To remedy this, we had to reinterpret what some of the operations did in various contexts. *Stack*, for example, works as one might expect with the case icon style used in Figures 11.5 to 11.8. However, there are other icon styles where the stack operation behaves a bit differently so as to produce reasonable displays. For example, icons can be changed to *fuse rectangular*, a style used to make histograms (see bottom of Fig. 11.9). In this case, *stack* not only places case icons on top of one another, but also widens them so that they extend across the entire length of the bin they occupy. With the icon style *fuse circular*, case icons become wedges that fuse together into a circle (pie graphs). In this case, *stack* has no function and thus if it is turned on, it does nothing. In general, the user is unaware of these differences, but pays no price for this ignorance.

We avoid using error messages to instruct students, primarily because we worried that they would erode the attitude we are working hard to create— that the student, not the software, is in control. In some cases, applying an operator does nothing to the plot, and the button dims to indicate that it is in a suppressed state (as happens with *stack* in the context of pie graphs). Again, this goes mostly unnoticed.

However, whenever we can, we show some change in the plot, even if it is of only limited use. For example, when a numeric attribute is fully separated on an axis, students can click the median button to display the location of the median below the axis (see top of Fig. 11.9.) With a binned dot-plot, however, it would be misleading to show the median as a specific point on an axis. But rather than have nothing happen when students turn on the median in this state, we display the median as a line running the length of the interval in which the median occurs (middle graph in Fig. 11.9). Although it does not provide much information about the value of the median, this display does help communicate the fact that when we place different values into the same bin we are, for the moment, considering them to be the same. This binned dot-plot can be changed into a histogram by selecting the icon style *fuse rectangular* (see bottom graph of Fig. 11.9). Now the median symbol once again appears at a precise location on a continuous axis. The animation from the binned dot-plot to the histogram shows the cases growing in width to the edges of the bin lines, hinting at yet another change in how we are thinking of the values in a common bin.

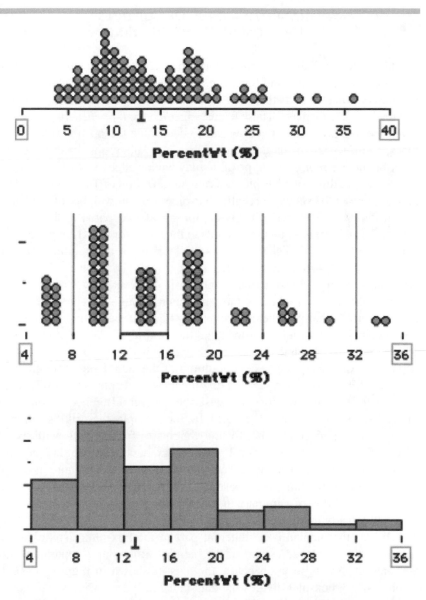

Figure 11.9   These graphs display the percentage the backpacks are of body weight. The top graph shows the location of the median (inverted T) at 13. In the binned dot-plot in the middle, the median now appears as a line below the bin, indicating that the median is in the interval 12–16. Changing the icon style to "fuse rectangular" makes a histogram, which now again displays the precise location of the median.

HAT-PLOT: A CASE OF BUILDING
UP FROM STUDENT THINKING

In addition to building *TinkerPlots* around a conceptual structure involving the operators *stack, order*, and *separate*, we also included features that were inspired by what we and others had observed students wanting to do in making and reading data displays. These features include the *reference line*, which students use to mark salient features and to determine the precise value of case icons, and *dividers* for partitioning of data into subgroups. In this section, I describe the *hat-plot*, a new type of display we introduce in *TinkerPlots*.

One way to think of a hat-plot is as a generalization of Tukey's (1977) box-plot. Figure 11.10 shows percentile hat-plots for the weights of students in four different grades. Each hat is composed of two parts: a "brim" and a "crown." The brim is a line that extends to the range for each group; the crown is a rectangle that, in this case, shows the location of the middle 50% of the data—the Interquartile Range (IQR). The particular hat-plots in Figure 11.10 are thus constructed using the same basic conventions of the box-plot. Whereas the whiskers of a box-plot are drawn through the center of the IQR rectangle, in the hat-plot the corresponding line is drawn along the bottom of this rectangle. We think that locating the central rectangle on top of the whiskers, or range line, helps emphasize what the center rectangle is depicting—the location of a central clump of the data. I say more about this later. In addition, our own sense is that the hat-like display that results makes it easier for students to notice and describe general differences in the shapes of the distributions. Note in Figure 11.10, for example, the striking difference in appearance between the hat for the weights of first-graders, with its relatively tall crown, and the hat for the seventh-graders, with its relatively short, but spreading, crown. The more skewed a distribution is, the more its hat-plot will appear as something like a baseball cap. We also think students will take quickly to the idea of summarizing distributions with hats, in part because they will already have a rich vocabulary for doing so.

Whereas the median is an inherent part of the box-plot display, it is not automatically displayed as part of the hat-plot. But using a separate control, you can display its location below the axis as shown in Figure 11.10. The result is that a box-plot divides the data into four parts, whereas the hat-plot divides it into three. We anticipate that this will have some pedagogical advantages as students already have a strong tendency to view many distributions as comprising three groups (see, e.g., Bakker & Gravemeijer, 2004).

A more fundamental difference between hat-plots and box-plots is that with hat-plots, you can change the setting for the brim edges to represent percentiles other than the box-plot's 25th and 75th percentiles. By clicking and

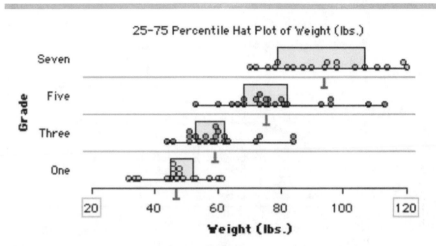

Figure 11.10 Superimposed percentile hat-plots for weight (in pounds) of students in grades 1, 3, 5, and 7. The edges of the hat crowns show the location of the 25th and 75th percentiles. The inverted T's under each group indicate medians. Thus these particular hat-plots show the same basic information as would box-plots, except that rather than retracting to display outliers, hat-plot brims extend to the minimum and maximum values.

dragging the edge of a brim, you can change these into, for example, 20th–80th percentile hats. Furthermore, each brim edge is adjusted independently, so you could set them to display 20th–76th percentiles. This allows students to make hat-plots that are initially tailored to a particular group of data, which they later can test on other groups.

You can also switch the metric of the brim from percentiles to ranges, average deviations or standard deviations. In Figure 11.11, I've used the range metric to construct hat crowns that extend from one third of the range to two thirds of the range.

Some have questioned our choice to include in *TinkerPlots* a display that is not among those listed in the NCTM Standards for the middle grades. There seems to be an implicit assumption in this question—that if something is not in the Standards, we should not include it in our learning objectives, curricula, or student tools. Although there are some grounds for taking this stance, we should reject it as a guiding principle.

The Standards are not a sacred canon but rather "a resource and guide" (NCTM, 2000, p. ix). NCTM describes the Standards as "part of an ongoing process of improving mathematics education" and believes that for the Standards "to remain viable, the goals and visions they embody must periodically be

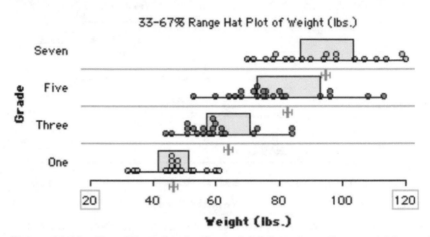

Figure 11.11 Range hat-plots for the weight of students (in pounds) in grades 1, 3, 5, and 7. These plots divide the range for each grade into equal thirds. The symbols below the bin lines indicate the midranges.

examined, evaluated, tested by practitioners, and revised" (p. x). Thus, it is contrary to the spirit of the Standards to use them to justify and support a rigid orthodoxy about what and how we should teach. As curriculum writers, researchers, and educators, we should be pushing ourselves to test and refine our vision of how students might learn to analyze data. Put another way, we should be thinking at least as much about what the next version of the Standards should say as we do about what this version says.

Instructional Role of Hat-Plots

In the following, I briefly present the rationale for including hat-plots in *TinkerPlots* and the reasons why I think they could play a helpful role in middle school data-analysis curricula. I also offer some tentative, and admittedly vague, ideas about how they might be used in a sequence of instruction, confident only in the fact that these ideas will change as a result of more thought and of trying them out in classrooms.

From the beginning, we struggled with the question of whether and how to implement box-plots in *TinkerPlots*. One of our objectives was to avoid using plot types as operational primitives. Our aim was to have standard displays, such as scatter-plots and histograms, be among the many possibilities that emerged as students progressively organized data using the basic operators *order*, *stack*, and *separate*. And as previously mentioned, the more general principle that informed the design of *TinkerPlots* was that, to the extent possible, we should build instruction on what students already know and are inclined to do.

Box-plots posed a problem to both these principles. First, the operational primitives in *TinkerPlots* worked well for producing most of the traditional displays included in the current middle school data analysis curricula, but they did not get us to box-plots. (This is another indication, by the way, of just how different box-plots are from most other statistical graphs. See Bakker, Biehler & Konold, 2005.) Second, regardless of how we imagined implementing box-plots in *TinkerPlots*, we could see no clear way of introducing box-plots to students other than as a convention some statisticians find useful. It should be clear at this point that despite what I said above about not allowing the Standards to co-opt educational choices, we as developers certainly feel a great deal of pressure to accommodate them. The fear is that if we do not, various decision-makers including publishers, school boards, and teachers, who themselves are often under the mandate to adopt "Standards-based" approaches, will elect not to use what we have developed. In this regard, the Standards get used both to facilitate and to stifle reform and innovation.

One of our early solutions to implementing box-plots was to adopt the approach used in the *Mini Tools* (see Cobb, 1999). In *Mini Tool 2*, students can overlay various types of groupings on top of stacked dot-plot displays. Creating four, equal-count groups is one of several options, and one that the Vanderbilt learning trajectory made special use of, because it could lead naturally into box-plots. This solved the first problem for us, in that box-plots could emerge in *TinkerPlots* as they did in the *Mini Tools* from the more basic act of dividing into groups.

However, there were aspects of teaching box-plots to students that we struggled with. In particular, it was not clear how to motivate students to make groups composed of roughly equal numbers of cases, and furthermore to make four such groups (rather than three or five or twenty). As Arthur Bakker put it in an e-mail exchange with us, "I have never found any activities with data sets that really begged to be organized by four equal [count] groups ..."

These reservations eventually led us to think about how we might build box-plot-like displays on the well-known tendency of students to summarize single, numeric distributions using "center" or "modal" clumps. These are ranges of values in the heart of a distribution that students use to indicate what is "typical" or "usual." Among the researchers who have reported the use of these sorts of "hills" or "clumps" are Bakker (2001); Cobb, (1999); Konold and Higgins (2003); Konold, Robinson, Khalil, Pollatsek, Well, Wing, et al. (2002); and Noss, Pozzi, and Hoyles (1999).

Inspired by this research, we included in *TinkerPlots* a divider tool that displays two lines on top of a distribution of values that students can freely

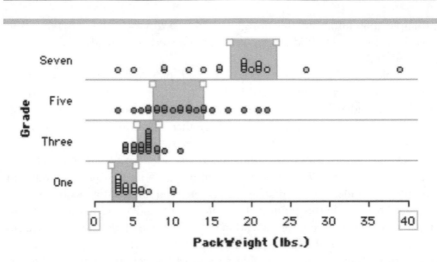

Figure 11.12 Stacked dot-plots of backpack weight (in pounds) of students in grades 1, 3, 5 and 7. Overlaid on each distribution is a pair of adjustable dividers that students can use to mark where data tends to be centered. As an option, they can display the number (and/or percent) of cases contained in each of the three divisions.

adjust (see Fig. 11.12). Our primary intention was that students would use these dividers to mark the location of modal clumps and, optionally, to display the number (or percent) of cases both inside and outside these clumps. Many researchers have commented on the difficulty students have using normative averages, including the mean and median, in meaningful ways (for a review, see Konold & Higgins, 2003). Modal clumps may provide a way for students to begin by using an average-like construct that does make intuitive sense to them. Furthermore, Cobb, Gravemeijer and their colleagues have described teaching sequences directed towards encouraging students to use these to compare groups by noting the relative positions of the "hills" in two distributions.

Figure 11.13 shows the added possibility in *TinkerPlots* of simultaneously seeing modal clumps and the location of means and medians. Seeing these together provides opportunities for helping students to develop more intuitive views of the standard measures of center. Freed from the role of representing what's average about the data, modal clumps might then provide students an informal way of describing the "average" variability in the data. Research by Konold et al. (2002) suggests in fact that the width of students' modal clumps is remarkably close to those of IQRs.

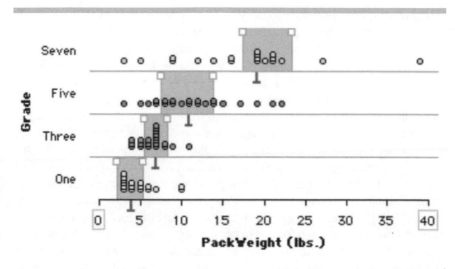

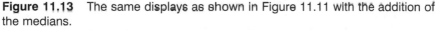

Figure 11.13   The same displays as shown in Figure 11.11 with the addition of the medians.

Our idea for hat-plots then emerged as a way for students to formalize their idea of modal clump, so that rather than fitting modal clumps *ad hoc* on the basis of how data happened to be distributed in a particular display, they could set them according to more objective, and previously agreed-to, criteria. Thus, our overall intention is that in analyzing data, students will naturally take to using the dividers provided in *TinkerPlots* as a way to indicate and communicate to others what they perceive as typical values in a distribution. Hat-plots will offer students a way of formalizing these modal clumps as part of establishing agreed on and objective criteria for using modal clumps to decide, for example, if two groups are different. That hat-plots divide a distribution into three components, just as dividers do, should facilitate the transition from dividers to hat-plots. It also fits with the observations of several researchers that students often initially perceive a distribution of values as comprising low, middle, and high values (e.g., see Bakker & Gravemeijer, 2004).

One reason for providing different metrics for hat-plots (e.g., where the three components split the distribution into different fractions of the range or into multiples of the average or standard deviation) is to encourage students to view hat-plots as a more general method for representing data. Another is to allow exploration of the relative strengths of various metrics. For many students, the range is a salient feature of distributions. We therefore expect that many students will initially choose to construct hat-plots by specifying fractions of the range, which is why originally we used the range metric as the default setting. Our hope was that with some exploration, students would discover some of the drawbacks of using the range. For example, it will often be the case that a range hat-plot that looks reasonable for the group on which it was constructed will not do a good job on other groups. Note that in Figure 11.11, the range hat-plots for students in grades 7 and 1 seem reasonable as summaries of the modal clumps; those for grades 5 and 3 do a fairly poor job. In contrast, the percentile hat-plots for the same data in Figure 11.10 fit the modal clumps of all of the groups reasonably well. Students might also discover using the range metric how one value can drastically affect the appearance of the hat-plot. Indeed, by dragging a single case on one of the extremes using the change-value tool in *TinkerPlots*, they can watch the entire hat slide upwards or downwards in pace with that case, making the range metric perhaps too fussy or sensitive for use in comparing groups. As an aside, we later changed the hat-plot default setting to percentiles when we observed many teachers using the hat-plot's range default setting but assuming that they were percentiles.

We have included in *TinkerPlots* both dividers and hat-plots in the hope that they may provide means for allowing students to build on intuitive ideas that they have about distributions. Our reasons for thinking these tools might be useful are based on recent research that has explored student reasoning and investigated various approaches to instruction that build on students' intuitive ideas. In the near future, we expect to learn from the curriculum developers, who are working in collaboration with the *TinkerPlots* development team, whether hat-plots and dividers are indeed useful, and what modifications or enhancements might make them more so.

CONCLUSIONS

In helping students learn a complex domain such as data analysis, we inevitably must find effective ways to restructure the domain into manageable components. The art is in finding ways to do this that preserve the essence and purpose of the pursuit. It is all too common in classrooms to find students succeeding at learning the small bits they are fed, but never coming to see the big picture nor experiencing the excitement of the enterprise. Of course, *TinkerPlots* by itself cannot change this, and much depends on how teachers and curriculum developers put it to use. Just as I have watched in frustration as students in traditional classrooms spend months learning to make simple graphs of single attributes and never get to a question they care about, I now have had the experience of watching students work through teacher-made worksheets to learn *TinkerPlots* operations one at a time, "mastering" each one before moving on to the next. This is despite the fact that the parts cannot be mastered in isolation or out of context.

After class, I spoke with the teacher who had created the worksheets and gently offered the observation that students could discover and learn to use many of the commands he was drilling them on as a normal part of pursing a question. He informed me that they didn't have time in their schedule to have students "playing around." Although his response added to my despair about the direction education in the United States seems to be heading under the pressures of the testing/accountability movement, I also took it as another indicator that we succeeded with *TinkerPlots* in developing the tool we had hoped to—that in the absence of the strict regime of a worksheet, students seem to actually enjoy using it to explore data.

ACKNOWLEDGMENTS

I thank Amy Robinson for her comments on portions of this chapter and Daniel Konold for drawing Figures 11.1 through 11.4. Portions of this chapter are from my article "Handling Complexity in the Design of Educational Software Tools," to appear in the *Proceedings of the Seventh International Conference on Teaching Statistics*. *TinkerPlots* is published by *Key Curriculum Press* and was developed with grants from the National Science Foundation (ESI-9818946, REC-0337675, ESI-0454754). Opinions expressed here are my own and not necessarily those of the Foundation.

REFERENCES

Bakker, A. (2002). Route-type and landscape-type software for learning statistical data analysis. In B. Phillips (Ed.), *Proceedings of the Sixth International Conference on Teaching of Statistics*. Voorburg, The Netherlands: International Statistical Institute.

Bakker, A., Biehler, R., & Konold, C. (2005). Should young students learn about box-plots? In G. Burrill & M. Camden (Eds.), *Curricular development in statistics education: International Association for Statistical Education 2004 Roundtable* (pp. 163–173). Voorburg, the Netherlands: International Statistical Institute.

Bakker, A., & Gravemeijer, K. P. E. (2004). Learning to reason about distribution. In D. Ben-Zvi & J. Garfield (Eds.), *The challenge of developing statistical literacy, reasoning, and thinking* (pp. 147–168) Dordrecht: Kluwer.

Biehler, R. (1997). Software for learning and for doing statistics. *International Statistical Review*, 65(2), 167–189.

Biehler, R. (1998). Students—statistical software—statistical tasks: A study of problems at the interfaces. In L. Pereira-Mendoza, L. S. Kea, T. W. Kee, & W. Wong (Eds.), *Proceedings of the Fifth International Conference on Teaching Statistics* (pp. 1025–1031). Singapore: International Statistical Institute.

Cobb, P. (1999). Individual and collective mathematical development: The case of statistical data analysis. *Mathematical Thinking and Learning, 1*(1), 5–43.

Cobb, P., McClain, K., & Gravemeijer, K. (2003). Learning about statistical covariation. *Cognition and Instruction, 21,* 1–78.

Falk, R., & Konold, C. (1997). Making sense of randomness: Implicit encoding as a basis for judgment. *Psychological Review, 104,* 301–318.

Flowers, J. H., & Hauer, T. A. (1992). The ear's versus the eye's potential to assess characteristics of numeric data: Are we too visuocentric? *Behavior Research Methods, Instruments, & Computers, 24(2),* 258–264.

Gee, J. P. (2003). *What video games have to teach us about learning and literacy.* New York: Palgrave Macmillan.

Harradine, A., & Konold, C. (2006). How representational medium affects the data displays students make. In A. Rossman & B. Chance (Eds.), *Proceedings of the Seventh International Conference on Teaching Statistics (ICOTS)* [CD-ROM]. Voorburg, The Netherlands: International Statistical Institute.

Konold, C. (1989). Informal conceptions of probability. *Cognition and Instruction, 6,* 59–98.

Konold, C. (2002). Teaching concepts rather than conventions. *New England Journal of Mathematics, 34(2),* 69–81.

Konold, C. (1995). *Datenanalyse mit einfachen, didaktisch gestalteten Softwarewerkzeugen für Schülerinnen und Schüler* [Designing data analysis tools for students]. *Computer und Unterricht, 17,* 42–49.

Konold, C., & Higgins, T. L. (2003). Reasoning about data. In J. Kilpatrick, W. G. Martin, & D. Schifter (Eds.), *A research companion to Principles and Standards for School Mathematics* (pp. 193–215). Reston, VA: National Council of Teachers of Mathematics

Konold, C., & Miller, C. (1994). *DataScope.* Santa Barbara: Intellimation Library for the Macintosh.

Konold, C., & Miller, C., D. (2005). *TinkerPlots: Dynamic data exploration.* Emeryville, CA: Key Curriculum Press.

Konold, C., Pollatsek, A., Well, A. D., Lohmeier, J., & Lipson, A. (1993). Inconsistencies in students' reasoning about probability. *Journal for Research in Mathematics Education, 24,* 392–414.

Konold, C., Robinson, A., Khalil, K., Pollatsek, A., Well, A., Wing, R., et al. (2002). Students' use of modal clumps to summarize data. In B. Phillips (Ed.), *Proceedings of the Sixth International Conference on Teaching of Statistics.* Voorburg, The Netherlands: International Statistical Institute.

National Council of Teachers of Mathematics. (2000). *Principles and standards for school mathematics.* Reston, VA: NCTM.

Noss, R., Pozzi, S. & Hoyles, C. (1999). Touching epistemologies: Meanings of average and variation in nursing practice. *Educational Studies in Mathematics, 40(1),* 25–51.

Pollatsek, A., Konold, C., Well, A. D., & Lima, S. D. (1984). Beliefs underlying random sampling. *Memory & Cognition, 12,* 395–401.

Rubin, A., Hammerman, J., Campbell, C., & Puttick, G. (2005). The effect of distributional shape on group comparison strategies. In K. Makar (Ed.), *Reasoning about distribution:*

A collection of current research studies. Proceedings of the Fourth International Research Forum on Statistical Reasoning, Thinking, and Literacy (SRTL-4). Brisbane: University of Queensland.

Thamel, P. (2003). Baseball; Red Sox' Checklist: Manager (Yes), Rodriguez (Maybe). *The New York Times*, December 5, 2003. Sec. D, p. 3.

Tufte, E. R. (1983). *The visual display of quantitative information.* Cheshire, CT: Graphics Press.

Tukey, J. W. (1977). *Exploratory data analysis.* Reading, MA: Addison-Wesley.

Well, A. D., Pollatsek, A., & Boyce, S. J. (1990). Understanding the effects of sample size on the variability of the mean. *Organizational Behavior and Human Decision Processes, 47*, 289–312.

12

Data-Analysis Skills: What and How Are Students Learning?

Marsha C. Lovett
Norma M. Chang
Carnegie Mellon University

The question of how to improve student learning is usually approached from one of two perspectives. The applied perspective focuses on what happens in the classroom in one particular domain and on what specific practices lead to better performance. The theoretical perspective embeds the domain under study in the larger context of general learning mechanisms and aims to understand student performance in terms of these mechanisms. Although this dichotomy is admittedly a caricature, there is still a commonly held view that applied and theoretical goals are in conflict. Stokes (1997) aptly describes this view: To be highly theoretical, work must give up on applied goals and vice versa.

The present chapter advocates a systematic combination of theoretical and applied emphases in the pursuit of understanding how students learn to analyze data. Through two studies of students' behavior during problem solving in both the laboratory and the classroom, we investigate students' mental representations of knowledge. Knowledge representation is an inherently theoretical construct, but students' knowledge representations have practical implications for how they learn and solve problems. By combining theoretical and applied perspectives, our approach leads to new insights that inform both. In one direction, learning theory can lead to predictions about how to improve instructional praxis, that is, applying learning theory to the case of data-analysis skills can lead to ideas for promoting students' learning in introductory statistics courses. In the other direction, studying what actually works in the classroom—especially when classroom results do not meet with theoretical predictions—can lead to refinements, revisions, or expansions to current theory. Thus, we see a synergistic relationship between the two perspectives akin to a cycle in which ideas and findings from one perspective feed into the other and, in turn, are fed back to continue the process.

Stokes (1997) argues convincingly in support of this approach after debunking the commonly held view of a conflict between the two perspectives. He reveals that applied and theoretical emphases need not be viewed as extremes of one continuum but rather as two separate dimensions. From this two-dimensional perspective, then, the most productive quadrant is the one in which work is both highly theoretical *and* highly applied (see Fig. 12.1).

In the case of students learning data analysis, we approach this integration from the applied side by studying students' learning in real (and realistic) classroom settings and by tapping familiar "applied" issues: How much do students improve with practice? Are students able to apply what they have learned to new problems and in new situations? What instructional interventions are effective for learning? We then tie these issues together by addressing a more theoretically framed question: What are students' internal representations of data-analysis knowledge and how do those knowledge representations change? This leads to an explicit articulation between theoretical issues (e.g., What knowledge representations would we expect? What would mechanisms of learning predict?) and domain-specific, educational issues (e.g., How do students approach data-analysis problems? What are the features of statistics problems that students represent? What kind of instructional experiences improve students' ability to solve data-analysis problems?). Note that the focus on students' knowledge representations also places an emphasis on characterizing the *nature* of student knowledge and learning. Our goal then is to maintain attention to the details and richness of learning in the domain of statistics while still pushing toward an abstract interpretation that speaks to general mechanisms of learning.

In the two studies that follow, we take up three specific research questions, all of which relate to *how students represent data-analysis skills.*

1. How do students decompose the task of data analysis?
2. What features do students incorporate in their strategies for choosing appropriate analyses?
3. How general are students' skills for choosing appropriate analyses?

Each question is explored in the context of students solving data-analysis problems. To address these questions, we employ a variety of methods: verbal protocol analysis, experimental intervention, and computational modeling. And for each question, we strive to explicate the specific results in the context of

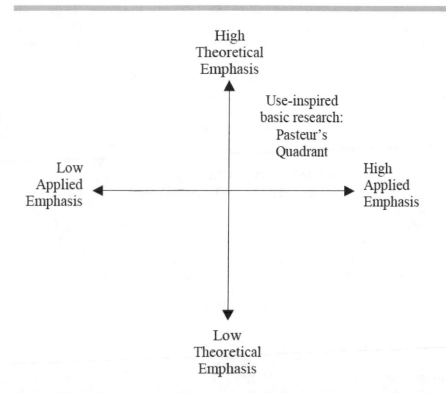

Figure 12.1 The separate dimensions of applied emphasis and theoretical emphasis, as discussed in Stokes (1997), span a two-dimensional space.

statistics education research and practice as well as to generalize from these results implications or further questions relevant to learning theory research.

In each case, the primary sample of participants comes from a pool of undergraduate students (mostly from Carnegie Mellon's College of Humanities and Social Sciences), who have either recently taken or are yet to take the introductory (one semester-long) course in statistics. Like many other "reformed" introductory statistics courses, this one emphasizes conceptual and critical understanding of statistics rather than memorization of formulas, and uses statistics software to minimize the computational mechanics students must implement. The main learning objectives of the course are that students come to understand and execute the processes of (1) designing a study and collecting data, (2) conducting exploratory analyses on a data set, and (3) making inferences from the sample about the population of interest. Our focus is on students' development of skills related to the second objective and also, but to a slightly lesser degree, the third. Note that these course objectives are also part of the Advanced Placement Statistics course, so many of the skills under study here would be relevant to an advanced high school statistics course.

In addition, although the participants in the following studies are primarily sampled from a university with a reputation for attracting "quantitative types," the students in our samples typically have modest mathematics and science backgrounds (e.g., no prior Calculus experience). In this regard, we have reason to believe that the results would generalize fairly well to other student populations and to other typical introductory statistics courses.

STUDY 1: HOW DO STUDENTS DECOMPOSE THE TASK OF DATA ANALYSIS?

To begin our investigation of students' knowledge representations for data analysis, it is important to understand how students conceive of the task at hand when they face analyzing a data set. In other words, what do students view as the important components of the process of solving data-analysis problems? This question attacks a theoretical issue of task decomposition—do students decompose the task of data analysis in a way similar to experts?—but it also relates to a practical issue of knowledge transfer—how well can students apply what they have learned in their statistics class to solve new data-analysis problems in a different context? Past research suggests that students often fail to adequately apply statistical concepts and skills outside their original learning context. So, we sought to analyze students' approach to data-analysis problems in a novel context in order to identify potential sources of this knowledge-transfer problem. To address these issues, we conducted a small-scale protocol analysis study (see Lovett, 2001, for additional details).

Methods

Participants. Student participants were 10 undergraduates between 18 and 20 years of age who had recently completed the introductory statistics class mentioned earlier and who had received an A or B as final grade. They were invited to participate in a single session that would involve solving various data-analysis problems and were paid for their participation. In addition to these student participants, three expert participants (two Statistics graduate students, both of whom had been teaching assistants for the introductory course, and one Statistics professor, the instructor of the course) completed a subset of the same problems.

Design and Procedure. Each participant was tested individually in a private room with a personal computer running the statistics package

Problem: A weather modification experiment was conducted to investigate whether "seeding" clouds with silver nitrate would increase the amount of rainfall. Clouds were randomly assigned to the treatment group (to be seeded) or to the control group (not to be seeded), and data were collected on the total rain volume falling from each cloud. The variable *group* indicates whether each cloud was seeded or not, the variable *rain* indicates each cloud's rain volume, and *day* is the day of the measurement. Use these data to see whether cloud seeding increases rainfall.

Solution: In addition to appropriate graphical displays (here, a side-by-side boxplot display of *rainfall* for each *group*), the solution includes these descriptive and inferential statistics.

	N	MEAN	MEDIAN	STDEV	MIN	MAX
Seeded	45	61.33	40	45.31	20	160
Unseeded	45	44.67	40	35.07	20	160

95% confidence interval for $\mu_{seeded} - \mu_{not}$: (0.02, 0.58)
t-statistic = 2.11, p = 0.038, df = 85

Figure 12.2 Sample problem (and solution) from Study 1.

(DataDesk) that had been used in the introductory statistics course. Participants received instructions on providing verbal protocols and completed a few mental arithmetic problems to practice talking aloud. Then, the first problem's data file was opened from within the statistics package, and students were given a description of the data set and a question to address with the data. Figure 12.2 shows an example problem and a sample of correct responses that would be consistent with the goals and content of the course. Note that this set-up differs from students' prior experience at solving data-analysis problems in the computer laboratory sessions from the course: In the course, students were given a set of instructions detailing the steps to take in analyzing a given data set and a series of questions to answer as they proceeded through the instructions. In the experiment, no such instructions or probing questions were given for this study, so participants had to decide on their own sequence of problem-solving steps and on their own definition of problem completion.

Each of the student participants completed three such data-analysis problems, while their verbal protocols and computer actions with the statistics software package were recorded. Each of the expert participants completed two such problems, while verbal protocols and computer actions were similarly recorded. The verbal protocols and computer software logs were time-stamped so that the two data streams could be synchronized for later analysis.

TABLE 12.1
Seven Steps of Highly Successful Statistics Solvers

Step	Student Performance
1. Translate question	20%*
2. Identify relevant variables	60%*
3. Characterize variable type	0%*
4. Select appropriate analysis	50%†
5. Conduct analysis	100%†
6. Interpret results	80%†
7. Evaluate evidence	60%†

Note. *Percentage of steps explicitly mentioning this goal in verbal protocol.
†Percentage of accurate steps, calculated assuming previous step was correct.

Results and Discussion

Experts' and Students' Goal Structure for Data Analysis. From the experts' protocols, we first identified the steps they consistently applied (verbally or through interaction with the statistics package). This analysis showed a common set of seven steps employed by all the experts (see the step labels in Table 12.1). Notice that the first three of these steps involve understanding the problem and planning the analysis and hence do not require overt behavior. (These steps are not represented explicitly in the solution of Fig. 12.2.) Steps 4 and 5 are explicitly enacted and thus necessarily have an observable component. Step 6 and to a lesser degree Step 7 are logically implied by the problem statement ("Use these data to see whether cloud seeding increases rainfall."), and yet the problem statement does not specify the level at which these subgoals would be considered complete. Note that these seven steps bear some resemblance to the data-modeling description of data analysis presented in Lehrer and Schauble (this volume) and to the domain-general scientific reasoning process outlined in Schunn and Anderson (1999).

The fact that these experts showed such consistency and thoroughness in their problem-solving process likely reflects the fact that they all had been involved in teaching the introductory statistics course according to a common plan. Moreover, they were probably accustomed to modeling this complete process as part of their teaching (either in office hours, recitations, or lecture). Under ordinary circumstances, however, an expert at their level would probably not articulate so many steps. For example, an expert might skip directly to some exploratory analyses without explicit planning. Given this, we take these steps as representing not necessarily a true "expert model" of data-analysis skill but rather a model of "good student" performance these instructors were (implicitly or explicitly) trying to promote in the course. Hence, we take these seven steps as a standard of comparison for the student participants' problem-solving processes.

To what degree did the student participants show evidence of having represented each of these seven steps as important subgoals in their process of solving data-analysis problems? To assess this, we transcribed students' verbal protocols and merged them with the logged statistics software data in appropriate temporal order. Each problem-solving step explicitly taken by the students—expressed either via a verbal protocol statement or a statistics software action or some combination of the two—was categorized as relating to one of the seven steps of "good student" performance.

Table 12.1 presents the percentages of steps categorized into each of the seven step categories. For the first three planning steps, these percentages reflect students' explicit mention of the step being completed and are quite low. Of course, it is possible that students actually considered these steps without explicitly mentioning them, so the numbers here may reflect an underestimate of the true percentages. Nevertheless, it is important to note that only 50% of the time did students choose the appropriate analysis or analyses—no better than a coin flip. This suggests that even if students were engaging the preliminary planning steps (1–3) in some covert way, their low performance on the fourth step still presents evidence of inadequate or inaccurate planning.

More detailed analyses of the fourth step, choosing an appropriate analysis, further support the idea that students lacked adequate planning. Even though two or three analyses should be the maximum number of appropriate analyses per problem, students performed, on average, 11 separate analyses per problem! Three of these, on average, were repeats of the same analysis. Needless to say, students in this study were completing many inappropriate or unnecessary analyses, consistent with previous results and indicating students' failure to transfer what they learned in class. Our interpretation of this result could be softened if students were choosing the most appropriate analyses first (indicating that their first choices were appropriately selected) or last (indicating that they knew to conclude their exploration after conducting the key analyses). However, neither of these ways of sequencing analyses captured a majority of participants' trials. So, it seems that the most reasonable interpretation is that students were making selections without a systematic approach. This is further supported by several protocol statements indicating students' use of arbitrary strategies for analysis selection and the fact that accurate selections were more likely to follow the presence of explicit planning steps than their absence (see Lovett, 2001, for more details).

In contrast to planning and selecting appropriate analyses, the last three steps showed much higher rates. Note that Table 12.1 presents a measure of percent correct for these three steps. But these percentages were computed assuming the preceding step had been correct. That is, 100% accuracy on Step 5 "conduct the analysis" merely implies that students always conducted the analysis they intended, regardless of whether it was appropriate or relevant. Finally, it is worth noting that the lowest accuracy rate on the last three steps is for Step 7 "evaluate the evidence." This percentage is low mainly because students often stated that they had completed the problem before mentioning any issues that would have related to evaluating the strength of evidence with respect to the question. That is, like the preliminary planning Steps 1–3, students appear to be skipping important steps in the process of analyzing data.

Another common feature of students' interpretations of evidence (in Steps 6 and 7) that contrasts with the experts' is that students did not contextualize their analysis interpretations in terms of the details of the problem but rather tended to mention unitless numbers and meaningless codes (e.g., "the mean of height for Group 1 was 60.3 and for Group 2 was 55.6" rather than "the mean height of men was 60.3 inches, whereas for women it was only 55.6 inches.

Implications for Statistics Education. Students' goal structures show several important differences from experts' goals. Students appear not to represent the subgoals involved in planning an appropriate analysis, skills that were explicitly taught in the course. In addition, there is anecdotal evidence from the verbal protocols that the features and skills students are representing in order to select an analysis are superficial (e.g., "when I'm stuck, I use box-plots") and nonrobust (e.g., guess-and-test without an appropriate stopping criterion). Finally, students often fail to evaluate the strength of evidence after describing the results of an analysis.

These particular gaps in students' goal structure suggest that students may benefit from additional explicit instruction and practice with feedback on the skills of planning and selecting appropriate analyses. Indeed, a computer-based tutor for data analysis whose design was largely based on these results shows evidence of improved learning outcomes in these areas (see Meyer & Lovett, 2002).

It is also worth noting that the aspect of data-analysis skill in which students showed greatest strength was the interpretation of results. Looking back to the course students took and how interpretation skills were taught—relative to planning, selecting analyses, and evaluating the strength of evidence—can also lead to suggestions for best practice in teaching data analysis. The most salient feature of how this course taught interpretation of results is that students had much more practice conducting and interpreting results *on their own* than they had at the other types of skills. Even in computer labs where students worked with data using a statistics package, the lab handouts often prescribed what analyses should be conducted and then asked for interpretation of those analyses' results. Reducing this "practice gap" between different skills is an adjustment that has recently been made to the course, and preliminary results suggest that it is having positive effects.

This idea of ensuring that students get ample practice executing the particular skills they are supposed to learn is a general lesson for instructional practice. In other words, here we have theory and practice advocating a common guideline: Give students practice at the skills you want them to learn. It is surprisingly easy to overlook this, perhaps because instructors are so expert at the task at hand that they cannot easily see the many distinct subskills a student must manage in order to complete an entire problem. And yet, the theory of transfer of skill (Singley & Anderson, 1989) explicates how specific the effects of skill practice are: practicing one skill, such as interpreting statistical analyses, will strengthen subsequent use of that skill, but it will not help seemingly related skills, such as selecting appropriate analyses and evaluating strength of evidence. Maintaining close alignment between the goals of instruction and the skill practices in which students engage, is therefore a key consideration for effective instructional design.

Implications of Results for Learning Theory

Besides applying these results to inform the practice of teaching statistics, we would like to be able to generalize from them to inform learning theory. Starting with the main result that students showed difficulty in planning an appropriate analysis, we can ask whether this result could have been predicted by existing theories.

A straightforward application of the mechanism of utility-based learning (cf. Anderson & Lebiere, 1998) offers an interesting prediction. According to utility-based learning, actions with high utility (high reward and low cost) are preferred over those with low utility. From Study 1, we saw that planning—though it was relatively rare—actually increased the likelihood of students' choosing an appropriate analysis. Indeed, the idea behind planning in any task is that it helps produce better outcomes. This would suggest that planning actions would eventually be associated with higher utility and would come to be preferred over alternatives. And yet, we saw the opposite result in Study 1; planning was rather rare even though it produced better outcomes.

This contradiction of a theoretical prediction suggests a need for refinement or elaboration of the utility-based learning mechanism, or more appealing, a broader perspective on how it applies. As for re-interpretation, it is worth noting that planning steps likely incur a higher cost, at least for novices, because they represent the newly taught skills that are more error prone and slower. This line of argument suggests that a useful instructional intervention would be to ensure that when students are beginning their practice, the problems they encounter should force failure or very low rewards when any nonrobust strategy is used, so that any planning-based strategy will dominate by comparison. In time, this will help the planning skills to benefit from utility learning, while at the same time getting faster and more accurate from practice.

One could argue that this is consistent with the approach taken by Koedinger and Anderson (1993) to address students' difficulty in learning planning skills in geometry problem solving. By making the planning skills explicit and giving feedback on students' execution of these skills, the instruction essentially enforces effective practice of those planning skills over less robust problem-solving approaches. So, we can see Study 1's statistics-specific result as one case of a more general learning phenomenon: Planning skills are difficult to learn; making them explicit, enabling feedback opportunities, and ensuring they are advantageous to performance aids learning.

Even in cases where these suggestions are followed, however, students can still be surprisingly resistant to planning outside of the original learning context. For example, Scott and Reif (1999) trained students to employ a systematic approach to solving Newtonian mechanics problems in introductory physics. Even though students were significantly more accurate (incurred greater rewards) and faster (paid lower costs) when using this systematic approach than not, they in large part resorted to their old, nonsystematic habits at post-test. One of the common themes in students' remarks in post-experimental debriefing was that the newly taught, planning-based procedure felt more effortful and they preferred steps that made them feel as if they were getting closer to a solution.

One way of dealing with the failure of utility-based learning to explain students' lack of planning is to recognize that the particular utility function influencing student learning might actually be more general than that typically implemented in computational models. For example, it is possible that because planning steps do not have an outwardly observable action, it is less likely that learners will attribute ultimate rewards to their planning steps. In addition, students' utility functions may include more than objective measures of cost, such as time and errors, but also subjective measures, such as mental effort. Recent studies are beginning to assess the dimension of cognitive load and include it in explanations of learning effects (cf. Paas, Renkl, & Sweller, 2003). But this is an area where studies of classroom learning could help refine the theory: What really does "count" as a success or a cost? How important is mental effort compared to objective measures of effort? These are empirical questions.

STUDY 2: WHAT FEATURES DO STUDENTS INCORPORATE IN THEIR STRATEGIES FOR CHOOSING APPROPRIATE ANALYSES?

Whereas Study 1 assessed students' knowledge of the goal structure for solving data-analysis problems after students had completed an introductory course in Statistics, Study 2 aimed to examine students during the course of instruction and to investigate more closely the nature of the data-analysis skills they are learning. Based on the previous study's results, it was clear that planning and selecting appropriate analyses was difficult for students. Study 2 aimed to explore the nature of those skills and the kind of practice that would be most helpful in promoting their learning. In sum, this study examined students' skills for selecting appropriate analyses under different learning conditions and analyzes various features of these skills.

We investigated these issues in the context of a statistics mini-course. The idea behind this context was that it would offer a good balance between the controlled conditions of a laboratory setting and the ecological validity of a real classroom. In particular, students without prior college-level statistics training were recruited to participate in the mini-course. These students then received instruction and practice in a classroom setting that was similar to the actual course setting, including a series of lectures and corresponding problem-solving practice similar to the course's computer laboratory sessions.

To keep the content of the mini-course reasonably small in scope, the possible analyses from which students could choose were restricted to the following exploratory displays: pie charts, histograms, box-plots, scatter-plots, and contingency tables. To select among these analyses, students need to learn to identify which of the variables provided in the problem statement are relevant to the question being asked, and then determine whether these variables take categorical or quantitative values. The combination of relevant variable types (e.g., one quantitative variable, two categorical variables, one categorical plus one quantitative, etc.) uniquely determines which statistical display is best for answering the question asked. Although students may spontaneously notice or deliberately consider other aspects of the problem, such as the cover story, specific key words or phrasing of the question, and so forth, these details are considered to be surface rather than deep features in that they do not decide the structure of the problem. However, some of the verbal protocol statements from Study 1 indicated that students were actually making reference to superficial features of the problem in selecting their analyses. Moreover, Study 1 provided ample evidence that students were not selecting analyses based on a systematic accounting of the relevant variables and their types (e.g., low percentages for Steps 2 and 3 from Table 12.1).

Thus, one specific question investigated in Study 2 was the degree to which students represent the deep features of the problem (e.g., the relevant variables' quantitative or categorical status) versus superficial features of the problem (e.g., cover story, phrasing of the question, etc.).

Other research has provided supporting evidence that students learn and use superficial features present in their training. As Ben-Zeev and Star (2001) have shown, students may be induced to favor one solution method over another equally effective method simply by the presence of familiar problem features that they learned to associate with that solution procedure. In that study, participants studied worked-out examples that presented one technique for simplifying algebraic expressions containing logarithms and a different technique for expressions containing radicals. Participants showed a subsequent preference for using the solution procedure that matched the symbols contained in the expressions based on their training, even though both procedures were equally valid and efficient for those problems.

Of even greater concern, Quilici and Mayer (1996) have demonstrated that spurious correlations between superficial and deep features may also decrease students' ability to correctly solve problems lacking the correlated features, beyond just influencing them to choose one correct strategy over another equally correct strategy. They found that students who were trained on data-analysis problems whose cover stories were spuriously correlated with the problem type were less successful at identifying the correct statistical analysis to perform on post-test problems. In interpreting these results, they recommended that data-analysis instruction should include supporting guidance that explicitly asks students to identify the independent and dependent variables and to classify each as categorical or quantitative. Since these suggestions have been incorporated into the training provided in the current study, we are particularly interested in ascertaining whether the detrimental effect of spurious correlations on students' problem solving is still as pronounced when explicit instructional support is provided.

Methods

Participants. We recruited 52 participants from Carnegie Mellon University and the University of Pittsburgh, all of whom were at most 2 years past the completion of their bachelor's degree. Participants were restricted to fluent English speakers with no prior coursework of statistics past the secondary-school level.

Design. This study employed a pretest, instruction, post-test design. The experimental manipulation was one component of the instructional phase, namely a difference in the set of problems solved by two separate groups of participants. This manipulation involved whether deep versus superficial features were correlated in the two groups' sets of training problems. One group of students worked through problems in which the surface features (cover story, question wording, and variable types in the data set) were spuriously correlated with the correct answer. For the other group, these features were systematically varied across all the problem types. Although the participants in the "spurious-correlation" (S) condition might perform better during training due to the ease of identifying the correct answer, we expected that ultimately participants in the "varied-features" (V) condition would surpass their counterparts on the post-test due to more robust understanding of the key concepts guiding their decision of the appropriate statistical analysis to apply.

The training problem features manipulated to create the *S* and *V* conditions were the cover story, question wording, and variable types in the data sets. *Cover story* refers to the general topic of the problem (e.g., demographics, entertainment, academics, money, medicine), whereas question wording was reflected in the particular words and phrasing used in the final question of the problem statement. Variable types indicate the number and combination of categorical and/or quantitative variables included in the data set accompanying the problem. (Note that the variable types included in the problem, a superficial feature, can be varied at least somewhat independently from the variable types that are relevant to solving the problem, a deep feature.) As previously noted, students must process all of these features in order to solve the problem, but these features do not determine the correct statistical analysis that will answer the question posed in the problem.

In the *S* condition, every problem of the same type (i.e., pie chart, histogram, box-plot, scatter-plot, or contingency table) also used the same topic for its cover story and the same wording in its final question. In five of the six problems of each type, the variables in the accompanying data set were exactly those variables needed to answer the question, so that the number and type (categorical vs. quantitative) of variables matched the requirements for the correct statistical analysis to be performed. The remaining problem provided a data set including three variables, with only one or two of them being relevant to the problem, so that these participants obtained some practice in having to select the relevant variables before solving the problem.

In the *V* condition, every problem type included at least one problem using each of the cover story topics. Although it was not possible to use all of the question wordings for all of the problem types, each problem type included a range of different wordings, with no problem type using the same wording twice. Half of the six problems for each type provided three variables in their data sets, whereas the other half included only those variables that were relevant to the problem. Although this necessitated increasing the correlation between the data set variables and the problem type, reducing the

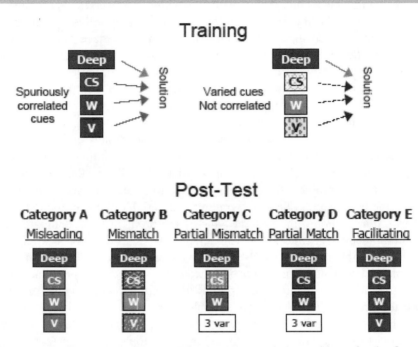

Figure 12.3 Illustration of the design of training and test problems for the *S* and *V* conditions in Study 2.

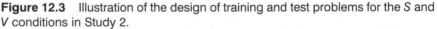

number of three-variable problems given in the *V* condition was intended to decrease the disparity in problem difficulty and skills practiced between the two conditions. Figure 12.3a illustrates the types of problems used during training in the *S* and *V* conditions.

Procedure. At the start of the experiment, participants completed two pretests measuring relevant statistical ability. The first pretest asked participants to categorize six data-analysis problems according to whatever scheme they found most compelling. This test was designed to tap the features students were processing as most important from the problem descriptions. The second pretest consisted of a paper-and-pencil skills assessment containing 28 multiple-choice questions measuring knowledge of basic statistical concepts and definitions.

The instructional component of the study extended across 4 consecutive days, with participants starting each day's session by watching a prerecorded video lecture of a statistics professor explaining how and when to use the data display of interest. This instruction included a demonstration of one or two examples of how to conduct and interpret results from the statistical analysis, as well as an explicit statement of the rules for deciding when to use each method of analysis. Up to this point, the training was identical across all conditions.

Following the video lecture on each day, participants were given a series of training problems to solve on their own via a computer interface. The computer interface presented the cover story for the problem (including the main question to be addressed using the data), a description of the variables measured, and then several questions about the data. In particular, immediately after reading the introductory problem statement, students had to identify which variables in the problem were relevant to the question asked (in cases where the problem included more variables than the question required), ascertain whether the relevant variables were categorical or quantitative, and identify specific values of the variables from the accompanying data set. The goal of these questions was to ensure that students were at least attending to the appropriate information before choosing the appropriate analysis for the data set and question. Study 1 had suggested that students were not explicitly commenting on these features, so these questions served as a way of confirming that, whether or not students selected analyses according to the deep features, we at least knew that students were able to identify these features correctly. After answering each of these questions in the computer interface, students received feedback on what the correct answer was so that they could continue with the rest of the problem. That is, in both conditions, students received the same feedback on each problem that specified the answers to all these questions, including the appropriate exploratory data analysis.

Note that the instructional manipulation just described applied only to the training problems. On days 2 through 4, each session began with a few training problems focusing on the new statistical display students had just learned (e.g., pie chart, histogram, box-plot, scatter-plot, or contingency table), and then continued with the additional problems reviewing all of the analysis methods they had learned so far. This resulted in participants solving more problems on the later days. Specifically, the 4 days of training provided students with 4, 7, 8, and then 11 problems on successive days, for a total of 30 training problems.

On the fifth day, participants completed several post-tests measuring their learning gains from the training. These included the same categorization task and skills assessment that had been done as pretests, as well as a comprehensive transfer problem-solving test requiring them to solve problems similar to those they had practiced during training. This test contained 30 problems in which participants again had to determine the appropriate statistical analysis to perform to answer a given question about a set of data, but with no supplementary questions or feedback guiding their solution process. The features of these problems were designed to make it easier to infer the extent of students' reliance on surface versus deep features as a function of their instructional conditions. Ten problems included the same combinations of surface features that had been present in the *S*-condition training, of which five were answered by the same statistical display that had been spuriously correlated with those features (Category E), and five were impossible to answer using the information given due to variables missing from the data set (Category A). The remaining 20 problems (Categories B, C, and D) utilized the same surface features presented during the *S*-condition training, but in conflicting combinations: for example, a problem might include a cover story that had been correlated with histograms, question wording that had been correlated with scatter-plots, and data set variables that had been correlated with box-plots, yet the problem would be correctly answered using a pie chart. Figure 12.3 illustates some of these aspects of the design of the transfer test.

Results and Discussion

Participants exhibited no significant differences between conditions on either of the pretest measures or in their improvement on those two measures from pre- to post-test. This null result was actually anticipated for the multiple-choice test, regardless of condition, since students were getting relatively little direct practice at recalling or using the definitions tested in this context. In contrast, we would have expected some difference between conditions in the problem-sorting task. For example, if students in one condition had become more sensitive to the problems' deep features, then their sorting might have shifted more to be based on those features. One possible explanation for the lack of difference in sorting behavior is that this task was simply not sensitive enough. Indeed, the transfer test was expected to be the most sensitive measure and the most ecologically valid measure as well. So, the remainder of this section discusses results of the transfer problems that were part of the post-test.

Differences between conditions did emerge on the 30-problem transfer test, where students had to solve additional problems without feedback ($M_S = .4958$, $SD_S = .1349$; $M_V = .6029$, $SD_V = .1210$; $t (45) = 2.860$, $p = .006$; 95%CI [.0317, .1825]). In particular, *V*-participants outperformed *S*-participants on all transfer problems except those where the correct answer had been spuriously correlated with all three of the surface features during the *S*-condition training (Fig. 12.3, Category E). This distinction suggests that although the *S*-participants may have performed adequately on their training problems, their understanding of the problems' structure was not sufficiently general to solve problems correctly in the absence of supporting surface features cuing them to the appropriate statistical analysis. Figures 12.4b and 12.4c summarize the difference in performance between conditions for all five categories of problems on the transfer test.

Analyzing the error patterns of S-condition participants revealed that they were indeed using the surface features to choose their analyses. On transfer problems where all three of the surface features had been correlated with the same incorrect data display (Fig. 12.3, Category A), S-participants were significantly more likely to choose that display as their answer than V-participants according to a 2 (condition) × 2 (matching vs. nonmatching errors) ANOVA (M_S = 3.25, SD_S = 1.391; M_V = 2.17, SD_V = 1.154; $t(45)$ = 2.880, p = .006). For problems whose surface features had been correlated with two or three different displays (Fig. 12.3, Categories B and C), S-participants made significantly more errors reflecting the influence of the cover story (CS) or question wording (Wd), as shown by a chi-square analysis of the number of errors made versus the number of possible errors ($\chi^2_{CS}(1)$ = 9.228, p_{CS} = .002; $\chi^2_W(1)$ = 6.525, p_W = .011). Figures 12.4b and 12.4c summarize the error patterns on the transfer test for S- and V-participants.

These differences in performance on the transfer test underscore the difference in what participants in the two conditions learned from their training: Problems whose answers were spuriously correlated with surface features led S-participants to learn surface features, whereas problems whose surface features varied across the range of possible answers led V-participants to learn the deep structure. According to further analyses of the knowledge structures that they appeared to be using to solve these problems, S-participants' knowledge of these spuriously correlated superficial features was stronger than their knowledge of the relevant information that determined the problems' deep structure (cf. Chang, Koedinger, & Lovett, in preparation). For example, on the transfer test, S-participants selected analyses in large part based on the cover story of the problem, even when this feature led to selecting an inappropriate display (i.e., when the cover story feature and the deep features were no longer correlated). In contrast, V-participants demonstrated stronger knowledge of deep structure than surface features.

The magnitude of the impact of this relatively mild manipulation shows a kind of perverse efficiency in students' learning, insofar as they learn—and learn quite well—exactly those features that are useful to their problem-solving success during training, and not the more general knowledge structures that were emphasized in explicit instruction but whose long-term utility has yet to be proven. Training that does not demand generalizing beyond these surface features is not likely to produce general knowledge; such training rewards short-term success achieved with an economy of mental effort.

Implications of Results for Instructional Practice

The superior transfer post-test performance by participants trained in the V condition highlights the importance of requiring that students practice the key skills

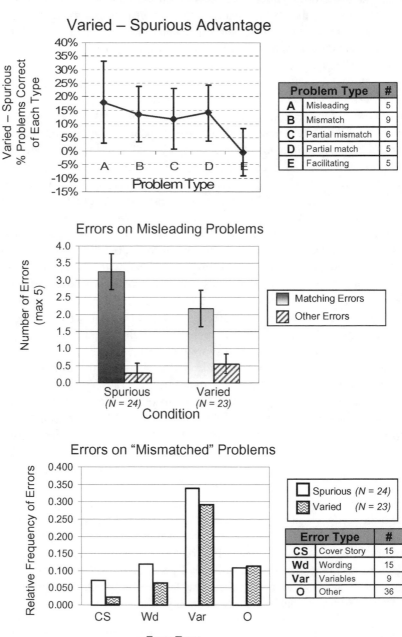

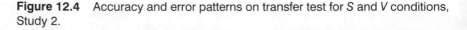

Figure 12.4   Accuracy and error patterns on transfer test for *S* and *V* conditions, Study 2.

involved in solving the problems, without spuriously boosting their success through helpful but superficial cues. The errors committed by *S*-participants indicate that students relied on these surface features to choose their answers on the post-test, a habit that may have developed and been reinforced during training, at the expense of building proficiency in identifying the deep structure of the problem. Thus, instruction that maximizes the utility of the instructed strategies and minimizes the utility of undesirable strategies will be most effective for student learning, especially in the case of planning skills.

This finding is consistent with the value of introducing desirable difficulty in promoting long-term retention and transfer (Bjork, 1994). Research from the domains of motor skills and verbal memory indicates that although increasing task variability during practice may initially depress performance, such a manipulation in fact improves transfer to different testing conditions (Schmidt & Bjork, 1992). The difficulty with which *S*-participants in this study generalized their knowledge to problems with different surface features offers another demonstration of this principle in a realistic educational setting.

A second implication of these results for instructional practice involves accurate assessment of student learning. The distinction in Study 2 between *S*-participants' apparent success during training and their poorer performance at the test belies the validity of relying solely on gross measures of accuracy and solution time to assess students' learning. Without explicitly assessing students' use of surface and deep knowledge in arriving at their answers, instructors may not be able to determine whether their students are reaching the right answers for the right reasons.

Implications of Results for Learning Theory

The promising results obtained from the feature-varying (*V*) training condition here invite further questions about the mechanisms underlying its effectiveness. One question is how this relates to cognitive load theory, which ordinarily would predict that increased variability risks overwhelming the learner with a high working memory load, thereby hindering the learning that can take place (Sweller, 1988). The learning benefits realized through the increased variability suggest that the additional difficulty contributes to germane rather than extraneous cognitive load, with students investing more effort in the construction of richer and more appropriate schemas. Other research within the framework of cognitive load theory confirms the value of increased variability in problem structure rather than surface features, and for worked examples but not conventional problem-solving (Paas & van Merriënboer, 1994). In light of these differences, the results of the current study suggest that it would be worthwhile to more clearly distinguish variability of problem structure and variability of irrelevant surface features to understand how each may affect learning.

Other research has described the value of limiting the variability in the problems students solve to a single dimension, while keeping the rest constant (e.g., Carnine, 1980; Gentner & Gunn, 2001; Linn, 2005; Scheiter & Gerjets, 2003; Schwartz & Bransford, 1998; Tennyson, 1972). Some of the arguments advanced in favor of this approach include reducing memory load and increasing the salience of the relevant feature. In situations where students examine two problems simultaneously, designing those problem pairs to vary on only one dimension may facilitate alignment of the problem structures or focus attention on the critical contrast. More recent research exploring these questions indicates that although the specific dimension that should vary may depend on the skills and learning goals of the students, novices exhibit a greater need to learn to discriminate between structures than to learn to generalize across surface features, so that they benefit more from comparisons that vary the problem structure (Chang, 2006).

Thus, in considering the implications of this research for theory, we have many questions: How much feature variability is beneficial? When in students' experience is it helpful to vary particular problem features? How does utility-based learning influence the likelihood that students will learn particular features? Are there domain-specific contributions that make it difficult to find adequate generalizations along these lines? Pursuing these questions will likely be productive for both improving theory and instructional practice.

STUDY 2 CONTINUED: HOW GENERAL ARE STUDENTS' SKILLS FOR CHOOSING APPROPRIATE ANALYSES?

Thus far in Study 2, the focus was on examining the degree to which and the conditions under which students incorporate deep rather than superficial features in their skills for analyzing data. The main finding was that students were more likely to learn and use the deep features of data analysis when they practiced their skills on problems where superficial and deep features were varied so as to avoid spurious correlations. Thus, when they engaged in this "varied" instruction, students began to exhibit a hallmark of expertise: representing problems according to their deep features (e.g., Chi et al., 1982). From the data collected in this study, we can also investigate an additional feature of students' knowledge representations that relates to expertise, namely, the generality of students' skills for choosing appropriate analyses.

When examining the instruction offered in the introductory course and looking back to the experts' protocols from Study 1, the representation of knowledge that seemed most consistent with experts' approach to exploratory data analysis reflected a single, general procedure for solving these problems. That is, regardless of which display was ultimately the one chosen, experts seemed to be engaging the same data-analysis skill. As well, in their teaching, they were advocating a single procedure for student to use in solving data-analysis problems. And yet, students' approach to the task of data analysis seemed much more constrained and less general: students used more arbitrary "guess and test" strategies for deciding on an analysis; they did not follow a systematic approach; and they relied heavily on superficial features of the problem when their training allowed (or encouraged) it.

Our additional goal for Study 2, then, was to investigate the degree to which students in the V condition were learning several specific skills for data analysis or one, more general skill. To accomplish this, we relied on the power-law of learning (Newell & Rosenbloom, 1981) and the fact that the more a particular skill is used, the more quickly and/or accurately that skill will be executed. Specifically, the power-law of learning is the finding that practicing a skill shows the same pattern of improvement across many different domains, namely that of a power function. A power function of practice expresses performance ($f(x)$) in terms of the number of practice opportunities (x) and several parameters (here, a and b), according to the following function: $f(x) = ax^{-b}$.

The logic of our analysis, then, is to fit two contrasting models to the V-participants' learning data, both of which make use of the power-law of practice. The difference between the two models lies in whether the skill that is taken to be practiced is a single, generic skill that applies across all the training problems or five separate skills, one for each of the five display types that students practiced on different subsets of the training problems. Then, we can evaluate which model fits the data better.

Method

The participants in this study are simply the V-participants from Study 2. The data used in answering this question of skill generality are simply their latency data on the training problems.

Results and Discussion

For each of the thirty training problems, we can calculate the time participants took to select the appropriate display and organize these latency data according to our two distinct models of skill representation: the *single skill* model and the *separate skills* model. In the single skill model, we organize the data in sequence from 1 to 30, for the 30 opportunities students had to practice the common selection skill—once for each training problem (see Fig. 12.5). In the "separate display skills" model, we organize the data according to the nth practice opportunity students had for each of the five separate skills (see Fig. 12.6). Note that in the "separate display skills" model, the maximum number of practice opportunities for any skill is six because each of the five display types was practiced equally often during training.

For each organization of the data, we fit a model that applies a power function to the latency data. For the single skill model, there are two free parameters (a and b), whereas for the separate skills model, there are several different ways we could parameterize the five different power functions. Initially, we chose to select a common b parameter for all five power functions but to let the a parameters vary. When the best-fitting parameter values for each of these models had b parameters close to 0.5, it seemed parsimonious to fit the single skill model by varying only the a parameter, and the separate skills model by varying only the five separate a parameters.

Still, the separate skills model has more free parameters than the single skill model. This can be accounted for by using a measure of fit (or in this case misfit) that penalizes the model for extra free parameters. The measure of misfit we used is the Bayes Information Criterion (BIC; Schwarz, 1978).

The results of our model fitting revealed that the separate skills model has a lower misfit measure (BIC = 25.1) compared to the single skill model (BIC = 31.0). That is, even after accounting for the separate skills model's greater number of free parameters, this model better accounts for students' latency data during learning.

The best-fitting function for the single skill model is $y = 13x^{-.05}$, and the best-fitting functions for the separate skills model are as follows: $y = 12x^{-.05}$ for histogram, $y = 10x^{-.05}$ for pie chart, $y = 10x^{-.05}$ for box-plot, $y = 4x^{-.05}$ for scatter-plot, and $y = 5x^{-.05}$ for contingency table. Note that the lower parameters for scatter-plots and contingency tables may suggest that students' prior experience with graphing in two dimensions and making frequency tables may have carried over to this study.

Implications of These Results for Practice and for Learning Theory

As just demonstrated, we were able to analyze students' performance according to the ideas of skill-based power-law speed-up. From this analysis, we found that the separate skills model (with one skill for each separate data display) fit students' data better than the single skill model. This suggests that students' knowledge representation is not yet as general as we would expect from experts. But this is not so surprising: These students have only studied data-analysis briefly in a mini-course with no other prior statistics coursework. The next questions for instructional application, then, are the following: When would we expect students to transition to the "more expert" single skill representation? What can we do to promote that transition? These questions deserve

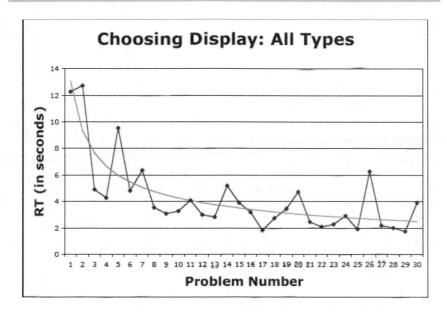

Figure 12.5   Practice effects on latency for the "single skill" model, plus best-fitting power-law function.

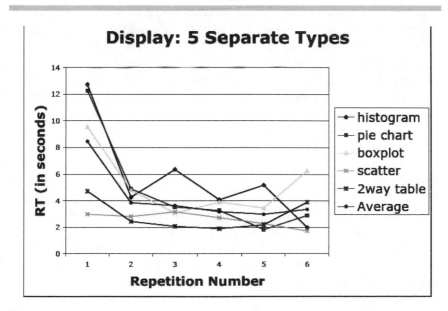

Figure 12.6   Practice effects on latency for the five separate display-selection skills.

more attention, especially as statistics education research moves beyond the introductory course.

Regarding current theory, there is not a well-supported mechanism for the process of generalization that would lead to specific guidelines for instruction in this regard. So, we are left with more open questions: How can we build a workable learning mechanism for generalization into current frameworks? How can we best use classroom research to inform theory in this regard? The issues of generalization and transfer are crucial, however, because there is so much to be gained if students can take what they have learned about statistical reasoning and carry it into their daily lives.

GENERAL DISCUSSION

The studies reported in this chapter were all aimed at better understanding students' knowledge representations in the area of exploratory data analysis. In Study 1, we revealed students' lack of explicit planning skills and their consequential difficulty in selecting appropriate exploratory analyses. We also showed that students often skipped the concluding step of data analysis—evaluating the strength of evidence. In Study 2, we found that when training problems present spurious correlations between superficial and deep features of the domain, students tend to learn to select analyses according to these superficial features rather than using the deep features to execute a more robust approach. When the training problems students solve offer a more varied set of features, without spurious correlations, students gain stronger representations of the deep features of the domain and can better transfer what they have learned to novel problems. Even these students, however, do not achieve a generalized representation of exploratory analysis skill (like that of an expert) but rather are refining several separate skills that apply in different data-analysis situations.

Although these knowledge representations can only be indirectly observed, they can have profound impact on students' direct performance. Indeed, the distinction between the theoretical construct of knowledge representation and its applied implications in student performance is a theme of this chapter and, at the same time, an underlying issue in teaching and learning. The teacher aims to help students develop more sophisticated internal knowledge structures, but can only observe and assess these through students' explicit behaviors. In addition, the teacher cannot directly adjust or refine students' knowledge structures but instead must present opportunities for students to engage in processing that will hopefully produce knowledge change.

Basic research in cognitive psychology has led to a variety of techniques for making inferences about internal knowledge representations. Some of these have been illustrated in the work presented here. But there are other techniques as well that could be used to complement our approach and to offer converging evidence of where students' knowledge representations are developing most and where there is greatest room for improvement. Some of these other techniques make use of the potential symmetry or asymmetry in students' abilities to perform a task in multiple ways. The simplest example of this is to test whether a paired associate "x goes with y" can be equally well retrieved from either item in the pair. This technique can also be applied in more skill-based settings (e.g., Anderson, Fincham, & Douglass, 1997). In the context of statistics instruction, one could ask: Are students as likely to inappropriately conduct a scatter-plot when they should use a box-plot as vice versa? Other factors that affect performance can also be analyzed to make inferences about knowledge representation, for example, the patterns of errors and accuracies, the impact of contextualization on performance, and the correlation between problem-solving performance and conceptual understanding. One argument implicit in this chapter is that conducting such analyses can not only reveal something about the nature of students' knowledge but about more effective practices for teaching.

Indeed, in each of the studies presented, in understanding statistics students' knowledge representations led to suggestions for improving instruction. Some of these have already been undertaken with positive results, and we can continue in these efforts. And, going in the other direction, instructional, classroom-based results offered valuable updates to current theory. Thus, the benefits of exploring students' knowledge representations can feed back to student learning and learning theory more generally.

REFERENCES

Anderson, J. R., & Lebiere, C. (1998). *The atomic components of thought*. Mahwah, NJ: Lawrence Erlbaum Associates.

Anderson, J. R., Fincham, J. M., & Douglass, S. (1997). The role of examples and rules in the acquisition of a cognitive skill. *Journal of Experimental Psychology: Learning, Memory, and Cognition, 23,* 932–945.

Ben-Zeev, T., & Star, J. R. (2001). Spurious correlations in mathematical thinking. *Cognition and Instruction, 19,* 253–275.

Bjork, R. A. (1994). Memory and metamemory considerations in the training of human beings. In J. Metcalfe & A. Shimamura (Eds.), *Metacognition: Knowing about knowing* (pp. 185–205). Cambridge, MA: MIT Press.

Carnine, D. W. (1980). Relationships between stimulus variation and the formation of misconceptions. *Journal of Educational Research, 74,* 106–110.

Chang, N. M. (2006). *Learning to discriminate and generalize through problem comparisons*. Unpublished doctoral dissertation. Carnegie Mellon University, Pittsburgh, PA.

Chang, N. M., Koedinger, K. R., & Lovett, M. C. (in preparation). *How spurious correlations influence students' learning*.

Chi, M. T. H., Glaser, R., & Rees, E. (1982). Expertise in problem solving, In R. S. Sternberg (Ed.), *Advances in the psychology of human intelligence* (pp. 1-75). Hillsdale, NJ: Lawrence Erlbaum Associates.

Gentner, D., & Gunn, V. (2001). Structural alignment facilitates the noticing of differences. *Memory & Cognition, 29,* 565–577.

Koedinger, K. R., & Anderson, J. R. (1993). Reifying implicit planning in geometry: Guidelines for model-based intelligent tutoring system design. In S. Lajoie & S. Derry (Eds.), *Computers as cognitive tools* (pp. 15–45). Hillsdale, NJ: Lawrence Erlbaum Associates.

Linn, M. C. (2005). WISE design for lifelong learning—pivotal cases. In P. Gärdenfors & P. Johansson (Eds.), *Cognition, education, and communication technology* (pp. 223–255). Mahwah, NJ: Lawrence Erlbaum Associates.

Lovett, M. C. (2001). A collaborative convergence on studying reasoning processes: A case study in statistics. In S. Carver & D. Klahr (Eds.), *Cognition and instruction: Twenty-five years of progress* (pp. 347–384). Mahwah, NJ: Lawrence Erlbaum Associates.

Meyer, O., & Lovett, M. C. (2002). Implementing a cognitive tutor in a statistical reasoning course: Getting the big picture. *Proceedings of the Seventh International Conference on Teaching Statistics.* Voorburg, the Netherlands: IASE.

Newell, A., & Rosenbloom, P. (1981). Mechanisms of skill acquisition and the law of practice. In J. Anderson (Ed.), *Cognitive skills and their acquisition* (pp. 1–55). Hillsdale, NJ: Lawrence Erlbaum Associates.

Paas, F., Renkl, A., & Sweller, J. (Eds.). (2003). Cognitive load theory *Educational Psychologist, 31(1).*

Paas, F. G. W. C., & Van Merriënboer, J. J. G. (1994). Variability of worked examples and transfer of geometrical problem-solving skills: A cognitive-load approach. *Journal of Educational Psychology, 86,* 122–133.

Quilici, J. L., & Mayer, R. E. (1996). Role of examples in how students learn to categorize statistics word problems. *Journal of Educational Psychology, 88,* 144–161.

Scheiter, K., & Gerjets, P. (2003). Sequence effects in solving knowledge-rich problems: The ambiguous role of surface similarities. In R. Alterman & D. Kirsh (Eds.), *Proceedings of the 25th Annual Meeting of the Cognitive Science Society* (pp. 1035–1040). Boston MA: Cognitive Science Society.

Schmidt, R. A., & Bjork, R. A. (1992). New conceptualizations of practice: Common principles in three paradigms suggest new concepts for training. *Psychological Science, 3,* 207–217.

Schunn, C. D., & Anderson, J. R. (1999). The generality/specificity of expertise in scientific reasoning. *Cognitive Science, 23*(3), 337–370.

Schwartz, D. L., & Bransford, J. D. (1998). A time for telling. *Cognition and Instruction, 16,* 475–522.

Schwarz, G. (1978). Estimating the dimension of a model. *Annals of Statistics, 6,* 461–466.

Scott, L., & Reif, R. (1999). *Teaching force-body diagrams systematically.* Unpublished masters' thesis, Carnegie Mellon University, Pittsburgh, PA.

Singley, M. K., & Anderson, J. R. (1989). *The transfer of cognitive skill.* Cambridge, MA: Harvard University Press.

Stokes, D. E. (1997). *Pasteur's quadrant: Basic science and technological innovation.* Washington, DC: Brookings Institution Press.

Sweller, J. (1988). Cognitive load during problem solving: Effects on learning. *Cognitive Science, 12,* 257–285.

Tennyson, R. D. (1972). A review of experimental methodology in instructional task sequencing. *AV Communication Review, 20,* 147–159.

13

Reconsidering Prior Knowledge

Daniel L. Schwartz
David Sears
Jammie Chang
Stanford University

An important goal of instruction is to prepare students for future learning. Educators hope that students will be prepared to learn from the next lesson, the next class, the next year, and opportunities beyond. Despite these hopes, assessment practices often overlook the goal of preparing people to learn, and this can make it difficult to judge the value of different learning experiences (Bransford & Schwartz, 1999). For example, televised interviews with recent Harvard graduates revealed serious misconceptions about the causes of the seasons. Under this assessment, their Ivy League educations seemed useless. This is a severe mismeasurement. If these students cared to learn about the cause of the seasons, they would be more prepared to do so than most young adults who never went to college. If the goal is to prepare people to learn, then it is important to design assessments that are sensitive to that goal. As we demonstrate in the following section, assessments of preparation for future learning can reveal the hidden value of educational experiences that can look poor by many standard assessments.

In this chapter, we use preparation for future learning assessments to work backwards to identify the types of prior knowledge that prepare students to learn. Most constructivist-inspired instruction attempts to make contact with students' prior knowledge so students will learn better. But what happens when students do not have the appropriate prior knowledge? We highlight how to develop a specific form of prior knowledge that many current models of learning and instruction do not address very well. The situation we emphasize occurs when people's prior knowledge is internally incommensurable. By *incommensurable* we mean that individuals cannot put information in the same rational system for combination or comparison. Incommensurables cannot be "measured" in the same terms. For example, young children who reason about the balance scale often see weight and distance as incommensurable. The notion of weight cannot be related to the distance dimension, and the notion of distance cannot be related to the weight dimension.

Incommensurable knowledge comes in many forms. With a contradiction, for example, the contradictory claims cannot both be rational, at least not according to one another. Here, we are particularly interested in cases where two or more measures of information cannot be related directly, and it is necessary to develop a higher order representation to relate them. An example from the domain of statistics can clarify. Consider how beginners often find the variability of a sample. One common solution we have observed is they sum the distances between the data points. Given 3, 5, 7, they might subtract 3 from 5, 3 from 7, and 5 from 7. They then sum the values of the pair-wise distances ($2 + 4 + 2 = 6$). This works quite well, until one needs to compare samples of different sizes. If one sample has more data points than the other, it will appear to have greater variability because there are more pair-wise distances. To make different sample sizes commensurable, most variability formulas divide by the sample size 'n.' This finds the average distance between points and permits a comparison across samples of different size.

We believe that a key challenge for statistics instruction is that people's relevant prior knowledge often consists of pieces that are tacitly or explicitly incommensurable. For example, how can one compare high jump scores with sprint times? Time and distance are different measurement systems. In this chapter, we provide several examples and describe how our instructional model helps students appreciate and work to reconcile incommensurables. The knowledge generated by our instruction often includes a critical early form of prior knowledge. By itself, the knowledge does not support independent problem solving. However, as we demonstrate, this early knowledge has a large pay-off because it prepares students to learn standard solutions quite well, which subsequently supports independent problem solving and flexible mastery.

EARLIER FORMS OF KNOWLEDGE

People learn by building on prior knowledge and abilities. This suggests it is important to design educational activities that are relevant to students' prior knowledge so they can treat lessons meaningfully. By the same token, students

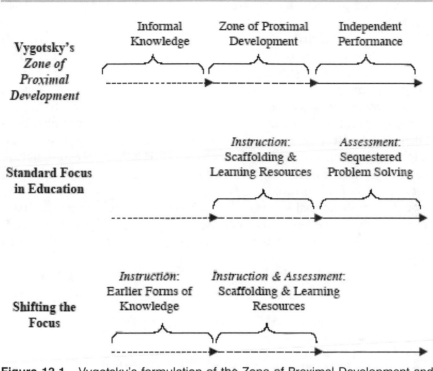

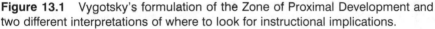

Figure 13.1 Vygotsky's formulation of the Zone of Proximal Development and two different interpretations of where to look for instructional implications.

need the right prior knowledge to start with. If students do not have useful prior knowledge, then there is a strong risk that they will build new knowledge on a faulty foundation; they may develop misconceptions or brittle behavioral routines. Our instructional goal is to develop forms of prior knowledge that can support learning. We will label these as "earlier" forms of knowledge to differentiate them from the prior knowledge that students already have.

To clarify the idea of earlier forms of knowledge, we borrow Vygotsky's (1934/1987) concept of the zone of proximal development. The top of Figure 13.1 shows that Vygotsky's construct comprises three zones. In the left-most zone, the child cannot complete a performance, even with help. For example, a child may be incapable of adding two numbers. In the zone of proximal development, the child can complete a mature performance with help, for example, if an adult holds up fingers on both hands to help the child count the combined quantities. Finally, experiences in the zone of proximal development can help a child move to a zone of independent performance—the child can add two numbers without help.

A common instructional interpretation of Vygotsky emphasizes the latter two zones, as shown in the middle panel of Figure 13.1. Educators embrace the zone of proximal development for its instructional implications; it is important to consider what types of scaffolds, learning resources, and activities can best build on children's prior abilities to support learning and subsequent independent performance. By this interpretation, the latter zone of independent performance is most relevant to issues of assessment. To find out if children have learned, educators can examine how well they complete tasks independently. Bransford and Schwartz (1999) referred to these assessments of independent performance as *sequestered problem solving*, because students are shielded from learning resources and scaffolds that can contaminate a test of independent performance.

A second educational interpretation of Vygotsky, which we propose here, shifts the focus to the left, as shown in the bottom panel of Figure 13.1. In this view, there is more attention to instructional activities that can expand the zone of proximal development so a child can learn from available resources. In addition, the zone of proximal development itself becomes highly relevant to issues of assessment. Vygotsky directly spoke to the assessment implications:

> Like a gardener who in appraising species for yield would proceed incorrectly if he considered only the ripe fruit in the orchard and did not know how to evaluate the condition of the trees that had not yet produced mature fruit, the psychologist who is limited to ascertaining what has matured, leaving what is maturing aside, will never be able to obtain any kind of true and complete representation of the internal state of the whole development..." (1934/1987, p. 200)

As Vygotsky pointed out, assessments of a child's zone of proximal development are a valuable way to estimate a child's developmental trajectory. These types of assessments are often called dynamic assessments (Feuerstein, 1979), because they examine how well a child can move along a trajectory of learning when given help. Focusing on learning rather than child maturation, Bransford and Schwartz (1999) referred to these types of assessments as tests of *preparation for future learning* (PFL). They argued that sequestered assessments of independent problem solving can be misleading when the question of interest is really whether people are in a position to continue learning.

The left-shift in our focus on Vygotsky's formulation also changes instructional perspectives. Rather than solely focusing on scaffolds or learning resources that support competent performance, it is also important to consider how to develop earlier forms of knowledge that prepare people to take advantage of future possibilities for learning.[1] For example, Martin and

Schwartz (2005) found that although certain learning materials did not affect independent performance, they did influence how prepared students were to learn from novel resources. In this study, the authors taught children to solve fraction addition problems using either pie wedges or tile pieces. Children in both conditions learned equally well to solve the problems using their base materials (pies or tiles). The children then received similar problems to the ones they had successfully learned to solve, but this time they had to solve them in their head without any materials. The students in both conditions did equally poorly. Thus, by this test of independent problem solving, the two methods of instruction performed the same. However, Martin and Schwartz also asked the children to retry the problems they could not do in their heads, this time using new physical materials (e.g., beans and cups, fraction bars, etc.). This PFL assessment, which included scaffolds in the form of new hands-on materials, revealed a different picture. The tile students learned to use the resources to solve 55% of the problems, whereas the pie students could only solve 35% of the problems. Thus the tile students were better prepared to learn how to use the new materials successfully, even though they could not solve these problems in their heads. Evidently, it is possible to develop forms of early knowledge that, although insufficient to support unaided performance, determine what learning resources will be within a student's zone of proximal development.

Developing earlier knowledge that can prepare people to learn is particularly important for statistics. The literature on judgment under uncertainty highlights the danger of not developing appropriate prior knowledge (Kahneman, Slovic, & Tversky, 1983). Statistics instruction can implicitly tap into inappropriate intuitions that have a surface similarity to statistics proper. People will use these intuitions to make sense of statistics instruction, but because the intuitions are not quite right, people will develop misconceptions.

For example, statistics often involves extrapolating from a rate of occurrence in a sample to make an estimate for a population. The proportionality of the sample ratio and the estimated population ratio taps into a notion of similarity, and people will think about probabilistic situations using similarity rather than likelihood. We recall a psychology professor answering the

---

[1]To our knowledge, the instructional possibility of developing earlier knowledge to expand children's zone of proximal development is not something Vygotsky addressed. Vygotsky was working on the proposal that culturally derived ("scientific") ideas can cause development, and therefore, he wanted to show that the introduction of these ideas in the zone of proximal development pushed a child's development forward. "Instruction is only useful when it moves ahead of development. When it does, it impells [sic] or wakens a whole series of functions that are in a stage of maturation lying in the zone of proximal development" (Vygotsky, 1934/1987, p. 212).

following question: If you need a sample of 50 people to get a reliable estimate for a population of 1,000, how large of a sample do you need if the population is 10,000?" The professor incorrectly replied that you would need a sample of 500 people (cf. Bar-Hillel, 1980). Though we are sure the professor had been taught the law of large numbers, this professor reasoned with similarity instead. One solution to this type of recurrent problem is to defuse misconceptions as they arise (e.g., Minstrell, 1989). For instance, it was pointed out, to our colleague's chagrin, that the reliability of the sample is independent of the size of the population. Another solution is to develop the right early knowledge to start with so people will learn more deeply when they are first taught. In the following section, we describe the type of earlier knowledge that we think prepares people to learn well in the domain of statistics.

TROUBLES IN PRIOR KNOWLEDGE

There are many different forms of prior knowledge that can support subsequent learning. In general, there are two common approaches to the role of prior knowledge that can help people learn. One takes a conceptual focus and attempts to build on students' prior intuitions and experiences. The other takes a procedural focus and aims for the mastery of component skills and the subsequent combination of those components. Both of these approaches are highly valuable, but here we highlight situations in which they appear insufficient. In particular, these methods have difficulty when prior knowledge holds incommensurables.

One Challenge of Building on Intuition and Everyday Experience

As stated before, people always build on prior knowledge to learn, and explicit efforts to leverage prior knowledge can be extremely valuable in instruction. A simple analogy can help clarify the structure of an otherwise foreign concept (e.g., atoms are like the solar system). This approach to instruction presupposes that the prior knowledge is already in place in the form of intuitions or grounded experiences. The challenge of instruction is to make contact with students' prior knowledge. If students cannot make sense of a lesson with their pre-existing knowledge, they will not understand.

There are cases, however, when people can encounter difficulty building correctly on prior intuitions because those intuitions are incommensurable in the learner's view. One example comes from an investigation of 12-year-olds' concepts of sampling. Schwartz, Goldman, Vye, Barron, and CTGV (1998) asked children to design sampling protocols for two different scenarios. In the

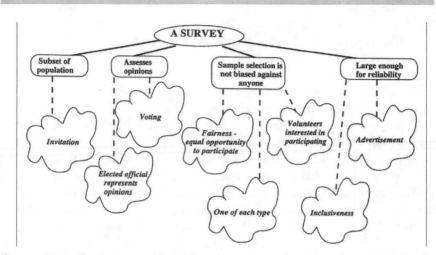

Figure 13.2 Twelve-year-old children have many intuitions that exhibit family resemblances to sampling, but none works quite right. (Schwartz et al., 1998, adapted with permission).

"fun booth" scenario, the children had to develop a plan to sample 40 students to find out what type of fun booth the 400 students at the school would prefer at a school fair. In the "gender" scenario, they had to develop a plan to sample 40 students to estimate how many boys and girls there were at their school of 400 students. The children understood the idea of using a sample to infer a population. They also drew on a variety of everyday concepts that exhibited family resemblances to the notion of sampling. Figure 13.2 provides a schematic summary of the different ways the children thought about taking a sample. The students had relevant prior knowledge, and the instructional challenge appeared to be how to connect this knowledge.

The children, however, also exhibited a strange inconsistency. For the gender scenario, 87% of the children generated relatively random sampling methods, such as standing at the front door at the beginning of the day and counting the number of boys and girls among the first 40. In contrast, for the fun booth scenario, 87% of the children generated biased sampling methods, selecting their sample based on whether the people had attributes relevant to a particular fun booth. For example, the children said they would sample the baseball players to see if they would come to a booth that involved throwing balls to dunk a teacher. The context of sampling influenced how the children reasoned about taking a sample. They appeared to be shifting interpretations of the task to make sense of these two situations.

Further examination revealed the problem. The children thought of cause and chance as incommensurable. The gender scenario did not involve any potential causal relations between the people sampled and the outcome. The scenario is like sampling marbles from an urn, where nothing apparently causes the color of the marble. In cases that do not involve potential causal relations (e.g., dice, spinners), the children accepted random sampling methods. In contrast, the fun booth scenario brought up a *covariance assumption*. The children thought in terms of how the attributes of the sampled people would cause (or co-vary) with their likely answer. This led to the biased sampling methods, because the children restricted their samples to the segment of the population most likely to be interested in a particular fun booth.

The distinction between random and causal situations was quite strong for the children. The children thought that random sampling methods could not apply to causal situations. As one student stated, "You don't just want to pick kids by chance, because you might get unlucky and end up getting kids who all like dunking booths." In retrospect, we should have known. For mature statistical reasoning, randomness has patterns (e.g., a normal curve), and capitalizing on these patterns permits causal inferences. But, how would children of this age have a conception of how randomness could be used to help infer causality when cause and randomness are seen as opposites (Piaget & Inhelder, 1975)?

In a subsequent study, Schwartz et al. (1998) tried to build on the children's prior conceptions. The authors had some successes, but overall they did not succeed as well as they would have liked. A new group of children worked for 2 weeks developing a plan to solve a Jasper Adventure that involved issues of sampling (CTGV, 1997). The Jasper Adventure, called "The Big Splash," presented students with a 20-minute video of a child who needed to develop a plan for a fair. The Jasper Series is an example of an excellent instructional model that attempts to build on children's prior knowledge. It develops a problem in an easily understood visual format that taps into children's own prior experiences. Even so, the children were never able to reconcile issues of cause and chance satisfactorily, and instead, they used another pre-existing concept that worked in many sampling situations shown in the video. They began to think of sampling in terms of "fairness." A fair sample gave everybody an equal chance of participating. Unfortunately, the concept of fairness is not adequate. On a posttest, the children liked the idea of leaving a survey on a table. They felt that any students who were interested could fill out the survey, so it was fair. This method of sampling leads to a self-selection bias; only those students interested in a dunking booth might choose to fill out the survey. Building on the children's prior knowledge was insufficient. The children never reconciled cause and chance, and as a result, they relied on prior concepts that were adequate for some situations, but manifested misconceptions in others.

Challenges to the Mastery of Skills

In contrast to building from prior intuitions, a mastery approach tries to develop the relevant prior knowledge. Mastery-focused instruction has learners memorize or master component skills that will later become part of a more complex performance. For example, an excellent way to learn to play a piano piece is to first learn the left hand of the first phrase, then the right hand, and finally put the two hands together before moving on to the next phrase. Much success has been achieved with this method of instruction. One of the primary methods of teaching children to read is to build component skills through phonics. In math, it is important for children to have mastered single-digit subtraction before taking on multidigit subtraction. Efficiency in component skills can free up cognitive resources for learning new materials and can prevent errors in execution. In these cases, the earlier knowledge that prepares people to learn also supports miniature independent performances, though these performances are restricted to tasks that fall short of the ultimate learning goal. Overall, the mastery model emphasizes independent performance as both the input and output of instruction.

An emphasis on independent performance is exceptionally valuable when the ultimate context of application comprises situations of high frequency and stability. Reading, for example, occurs over relatively conventional forms of text. Educators can count on these stable textual contexts when designing instruction (words are grouped horizontally, reading goes left to right, periods signal the end of an idea unit). The same is true of many apprenticeships and jobs that involve stable practices and few opportunities for mobility. It is also true for the recurrent problem formats that occur in highly stylized curricula, like problem work sheets. In these cases, the goal is not to prepare people to continue learning given changing circumstances, but rather, the appropriate goal is to build a set of self-contained independent performances.

Efficient mastery of facts, skills, and concepts is important in all domains, including contexts that require innovation (Schwartz, Bransford, & Sears, 2005). Yet, there are perils associated with a unitary emphasis on mastery. One limitation is that mastery approaches may not always develop people's zone of proximal development as well as they might. People may master knowledge for one form of independent performance, but this does not increase their abilities to learn in new situations. Except for high-stability and high-frequency application contexts, it is hard to guarantee that instruction for one form of independent performance will fit the type of performance needed for a new situation.

For example, Schwartz and Bransford (1998) asked college students in one experimental condition to write a summary of a chapter on classic studies of memory. In a second condition, students received simplified data sets from the studies, but they never saw the chapter. Their task was to graph what they thought constituted the important patterns in the data. On a subsequent true–false test, the summarize students did much better than the graphing students. They had a better mastery of the facts. However, this mastery was limited to simple retrieval performances, and it did not help them learn. Evidence to this point came from a second part of the study. The students from both conditions later heard a common lecture that reviewed the studies and their implications for broader human behavior. On a test a week later, the students received a description of a new experiment and had to predict the results. Students who had completed the graphing activities produced twice as many correct predictions as the summarize students with no increase in wrong predictions. The graphing students had been more prepared to learn from the lecture and then use this learning in a new situation. We know the graphing students learned from the lecture, because other graphing students who did not receive the lecture did quite badly on the prediction problem. One explanation of these results is that the graphing activity, which did not yield mastery on the true–false memory test, still developed important forms of early knowledge that prepared students to learn deeply from the lecture and apply this knowledge flexibly. A second explanation is that the summarize students thought they had already mastered the chapter, and therefore they did not listen as carefully. In either case, activities that overly emphasize mastery for specific forms of performance may not be ideal for situations that depend on learning related ideas that may take a slightly but significantly different form.

A second example of the strengths and limitations of mastery for future learning comes from a study by Schwartz and Martin (2004). They taught roughly 200 high school students how to compute variability using the mean deviation and to understand why the mean deviation divides by 'n.' After instruction, the students received a test that examined their mastery, their "insight," and their preparation for future learning. The mastery item asked them to compute the mean deviation for a set of numbers. The insight item showed the students the mean deviation formula and asked why it divides by 'n.' Their answers to this latter question indicated whether they appreciated that dividing by 'n' provides a way to compare samples of different sizes. The PFL item asked students to determine which of two basketball players was more consistent in their points-per-minute scoring. They had to determine the variability (covariance) of bivariate data (points and minutes played). These students had only learned about univariate data, so working with bivariate data was something new and would require learning how to put two incommensurable dimensions-points and minutes-played, within a single structure.

Figure 13.3 shows the percentages of students who learned to solve the bivariate problem during the test. The results are broken out by whether the

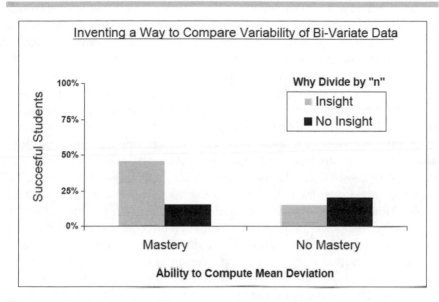

Figure 13.3 Students' abilities to learn how to compare covariance without instruction. Results are broken out by student mastery of a formula for computing univariate variability and their insight on how the univariate formula resolves problems of making different sample sizes commensurable.

students showed mastery and/or insight into the mean deviation formula. The notable finding is that mastery of the mean deviation formula by itself was not optimal for helping students learn. The students also needed insight on issues of incommensurability (i.e., why it is important to divide by 'n'). At the same time, insight alone was not optimal either. Students needed both forms of knowledge to help them solve this very difficult transfer problem that required going beyond what they had learned before. This is correlational evidence—later we provide relevant experimental evidence. For now, the take-home message is that mastery is important, but there are other forms of earlier knowledge that prepare people to learn. In particular, explicit early knowledge about incommensurables can be helpful in the domain of statistics.

Inconsistency in Prior Knowledge for Learning

To summarize, there is a large family of learning theories that presuppose commensurable prior knowledge or intuitions. However, in the study of children's notions of sampling, we found that the children had incommensurable prior knowledge, and that replacing these concepts with yet a third piece of knowledge (fairness) did not lead to a mature understanding. Modern associative theories of learning propose that learning is characterized by the aggregation of component prior knowledge. This mastery view of learning works well, until people have implicitly inconsistent knowledge that cannot be easily associated. Though it may be possible to teach people the right performance, the underlying inconsistencies may remain and yield misconceptions or interfere with their abilities to learn subsequently.

A different view of learning, that does not presuppose consistent prior knowledge, explicitly emphasizes the reconciliation of inconsistent or incommensurable knowledge. Chi, De Leeuw, Chiu, and LaVancher (1994), for example, found that one benefit of self-explanation is that it helps learners work through inconsistencies in their knowledge. Piaget, in particular, described development in these terms. Children discover that their beliefs are internally inconsistent, which causes a disequilibrium. Through a process of reflexive abstraction that resolves the disequilibrium, the children develop more mature knowledge. Piaget, however, did not write very much about instruction. He also did not consider situations where implicit contradictions and incommensurables do not cause disequilibrium, which we think is often the case, especially in statistical reasoning. We have attempted to develop a model of instruction that directly helps students see incommensurables and try to handle them. In turn, this early knowledge prepares students to learn the canonical solutions invented by experts.

LEARNING AS RECONCILIATION

The significance of reconciling incommensurables for learning was first developed in detail by Plato to address the learning paradox. The learning paradox asks how people can possibly learn something if they do not already know it in some form, thus raising the very question of whether it is possible to develop new knowledge, or whether all knowledge growth needs to presuppose complete prior knowledge. Accepting the paradox leads to a view of learning that emphasizes the refinement of prior knowledge (e.g., innate concepts, forms, language modules, intuitions, and so forth). Meno formulates two aspects of the paradox specifically:

> But how will you look for something when you don't in the least know what it is? How on earth are you going to set up something you don't know as the object of your search? To put it another way, even if you come right up against it, how will you know that what you have found is the thing you didn't know? (Meno, in Plato, 1961, 80.d)

The first half of the paradox asks how people can look for knowledge if they do not already know what they are looking for. Plato's solution is that incommensurables alert people to the need for learning. As we mentioned, the term incommensurable refers to the situation where multiple elements cannot be accommodated by the same rational system. An example comes from an isosceles right triangle. If we define the length of the sides as one unit, the hypotenuse yields an irrational number. Alternatively, if we define the hypotenuse length as the unit, the sides will yield an irrational number. Thus, a failure in a measurement system can let one know where to look for new knowledge. It causes the disequilibrium that begins the search for resolution.

The second half of the paradox asks how people can recognize that they have found knowledge if they did not know it already. The solution to this half of the paradox is that people will know they have found new knowledge when the incommensurables can be explained by the same system. So, in the case of the right triangle, the resolution comes by squaring the sides, which can then be measured in the same unit system. One knows they have "found knowledge" because it explains previously incommensurable elements.

There are three elements of this account that we take to heart in our instruction. First, it is important to help students sufficiently differentiate the elements of a problem so they notice there are incommensurables. Second, we provide students with the impetus and means to work on reconciling the incommensurables into a higher order structure. Finally, we provide students with the canonical solution. It is unrealistic to expect students to develop conventional solutions that took trained experts many years to invent. The first two elements of our instruction create the earlier knowledge that prepares the students to deeply understand the "ideal" solution when it is presented to them.

In the Meno, Socrates demonstrates the resolution to the learning paradox by leading Meno's slave through a geometry problem similar to the right triangle example. The slave never resolves the incommensurables on his own. Ultimately, Socrates provides the solution to the slave who, debatably, is in a position to recognize the significance of the solution ("Yes, you are right Socrates"). In other words, the process of noticing incommensurables and trying to reconcile them sets the stage for appreciating the solution when it appears—whether through personal discovery, the grace of the gods, or in the more typical case, by being told. Thus, we adopt the aims of the Socratic method, but we do not adopt the Socratic method of question asking, which only the most talented of people can wield successfully.

DEVELOPING EARLIER FORMS OF KNOWLEDGE

In our instructional model, students develop an appreciation of incommensurables at the same time as they attempt to reconcile them. This simultaneity is important, because students co-evolve their ability to identify the incommensurable features with their ability to handle them. The two processes fuel one another. However, for discussion, we can distinguish them analytically.

Noticing Incommensurables Through Contrasting Cases

The first component of our instruction is built into the instructional materials and helps students perceive the features that enter into an incommensurable relation. When people enter a new domain, their prior knowledge can be too vague to support the appreciation of lurking incommensurables. Therefore, we help them develop more precise early knowledge. To do this, we rely on contrasting cases. Contrasting cases are a powerful way to help people notice specific features they might otherwise gloss over (Bransford, Franks, Vye, & Sherwood, 1989; Gibson, & Gibson, 1955; Marton & Booth, 1997). For instance, Howard Gardner (1982) describes an art exhibit that juxtaposed original paintings and forgeries. At first people could not tell the difference, but through careful comparison, they began to notice the features that differentiated the originals. Similarly, in our materials, students learn to discern relevant features by comparing data sets. Contrasting cases of small data sets that highlight key quantitative distinctions can help students differentiate important quantitative features.

Figure 13.4 provides one example of how we do this for the topic of variability. Each grid shows the result of a test using a different baseball-pitching machine. The black circles represent where a pitch landed when aimed at the target X. The grids create a set of contrasting cases that alert learners to important features of distributions. For example, when most students come to variability, they over-assimilate the concept of variability to their well-developed notion of accuracy. Variability is viewed as a lack of accuracy, rather than deviations around the mean. The pitching grids specifically include an example where all the pitches are extremely close together, yet they are far from the target. This helps the students notice that variability and lack of accuracy are distinguishable properties. The contrasts between the four machines also draw attention to issues of sample size, outliers, and density.

Working Toward a Higher Order Structure

Helping students differentiate key quantitative features is an important component of our instructional model, but it is not sufficient for developing the types

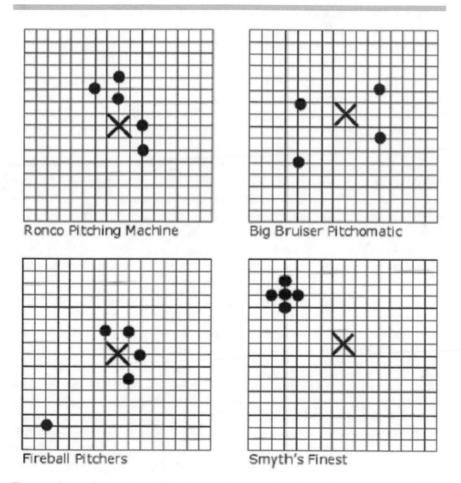

Figure 13.4   Contrasting cases for noticing and dealing with incommensurables in variability. Students invent a reliability index. (Schwartz & Martin, 2004, adapted with permission).

of earlier knowledge that we think prepare people to learn. Well-differentiated knowledge may only yield a set of discrete observations. But, the goal of most statistics instruction is for students to understand the structure that can accommodate all the features. For example, the grids include a number of incommensurable properties that models of variance have been designed to handle. For instance, sample size and distance from the mean are incommensurable features. One does not naturally measure distance in terms of sample size or vice versa. Variance formulas provide a structure so that sample size and distance can be put in the same rational system. For example, with the pitching grids, one can divide the total distances between the pitches by the sample size to get the average distance between pitches. We think students need to recognize the incommensurable that dividing by 'n' resolves so elegantly.

We doubt that simply pointing out that two components are incommensurable is going to work very well, because students will still not know how to reconcile them. It is important to have students work to reconcile the incommensurable elements into a single structure. The recognition of incommensurable features without the effort or means to reconcile them can cause people to simply fall back to one dimension or the other when put in a situation that requires both. One example of this behavior comes from the children who flipped between random and covariant sampling methods above. Another example comes from work conducted with children learning about the balance scale. Schwartz, Martin, and Pfaffman (2005) provided 9–10 year-old children with a series of balance scale problems that varied the distances and number of weights on either side of the fulcrum. For each problem, the children chose what they thought would happen (tilt left, balance, tilt right), and they justified their prediction. They then received feedback by seeing the true behavior of the scale, and they were asked to re-justify the result if they had predicted incorrectly. Half of the children were told to use words and half were told to "invent math" to justify their choices. The children told to use words performed like average children of this age, using one dimension, for example "more weight," to justify their choice. If their choice was wrong, they simply switched to the other dimension ("more distance"). Only 19% of the children included both distance and weight in the same justification, and the children did not appreciably improve in their ability to predict the behavior of a balance scale.

The children who were told to invent math showed a much different pattern. They explored different types of mathematical structures across problems including addition, subtraction, and multiplication. All told, 68% of these children included both dimensions of information in their justifications. The "invent math" children tried to find a way to reconcile the different dimensions of information, and ultimately, they learned to solve balance scale problems at the rate of adults.

One take-home message from the balance scale study is the following: To help students work towards reconciling dimensions, it is important to provide tools that can help them make headway. The "word" children in the balance scale study knew they were flipping back and forth between dimensions, but they had no way to do anything about it. Young children lack the cultural structures and artifacts that can help organize the complexity of incommensurables into a higher order structure. One cultural structure that is particularly good for handling complexity is mathematics. Thus, when we have students work with statistical notions, we do not ask them simply to notice things qualitatively.

We encourage them to use math to help find a way to manage the high complexity of distributions.

To return to the pitching grid example (Fig. 13.4), we included a task structure that ensured the students would recognize and attempt to reconcile the different quantitative features. The students' task was to develop a mathematical procedure that computes a single value to help shoppers compare consistency between the machines, much as an appliance receives an energy index. By providing the students the goal of comparison, they notice contrasts in the data from each machine, and they work to innovate a common measurement structure that incorporates all of these dimensions in making comparative decisions.

Delivering a Canonical Solution Once Students are Prepared to Learn

Finally, per our three-component instructional model, we assume that noticing and working to reconcile incommensurables creates the earlier knowledge that prepares students to learn the higher order structure created by experts. So, even though no students invented an ideal solution to the pitching grid problem, they developed the earlier knowledge that creates a time for telling (Schwartz & Bransford, 1998). For example, given a lecture, the students can appreciate the significance of what the lecture has to offer. Lectures and other forms of direct instruction are not inherently less valuable than hands-on activities. Their value depends on the knowledge that students can bring to the exposition, and we assume that the first two components of our instructional model help create the relevant earlier knowledge.

This assumption appears to be borne out. For example, Schwartz and Martin (2004) provided ninth-grade students with a 5-minute lecture on the mean deviation after they completed the pitching grid activity (plus one more). The authors' assumption was that the lecture would be within the students' zone of proximal development, and they would learn well and master the procedure. Pre- and posttests suggested this was the case. On posttest, 86% of the students could compute a measure of variance compared to 5% on pretest, which is impressive given that the students heard the complicated lecture in a very brief presentation and only practiced for 10 minutes. On a delayed posttest a year later, and without any intervening practice, the students still performed at 57%. This is well above the 0% the authors found in a sample of university students who had completed a semester of college statistics within the past year. It is important to note, however, that asking the college students to compute a measure of variance was like asking them the cause of the seasons—it was a potential mismeasurement of what they had learned. We only present the college benchmark to show how well the ninth-graders had been prepared to learn from the lecture, and at the end of the next section, we provide a better measure of the college students' understanding.

A DEMONSTRATION OF INSTRUCTION
THAT PREPARES PEOPLE TO LEARN

The preceding claim that our instruction prepared students to learn from the brief lecture is only a plausible inference. The students had limited exposure to the conventional solution, and they showed abilities quite above what we had previously observed among college students. Nevertheless, we did not compare how well these students learned from the lecture versus students who had not completed our preparation activities. Therefore, it is important to develop evidence in a more compelling research design. In this section, we describe that evidence.

The experiment arose from a concern that most current assessments of knowledge focus on mastery or independent performance. These assessments use tests of sequestered problem solving, where students have no chance to learn to solve problems during the test. We were worried that this assessment paradigm had created a self-reinforcing loop. Educators use methods of procedural and mnemonic instruction that support mastery as measured by these sequestered tests, and therefore, the tests generate continued feedback that tells educators their methods of instruction are effective. Our concerns were two-fold. One was that sequestered tests tend to measure mastery, but we suppose that a goal of secondary instruction is to increase students' zone of proximal development so they can continue to learn. Our second concern was that these sequestered tests were likely to miss the benefits of activities that engage students in innovating their own solutions. Students often do not generate the canonical solutions that sequestered tests evaluate, and therefore, they perform badly. However, we thought well-designed innovation activities may prepare students to learn efficient solutions once they appear. Therefore, we thought it was important to work on a form of dynamic assessment that included resources for learning during the test and could evaluate students' preparation for future learning.

The instructional content of the experiment tried to help students learn how to reconcile yet another incommensurable common to statistics: normalizing data using standardized scores. Standardized scores make seemingly incommensurable data comparable (e.g., comparing athletes from different sports or eras), and they are one key measure in inferential statistics. The experiment began on the last day of two weeks of instruction (Schwartz & Martin, 2004). During the prior 2 weeks all the students had completed a number of "noticing and reconciliation" tasks and received direct instruction on canonical solutions in the domain of descriptive statistics. For the experiment on learning standardized scores, students from multiple classes were divided into two different instructional treatments: a tell-and-copy condition and an invention condition.

Both conditions began with a front-of-the-class presentation on the problem of comparing grades from students in different classes. The presentation showed how an 85% could be an average grade for one teacher's class, but it could be an outstanding performance in a second teacher's class. Students quickly observed that it did not seem fair for students in each class to receive the same grade. The teacher explained that the problem is to find a way to determine who did better when one cannot simply use percentage correct. The teacher explained that "grading on a curve" was a way to solve this problem, and that it did not simply mean shifting the scale so everybody does better (a common misconception among students).

In the tell-and-copy condition, the teacher continued on and showed a visual solution to the problem. This solution involved finding the mean deviation and then marking out deviation regions on a histogram to determine which region a student falls into. This is the visual equivalent of finding how many Z-scores or deviation units an individual is from the mean. In the invention condition, students did not receive any instruction for how to solve the problem of comparing scores from different distributions. Their lesson simply ended with the challenge of comparing scores from different distributions.

Afterwards, the students in both treatments received raw data sets that required comparing individuals from different distributions to see who did better. For example, in one activity, the students had to decide if Bill broke the high jump world record more than Joe broke the long jump record, given scores for the top high jumps and long jumps that year. In the tell-and-copy treatment, students worked with data to use the procedure they had just learned. If necessary, the students received corrective feedback whenever the teacher walked by their desk. The goal was to help them develop mastery of the visual procedure. In the invention condition, students had to innovate their own way to solve this problem of comparing incommensurable performances. They did not receive any feedback. The goal was for them to further notice the problem of incommensurables and work to reconcile it. By hypothesis, this would create the earlier form of knowledge that would prepare them to learn.

To compare whether the invention or the tell-and-copy conditions better prepared the students to learn, the study included a second factor that controlled whether the students received a worked-out example embedded in a posttest given a few days later. The worked example showed how to compute standardized scores given descriptive measures only (e.g., means, variances), rather than using raw data as in the classroom activities. The example showed how Cheryl determined if she was better at the high dive or low dive. The students had to follow the example to determine if Jack was better at high jump or javelin. Half of the students from each instructional condition received this worked example as part of their posttest and nearly every student who received the worked example followed it correctly, demonstrating excellent mastery. The question was whether the students would learn what this worked example had to offer, or whether they would simply see it as a "plug and chug" problem. To detect if students learned from the worked example, there was a target transfer problem several pages later in everybody's posttest. Like the worked example, the target transfer problem required calculating standardized scores from descriptive measures rather than raw data, but used a different context (e.g., comparing home run hitters from different eras).

Figure 13.5 shows the percentages of students who solved the target transfer problem. Students who invented their own methods for standardizing data learned from the worked example embedded in the test and spontaneously transferred this learning to solve a novel problem. They performed better on the transfer test than inventing students who did not receive the embedded resource. They also performed better than students in the tell-and-copy condition, who exhibited no benefit when they had the embedded resource. A closer look at Figure 13.5 helps to locate the effect more precisely. An answer to the transfer problem was considered correct when a student gave a quantitatively precise answer or when a student gave a good qualitative or visual answer. Figure 13.5 shows that the inventing students used the quantitative technique from the worked example three times more often than the other conditions.

The study provides two bits of information. The first is that noticing and working to reconcile incommensurables can develop the earlier knowledge that prepares people to learn mature canonical solutions. Interestingly, the invent students were able to transfer across the different surface forms of the initial classroom instruction, the worked example, and the target transfer problem. Across this study and a subsequent replication, there was no evidence that surface form or problem topic influenced transfer. Working to reconcile incommensurables appears to help students learn the high-order structure that makes problem solving possible and it enables them to see that structure in new situations.

The second bit of information is that dynamic assessments that include resources for learning during a test can be sensitive measures of earlier forms of understanding. These forms of understanding are insufficient for independent problem solving—the students who did not receive the embedded worked example did not do very well. Even so, these earlier forms of knowledge can support the acquisition of more mature forms of understanding. Dynamic

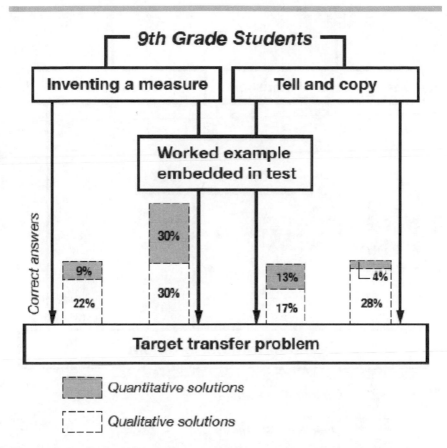

Figure 13.5 Design of assessment experiment and results for ninth-graders.

assessment like PFL tests indicate what is within the students' zone of proximal development, and they help reveal the value of instructional methods that are overlooked by tests of independent problem solving. The two forms of instruction in our study, inventing measures versus tell-and-copy, would have appeared equivalent had we not included the resource item from which students could learn.

The value of PFL assessments is further amplified by considering college students. Above, we reported that college students who had taken a full semester of statistics utterly failed to compute a measure of variability. By this measure of mastery, their semester of statistics was useless. However, this is a mismeasurement. Figure 13.6 presents a different story. We gave these same college students the assessment that we gave to the ninth-graders in the same testing format. We also included a sample of college students who had

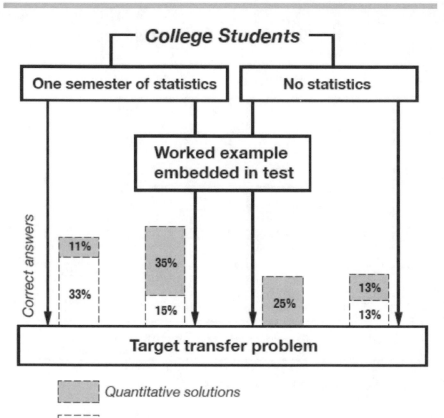

Figure 13.6 Performance of college students with and without college statistics who received the same test as the ninth-graders.

not taken any statistics. Although the college students performed more poorly than the ninth-graders, they were able to take advantage of the worked example in the test to learn the quantitative technique, and students who had taken a semester of statistics were most likely to learn from this resource. So, even though the college students failed to show mastery on basic statistical procedures, they were able to learn given a worked example. We assume this is a consequence of their college experiences and the statistics course, although it is always possible that the ability to learn well from worked examples is what got them into college in the first place. In either case, PFL assessments can reveal important forms of knowledge that tests of brute memory or sequestered mastery can miss.

CONCLUSIONS

In this chapter, we have tried to reconsider the role of prior knowledge in learning. The importance of prior knowledge in learning is well documented, but existing models tend either to presuppose the prior knowledge (intuitions) or to ignore prior knowledge that does not support independent problem solving (mastery). We think that it can be problematic to leave prior knowledge untouched in situations where prior knowledge is inconsistent. Intuitions sometimes contain tacit conflicts that, if left unresolved, become shaky foundations for further learning. For example, we described 12-year-olds whose notion of chance and cause as opposites made it difficult for them to understand random sampling. Mastery of independent problem solving routines, although a critical part of building expertise, can yield inflexible knowledge that cannot adapt to variations in problem context and new learning situations. High school students who mastered the mean deviation formula but did not have insight into its properties (why the formula divides by 'n') were less able to adapt their knowledge to a bivariate problem. We suspect that methods emphasizing intuition or mastery are insufficient because they do not help students notice and reconcile incommensurables in their prior knowledge, especially in a domain like statistics where incommensurables abound.

Borrowing from Piaget's notion of disequilibrium and one of Plato's resolutions to the learning paradox, we proposed a different approach to prior knowledge. We shifted the focus of instruction to help learners develop "early" knowledge that they did not already have, and we shifted assessment procedures away from independent performances towards evaluating a learner's zone of proximal development. Our proposal is that noticing and reconciling incommensurables prepares students to understand canonical solutions when given an opportunity to learn, and the best way to assess this readiness to learn is to use measures of preparation for future learning.

Our instructional model (Designs for knowledge evolution, Schwartz, Martin, & Nasir, 2005) incorporates three key elements. First, we use contrasting cases to draw students' attention to key features that produce the incommensurables, such as different sample sizes in the pitching grid task. Second, we provide students a task structure and set of cultural tools (e.g., mathematics, graphing) that help them try to reconcile incommensurable elements. For example, we showed that young children learned about balance when they tried to apply math to understand the behavior of the balance scale. Third, we teach students the expert solutions that they are now in better position to understand at a deep structural level.

To bring these points together, we described an experiment with ninth-graders that showed the benefit of inventing compared to tell-and-copy activities.

Students who tried to innovate a standardization procedure for comparing incommensurable data sets were better prepared to learn from a worked example in a posttest and to spontaneously transfer this knowledge to a target problem later in the test. Notably, without a learning resource in the test, the inventing students looked the same as students who received the more mastery-oriented instruction. The invention activity created an earlier form of knowledge that did not support independent performance but did provide the knowledge necessary to learn.

Knowing which forms of early knowledge are useful and how to develop them seems like an important goal of the learning sciences that has been neglected by both the developmental and cognitive science literatures. The developmental literature emphasizes maturation over knowledge, so the question is rarely what specific instructional conditions can develop early readiness. This is Vygotsky's allure to educators. His work provides a developmental perspective that emphasizes the value of particular circumstances for learning—circumstances that educators can sometimes control. The cognitive science literature and the derivative educational literature have largely examined the forms of knowledge and concepts that support mature and expert performance. Perhaps because they are hard to assess with standard instruments, cognitive science has paid less attention to the role of earlier forms of knowledge. However, we think that assessing early knowledge with PFL instruments can be accomplished with some simple modifications to standard procedures.

For example, a standard transfer paradigm has students learn by one of two methods and then measures their success on a target transfer problem. In our final experiment with ninth-graders learning how to standardize scores, we made a simple modification that created a "double transfer" paradigm. Students needed to spontaneously "transfer in" what they learned from the class activities to learn from the worked example embedded in the posttest. Then, they needed to spontaneously "transfer out" this new learning to solve the target transfer problem later in the test. In contrast to most transfer experiments, the manipulation of interest was not how we presented the target procedure itself (which was the same worked example across conditions), but rather, how we differentially prepared students to learn from the worked example. We propose this "double transfer" instrumentation is a more ecologically valid measure of transfer, where the transfer of one's earlier knowledge determines what one learns, and what one learns determines what is transferred to solve a subsequent problem.

We suspect there are other ways to assess preparation for future learning, and expanding our repertoire of these instruments will enable us to further reconsider the possibilities for developing the earlier knowledge that prepares people to learn. We have chosen one form of early knowledge here that we think is particularly important for learning higher order knowledge, because many higher order concepts in the sciences solve the problem of how to relate ideas that are otherwise incommensurable (e.g., mass and velocity). And as we have tried to indicate, statistics is filled with incommensurables that catch people unaware. Nisbett, Krantz, Jepson, and Kunda (1983) demonstrated that people can learn statistical concepts with relatively simple instruction when those concepts work in accordance with people's prior knowledge. In light of that, we could limit our instructional aspirations to those topics for which people have good prior knowledge. Or, we could develop the right early knowledge to start with.

ACKNOWLEDGMENTS

We thank Janet Go for her last-minute heroics. This material is based on work supported by the National Science Foundation under Grants No. BCS-021458 & REC-0196238. Any opinions, findings, and conclusions or recommendations expressed in this material are those of the authors and do not necessarily reflect the views of the National Science Foundation.

REFERENCES

Bar-Hillel, M. (1980). What features make samples seem representative? *Journal of Experimental Psychology: Human Perception and Performance, 6*, 515–550.

Bransford, J. D., & Schwartz, D. L. (1999). Rethinking transfer: A simple proposal with multiple implications. In A. Iran-Nejad & P. D. Pearson (Eds.), *Review of Research in Education,* (vol. 24; pp. 61–100). Washington, DC: American Educational Research Association.

Bransford, J. D., Franks, J. J., Vye, N. J., & Sherwood, R. D. (1989). New approaches to instruction: Because wisdom can't be told. In S. Vosniadou & A. Ortony (Eds.), *Similarity and analogical reasoning* (pp. 470–497). New York: Cambridge University Press.

Chi, M. T. H., de Leeuw, N., Chiu, M-H., & LaVancher, C. (1994). Eliciting self-explanations improves understanding. *Cognitive Science, 18*, 439–477.

CTGV [Cognition and Technology Group at Vanderbilt]. (1997). *The Jasper Project: Lessons in curriculum, instruction, assessment, and professional development.* Mahwah, NJ: Lawrence Erlbaum Associates.

Feuerstein, R. (1979). *The dynamic assessment of retarded performers: The learning potential assessment device, theory, instruments, and techniques.* Baltimore: University Park Press.

Gardner, H. (1982). *Art, mind, and brain: A cognitive approach to creativity.* New York: Basic Books.

Gibson, J. J., & Gibson, E. J. (1955). Perceptual learning: Differentiation or enrichment. *Psychological Review, 62*, 32–51.

Kahneman, D., Slovic, P., & Tversky, A. (Eds.) (1983). *Judgment under uncertainty: Heuristic and biases.* New York: Cambridge University Press.

Martin, T., & Schwartz, D. L. (2005). Physically distributed learning: Adapting and reinterpreting physical environments in the development of the fraction concept. *Cognitive Science, 29*, 587–625.

Marton, F., & Booth, S. (1997). *Learning and awareness*. Mahwah, NJ: Lawrence Erlbaum Associates.

Minstrell, J. A. (1989). Teaching science for understanding. In L. B. Resnick & L. E. Klopfer (Eds.), *Toward the thinking curriculum: Current cognitive research* (pp. 129–149). Alexandria, VA: ASCD

Nisbett, R. E., Krantz, D., Jepson, C., & Kunda, Z. (1983). The use of statistical heuristics in everyday inductive reasoning. *Psychological Review, 90*, 339–363.

Piaget, J., & Inhelder, B. (1975). *The origin of the idea of chance in children*. (L. Leake, Jr., P. Burrell, & H. D. Fischbein, Trans.). NY: Norton.

Plato (1961). *Collected dialogs of Plato including the letters*. (E. Hamilton & H. Cairns, Eds.) Princeton, NJ: Princeton University Press.

Schwartz, D. L., & Bransford, J. D. (1998) A Time for telling. *Cognition & Instruction, 16*, 475–522.

Schwartz, D. L., Bransford, J. D., & Sears, D. A. (2005). Efficiency and innovation in transfer. In J. Mestre (Ed.), *Transfer of learning from a modern multidisciplinary perspective* (pp. 1–52). Greenwich, CT: Information Age Publishing.

Schwartz, D. L., Goldman, S. R., Vye N. J., Barron, B. J., & CTGV. (1998). Aligning everyday and mathematical reasoning: The case of sampling assumptions. In S. Lajoie (Ed.), *Reflections on statistics: Agendas for learning, teaching and assessment in K–12* (pp. 233–274). Mahwah, NJ: Lawrence Erlbaum Associates.

Schwartz, D. L., & Martin, T. (2004). Inventing to prepare for learning: The hidden efficiency of original student production in statistics instruction. *Cognition & Instruction, 22,* 129–184.

Schwartz, D. L., Martin, T., & Nasir, N. (2005). Designs for knowledge evolution: Towards a prescriptive theory for integrating first- and second-hand knowledge. In P. Gardenfors & P. Johansson (Eds.), *Cognition, education, and communication technology* (pp. 21–54). Mahwah, NJ: Lawrence Erlbaum Associates.

Schwartz, D. L., Martin, T., & Pfaffman, J. (2005). How mathematics propels the development of physical knowledge. *Journal of Cognition and Development, 6*, 65–88.

Vygotsky, L. S. (1987). *The collected works of L. S. Vygotsky*. (R. Rieber & A. Carton, Eds.). NY: Plenum.

14

Discussion of Part II: Statistical Reasoning and Data Analysis

Kenneth R. Koedinger
Carnegie Mellon University

This chapter discusses chapters 8 to 13. I organize my discussion of these chapters by first summarizing each in terms of the following four features of a scientific argument: (1) the main research question, (2) the hypothesis or claim, (3) the theoretical argument for the hypothesis, and (4) the empirical evidence for the hypothesis. As appropriate, I integrate comments, connections, and criticisms. I conclude by reviewing some general lessons that I found particularly enlightening from these chapters in hopes that they are also enlightening to the reader of this discussion.

DO NAÏVE THEORIES EVER GO AWAY? CHAPTER BY DUNBAR, FUGELSANG, AND STEIN

The key research question addressed by the Dunbar, Fugelsang, and Stein chapter is "Do naïve theories ever go away?" The hypothesis is that no, naïve theories do not go away. The theoretical argument for this hypothesis is that these theories do not go away because students have trouble processing (encoding and integrating) new information about the correct theory because their existing, naïve theory does not provide a structure into which the encoding and integration can occur.

345

The empirical evidence for the hypothesis comes from three sources. First, despite classroom instruction, even college students at prestigious institutions like Harvard and Dartmouth maintain (or return to) the naïve theory that, for example, the seasons are caused by the earth's proximity to the sun rather than explaining that the tilt of the earth leads one hemisphere to experience winter when the sun hits it at a more oblique angle and thus the energy is "spread out." Further, in a short instructional experiment, college students showed essentially no improvement after watching an instructional video explaining why we have seasons. Data from student responses are consistent with the theoretical claim that students "did not encode the relevant information that was inconsistent with their theory" and more specifically "fail[ed] to integrate different sources of information correctly."

A second source of empirical evidence further probes why naïve theories do not go away by using experiments that manipulate whether students are presented with data that are consistent or inconsistent with their theories. Brain imaging revealed that consistent data activates learning areas (caudate and parahippocampal gyrus) whereas inconsistent data activates error detection and inhibition areas (anterior cingulate, precuneus, and dorsolateral prefrontal cortex). These results are interpreted as demonstrating that "when people receive information that is inconsistent with their preferred theory learning does not easily occur." This interpretation is argued to follow from the lack of activation of the learning areas by the inconsistent data. Just because students notice a discrepancy with their existing naïve theory, does not mean that they can immediately discover, learn, or evoke the correct theory. Indeed, some advocates for presenting inconsistent data also recommend extended classroom discussions around inconsistent data that makes explicit why the naïve theory does not work and why the correct theory does. For instance, Minstrell and Kraus (2005) suggest that "we need to acknowledge students' attempts to make sense of their experiences and help them confront inconsistencies in their sense making" (p. 476). Presumably, in such successful instructional manipulations, learning areas in the brain (caudate and parahippocampal gyrus) are activated. One might wonder, though, whether *other* brain areas are activated when learning requires theory restructuring— an interesting opportunity for further research.

It is worth noting that the authors' discussion of educational interventions includes mention of "presenting students with either large amounts of data, key anomalies, and new theories," but it does not mention getting students to provide rationalizations or explanations for why a naïve theory is wrong and cannot explain anomalous data. Such an intervention is indeed recommended by some (Minstrell & Kraus, 2005) and some experimental evidence exists for consequent learning benefits (cf., Mathan & Koedinger, 2005; Siegler, 2002).

A third source of empirical evidence investigates the behavioral and brain differences between learners who have achieved theory restructuring from those who have not. This evidence comes from studies of students' naïve "impetus" theories of physical motion. Again, students were presented with data inconsistent with the naïve theory (two balls of different sizes dropping at the same rate) under fMRI brain imaging. In this study, however, advanced students did not activate error correction areas (anterior cingulate) for data inconsistent with the naïve theory; rather they did so for data inconsistent with correct "Newtonian" theory. In other words, the brain imaging results are consistent with the behavioral data that such students have successfully restructured their conceptions.

Interestingly, among the nonphysics students, about half *behaved* in accord with Newtonian theory (saying two different-sized balls falling at the same rate is correct), but nevertheless had anterior cingulate activation indicating some remaining residual of the naïve theory. The authors interpret this result to reveal "that the students had not undergone the deep conceptual change needed to produce the correct answer for the right reasons." However, more direct evidence of that claim would be to find that these students could not correctly explain their conclusions. I, for one, am not convinced that lack of anterior cingulate activation in these circumstances (i.e., when presented with naïve-theory-inconsistent data) is necessary for "deep conceptual change." It seems possible that a student can have made the conceptual change in a more deliberate or metacognitive fashion (perhaps mediated by the prefrontal cortex) yet still requires more practice be *fluent* in applying the theory. Such a student would be able to provide a correct explanation, but would still need to overcome a "that doesn't seem right" reaction to data inconsistent with their prior naïve theory.

INTRICACIES OF STATISTICAL INFERENCE AND TEACHERS' UNDERSTANDING OF THEM: CHAPTER BY THOMPSON, LIU, AND SALDANHA

The key research question addressed by the Thompson, Liu, and Saldanha chapter is "Are there intricacies of statistical inference that teachers have great difficulty understanding?" The main hypothesis is that teachers do not develop a deep or complete enough conception of sampling logic behind hypothesis testing to apply it spontaneously to new problem situations. The theoretical argument for this claim is that sampling logic is complex, placing many cognitive demands on the learner. First, a learner must think of samples both as composed of individuals and as "items in themselves," that is, a sample is both a process and an object (cf. Sfard, 1991). Second, a learner must develop an understanding "that repeatedly collecting samples has the result that the values of a statistic [computed on each of those samples] are distributed somehow within a range of possibilities." Third, a learner must build this understanding on the idea of randomness, "which is known to be troublesome for people of all ages," and, to understand hypothesis testing, on the notoriously difficult idea of proof by contradiction.

The empirical evidence for this chapter's claim comes from pre- and post-instruction interviews of eight experienced high school mathematics teachers surrounding a 2-week professional development seminar as well as from observations during the seminars. On the pre-interview, all but two of the teachers expressed a misconception, as stated by one of them, that the "difference between population mean and sample mean will be less than the difference between individual measurements and the population mean."

It is difficult to gauge whether the seminar led to a reduction (at least temporary) in this misconception because the post-interviews did not have a directly parallel question. However, it does seem clear that although teachers may have improved their understanding of the logic of hypothesis testing, "they did not understand its functionality." For instance, seven of the eight teachers "did not employ spontaneously the method of hypothesis testing" when given a typical scenario for the application of hypothesis testing. They wanted more or better samples instead of simply concluding that the current sample was such that the null hypothesis could not be rejected.

One simple, albeit inadequate, instructional recommendation of this research is that textbooks should explicitly deny the common misconception identified here with a clearly highlighted (and perhaps three times-repeated) statement like "The mean of a sample is *not* more likely to be closer to the population mean than individual items, rather it is the mean*s* of sample*s* that are more likely to be closer to the populations mean." In a similar way, a research methods textbook by Trochim (2005) addresses common misconceptions head on, for instance, by emphasizing (repeatedly) that random *assignment* to conditions is not the same as random *sampling*. In my experience, such statements at least slow some students down and lead them to some reflection on the subtle, but crucial, wording differences between the two statements. Of course, by no means are such explications enough, but they are a reasonable start. Further efforts, for instance, might incorporate techniques, like those discussed earlier (Mathan & Koedinger, 2005; Minstrell & Kraus, 2005; Siegler, 2002), for having students confront situations where their misconceptions lead to incorrect conclusions.

The fact that fundamental notions of sampling and hypothesis testing are difficult for high school mathematics teachers, even after an intensive multiday seminar, is a sobering observation that we must keep in mind as we work to tackle the greater challenge of helping these teachers' *students* understand and effectively use these ideas.

MIDDLE SCHOOL STUDENTS' USE OF APPROPRIATE AND INAPPROPRIATE EVIDENCE IN WRITING SCIENTIFIC EXPLANATIONS: CHAPTER BY MCNEILL AND KRAJCIK

McNeill and Krajcik explicitly state their research questions as: "What difficulties do middle school students have using evidence and reasoning when constructing scientific explanations? How does content area influence students' use of evidence and reasoning?" A key hypothesis is that students have difficulty learning to generate appropriate scientific explanations, such as explaining why two substances are chemically different in terms of differences in their chemical properties (e.g., densities) rather than in the objects' properties (e.g., mass). A second hypothesis is that such explanation skills are content specific, yielding different kinds of errors for different content areas.

A theoretical rationale for why students may have difficulty learning to generate scientific explanations is not clearly stated in the chapter; however, I suspect that part of the reason may be that much human learning is implicit (Dienes & Perner, 1999). We can learn to derive conclusions or claims from past experience and examples and do not always initially have explicit easy-to-verbalize knowledge of how we arrived at those conclusions or why we believe (and should believe) those claims.

The empirical evidence that students have difficulty learning to provide good scientific explanations comes from post-test data showing that "students' evidence and reasoning [scores] were still lower than their claim scores and low at an absolute level." Students improved substantially from pre- to post-test on several measures, but their mean post-test scores were still low; 51% (2.1 of 4) for claims, 21% (1.3 of 6) for evidence, and 11% (1.0 of 9) for reasoning after 5 to 8 weeks of instruction.

The empirical evidence that explanation skills are content specific comes from finding differences in these scores across different content areas, namely substance and property versus chemical reactions. Students had much higher claim than evidence and reasoning scores on the chemical reaction question than on the substance and property question. It turned out that it was possible on the chemical reaction question for students to make the correct claim using inappropriate evidence—they concluded that the chemical reaction occurred (correct claim) because the mass or volume changed (wrong evidence).

Interpreting this data relative to the hypothesis, I would submit that the difference in score profile is less an issue of the content area and more about the specific design of the assessment question. One could create a substance and property question where incorrect reasoning leads to a correct response and a chemical reaction task where incorrect reasoning does not lead to a correct response. Extending a point made in the Lovett and Chang chapter summarized in the following section, not only is "ensuring that students get ample practice executing the particular skills they are supposed to learn ... surprisingly easy to overlook," but so is making sure that instructional or assessment activities do not allow students get by without deep understanding. The McNeill and Krajcik chapter nicely illustrates how careful research and data analysis can overcome such oversights and lead to better instructional and assessment designs. It is also highlights how assessments that request explanations are much more likely to identify, for teachers as well as researchers, situations where students correct answers hide a deeper lack of understanding.

As a final point about this chapter, McNeill and Krajcik discuss their "learning goals-driven design process," which focuses first on identifying learning goals, then on developing "learning performances" that show whether students have acquired those goals, and finally on activities and assessments that support these performances. I think this approach of reasoning backward from a clear articulation of the learning goals to be achieved to an instructional design is all too often not employed. However, as argued by Konold in the next chapter, there is also merit in reasoning forward from what beginning students know and do not know.

DESIGNING A DATA ANALYSIS TOOL FOR LEARNERS: CHAPTER BY KONOLD

The Konold chapter begins by addressing the research question: "What are the statistical capabilities that today's citizens need, and what will they need 25 years from now?" His major point is that we should not think of statistics instruction in schools as a stripped-down version of college-level statistics. He points out that many more people work with data than ever before and few of them are formally trained statisticians. Rather than being "number crunchers," people are more often "plot wringers" who visualize, manipulate, analyze and "mine" data using computers and dynamic displays of that data.

In reasoning about the potential needs of future citizens, Konold astutely points out that the "underlying concepts" of statistics, like covariation and density, are more likely to be around than existing methods for representing them, like scatter-plot displays and histograms. This observation opens the door for Konold's interesting rethinking of today's representation methods.

In the rest of the chapter, Konold focuses on the question of "How do we start early in young peoples' lives to develop [the statistical] capabilities [that current and future citizens need]?" He introduces his *TinkerPlots* software environment and the "hat-plot" data display in particular. One can view the hat-plot as resulting from a fundamental strategy for effective communication and instruction, which is to minimize irrelevant or less important features or details so as to highlight the relevant and most important features. The hat-plot is a substitute for the box-plot and incorporates features of the histogram. Hat-plots eliminate the arguably less important feature of a box-plot: the four-part quartile division of the data and, in particular, the separation of the middle quartiles. Instead, hat-plots divide data into three parts, the hat is the middle 50% of the data and the "brims" represent the two remaining 25% pieces on either side. The relevant or most important feature that a box-plot intends to highlight is the "modal clump" or "central bulk" (as I prefer to call it) of the data set, that middle 50% ("interquartile range") that is most "typical" or representative of the data set.

The importance of this "central bulk" derives primarily, so it seems, from the frequent need to compare data sets to determine whether one tends to have greater values than another. One can reason about whether one set of data values tend to be bigger than another by visualizing the extent that the central bulk of the first set is more to the right of (on a number line) and more separated from the central bulk of the second set. That a box-plot divides the middle 50% into two parts distracts attention from this central bulk that is most typical or most representative of the data. Konold cites evidence that students left to choose central bulks of data sets (e.g., displayed in a stacked dot-plot) will tend to chose hat sizes that are remarkably close to the middle 50%.

In contrast to McNeill and Krajcik's learning goals-driven design process, Konold puts less emphasis on starting with instructional objectives: "We should be thinking at least as much about what the next version of the Standards should say as we do about what this version says." He puts more emphasis on "pushing ourselves to test and refine our vision of how students might learn," that is, designing instructional activities and software as much from building up from students' existing partial knowledge as from building down from normative instructional goals.

DATA-ANALYSIS SKILLS: WHAT AND HOW ARE STUDENTS LEARNING? CHAPTER BY LOVETT AND CHANG

The key research question addressed by Lovett and Chang is how do students approach the task of exploratory data analysis and, in particular, learn features for selecting data display that appropriately generalize across data analysis tasks. The key hypothesis is that students select plots largely by guessing with little analysis of why and are susceptible to acquiring superficial selection features (e.g., use pie charts for demographic data) from spurious correlations in instructional examples and problems.

The theoretical rationale for this hypothesis is first that, consistent with the ACT-R theory (Anderson & Lebiere, 1998), students try to maximize the utility of their actions by seeking low cost/effort methods that (appear to!) achieve their goals. Second, again consistent with ACT-R, students acquire new knowledge through analogy to examples and past problem-solving experiences and, like any inductive learning mechanism, analogy will pick up on features that are correlated with successful choices. If instructional examples and practice problems contain spurious (nonsolution-related) correlations, the analogy process is likely to pick up on these and associate superficial features with particular responses. Also, because the analogy mechanism tends to be conservative in its generalizations, students are likely to acquire knowledge that is of somewhat limited generality—likely to be specific to particular problem categories (e.g., when to select a box-plot) and not generalize across all data analysis problems (e.g., when to select data displays in general).

The empirical evidence that students do not appropriately plan (e.g., identify relevant variables and whether they are categorical or numeric) before selecting a data display comes from a contrast between expert and student think-aloud data and the fact that students neither verbalize such a plan (whereas experts do) nor are they accurate or efficient in selecting a display.

The empirical evidence that students acquire superficial features for data display selection comes from an experiment that contrasted a curriculum of problems designed to have spurious correlations with one that was designed with wide variation in superficial features to avoid spurious correlations. Students in the spurious condition not only learned more poorly, but also behaved at post-test in a way that is consistent with the hypothesis that they acquired these superficial features. Namely, they did relatively well on problems that honored these superficial features (e.g., a problem with demographic data where a pie chart was appropriate)—on par with students in the varied condition, but worse on other problems.

Further data supporting the notion that student knowledge acquisition tends toward more specific conceptions rather than the broader and transferable generalization we would like students to acquire comes from analysis of "learning curves." Learning curves are generated by comparing the relationship between opportunities to learn a knowledge component over time and student performance, as measured in time or error rate, on tasks exercising that component. Lovett and Chang found a more parsimonious fit for a more specific knowledge component model that has a component for each correct data display choice than for a general model that has a single component that can select any display. Coming up with new methods and algorithms to use learning curves to assess students' level of generality in different instructional conditions is an active area of research in my lab (Cen, Koedinger, & Junker, 2006). One interesting thing to try would be to see whether an even more specific model (that incorporates superficial features) fits the learning curves of students in the spurious condition whereas a more general (and more expert) model may better fit students in the varied condition.

RECONSIDERING PRIOR KNOWLEDGE: CHAPTER BY SCHWARTZ, SEARS, AND CHANG

Schwartz, Sears, and Chang explore the interesting question of whether certain types of instructional activities can create prior knowledge that better prepares people to learn from subsequent instruction. They hypotheses that prior instruction that helps students gain insight on "incommensurables" in a topic domain should better prepare those students to learn from future instruction on that topic. The authors provide numerous examples of incommensurables, but to provide one of my own, one faces an incommensurability challenge when adding two fractions with unlike denominators, like ¼ and 1/5—one cannot directly add fourths to fifths. The common denominator procedure, converting both fractions to twentieths, solves the incommensurability. The authors' hypothesis is that helping students to see such procedures as resolving an incommensurability challenge should prepare them to better learn this and related procedures.

The theoretical argument for their hypothesis is essentially that many hard ideas, particularly in statistics, are mathematical solutions to the general problem of making incommensurable quantities commensurable, that is, transforming quantities that cannot be directly compared or combined so that they can be. And if students are not prepared to recognize this incommensurability and grapple with the challenge it poses, they will not understand the solution that statisticians have invented to solve it. If they are prepared to recognize incommensurability, they will not only understand statistics more deeply, but also be better prepared to learn new statistics. This better learning can be assessed at a post-test in a "preparation for future learning" (PFL) assessment by presenting new material to learn (e.g., by a worked example) on the test itself followed by a question about that material.

It can be productive to think of a scientific principle or method as a "reasonable solution to a reasonable problem." Unless students understand what the reasonable problem is that a method is trying to solve, they will have difficulty learning that method. Schwartz, Sears, and Chang claim that often the problem in statistics is how to combine otherwise incommensurable measures.

One initial form of empirical evidence is a correlational result. Some 200 high school students were instructed on mean deviation. Those students who both (1) better mastered computation of mean deviation *and* (2) better understood why dividing by n is useful learned more from instruction on finding variability (covariance) in bivariate data. They learned more than students who had just done one of (1) or (2). In other words, these data are consistent with the idea that with prior knowledge of *both* basic building blocks and a "metarecognition" of how dividing by n solves the incommensurability, students were in a better position to learn covariance.

Experimental evidence supporting the hypothesis that prior understanding of incommensurability supports future learning comes from Schwartz and Martin's (2004) study of instruction on variance. Here students were presented with the incommensurability challenge through "contrasting cases" that illustrated, in particular, that a naïve measure of variance that ignores sample size (e.g., add all the distances between points) yields a smaller result for one data set (A) than another (B) when visually it is clear that A has a larger variance than B. This happens because A has fewer data points than B. Toward getting students "working towards a higher order structure," students were asked to invent a measure of variance. Unlike discovery learning approaches where such an activity is intended to lead students to come up with a measure, in this approach it is sufficient that students grapple with the problem. Indeed, none invented an adequate measure. However, the experience had lasting impact. Students who had experienced this "problematizing" were better able to learn from future instruction than those who had not.

One area for improvement in the theoretical rationale is in a clearer explication of what knowledge it is that students acquire through this approach. The authors say that "working to reconcile incommensurables appears to help students learn the higher order structure that makes problem solving possible" (p. XX). But, what is this "high-order structure"? And how does it get brought to bear when students are using the learning resources in the PFL dynamic assessment? What do they know or do that students who have not had the reconciliation experience do not know or do?

I like this notion of incommensurabilities and can see its potential application in some of my own instructional design work, for instance, in preparing students to learn the common-denominator procedure for adding fractions (cf., Koedinger, 2002) as just illustrated.

The authors' emphasis on preparation for future learning assessments leads them to a different view on the Harvard students, described in the Dunbar et al.

chapter, who could not correctly describe how the seasons work. If these students were, as Schwartz et al. believe, better able to learn from instruction on the seasons than other less educated students, then we should perhaps not count this a failure of our education system. Indeed, it is clearly not possible for schools to teach all that is known to all students. According to Schwartz et al., schools should not only provide students with basic building blocks, skills. and concepts, for future learning (via "vertical transfer"; Singley & Anderson, 1989), but should also provide concepts that facilitate better building with those basic blocks (via "horizontal transfer"). Such concepts may well include knowing that some scientific ideas, especially in statistics, are designed to tackle the problem of incommensurability.

CONCLUSIONS

These chapters provided multiple dimensions of insight into statistics learning and teaching. One dimension is rethinking of the goals of statistics instruction. Thompson et. al showed how difficult the logic of hypothesis testing is, even for high school mathematics teachers and made it clear that more emphasis is needed on design of instruction to bring that logic home to learners. Konold emphasizes experiences for young learners that target key concepts like covariation and density and interactive data displays that highlight these key concepts. Schwartz et. al recommended more use of assessments that test whether students are prepared for future learning and more focus on getting students attuned to the higher order structures and design goals (e.g., resolve incommensurables) of statistical methods. A second dimension of insight is results of experiments that tap into the causal mechanisms underlying student learning of statistics and this dimension was well illustrated by the Dunbar, Lovett, and Schwartz chapters. A third dimension is the illustration of use of alternative research methods including fMRI (Dunbar), interviews (Thompson), and classroom studies (McNeill). A fourth dimension is the introduction the use of software in the statistics learning and research in which Konold provided a description of compelling software for early statistics learners and Lovett illustrated the use of software not only in performing statistics, but also to collect log data on student actions and latencies to draw learning curves.

REFERENCES

Anderson, J. R., & Lebiere, C. (1998). *The atomic components of thought*. Mahwah, NJ: Lawrence Erlbaum Associates.

Cen, H., Koedinger, K. R., & Junker, B. (2006). Learning factors analysis: A general method for cognitive model evaluation and improvement. In M. Ikeda, K. D. Ashley, T. -W. Chan (Eds.), *Proceedings of the Eighth International Conference on Intelligent Tutoring Systems*, pp. 164–175. Berlin: Springer-Verlag.

Dienes, Z., & Perner, J. (1999). A theory of implicit and explicit knowledge. *Behavioral and Brain Sciences, 22*(5), 735–808.

Koedinger, K. R. (2002). Toward evidence for instructional design principles: Examples from Cognitive Tutor Math 6. In D. S. Mewborn, P. Sztajn, D. Y. White, H. G. Wiegel, R. L. Bryant, & K. Nooney (Eds.), *Proceedings of the 24th annual meeting of the North American Chapter of the International Group for the Psychology of Mathematics Education,* Vol. 1, pp. 21–49. Columbus, OH: ERIC Clearinghouse for Science, Mathematics, and Environmental Education.

Mathan, S. A., & Koedinger, K. R. (2005) Fostering the intelligent novice: Learning from errors with metacognitive tutoring. *Educational Psychologist. 40* (4), 257–265.

Minstrell, J., & Kraus, P. (2005). Guided inquiry in the science classroom. In S. Donovan & J. Bransford (Eds.), *How students learn.*(pp. 475–513) Washington, DC: National Academy Press.

Schwartz, D. L., & Martin, T. (2004). Inventing to prepare for learning: The hidden efficiency of original student production in statistics instruction. *Cognition & Instruction, 22,* 129-184.

Sfard, A. (1991). On the dual nature of mathematical conceptions: reflections on processes and objects as different sides of the same coin. *Educational Studies in Mathematics, 22,* 1–30.

Siegler, R. S. (2002). Microgenetic studies of self-explanation. In N. Garnott & J. Parziale (Eds.), *Microdevelopment: A process-oriented perspective for studying development and learning* (pp. 31–58). Cambridge, MA: Cambridge University Press.

Singley, K., & Anderson, J. R. (1989). *The transfer of cognitive skill.* Cambridge, MA: Harvard University Press.

Trochim, W. M. K. (2005). *Research methods: The concise knowledge base.* Ohio: Atomic Dog Publishing.

III

Learning From and Making Decisions With Data

15

Causal Learning From Observations and Manipulations

David Danks
Carnegie Mellon University

Data from the world only have value if we can use them in some way. For many uses, such as predicting the weather, we only need to understand the correlational structure among the various features. For other purposes, though, we must know something about the causal structure of the environment, including other people. For example, to make accurate decisions, we must know the likely effects of our actions; to explain events in the world, we need to know what could have caused them; to predict other people's actions, we must know how their beliefs, desires, and so on, cause them to act in particular ways. We extract causal beliefs from the patterns we see in the world, even though we never directly observe causal influence (Hume, 1748), and then use those beliefs systematically in our cognizing (Sloman, 2005). We are thus faced with a fundamental psychological problem: How do we, in fact, learn causal relationships in the world, which we then use in myriad ways to adjust or control our environment?

In particular, we focus here on the problem of learning novel causal relationships given only data from the world, and where our prior knowledge does not significantly aid our causal learning.[1] The paradigmatic learning situation involves trying to determine the causal relationships among a set of

---

[1]Alternately, one could ask how we exploit prior causal knowledge to infer novel causal relationships. That is, how do we leverage our prior knowledge in novel situations and environments to draw

variables (e.g., hormone levels and a disease, or fertilizers and plant growth) given a series of cases, where they are observed one at a time, or perhaps in a summary. Most of the theories we discuss further assume that the variables are binary (typically present/absent), and that we can use prior knowledge (including temporal information) to label the variables as either potential causes or the effect. Thus, we have a quite well-defined situation and experimental design: given observations of a series or summary of cases of binary potential causes and effect, determine the causal "influence" of each potential cause on the effect (where "influence" is deliberately being left vague).

A number of different theories have been proposed to explain just how people solve this problem, and though there are some known theoretical results connecting pairs of theories, they are widely scattered. In addition, recent surveys of the literature (e.g., De Houwer & Beckers, 2002; Shanks, 2004) have primarily focused on comparisons of the theories to empirical work, rather than the interesting connections among the theories themselves. Understanding these connections is particularly important from an experimental design perspective, because that enables us to determine the class of problems on which the various theories make different predictions. This chapter is aimed at providing just such a unification of the theory space, rather than an answer to the question of which theory best fits the empirical data. The latter task is particularly challenging given the growing evidence that a range of learning strategies occur in experimental populations (Lober & Shanks, 2000; White, 2000).

The central problem just identified is underspecified in certain ways. In particular, the temporal relationships of the variables seem to be relevant— positively and negatively—for people's ability to learn causal relationships (Buehner & May, 2002, 2003, 2004; Hagmayer & Waldmann, 2002; Lagnado & Sloman, 2004). For example, if no prior knowledge is provided and the potential causes occur significantly prior to the effect, people will tend not to infer a causal relationship. Also, people's understanding of causal relationships seems to be partially task-dependent, as their experimental responses depend systematically on the probe question, particularly counterfactual versus "influence" terminology (Collins & Shanks, 2006). These complications and subtleties in causal inference are clearly relevant from a theoretical point of view, but they have not been a central focus of theoretical work to this point, and so we set them aside for the remainder of this chapter.

---

interesting causal conclusions? This question has been studied extensively by Woo-Kyoung Ahn and her colleagues under the heading of "mechanism theory" (Ahn & Bailenson, 1996; Ahn, Kalish, Medin, & Gelman, 1995; see also Lien & Cheng, 2000). Although not addressed here, there are potentially interesting connections with the work discussed here (Danks, 2005; Glymour, 1998), and it is important to recognize that data-driven causal learning is not the only kind.

The study of data-driven induction of causal beliefs has recently grown substantially in both experiments and theories: at least 12 substantively different theories have been independently proposed just in the last 10 years. Roughly speaking, there are two major dimensions on which theories of human causal learning vary: whether they describe dynamic or long-run learning; and whether they describe learning of causal parameters or of causal structure. The first dimension is quite natural and obvious: (a) "dynamic," if the theory describes changes in causal belief after each observed case; or (b) "long-run," if the theory describes the causal beliefs that the individual will hold after observing a "sufficiently long" sequence (i.e., when the causal beliefs have stabilized).[2] The second dimension—parameter versus structure inference—is roughly the distinction between learning "C causes E" and learning "how strongly C causes E." Unfortunately, this characterization is not quite right, because parameter learning is a kind of structure learning: learning that C has a nonzero (or zero) causal strength implies having learned that C causes (or does not cause) E.

To get a more accurate picture of this second distinction, we need to make a brief excursion in the third section of the chapter into causal Bayesian networks (or simply, causal Bayes nets), a mathematical framework from computer science, statistics, and philosophy that has emerged in the past 20 years as a normative framework for modeling causal systems. We return to the parameter/structure distinction in more detail in that section. Before that, however, we survey a variety of dynamical and long-run causal learning theories proposed in the psychological literature in the second section of the chapter. The third section describes the framework of causal Bayes nets, and details more of the substantial relationships between the various theories. For all of these theories, we focus on inference from observational data. The final, fourth, section turns to focus on the problem of inference from our manipulations and actions in the world around us. This shift in data source reveals further interesting connections among the various theoretical accounts of human causal learning.

A MENAGERIE OF MODELS

Many psychological theories of human causal learning can be placed into four families of theories, centered on: the well-known Rescorla-Wagner

---

[2]Some recent summaries (e.g., De Houwer & Beckers, 2002) seem to use "associative" versus "non-associative" (or "probabilistic") where I use "dynamic" versus "long-run." However, that work interprets the two classes of theories as competing, whereas I argue that they are complementary. In addition, they rarely provide an explicit characterization of "associative," and so classification of new theories is not always obvious.

TABLE 15.1
Metatheoretic Structure With Equation Numbers

Dynamical Model	Long-Run Model	Causal Bayes Net Function
R-W and variants (15.1)	Conditional ΔP (15.2)	Sum of present cue strengths (15.10)
(Generalized) Pearce (15.3)	One-cue: (15.4) & (15.5); Multiple-cue: General procedure, but no equations	One-cue: Equation (15.12); Multiple-cue: Unknown
Equation (15.7)	Power PC (15.6)	Noisy-OR/AND (15.11)
Equation (15.9)	pCI/belief adjustment (15.8)	None exists
Bayesian updating; dynamic estimation of independencies and associations; testing the current causal model	Arbitrary causal Bayes net structure learning	Various possible functions, depending on prior knowledge or biases

model, a configural cue version of Rescorla-Wagner, Cheng's causal power approach, and hypothesis confirmation testing. In this section, we focus on characterizing these families in terms of the within-family relationships: connecting dynamical and long-run theories that share certain crucial features. In the third section of this chapter, we return to the cross-family comparisons, as well as describing the causal Bayes net psychological theories. One historical note: although many of these theories are presented here as dynamical/long-run versions of each other, these connections were almost all established only after each individual theory had independently been proposed. This section is geared towards theoretical clarity, not historical accuracy. A summary of the theoretical relationships is provided in Table 15.1.

Rescorla-Wagner, Its Descendants, and Probabilistic Contrasts

The Rescorla-Wagner (1972) model (henceforth, the R-W model) is the paradigmatic instance of an associationist learning theory: people have beliefs about the associative strengths between cues and an outcome, and given a novel case (i.e., a set of cues and an outcome), they change their beliefs based on the error in the prediction made by their current beliefs. More precisely, if V_i^t is the associative strength of cue i after case t, the R-W model predicts that V_i after the next case will be given by $V_i^{t+1} = V_i^t + \Delta V_i^{t+1}$, where the latter term is:

$$\Delta V_i^{t+1} = \begin{cases} \alpha_i \beta_1 \left(\lambda - \sum_{\text{cue } j \text{ appears}} V_j^t \right), \text{ if } V_i \text{ and the outcome both occur} \\\\ \alpha_i \beta_2 \left(0 - \sum_{\text{cue } j \text{ appears}} V_j^t \right), \text{ if } V_i \text{ occurs and the outcome does not} \\\\ 0, \text{ if } V_i \text{ does not occur} \end{cases} \quad (15.1)$$

where λ is the maximum association supported by the outcome (usually assumed to be 1); α_i is the salience of cue i; and β_1 and β_2 are the learning rates when the outcome is present and absent, respectively (typically with $\beta_1 \geq \beta_2$). In the R-W model, associative strengths only change when their corresponding cues occur, and the change is proportional to the "error" between the actual occurrence (or absence) of the outcome and the predicted value of the outcome (given by the linear sum of associative strengths).

The R-W model has proven to be a very good model of many animal associative learning phenomena (Miller, Barnet, & Grahame, 1995), and has been proposed as a model of human causal induction by reinterpreting the associative strengths as perceived causal strengths, in which case "cues" are potential causes (Baker, Mercier, Vallee-Tourangeau, Frank, & Pan, 1993; Lober & Shanks, 2000; Shanks, 1995; Shanks & Dickinson, 1987).[3] The R-W model cannot be the correct model of human causal learning, however, because it mistakenly predicts that people will not update their causal beliefs about a potential cause after a case in which it is absent. Retrospective revaluation seemingly only occurs in animals in special conditions (e.g., Blaisdell, Denniston, & Miller, 2001; Blaisdell & Miller, 2001), but has been found multiple times in human causal learning (e.g., Chapman, 1991; Van Hamme & Wasserman, 1994; Wasserman et al. 1996). Van Hamme and Wasserman (1994; henceforth, VHW) and Tassoni (1995) have proposed modified R-W models in which associative strengths can change even when a cue is not presented. Although these theories differ in exact details, the basic intuition is the same: given information about the occurrence or non-occurrence of other cues and the outcome, the *absence* of a cue can be informative, and so we may need to "error correct" a cue's associative strength even when it does not

---

[3]There is significant debate about whether this causal interpretation is a legitimate use of the R-W model. Michael Waldmann and his colleagues (Waldmann, 2000, 2001; Waldmann & Holyoak, 1992; Waldmann, Holyoak, & Fratianne, 1995) have argued that cues in the R-W model must be the variables learned about first, and so are not mapped onto potential causes in cases of diagnostic learning (that is, reasoning from effects to causes). On this more narrow view of the R-W model, the dynamic theory I discuss here corresponds to an analogue of the R-W model, not to the model itself.

occur. The short-run behavior of these descendants of the R-W model has only been partially explored.

There has been a long history of research into the behavior of the R-W model in the long run (a very limited sample of the research is: Chapman & Robbins, 1990; Cheng, 1997; Danks, 2003; Gluck & Bower, 1988; Sutton & Barto, 1981). For many interesting cases, the R-W model does not have well-defined asymptotic behavior.[4] Instead, we can only talk of equilibrium states, which are themselves sometimes quite difficult to calculate; Danks (2003) provides their most general characterization, as well as a general algorithm for determining them. With experimental designs and parameter values that are typical of standard practice, the R-W model ends up living in the neighborhood of the equilibrium value in the long run. And for a large class of problems described in the following paragraphs, the R-W model's equilibrium state turns out to be the conditional probabilistic contrasts for each variable, which were *independently* proposed as the basis for a long-run theory of human causal learning (Cheng & Novick, 1990, 1992; Spellman, 1996).

The conditional probabilistic contrast, often called conditional ΔP, is essentially a measure of conditional association, and the conditional ΔP theory proposes that people's judgments of causal influence for each variable will be proportional to that variable's conditional ΔP (Cheng & Novick, 1990, 1992; Spellman, 1996). Suppose Q is some specification of cue values for every cue *except* cue i: for example, Cue 1 is present, Cue 2 is absent, and so on. Because we have n cues, there are 2^{n-1} different Q's. Given some particular Q, the conditional probabilistic contrast for cue i is:

$$\Delta P_{i.Q} = P(E \mid i \text{ \& } Q) - P(E \mid \neg\, i \text{ \& } Q). \qquad (15.2)$$

In other words, the conditional probabilistic contrast is the change in the outcome probability between the i-present and i-absent cases, conditional on Q.

The various conditional probabilistic contrasts for a particular cue need not all be equal, but might differ depending on the particular variable values in the conditioning set. In these cases, the conditional ΔP model does not make a determinate prediction. However, if the conditional probabilistic contrasts for each variable are defined and equal, then the R-W model's equilibrium state for that problem is exactly conditional ΔP (Danks, 2003). That is, whenever the conditional ΔP theory is well-defined, the R-W model makes the same long-run prediction. Moreover, in these cases, the VHW and Tassoni variations have the same equilibrium states as the R-W model (Danks, 2003); they all make the same long-run predictions as the conditional ΔP theory

---

[4]The R-W model only has well-defined asymptotes for systems that are (1) deterministic; and (2) have a perfect equilibrium (Danks, 2003).

whenever the latter theory makes any prediction at all. We can thus naturally think of the R-W model and its descendants as dynamical implementations of the conditional ΔP theory.

Pearce and Configural Cues

In the R-W model, each cue has its own associative strength, and the associative strength of compound cues (e.g., A and B both occur) is just the sum of the individual associative strengths. Pearce's (1987) theory of associative learning reverses this picture: each compound cue has its own associative strength, and the associative strength of individual cues is derived from those compound cue strengths. This theory was originally proposed in the animal learning literature, but it has since been proposed as a model of human causal learning (Lopez, Shanks, Almaraz, & Fernandez, 1998; Perales & Shanks, 2003). More formally, using notation slightly different from Pearce, we define $S(Q \rightarrow R)$ to be the extent of generalization from compound Q's strength to compound R's strength. So, for example, if V_{XC} is the associative strength for the compound cue XC (and this is the only compound cue in which C occurs), then the associative strength for the individual cue C (due to XC's associative strength) is given by $S(XC \rightarrow C) \times V_{XC}$. Pearce (1987) assumed the generalization parameters were symmetric; Perales and Shanks (2003) remove that assumption.

The associative strength of a compound cue changes only when that compound is presented. If we let $\delta(E) = 1$ if the outcome occurs and 0 otherwise, then given the presentation of compound cue Q on trial $t+1$, the change in the strength of Q^t is given by:

$$\Delta V_Q^{t+1} = \beta\left(\lambda\delta(E) - \left(V_Q^t + \sum_{R \in Compounds} S(Q \rightarrow R)V_R^t\right)\right) \qquad (15.3)$$

Given some set of updated compound cue associative strengths, the associative strength for some individual cue C is the weighted (by the generalization parameters) sum of the associative strengths of all compound cues containing C. As with the R-W model, this model only rarely has true asymptotics, but has well-defined equilibrium states. The equilibrium states for one individual cue C and a constant background X were given in Perales and Shanks (2003), and in our notation, they are:

$$V_C = S(CX \rightarrow C) \times \frac{\lambda(P(E \mid C) - S(CX \rightarrow X)P(E \mid \neg C))}{1 - S(CX \rightarrow X)S(X \rightarrow CX)} \qquad (15.4)$$

$$V_X = \frac{\lambda(P(E \mid \neg C) - S(X \to CX)P(E \mid C))}{1 - S(CX \to X)S(X \to CX)} \tag{15.5}$$

The equilibrium states for more complicated situations involving multiple individual cues have not been determined, but can easily be calculated using the matrix method of Danks (2003), because we will again have n equations in n unknowns (though here the n unknowns are the compound cue strengths, rather than the individual ones). There are currently no known equivalencies between the equilibrium states of Pearce's model and any other independently proposed long-run theories of causal or associative learning (except the connection with causal Bayes net parameter estimation provided in the third section).

Causal Power Estimation

The R-W, ΔP, Pearce, and other models all essentially try to model the observed statistics. No particular metaphysics is proposed to explain the occurrence of those statistics; they are simply learned. Patricia Cheng's power PC theory incorporates a quite different picture of human causal learning: it posits that humans assume (or operate as if making the assumption) that the influence of a cause on its effect cannot be directly observed, and so the task of causal learning is to determine the strength of that unobserved influence (Buehner & Cheng, 1997; Buehner, Cheng, & Clifford, 2003; Cheng, 1997; Novick & Cheng, 2004). Focusing on generative causes (i.e., those that cause the effect to occur, rather than prevent it), each is presumed to have some capacity—in the sense of Cartwright (1989)—to bring about the effect. Moreover, the presence of the cause is necessary, but not sufficient for the operation of the capacity; the cause's capacities might sometimes fail to operate.[5] We also suppose that there is some always-present, generative background cause (whose capacity to produce the effect also operates only probabilistically). If the occurrence of C and the operation of its capacity are independent of the operation of the background cause's capacity, then p_C, the probability that C's capacity operates, can be estimated from purely observational data using the following equation derived in Cheng (1997):

$$p_C = \frac{\Delta P_C}{1 - P(E \mid \neg C)} \tag{15.6}$$

---

[5]For those who favor a purely deterministic metaphysics, the theory works out exactly the same if we suppose that each generative cause always brings about the effect, unless there is a cause-specific, unobserved, not-always-present preventive cause that disables (in some way) the generative cause's operation.

p_C is a corrected ΔP, where the correction factor accounts for the fact that some instances of C's capacity operating will also be instances in which the background cause's capacity was operating. That is, sometimes E will be doubly produced, and so any estimate of C's causal influence must include some information about the likelihood of E's being doubly caused. A slightly different equation is used to estimate preventive causal power.

In the power PC theory, the estimation in Equation 15.6 does not necessarily occur over all cases, but only over those in a "focal set": a set of cases in which the reasoner judges the cause's occurrence and operation to be independent of the background's operation. The focal set also supports the extension of the power PC theory to multiple potential causes: for each variable, causal power is estimated for a set of cases in which the reasoner judges the various causes' occurrences and operation to be independent of each other. Typical examples of focal sets are: all cases; all cases in which one potential cause is always present; all cases in which a potential cause is always absent; and so on. No fully specified dynamical theory for focal set selection has been proposed.

The power PC theory is an asymptotic theory: it predicts people's beliefs in the long-run, when those beliefs have stabilized. Equation 15.7 gives a dynamical theory whose equilibrium states are the power PC predictions, where the V_k's are generative causes, and the V_j's are preventive causes (Danks, Griffiths, & Tenenbaum, 2003).

$$\Delta V_i = \alpha_i \beta_{\delta(E)} \left(\lambda \delta(E) - \prod_{\delta(V_k)=1} (1 - V_k) \left[1 - \prod_{\delta(V_j)=1} (1 - V_j) \right] \right) \qquad (15.7)$$

This dynamical theory is analogous to the VHW and Tassoni variations on the R-W model, except that a different prediction function is used. Rather than simply taking the sum of the present potential causes' strengths, we integrate the present potential causes according to the underlying metaphysics of the power PC theory.

Dis/Confirming Evidence

A quite different way of approaching the problem of causal inference is to suppose that people are explicitly testing the hypothesis that C causes E. The most direct way to do so is to track one's evidence for and against the hypothesis (Catena, Maldonado, & Candido, 1998; White, 2003a, 2003c). The cases that confirm the hypothesis are those in which both C and E are either present or absent, and cases that disconfirm it are those in which C and E differ on presence/absence. More specifically, White's proportion of Confirming Instances (pCI) theory predicts that judgments of C's causal strength will be proportional to:

$$pCI = [P(C \& E) + P(\neg C \& \neg E)] - [P(C \& \neg E) + P(C \& \neg E)] \quad (15.8)$$

That is, causal judgments are predicted to be proportional to the difference between the relative frequencies of confirming and disconfirming instances. (The theory's name is thus a little misleading.) We can also consider a version of pCI in which the various probabilities are differentially weighted (White, 2003c) to reflect the possibility that some kinds of evidence might be more important than others, perhaps because of rarity or some other asymmetry (McKenzie & Mikkelsen, 2000; see also White, 2003b). These weights can easily be incorporated into Equation 15.9 that follows, and do not make a substantial theoretical difference, and so we ignore them for the present purposes.

In Catena et al.'s (1998) belief adjustment model, the judgment of C's causal strength is given by an updating equation: $J_i = J_{i-1} + \gamma (NewEvidence - J_{i-1})$, where γ is a learning rate parameter (called β by Catena et al.), and *NewEvidence* is just pCI (or possibly weighted pCI) for the cases seen since J_{i-1}. That is, the belief adjustment model says that people do not track causal strength based on a whole sequence of cases, but rather update their beliefs based on the difference between their last judgment and the evidence seen since that judgment. When people only make one judgment for a whole series, then the belief adjustment model makes the same predictions as the (weighted) pCI model. If people make multiple judgments during observation of a series, then γ controls the importance of recent cases: if $\gamma = 0$, then no learning occurs from one judgment to the next; if $\gamma = 1$, then only cases observed since the last judgment matter; intermediate values correspond to various weightings of recent versus past data. If the interjudgment observation distribution is stationary (i.e., the number of cases of each type is the same in every between-judgment interval), then γ indicates how rapidly the belief adjustment model converges to the (weighted) pCI value. The belief adjustment model obviously depends crucially on people's judgment frequencies, but no non-experimental account of judgments has been provided; that is, Catena et al. (1998) do not say when multiple judgments occur in the real world. We thus focus on the pCI theory because it simultaneously functions as a critical part of the belief adjustment model, and is fully specified for more realistic learning situations.

A shortcoming shared by both pCI and the belief adjustment model is that neither has been extended to more complicated situations in which there are multiple potential causes. This extension is critical, given the range of experimental phenomena that require multiple causes (such as blocking phenomena). One natural extension of the theories would be to continue using the pCI equation in its current form, where the various probabilities now must be computed by summing over the different possible states of the other potential causes. This extension determines a value we can call the "unconditional pCI" for each potential cause. We could also consider extensions to "conditional pCI": the unconditional pCI given a fixed specification of the other variable values. As with conditional ΔP, there will be multiple conditional pCIs for a single variable. When that value is well-defined, the behavior of the conditional pCI theory is easily determinable. Its behavior in other conditions will depend substantially on the way the theory is cashed out. To our knowledge, none of these extensions has been endorsed or tested by proponents of the pCI or belief adjustment theories.

Notwithstanding the above concerns, we can naturally inquire about the existence of a dynamical theory for estimating pCI.[6] As with the dynamical theories for conditional ΔP (i.e., R-W and variants) and power PC, we require an updating equation for the strength estimate for the potential cause given the observation of some case. For the pCI theories, we update C_j's strength estimate with the following equation:

$$\Delta V_j^{i+1} = \beta\left((-1)^{|\delta(E)-\delta(C_j)|}\lambda - V_j^i\right) \qquad (15.9)$$

That is, we update the strength estimate based on the difference between the current estimate for C_j and either (i) λ, if C_j and E's presence/absence is the same; or (ii) $-\lambda$, if their presence/absence is different. Note that the presence or absence of other potential causes is completely irrelevant to the estimate for C_j. The equilibrium states for this updating function are the unconditional pCI values for the particular causal learning situation.

Unfortunately, the pCI theory simply cannot work in the real world as it is currently stated, for the same reason that Hempel's (1965) theory of scientific confirmation failed: for some "C causes E" claim, there will be many $\neg C, \neg E$ things, but very few of those instances will actually provide any meaningful confirmation of the causal hypothesis.[7] As an extreme example, consider the causal claim that dropping objects on the moon (C) causes them

---

[6]To my knowledge, this is the first appearance of a dynamical theory for pCI or the between-judgment periods in the belief adjustment model.

[7]A similar problem arises for the ΔP theory. Because almost all real-world cases will be $\neg C$ (and many will be $\neg E$), an unrestricted application of the P theory should lead to $P(E \mid \neg C) \approx P(E)$, which will be approximately zero for many E. But this is clearly not the intended application of the ΔP theory (Shanks, 1993). The power PC theory and probabilistic contrast models avoid this problem by appealing to "pragmatically determined focal sets." The various associative theories either (1) ignore cases in which the cause is absent (e.g., R-W and Pearce); or (2) only update on unexplained, "salient" absences of the cause (e.g., VHW and Tassoni).

to turn into wedges of green cheese (E). Every experience that I have had in my lifetime is an instance of $\neg C$, $\neg E$ with respect to this causal claim. Therefore, because the evidential weight of $\neg C$, $\neg E$ cases is supposed to be at least the same order of magnitude as for C, E cases in the pCI theory, I should think it highly likely that the causal claim is true. But clearly these $\neg C$, $\neg E$ observations in fact give me no real information at all about the causal claim. In order to save the pCI theory, we need to provide some account of which $\neg C$, $\neg E$ instances count as relevant for judgments about "C causes E"; this is essentially another version of the "frame problem" (McCarthy & Hayes, 1969). Of course, there is no ambiguity in experimental settings about which cases are relevant, but the real world is substantially more complicated. One natural move would be to use only pragmatically selected cases; unfortunately, no well-specified theory of the relevant pragmatics has been offered.

Moreover, even if we restrict our attention to artificial situations in which the pCI theory is closer to being well-defined (e.g., an experiment), it still has a strange implication: there must be a deep flaw in one (or both) of (i) our psychological experiments, or (ii) our actual causal cognition. Specifically, suppose that we have equal weights on the four terms in the pCI sum (unequal weights are discussed in footnote 9). Except in very particular circumstances (specifically, $P(C) = 0.5$), if C and E are statistically independent, then pCI 0; and if they are associated, then there is a range of cases for which pCI $= 0$.[8] For the highly specific situations tested in an experiment—only two, temporally ordered, variables, no unobserved common causes, no other anomalous circumstances—every plausible theory of actual causal influence says that C causes E if and only if C and E are associated. Thus, the pCI theory says: when $P(C) \neq 0.5$, (a) if C does not cause E, then people will conclude C *does* cause E, because pCI $\neq 0$; and (b) sometimes when C does cause E, people will conclude the opposite, because pCI $= 0$. So even if the pCI theory is the best explanation of people's responses in certain experiments (and there is reason to doubt this; see Griffiths & Tenenbaum, 2005), either our experiments are not measuring what we think, or else people are systematically wrong in their causal attributions.[9] The latter possibility, systematic error, would be quite surprising in light of our success in moving through our world.

---

[8]The derivation is straightforward: pCI and ΔP make the same prediction if and only if $P(C) = 0.5$. Because $\Delta P = 0$ if and only if C and E are statistically independent, we can conclude: if $P(C) \neq 0.5$, then if pCI $= 0$, then C and E are associated. The converse does not hold, because there are many ways for pCI to differ from a nonzero ΔP, but still be nonzero itself. Nevertheless, there are some cases in which pCI $\neq 0$, but C and E are independent.

[9]One might hope to save pCI by using unequal weights. Although this move helps somewhat for the $P(C) \neq 0.5$ situation, it actually harms the theory for the $P(C) = 0.5$ situation. Specifically, regardless of $P(C)$, we have: (i) For all situations and a measure one set of weights, [statistical independence $\Rightarrow$ pCI $\neq 0$; and (ii) there are situations and a measure zero set of weights such that [statistical association $\Rightarrow$ pCI $= 0$].

CAUSAL LEARNING WITH BAYES NETS

The previous section focused on a variety of psychological theories of human causal learning. We now turn to consider a normative framework for representing causal structures: causal Bayes nets. The causal Bayes net framework originally emerged from a mixture of statistics, computer science, and philosophy, and has successfully been applied in a variety of contexts (examples from a wide range of fields include: Bessler, 2003; Conati, Gertner, Van Lehn, & Druzdzel, 1997; Cooper, Fine, Gadd, Obrosky, & Yealy, 2000; Lerner, Moses, Scott, McIlraith, & Koller, 2002; Ramsey, Gazis, Roush, Spirtes, & Glymour, 2002; Shipley, 2000; Smith, Jarvis, & Hartemink, 2002; Waldemark & Norqvist, 1999). In this section, I first outline the causal Bayes net framework, and several psychological theories of human causal learning that have been based on it. This discussion is not intended as a formal introduction to causal Bayes nets; many other, more comprehensive introductions are available elsewhere (e.g., Glymour & Cooper, 1999; Pearl, 2000; Spirtes, Glymour, & Scheines, 1993). I then show how Bayes nets provide a powerful *lingua franca* in which to express almost all of the other extant psychological theories. Also, one of the real strengths of causal Bayes nets is their ability to model manipulations in the causal system. We return to that issue in more detail in the last section of this chapter. One final note before continuing: the term "Bayesian" has become loaded with substantial theoretical baggage, and it is important to realize that the word "Bayes" in the framework name is due only to historical accident[10]; there is nothing intrinsically Bayesian about causal Bayes nets.

An Introduction, and Applications to Human Causal Learning

Suppose we have a set of variables.[11] In this setting, the variables might be the various cues and outcomes, and the possible values for each variable would be present or absent; more complicated sets of variables are also possible. Additionally, if we have time series data, the variables might be time-indexed. A causal Bayes net is composed of two related pieces: (1) a directed acyclic graph (DAG) over the variables; and (2) a probability distribution over the variables. In the DAG, there is a node for each variable, and $X \rightarrow Y$ means "X causes Y," though no particularly strong metaphysical theory of causation is required; Woodward (2003) carefully explores the metaphysical commitments

---

[10]They were originally used to improve performance on Bayesian updating, principally in medical diagnosis.

[11]I assume throughout that the variables are discrete. Structural equation models are the continuous-variable analogues of causal Bayes nets, and every claim in this chapter also holds for them.

of causal Bayes nets. The probability distribution is a specification of the probability of all possible combinations of variable values. These two components are connected by two assumptions:

Causal Markov Assumption: Every variable is independent of its non-effects conditional on its direct causes.

Causal Faithfulness Assumption: The only probabilistic independencies are those entailed by the causal Markov assumption.

These two assumptions are essentially claims about the ways in which causal structure reveals itself in observable statistics or probabilities. They could be empirically false in certain domains, but there are reasons to think that they hold of many systems (Glymour, 1999). Moreover, there is growing evidence that people naturally make these assumptions, particularly the causal Markov assumption (Gopnik, Glymour, Sobel, Schulz, Kushnir, & Danks, 2004).

The two components of a causal Bayes net describe different kinds of causal information: the DAG encodes the qualitative causal structure; and the probability distribution encodes the quantitative types and strengths of (i.e., the parameters for) the various causal influences. Thinking about causal Bayes nets in this way helps illuminate the two assumptions: the causal Markov assumption says (roughly) that we don't need to determine the parameters for variables not connected by an edge because there is no direct causal influence; the causal Faithfulness assumption says (roughly) that the parameter values do not obscure the causal structure, for example by multiple causal pathways exactly offsetting each other. In this framework, the distinction drawn at the end of the first section between structure and parameter learning corresponds to learning about the DAG and probability distribution, respectively.

In addition to modeling known causal structures, a causal Bayes net can be learned from purely observational data given the causal Markov and Faithfulness assumptions (experimental and mixed data are discussed in the next section). That is, given purely observational data and these two assumptions about the way in which causation reveals itself in associations, we can often recover substantial parts of the actual causal structure. This result is perhaps surprising, given the oft-repeated mantra that "correlation does not imply causation." Although this statement is true for single pairs of variables, it is not true for *patterns* of correlations (given these two assumptions). A simple example might help to show why. First, define a "causal connection" between X and Y to be one or more of: (1) X causes Y; (2) Y causes X; or (3) there is an unobserved common cause of X and Y. Now suppose that we have three variables, A, B, and C, and that the only independence among these variables is between A and C, unconditionally. From these data, we can conclude that (1) there is a causal connection between A and B, as well as B and C; but (2) B does not cause either A or C; and (3) there is no causal connection (direct or indirect) between A and C. To illustrate just one of these conclusions, consider (2), and suppose instead that B causes C. That implies that there must be an indirect causal connection between A and C, where the exact nature of the connection depends on the causal connection between A and B. But an indirect causal connection implies unconditional association (because of the causal Faithfulness assumption), which contradicts the known data. Hence, we can conclude that B does not cause C.

A variety of learning algorithms have been developed within the machine learning community over the past 15 years that exploit this fact that we can infer some causal structure from patterns of correlations (Chickering, 2002; Heckerman, 1998; Spirtes et al., 1993). Although the algorithms differ in important details, they all infer possible causal structures from patterns of conditional and unconditional associations and independencies. That is, the algorithms determine (in varying ways) the set of causal structures that could have, or were likely to have, produced data such as that actually observed. Roughly speaking, these algorithms divide into two camps: constraint-based algorithms determine the full set of possible causal Bayes nets (including those with unobserved common causes) from the pattern of statistically significant independencies and associations; Bayesian and score-based algorithms search through the space of graphs, typically in a heuristic manner, to find causal structures that are highly probable, given the observed data. Recovering causal connections from observation correlations using these algorithms is more than a theoretical possibility: Causal Bayes nets have been applied in a wide range of domains for both causal discovery and various types of inference (see references in the introduction to this section). That being said, they are not an ideal representation for some domains, such as feedback or epidemiological models. Perhaps more importantly for cases of human causal learning, causal Bayes nets do not currently provide good models of continuous time phenomena, though continuous time Bayes nets are the subject of ongoing research (Nodelman, Shelton, & Koller, 2002, 2003).

For other situations, causal Bayes nets provide an excellent representational framework for causal relationships; the causal learning situations modeled by psychological theories form one such class of suitable situations. Thus, a natural strategy would be to test whether people represent and learn these causal structures as though they were causal Bayes nets. A number of different researchers have pursued this line of thinking, which has resulted in essentially two different kinds of causal Bayes net-based psychological theories. One approach has been to use causal Bayes net learning algorithms to provide a computational-level account (or a rational analysis) of causal learning (Gopnik & Glymour, 2002; Gopnik et al., 2004; Gopnik, Sobel, Schulz, & Glymour, 2001; Griffiths & Tenenbaum, 2005; Steyvers, Tenenbaum, Wagenmakers, & Blum, 2003; Tenenbaum & Griffiths, 2001, 2003).[12] That is, this work focuses on understanding the high-level relationship between the observed cases and people's causal judgments, without necessarily arguing for any particular algorithm by which those judgments are reached. Although specific learning algorithms are, of course, used in deriving predictions, no particular descriptive claim is intended by their use. Rather, the claim here is that people act rationally (i.e., according to the normative prescriptions of causal Bayes net learning algorithms), even though they might not actually be using causal Bayes net learning algorithms. For example, Tenenbaum & Griffiths (2001) argue that people make judgments as though they are Bayesian learners of causal Bayes nets, but note that χ^2 estimates are a simple, close approximation of the "rational" prediction, and would be indistinguishable for all of their experiments.

A quite different use of the causal Bayes net framework is to argue that people are essentially doing top-down search over causal Bayes net structures (Lagnado & Sloman, 2002, 2004; Waldmann, 2000, 2001; Waldmann & Martignon, 1998). Sometimes referred to as "causal model theory," the representation of causal beliefs was inspired in part by causal Bayes nets (particularly Pearl, 1988), but uses an independently developed learning mechanism (Waldmann, 1996; Waldmann & Holyoak, 1992; Waldmann, Holyoak, & Fratianne, 1995). Specifically, learning is top-down: people use prior beliefs (e.g., beliefs about temporal order, intervention status, or other prior domain knowledge) to determine an initial causal structure, estimate the strengths of influences based on that structure, and then revise their beliefs about the underlying causal structure only as necessary. This last step is obviously of central importance, but has not been significantly explored. This approach can also be represented as a set of restrictions on the learning process in the rational analysis approach (e.g., as a highly skewed prior distribution for Bayesian learning of causal Bayes nets).

The causal Bayes net approaches are not necessarily direct competitors of the other psychological theories. In particular, both of the causal Bayes net approaches typically assume some situation-dependent prior knowledge

---

[12]These papers use a mix of constraint-based and Bayesian learning algorithms. However, the differences are not as great as they might appear. In particular, because constraint-based algorithms do not care about the source of the association/independence judgments, one could easily use Bayesian statistics to calculate the associations and independencies. See Danks (2004) for more details.

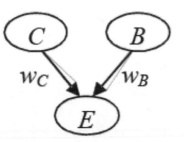

Figure 15.1 Causal Bayes net for parameter estimation.

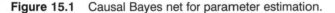

constraints on the particular form(s) that causal influence can take, where these restrictions often correspond to one of the other extant psychological theories. That is, the causal Bayes net approaches typically agree with one or another of the other psychological theories about causal influence estimation *once the causal structure has been learned.* The causal Bayes net approaches differ in that they posit a structure learning step that is conceptually—and sometimes algorithmically—prior to the parameter learning step. They argue that people do not infer the quantitative causal influence (the parameters) until they determine that there is a qualitative causal influence (the graphical structure). We return to this connection in the final section of the chapter.

A Metatheoretic Structure Based on Causal Bayes Nets

This connection between the causal Bayes net approaches and the other extant psychological theories points to an idea: perhaps *all* of the other psychological theories can be completely explained as doing parameter estimation on some fixed causal structure. This intuition turns out to be exactly right, as we can represent the range of theories in a single, metatheoretical structure using the causal Bayes net framework. Consider the DAG in Figure 15.1, where B is some always-occurring background variable, and w_C and w_B are parameters associated with the edges.

To turn this DAG into a causal Bayes net, we must also provide a probability distribution for C and E. Because C is an exogenous variable (i.e., one with no cause within the system), we need provide only its base rate. For the distribution for E, we can specify a function whose "free parameters" are the w_B and w_C parameters in Figure 15.1, and whose input variables are whether

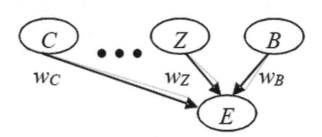

Figure 15.2   Full one-layer causal Bayes net for parameter estimation.

each parent variable occurs.[13] For example, the probability of E might be given by w_B, plus w_C when C occurs: $P(E) = w_B + w_C\delta(C)$. (Remember that $\delta(X) = 1$ if X is present, 0 otherwise, and that B is always present.) For this function for $P(E)$, ΔP_C is the maximum likelihood estimate of w_C (Tenenbaum & Griffiths, 2001).[14] That is, the one-potential cause ΔP theory can be interpreted as a maximum likelihood estimate of a parameter in a fixed-structure causal Bayes net with a particular functional form.

In fact, we can provide an even stronger result. Consider the DAG shown in Figure 15.2. The conditional ΔP for variable X is a maximum likelihood estimate of w_X when the probability of E is the sum of the w-parameters for the occurring variables (Tenenbaum & Griffiths, 2001):

$$P(E) = \Sigma w_X \times \delta(X) \qquad (15.10)$$

And given the equivalence between conditional ΔP and the equilibrium states of the R-W model (and VHW and Tassoni variations), we can reinterpret these dynamical theories as algorithms for learning the maximum likelihood values of the parameters. That is, all of the theories in the first part of the second section of the chapter are slightly different ways to do parameter estimation in a fixed-structure, fixed-functional form causal Bayes net.

Alternately, suppose the functional form for $P(E)$ in Figure 15.1 is given by:

$$P(E) = w_C \times \delta(C) + w_B - w_C \times w_B \times \delta(C) \qquad (15.11)$$

---

[13]This is not the only way to specify $P(E)$, but it is convenient for our purposes.

[14]All proofs are omitted due to space considerations, but are available on request from the author.

The causal power in Cheng's power PC theory is the maximum likelihood estimate of w_C in this function (Glymour, 1998; Tenenbaum & Griffiths, 2001). For multiple causes, causal power is the maximum likelihood estimate of the w-parameters in Figure 15.2, where the functional form is the natural multivariate extension of equation (15.11): a multivariate noisy-or gate for generative causes, or a noisy-and gate for preventive causes (Danks et al., 2003). No results are known about the "parameter estimation properties" of the recent extension of the power PC theory to interactive causes (Novick & Cheng, 2004). The power PC theory and corresponding dynamical theory are thus maximum likelihood parameter estimators for the exact same causal structure as the conditional ΔP theory; they make different predictions because they assume different functional forms for $P(E)$ in that causal Bayes net.

The story is a bit more complicated for Pearce's theory and its equilibrium states because of the generalization parameters. For one potential cause (Fig. 15.1), V_C in Pearce's theory is the maximum likelihood estimate of the w_C term (and V_X for the w_B term) for the $P(E)$ function:

$$P(E) = S(CB \rightarrow B)^{\delta(C)} \times w_B + \frac{S(B \rightarrow CB)^{(1-\delta(C))}}{S(CB \rightarrow B)} \times w_C. \qquad (15.12)$$

That is, in Pearce's theory, the probability of the effect is a weighted sum of both w-parameters, where the weights depend on whether C is present or absent. It is currently unknown whether the above equation for $P(E)$ can be extended to the multiple-cause situation depicted in Figure 15.2.

Not all of the previously discussed theories can be represented in this way, however. In particular, the pCI theory cannot be represented as a parameter estimator for the causal Bayes net in Figure 15.1. Because it is unclear how to extend pCI to multiple potential causes, we focus here on the one-cause situation. In the causal Bayes net framework, if C and E are unconditionally independent, then the causal Faithfulness assumption implies that there cannot be a graphical edge between them (i.e., C does not cause E), and so there must be a zero w-parameter in Figure 15.1. Therefore, for any theory that can be represented as a causal Bayes net parameter estimator, it must be the case that unconditional independence between C and E (in the one-cause situation) implies a zero w-parameter. pCI fails this requirement: as noted earlier, if $P(C) \neq 0.5$ and C and E are independent, then pCI $\neq 0$. Therefore, there cannot be a (Faithful) functional form for the causal Bayes net such that pCI is the maximum likelihood estimate of w_C.[15]

---

[15]Griffiths & Tenenbaum (2005) have provided a rational "approximate justification" of pCI as causal Bayes net structure learning, but their reconstruction requires one to make highly implausible assumptions.

Given all of these results, we can place these various theories into three distinct columns in the single, metatheoretic structure shown in Table 15.1, where names are provided for the more common theories. (Literature references for each cell can be found in the sections above. Numbers in parentheses indicate equations.)

Each row of the table represents a class of theories: the first four rows contain various parameter estimators, and the fifth row describes the "native" causal Bayes net structure learning algorithms. For the parameter estimators (the first four rows), there are shared relationships between the columns: (1) the long-run behavior (typically, the equilibrium state) of the dynamical models is the asymptotic model; (2) the asymptotic model is a maximum likelihood estimate of the w-parameters in the Bayes net function (for the causal Bayes net of Fig. 15.2); and (3) the Bayes net function is—for the first three rows—the prediction function for the error-correction term of the dynamical models. For the structure learning algorithms, the relationships are a bit different, because they are also learning the graphical structure of the causal Bayes net. That row is included primarily to highlight the contrasts with the parameter estimation theories.

NOT ALL DATA ARE CREATED EQUAL: LEARNING FROM MANIPULATIONS

The data used by the theories described in this chapter are purely observational: cases where we only see the naturally occurring values of each variable. But we often get data from our manipulations of the causal systems around us; a simple example is flipping a light switch to figure out what it causes. Moreover, there can be a substantial difference between observing and manipulating a variable. The observation that someone has nicotine stains on her fingers licenses the inference that she (probably) smokes; intervening to force someone to have nicotine stains on her fingers eliminates the support for the inference to her smoking. The variable values in an observation are due to the causal structure that is "in the world"; in contrast, manipulating a variable changes the causal structure so that a variable's value depends on us, rather than its normal causes. In this example, the nicotine stains in the second case are due solely to our manipulation, which is why we cannot infer anything about the person's smoking behavior.

In this example, the manipulation yielded less information than the observation, but sometimes manipulations are more informative. Consider the simple case in which X and Y are observed to be associated. All we can conclude is that there is some causal connection between X and Y, but we don't know

TABLE 15.2
Possible Causal Models Given Manipulations

	Independent After Y Manipulation	Associated After Y Manipulation
Independent after X manipulation	Unobserved common cause	*Y* causes *X*; and perhaps an unobserved common cause
Associated after X manipulation	*X* causes *Y*; and perhaps an unobserved common cause	Each one causes the other (feedback loop); and perhaps an unobserved common cause

what it is: (1) *X* causes *Y*; (2) *Y* causes *X*; (3) an unobserved common cause of *X* and *Y*; or some combination of these possibilities. Now suppose that we can manipulate *X* and *Y* independently, and then check whether they are associated. The outcomes of the manipulations will depend on the underlying causal structure, and so we summarize the inferences we can make in each possible outcome pair in Table 15.2.

For example, suppose that *X* = nicotine stains (present or absent) and *Y* = smoking (present or absent). These variables will be associated if we manipulate *Y*, but not if we manipulate *X* (for the reasons discussed earlier). We are thus in the upper right-hand cell of the table, and so we can (correctly) conclude that smoking causes nicotine stains, and that there might also be an unobserved common cause of the two variables. Observations alone would only tell us that there is some causal connection between them, but not its form. Being able to manipulate the variables thus led to more learning than given observations. In general, manipulations give us more information, particularly about direction, for individual causal connections, but at the cost of changing the causal structure. Observations show us the full causal structure, but at the cost of reduced information about the specific causal connections. Sometimes manipulations are the best way to learn; sometimes observations are superior; often, a combination is best.

We might wonder whether people can exploit this informational difference in learning. In fact, recent research suggests that we learn causal structure substantially *better* when we can manipulate the causal system (Gopnik et al., 2004; Kushnir, Gopnik, Schulz, & Danks, 2003; Lagnado & Sloman, 2004; Schulz & Gopnik, 2004; Sloman & Lagnado, 2004; Sobel & Kushnir, 2003, 2006; Steyvers et al., 2003). Furthermore, we can understand this advantage by considering the representation of manipulations within the causal Bayes net

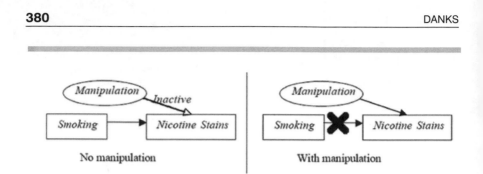

No manipulation   With manipulation

Figure 15.3   Example of manipulation representation.

framework (Pearl, 2000; Spirtes et al., 1993). A manipulation on target X is represented by the introduction of a new direct cause of X that represents the manipulation occurring or not. When the manipulation does not occur, the causal system functions as normal; the causal influence of the manipulation is simply inactive. When the manipulation occurs, the other causes of the manipulated variable no longer matter, and so we can remove (or "break") those edges in the causal Bayes net.[16] This transition is shown in Figure 15.3.

And notice that smoking and nicotine stains will be independent in the right-hand causal system, because there is no causal connection between the two. The causal Bayes net representation of manipulations thus correctly captures our intuitions.

In addition to providing an excellent representation of the impact of manipulations, the causal Bayes net framework also gives a natural account of learning from manipulations. That is, the learning algorithms discussed in the previous section can be straightforwardly adjusted to incorporate exclusively postmanipulation data, or even mixtures of observational and manipulation data. Moreover, there are also causal Bayes net accounts of "active learning": choosing the manipulation or experiment (or series of manipulations) that maximally reduces one's uncertainty about the underlying structure (Eberhardt, Glymour, & Scheines, 2006; Tong & Koller, 2001). Because of this natural integration of manipulations into the causal Bayes net framework, no adjustment is needed for any of the psychological accounts of human causal learning that are based directly on that framework.

The story is more complicated for the "traditional" psychological theories discussed in the second section of the chapter because none of them explicitly

---

[16]As a technical aside, a variable being "edge-breaking" is actually sufficient but not necessary for it to count as a "manipulation" on this scheme. A more precise characterization of 'manipulation' can be given in terms of sources of variation in the target variable that are independent of the other variables in the system. See the Manipulation Theorem of Spirtes et al. (1993) for a precise statement.

discuss the observation/manipulation distinction. In fact, the lack of this distinction in the traditional theories, and the importance of the distinction in the causal Bayes net framework, has been a crucial motivation of much recent experimental research on human causal learning. However, the re-description of those theories in terms of parameter estimation in a specific causal Bayes net provides one explanation for the lack of focus on this distinction: namely, that there is no observation/manipulation distinction for the potential causes in the fixed causal Bayes net in Figure 15.2. Given that we know (or assume) that the causal system has the structure in Figure 15.2, we can make exactly the same inferences—either about the parameters or about the likelihood of the effect occurring—given either (a) observations that the potential causes have some values; or (b) manipulations to force the potential causes to have exactly the same values. In addition, if we want to know which variable to manipulate to bring about the effect, we can simply use the observational probabilities to determine which variable would be most efficacious. This result might seem a bit surprising, but notice that the manipulations all take place on variables that have no edges directed into them, and so the manipulation does not break any causal connections (within the system). The manipulation/observation distinction only matters when the manipulation is on some variable that has causes in this causal structure. None of the potential causes in Figure 15.2 meets this requirement, and so the distinction is not relevant for learning or inference. Of course, the parameter estimation theories could resist this reinterpretation, but then they must provide some explanation of the observation/manipulation distinction, which seems to be quite important in human causal learning.

If we apply this reinterpretation to the traditional psychological (parameter estimation) theories, then they can explain the manipulation data and experiments, though at a cost. First, there is a potential rhetorical cost. Several of the theories were originally developed within the animal learning community (e.g., Pearce, 1987; Rescorla & Wagner, 1972), and so are sometimes accompanied by rhetoric about there being no distinction between learning covariations and causation, or about causal learning being just a type of covariation learning (De Houwer & Beckers, 2002). That rhetoric is no longer legitimate in this reinterpretation of the parameter estimation theories, because the observation/manipulation distinction is now being explicitly drawn in the framework. We just happen to know (or assume) a causal structure in which we can learn, predict, and make decisions equally well given the two kinds of information. In this framework, there really is a difference between beliefs about correlations and beliefs about causation, but they happen to coincide in these particular learning situations.

More importantly, the traditional psychological theories must make a choice about theoretical scope in this reinterpretation. One option is to argue that the parameter estimation theory explains and predicts all parts of data-driven causal learning. That is, to argue that people assume the causal structure in Figure 15.2, and so cannot learn different causal structures. This strategy is unlikely to succeed, because there is substantial experimental evidence that people can learn other causal structures, such as a chain, or a common cause (Lagnado & Sloman, 2002; Steyvers et al., 2003; Waldmann et al., 1995), and even that rats can learn such structures (Blaisdell, Sawa, Leising, & Waldmann, 2006). Alternately, one could narrow the scope of the parameter estimation theory to apply only *after* the causal structure has been determined (where some other mechanism handles the structure learning). This option results in a theory such as Waldmann and Martignon (1998), in which people estimate each "edge parameter" according to the power PC theory, but use another algorithm to determine the structure in which estimation occurs (see also Danks et al., 2003; Tenenbaum & Griffiths, 2003). In this option, the parameter estimation theories explain less than has previously been thought.

CONCLUSION

Many of our cognitive activities presuppose beliefs about causal relationships in the world, and a range of theories have been proposed to explain how we make causal inferences from our observations and manipulations of the world around us. The primary concern in the psychological literature to this point has been on the successes and failures of these theories at predicting various experimental data. This focus has led to less exploration of the relationships among the theories. Despite the fact that many of the theories were independently proposed, there are numerous interesting relationships among them. In particular, many of the theories are dynamical or long-run versions of each other; there are connections across explanatory levels that provide a better understanding of the "theory space," as well as support the design of better crucial experiments among the theories. For example, we can see that there is little point to performing an experiment to distinguish between the R-W model and (the long-run version of) the conditional ΔP theory, because the former is a dynamical version of the latter.

More importantly, we can use the framework of causal Bayes nets to demonstrate that most of the extant psychological theories have essentially the same structure: they are parameter estimators for a fixed-structure, fixed-functional form causal Bayes net, where the precise functional form differs between the theories. These theories (almost) all focus on the estimation of quantitative strengths of causal influence, and thereby infer causal structure only indirectly (through inference of zero causal strength).

Moreover, various theoretical considerations—particularly the observation/ manipulation distinction—point towards the vital importance of correct inference of causal structure. But rather than concluding (as one might) that the lack of structure learning in the parameter estimation theories implies that they are deeply flawed, we can again use the causal Bayes net framework to show the vital role played by these theories: they provide accounts of the types of causal "functions" that people will consider when inferring causal structure. The "theory space" of functional forms has been extensively explored in the past 15 years of research on human causal learning; distinguishing the various possible structure learning algorithms and determining their empirical accuracy remains a substantial open research problem.

ACKNOWLEDGMENTS

Maralee Harrell, Clark Glymour, Alison Gopnik, and Michael Waldmann provided useful comments on earlier drafts. Thanks also to the audience of the 33rd Carnegie Symposium on Cognition, particularly Luis Barrios, Christian Schunn, and Priti Shah, for valuable questions and comments.

REFERENCES

Ahn, W.-K., & Bailenson, J. (1996). Causal attribution as a search for underlying mechanisms: An explanation of the conjunction fallacy and the discounting principle. *Cognitive Psychology, 31*, 82–123.

Ahn, W.-K., Kalish, C. W., Medin, D. L., & Gelman, S. A. (1995). The role of covariation versus mechanism information in causal attribution. *Cognition, 54*, 299–352.

Baker, A. G., Mercier, P., Vallee-Tourangeau, F., Frank, R., & Pan, M. (1993). Selective associations and causality judgments: Presence of a strong causal factor may reduce judgments of a weaker one. *Journal of Experimental Psychology: Learning, Memory, & Cognition, 19*, 414–432.

Bessler, D. A. (2003). *On world poverty: Its causes and effects.* Rome: Food and Agricultural Organization of the United Nations.

Blaisdell, A. P., Denniston, J. C., & Miller, R. R. (2001). Recovery from the overexpectation effect: Contrasting performance-focused and acquisition-focused models of retrospective revaluation. *Animal Learning & Behavior, 29*, 367–380.

Blaisdell, A. P., & Miller, R. R. (2001). Conditioned inhibition produced by extinction-mediated recovery from the relative stimulus validity effect: A test of acquisition and performance models of empirical retrospective revaluation. *Journal of Experimental Psychology: Animal Behavior Processes, 27*, 48–58.

Blaisdell, A. P., Sawa, K., Leising, K. J., & Waldmann, M. R. (2006). Causal reasoning in rats. *Science, 311*, 1020–1022.

Buehner, M. J., & Cheng, P. W. (1997). Causal induction: The Power PC theory versus the Rescorla-Wagner model. In M. G. Shafto & P. Langley (Eds.), *Proceedings of the 19th annual conference of the cognitive science society* (pp. 55–60). Mahwah, NJ: Lawrence Erlbaum Associates.

Buehner, M. J., Cheng, P. W., & Clifford, D. (2003). From covariation to causation: A test of the assumption of causal power. *Journal of Experimental Psychology: Learning, Memory, & Cognition, 29*, 1119–1140.

Buehner, M. J., & May, J. (2002). Knowledge mediates the timeframe of covariation assessment in human causal induction. *Thinking & Reasoning, 8*, 269=295.

Buehner, M. J., & May, J. (2003). Rethinking temporal contiguity and the judgment of causality: Effects of prior knowledge, experience, and reinforcement procedure. *The Quarterly Journal of Experimental Psychology, 56A*, 865–890.

Buehner, M. J., & May, J. (2004). Abolishing the effect of reinforcement delay on human causal learning. *The Quarterly Journal of Experimental Psychology, 57B*, 179–191.

Cartwright, N. (1989). *Nature's capacities and their measurement.* Oxford, UK: Oxford University Press.

Catena, A., Maldonado, A., & Candido, A. (1998). The effect of the frequency of judgment and the type of trials on covariation learning. *Journal of Experimental Psychology: Human Perception and Performance, 24*, 481–495.

Chapman, G. B. (1991). Trial order affects cue interaction in contingency judgment. *Journal of Experimental Psychology: Learning, Memory, & Cognition, 17*, 837–854.

Chapman, G. B., & Robbins, S. J. (1990). Cue interaction in human contingency judgments. *Memory & Cognition, 18*, 537–545.

Cheng, P. W. (1997). From covariation to causation: A causal power theory. *Psychological Review, 104*, 367–405.

Cheng, P. W., & Novick, L. R. (1990). A probabilistic contrast model of causal induction. *Journal of Personality and Social Psychology, 58*, 545–567.

Cheng, P. W., & Novick, L. R. (1992). Covariation in natural causal induction. *Psychological Review, 99*, 365–382.

Chickering, D. M. (2002). Optimal structure identification with greedy search. *Journal of Machine Learning Research, 3*, 507–554.

Collins, D. J., & Shanks, D. R. (2006). Conformity to the Power PC theory of causal induction depends on the type of probe question. *The Quarterly Journal of Experimental Psychology, 59*, 225–232.

Conati, C., Gertner, A., Van Lehn, K., & Druzdzel, M. J. (1997). On-line student modeling for coached problem solving using Bayesian networks. In A. Jameson, C. Paris, & C. Tasso (Eds.), *Proceedings of the 6th international conference on user modeling* (pp. 231–242). Vienna: Springer-Verlag.

Cooper, G. F., Fine, M. J., Gadd, C. S., Obrosky, D. S., & Yealy, D. M. (2000). Analyzing causal relationships between treating clinicians and patient admission and mortality in low-risk pneumonia patients. *Academic Emergency Medicine, 7*, 470–471.

Danks, D. (2003). Equilibria of the Rescorla-Wagner model. *Journal of Mathematical Psychology, 47*, 109–121.

Danks, D. (2004). Constraint-based human causal learning. In M. Lovett, C. Schunn, C. Leviere & P. Munro (Eds.), *Proceedings of the 6th international conference on cognitive modeling* (pp. 342–343). Mahwah, NJ: Lawrence Erlbaum Associates.

Danks, D. (2005). The supposed competition between theories of human causal inference. *Philosophical Psychology, 18*, 259–272.

Danks, D., Griffiths, T. L., & Tenenbaum, J. B. (2003). Dynamical causal learning. In S. Becker, S. Thrun, & K. Obermayer (Eds.), *Advances in neural information processing systems 15* (pp. 67–74). Cambridge, MA: The MIT Press.

De Houwer, J., & Beckers, T. (2002). A review of recent developments in research and theories on human contingency learning. *The Quarterly Journal of Experimental Psychology, 55B*, 289–310.

Eberhardt, F., Glymour, C., & Scheines, R. (2006). N-1 experiments suffice to determine the causal relations among N variables. In D. Holmes & L. Jain (Eds.), *Innovations in machine learning*. Berlin: Springer-Verlag.

Gluck, M. A., & Bower, G. H. (1988). From conditioning to category learning: An adaptive network model. *Journal of Experimental Psychology: General, 117*, 227–247.

Glymour, C. (1998). Learning causes: Psychological explanations of causal explanation. *Minds and Machines, 8*, 39–60.

Glymour, C. (1999). Rabbit hunting. *Synthese, 121*, 55–78.

Glymour, C., & Cooper, G. F. (1999). *Computation, causation, & discovery*. Cambridge, MA: AAAI Press & The MIT Press.

Gopnik, A., & Glymour, C. (2002). Causal maps and Bayes nets: A cognition and computational account of theory-formation. In P. Carruthers, S. Stich, & M. Siegal (Eds.), *The cognitive basis of science* (pp. 117–132). Cambridge, UK: Cambridge University Press.

Gopnik, A., Glymour, C., Sobel, D. M., Schulz, L. E., Kushnir, T., & Danks, D. (2004). A theory of causal learning in children: Causal maps and Bayes nets. *Psychological Review, 111*, 3–32.

Gopnik, A., Sobel, D. M., Schulz, L. E., & Glymour, C. (2001). Causal learning mechanisms in very young children: Two, three, and four-year-olds infer causal relations from patterns of variation and covariation. *Developmental Psychology, 37*, 620–629.

Griffiths, T. L., & Tenenbaum, J. B. (2005). Structure and strength in causal induction. *Cognitive Psychology, 51*, 334–384.

Hagmayer, Y., & Waldmann, M. R. (2002). How temporal assumptions influence causal judgments. *Memory & Cognition, 30*, 1128–1137.

Heckerman, D. (1998). A tutorial on learning with Bayesian networks. In M. I. Jordan (Ed.), *Learning in graphical models* (pp. 301–354). Boston: Kluwer.

Hempel, C. (1965). *Aspects of scientific explanation*. New York: Free Press.

Hume, D. (1748). *An enquiry concerning human understanding*. Oxford, UK: Clarendon.

Kushnir, T., Gopnik, A., Schulz, L. E., & Danks, D. (2003). Inferring hidden causes. In R. Alterman & D. Kirsh (Eds.), *Proceedings of the 25th annual meeting of the cognitive science society* (pp. 699–703). Boston: Cognitive Science Society.

Lagnado, D. A., & Sloman, S. A. (2002). Learning causal structure. In W. D. Gray & C. D. Schunn (Eds.), *Proceedings of the 24th annual conference of the cognitive science society*. Mahwah, NJ: Lawrence Erlbaum Associates.

Lagnado, D. A., & Sloman, S. A. (2004). The advantage of timely intervention. *Journal of Experimental Psychology: Learning, Memory, & Cognition, 30*, 856–876.

Lerner, U., Moses, B., Scott, M., McIlraith, S., & Koller, D. (2002). Monitoring a complex physical system using a hybrid dynamic Bayes net. In A. Darwiche & N. Friedman (Eds.), *Uncertainty in artificial intelligence: Proceedings of the 18th conference* (pp. 301–310). San Francisco: Morgan Kaufmann.

Lien, Y., & Cheng, P. W. (2000). Distinguishing genuine from spurious causes: A coherence hypothesis. *Cognitive Psychology, 40*, 87–137.

Lober, K., & Shanks, D. R. (2000). Is causal induction based on causal power? Critique of Cheng (1997). *Psychological Review, 107*, 195–212.

Lopez, F. J., Shanks, D. R., Almaraz, J., & Fernandez, P. (1998). Effects of trial order on contingency judgments: A comparison of associative and probabilistic contrast accounts. *Journal of Experimental Psychology: Learning, Memory, & Cognition, 24*, 672–694.

McCarthy, J., & Hayes, P. J. (1969). Some philosophical problems from the standpoint of artificial intelligence. In D. Michie & B. Meltzer (Eds.), *Machine intelligence 4* (pp. 463–502). Edinburgh: Edinburgh University Press.

McKenzie, C. R. M., & Mikkelsen, L. A. (2000). The psychological side of hempel's paradox of confirmation. *Psychonomic Bulletin & Review, 7,* 360–366.

Miller, R. R., Barnet, R. C., & Grahame, N. J. (1995). Assessment of the Rescorla-Wagner model. *Psychological Bulletin, 117,* 363–386.

Nodelman, U., Shelton, C. R., & Koller, D. (2002). Continuous time Bayesian networks. In A. Darwiche & N. Friedman (Eds.), *Proceedings of the 18th international conference on uncertainty in artificial intelligence* (pp. 378–387). San Francisco: Morgan Kaufmann.

Nodelman, U., Shelton, C. R., & Koller, D. (2003). Learning continuous time Bayesian networks. In C. Meek & U. Kjaerulff (Eds.), *Proceedings of the 18th international conference on uncertainty in artificial intelligence* (pp. 451–458). San Francisco: Morgan Kaufmann.

Novick, L. R., & Cheng, P. W. (2004). Assessing interactive causal influence. *Psychological Review, 111,* 455–485.

Pearce, J. M. (1987). A model for stimulus generalization in Pavlovian conditioning. *Psychological Review, 94,* 61–73.

Pearl, J. (1988). *Probabilistic reasoning in intelligent systems: Networks of plausible inference.* San Francisco: Morgan Kaufmann Publishers.

Pearl, J. (2000). *Causality: Models, reasoning, and inference.* Cambridge, UK: Cambridge University Press.

Perales, J. C., & Shanks, D. R. (2003). Normative and descriptive accounts of the influence of power and contingency on causal judgement. *The Quarterly Journal of Experimental Psychology, 56A,* 977–1007.

Ramsey, J., Gazis, P., Roush, T., Spirtes, P., & Glymour, C. (2002). Automated remote sensing with near infrared reflectance spectra: Carbonate recognition. *Data Mining and Knowledge Discovery, 6,* 277–293.

Rescorla, R. A., & Wagner, A. R. (1972). A theory of Pavlovian conditioning: Variations in the effectiveness of reinforcement and nonreinforcement. In A. H. Black & W. F. Prokasy (Eds.), *Classical conditioning II: Current research and theory* (pp. 64–99). New York: Appleton-Century-Crofts.

Schulz, L. E., & Gopnik, A. (2004). Causal learning across domains. *Developmental Psychology, 40,* 162–176.

Shanks, D. R. (1993). Associative versus contingency accounts of causal learning: Reply to Melz, Cheng, Holyoak, and Waldmann (1993). *Journal of Experimental Psychology: Learning, Memory, & Cognition, 19,* 1411–1423.

Shanks, D. R. (1995). Is human learning rational? *The Quarterly Journal of Experimental Psychology, 48A,* 257–279.

Shanks, D. R. (2004). Judging covariation and causation. In N. Harvey & D. Koehler (Eds.), *Blackwell handbook of judgment and decision making.* Oxford, UK: Blackwell.

Shanks, D. R., & Dickinson, A. (1987). Associative accounts of causality judgment. In G. H. Bower (Ed.), *The psychology of learning and motivation, vol. 21* (pp. 229–261). San Diego: Academic Press.

Shipley, B. (2000). *Cause and correlation in biology: A user's guide to path analysis, structural equations and causal inference.* Cambridge, UK: Cambridge University Press.

Sloman, S. A. (2005). *Causal models: How people think about the world and its alternatives.* Oxford, UK: Oxford University Press.

Sloman, S. A., & Lagnado, D. A. (2004). Causal invariance in reasoning and learning. In B. H. Ross (Ed.), *The psychology of learning and motivation, vol. 44* (pp. 287–325): Elsevier.

Smith, V. A., Jarvis, E. D., & Hartemink, A. J. (2002). Evaluating functional network inference using simulations of complex biological systems. *Bioinformatics, 18,* S216–224.

Sobel, D. M., & Kushnir, T. (2003). Interventions do not solely benefit causal learning: Being told what to do results in worse learning than doing it yourself In R. Alterman & D. Kirsh (Eds.), *Proceedings of the 25th annual meeting of the cognitive science society.* Boston: Cognitive Science Society.

Sobel, D. M., & Kushnir, T. (2006). The importance of decision-making in causal learning from interventions. *Memory & Cognition, 34,* 411–419.

Spellman, B. A. (1996). Conditionalizing causality. In D. R. Shanks, K. J. Holyoak & D. L. Medin (Eds.), *Causal learning: The psychology of learning and motivation, vol. 34* (pp. 167–206). San Diego, CA: Academic Press.

Spirtes, P., Glymour, C., & Scheines, R. (1993). *Causation, prediction, and search.* Berlin: Springer-Verlag.

Steyvers, M., Tenenbaum, J. B., Wagenmakers, E.-J., & Blum, B. (2003). Inferring causal networks from observations and interventions. *Cognitive Science, 27,* 453–489.

Sutton, R. S., & Barto, A. G. (1981). Toward a modern theory of adaptive networks: Expectation and prediction. *Psychological Review, 88,* 135–170.

Tassoni, C. J. (1995). The least mean squares network with information coding: A model of cue learning. *Journal of Experimental Psychology: Learning, Memory, & Cognition, 21,* 193–204.

Tenenbaum, J. B., & Griffiths, T. L. (2001). Structure learning in human causal induction. In T. Leen, T. Deitterich, & V. Tresp (Eds.), *Advances in neural information processing systems 13* (pp. 59–65). Cambridge, MA: The MIT Press.

Tenenbaum, J. B., & Griffiths, T. L. (2003). Theory-based causal inference. In S. Becker, S. Thrun & K. Obermayer (Eds.), *Advances in neural information processing systems 15* (pp. 35–42). Cambridge, MA: The MIT Press.

Tong, S., & Koller, D. (2001). Active learning for structure in Bayesian networks. In H. Levesque (Ed.), *Proceedings of the 17th international joint conference on artificial intelligence* (pp. 863–869). Seattle: AAAI Press.

Van Hamme, L. J., & Wasserman, E. A. (1994). Cue competition in causality judgments: The role of nonpresentation of compound stimulus elements. *Learning and Motivation, 25,* 127–151.

Waldemark, J., & Norqvist, P. (1999). In-flight calibration of satellite ion composition data using artificial intelligence methods. In C. Glymour & G. F. Cooper (Eds.), *Computation, causation, & discovery* (pp. 453–480). Cambridge, MA: AAAI Press & The MIT Press.

Waldmann, M. R. (1996). Knowledge-based causal induction. In D. R. Shanks, K. J. Holyoak, & D. L. Medin (Eds.), *Causal learning: The psychology of learning and motivation, vol. 34* (pp. 47–88). San Diego, CA: Academic Press.

Waldmann, M. R. (2000). Competition among causes but not effects in predictive and diagnostic learning. *Journal of Experimental Psychology: Learning, Memory, & Cognition, 26,* 53–76.

Waldmann, M. R. (2001). Predictive versus diagnostic causal learning: Evidence from an overshadowing paradigm. *Psychonomic Bulletin & Review, 8,* 600–608.

Waldmann, M. R., & Holyoak, K. J. (1992). Predictive and diagnostic learning within causal models: Asymmetries in cue competition. *Journal of Experimental Psychology: General, 121,* 222–236.

Waldmann, M. R., Holyoak, K. J., & Fratianne, A. (1995). Causal models and the acquisition of category structure. *Journal of Experimental Psychology: General, 124,* 181–206.

Waldmann, M. R., & Martignon, L. (1998). A Bayesian network model of causal learning. In M. A. Gernsbacher & S. J. Derry (Eds.), *Proceedings of the 20th annual conference of the cognitive science society* (pp. 1102–1107). Mahwah, NJ: Lawrence Erlbaum Associates.

Wasserman, E. A., Kao, S.-F., Van Hamme, L. J., Katagiri, M., & Young, M. E. (1996). Causation and association. In D. R. Shanks, K. J. Holyoak & D. L. Medin (Eds.), *Causal learning: The psychology of learning and motivation, vol. 34* (pp. 207–264). San Diego: Academic Press.

White, P. A. (2000). Causal judgment from contingency information: Relation between subjective reports and individual tendencies in judgment. *Memory & Cognition, 28,* 415–426.

White, P. A. (2003a). Causal judgment as evaluation of evidence: The use of confirmatory and disconfirmatory information. *The Quarterly Journal of Experimental Psychology, 56A,* 491–513.

White, P. A. (2003b). Effects of wording and stimulus format on the use of contingency information in causal judgment. *Memory & Cognition, 31,* 231–242.

White, P. A. (2003c). Making causal judgments from the proportion of confirming instances: The pci rule. *Journal of Experimental Psychology: Learning, Memory, & Cognition, 29,* 710–727.

Woodward, J. (2003). *Making things happen: A theory of causal explanation.* Oxford, UK: Oxford University Press.

16

Statistical Reasoning: Valid Intuitions Put To Use

Peter Sedlmeier
Chemnitz University of Technology

Is it true that human minds "are not built (for whatever reason) to work by the rules of probability" as Gould (1992, p. 469) contends? Do we have to "stumble along ill-chosen shortcuts to reach bad conclusions" when we have to reason statistically as McCormick (1987, p. 24) thinks? Until recently, the answer of the majority of researchers in the field of judgment and decision making might have been summarized as a resounding "yes." The main reason for the negative answer has been expressed by Kahneman and Tversky (1973): "In making predictions and judgments under uncertainty, people do not appear to follow the calculus of chance or the statistical theory of prediction. Instead, they rely on a limited number of heuristics, which sometimes yield reasonable judgments and sometimes lead to severe and systematic errors" (p. 237). Such systematic errors or *biases* have indeed been shown again and again in people's judgments (e.g., Kahneman, Slovic, & Tversky, 1982; Piattelli-Palmarini, 1994) and have been accorded the status of *cognitive illusions* (Kahneman & Tversky, 1996). Because of the persistence of these cognitive illusions, there has been little hope for the effectiveness of training programs: "Attempts to train people not to think representatively and not to be influenced by availability or other biases have not been very successful," perhaps because "it is impossible for us to think in a way we do not think" (Dawes, 1988, p. 142). Heuristics can be seen as intuitive reactions that arise when one is asked to solve statistical reasoning problems (see Tversky & Kahneman, 1974, p. 1124). The not very encouraging résumé might then be: When reasoning statistically, we often rely on invalid intuitions that lead to errors and that are immune to training attempts.

Is this really so? My main argument in this chapter is that although invalid intuitions may lead to errors in statistical reasoning, even statistically naïve persons hold valid statistical intuitions that can help them to solve probability problems spontaneously, given that the problems are presented in a suitable representational format. Moreover, these valid intuitions can be of much help in designing efficient training programs to teach different aspects of statistical reasoning. I begin with a broad perspective on intuitive problem solving, to show that valid statistical intuitions are just a special case of a general connection between representational format and intuitive abilities. I then illustrate this idea with two types of problems commonly used in research on statistical reasoning: Bayesian inference and the impact of sample size.[1] Then I propose an associative learning explanation for why and when we have valid statistical intuitions at our disposal. Finally, I discuss the possible uses of these intuitions in training programs.

VALID INTUITIONS IN EVERYDAY PROBLEM SOLVING

A large number of our daily, routine problem-solving activities happen in an intuitive manner (Sedlmeier, 2005). The argument I later apply to statistical reasoning is that a crucial precondition for triggering valid intuitive responses is a suitable external representational format.[2] To clarify this idea and to show how general the phenomenon is, let us look at some examples.

"Everyday Things"

Norman (1988) presented numerous examples from daily life in which the "affordances" of things dramatically change with the way these things are represented. For instance, the way a door handle is connected to a door may evoke the intuitive response to push or to pull or may not evoke any reasonable response at all. Or, consider the light switches for a big lecture hall: in their usual vertical arrangement they do not evoke a clear intuitive response if you want to switch on a certain row of lamps. If the arrangement of light switches instead maps the locations of the lamps, the task of switching on the right lamps can be solved intuitively, as Norman (1988) demonstrated. This principle of mapping, that is, arranging switches or controls according to the spatial locations

---

[1] The same argument can also be made for two other types of commonly used statistical problems: reasoning about the probability of conjunctive events and about simple conditional probabilities (see Sedlmeier, 2000).

[2] Intuitive responses are "reached with little apparent effort, and typically without conscious awareness. They involve little or no conscious deliberation" (Hogarth, 2001, p. 14).

of the things to be turned on and off, describes a very powerful way of evoking intuitive responses. Further examples are the mapping of stove burners and controls (for standard stoves, there is no satisfactory mapping) and the mapping between faucets and showers (finding the hot water on the first attempt is sometimes not easy). Norman (1993) also calls this the *naturalness principle*: "Experiential cognition is aided when the properties of the representation match the properties of the thing being represented" (p. 72).

Logic

Consider the following two problems (adapted from Cosmides, 1989, p. 192):

Problem A:
Part of your new clerical job at the local high school is to make sure that student documents have been processed correctly. Your job is to make sure the documents conform to the following alphanumeric rule: "If a person has a 'D' rating, then his documents must be marked code '3'." You suspect the secretary you replaced did not categorize the students' documents correctly. The cards below have information about the documents of four people who are enrolled at this high school. Each card represents one person. One side of a card tells a person's letter rating and the other side of the card tells that person's number code.

Now four cards were shown to the participants, labeled with "D," "F," "3," and "7," and participants are asked to indicate those card(s) one definitely needs to turn over to see if the documents of any of these people violate the above rule. Only 4–25% of college students chose the two correct cards, "D" and "7."[3] However, the proportion of correct solutions rose to 75% in the following problem:

Problem B:
In its crackdown against drunk drivers, Massachusetts law enforcement officials are revoking liquor licenses left and right. You are a bouncer in a Boston bar, and you'll lose your job unless you enforce the following law. "If a person is drinking beer, then he must be over 20 years old." The cards below have information about four people sitting at a table in your bar. Each card represents one person. One side of a card tells what a person is drinking and the other side of the card tells that person's age. Indicate only those card(s) you definitely need to turn over to see if any of these people are breaking this law.

---

[3]This is a version of the famous "Wason selection task." The logical conclusion "If *P* then *Q*" can be falsified if *P* is true but *Q* is not. The four cards in the problem represent *P* (D), *not-P* (F), *Q* (3), and not-Q (7). There are two ways in which the rule can be falsified: either it turns out that on the other side of the D card there is a 7 (*not-Q*), or that on the other side of the 7, there is a D (*P*).

The cards presented to the participants now read "drinking beer," "drinking coke," "25 years old," and "16 years old." It is almost immediately clear to most people that one has to check whether that person drinking beer is over age, and whether the 16-year-old is drinking beer. Although the two problems are both variants of the same type of logical problem, the content makes a big difference. The first situation is very unfamiliar and does not evoke intuitive responses whereas one does not need logical conclusions to arrive at the logical solution in the second problem: it comes intuitively.

School Math

Fischbein and his collaborators examined mathematical intuitions in young students. One set of problems they used consisted of the following two questions (Fischbein, 1994, p. 234):

1. From 1 quintal of wheat, you get 0.75 quintals of flour. How much flour do you get from 15 quintals of wheat?
2. 1 kilo of a detergent is used in making 15 kilos of soap. How much soap can be made of 0.75 kilos of detergent?

These two problems have the same solution: one just has to multiply two numbers, 15 and 0.75. However, the solution rates across fifth-, seventh-, and ninth-grade students, although they did not differ so much across age groups, were quite different for these two problems: about 75% correct solutions for the first problem and about 25% for the second. Why? Fischbein (1994) explains the difference with students applying the intuition that "multiplication makes bigger." If the second number—the number by which the first is multiplied—is larger than 1, this means that the result of the multiplication is larger than the first number: multiplication makes bigger. This intuition can be applied to the first problem but not the second. Note that the crucial difference between these two problems seems to be just the order in which information is presented.

General Principle

There are many other areas where one can find similar results. Here is one more example: Many studies in South America have shown that children and adolescents, as well as carpenters and fishermen with almost no schooling, are successfully able to sell fruit, build houses, and charge correct fish prices in an intuitive way—with *street math*. However, this ability breaks down if the same persons are given the identical tasks formulated in versions used in school training (Nunes, Schliemann, & Carraher, 1993). What do all these examples show? Although they are quite different, the general principle is the same: The external representational format can make a big difference. The difference may consist in spatial arrangement, matters of content or context, or even the order of numbers—if the external representation matches a valid intuition, the corresponding decisions are made quickly (and correctly) and problems can be solved easily.

VALID STATISTICAL INTUITIONS

The idea exemplified in the last paragraph—that the right representational format may help in intuitive problem solving—will now be applied to statistical reasoning. For illustration, I have chosen two classes of problems that are often used in research on statistical reasoning: Bayesian problems and sample-size problems. For each of the two classes of problems, I first present the (standard) difficult version and then show how slight changes in representational format make them easier. Then I describe the valid intuition that makes the problems easier, in each case. The intuition that I postulate to work in the case of Bayesian problems I call *ratio intuition*; and the intuition that is assumed to work in the case of sample-size tasks is the *size-confidence intuition*.

Bayesian Problems, Difficult Version

In Bayesian problems the probability of an event is revised in the light of new information. Here is an example, the *mammography problem*, originally examined by Casscells, Schoenberger, and Graboys (1978), in an adapted version (part headings inserted for discussion only):

Introductory text
A reporter for a women's monthly magazine would like to write an article about breast cancer. As a part of her research, she focuses on mammography as an indicator of breast cancer. She wonders what it really means if a woman tests positive for breast cancer during her routine mammography examination. She has the following data:
Base rate (prior probability)
The probability that a randomly chosen woman who undergoes a mammography exam will have breast cancer is 1%.
Hit rate
If a woman undergoing a mammography exam has breast cancer, the probability that she will test positive is 80%.
False alarm rate
If a woman undergoing a mammography exam does not have breast cancer, the probability that she will test positive is 10%.

Question

What is the probability that a woman who has undergone a mammography exam actually has breast cancer, if she tests positive?

The event in question is that a randomly chosen woman has breast cancer. Without any further knowledge, the (prior) probability for that to be true is 1% or .01—the base-rate information given in the problem. The new information is that the mammography test was positive. This information is connected to two other pieces of information: the hit rate, p(positive test|cancer), and the false alarm rate, p(positive test|no cancer), which are given in the problem as 80% and 10%, respectively. How should the prior probability be revised to arrive at the sought for posterior probability, p(cancer|positive test)? Bayes' theorem provides the solution: equation 1.

The available evidence indicates that Bayesian problems of this and other types are very difficult for laypeople as well as professionals, with correct solution rates of usually less than 10% (e.g., Casscells et al., 1978; Eddy, 1982; Kahneman & Tversky, 1972; Koehler, 1996). The main problem seems to be that often people do not take the base rate into account, a neglect that has been termed the base-rate fallacy. The conclusion is clear: "The genuineness, the robustness, and the generality of the base-rate fallacy are matters of established fact" (Bar-Hillel, 1980, p. 215).

$$p(cancer|pos.) = \frac{p(cancer)p(pos.|cancer)}{p(cancer)p(pos.|cancer) + p(no\ cancer)p(pos.|no\ cancer)} \qquad (1)$$

$$= \frac{.01 \cdot .8}{.01 \cdot .8 + .99 \cdot .1}$$

$$= .075$$

Bayesian Problems Made Easier

How can Bayesian problems be made easier? Gigerenzer and Hoffrage (1995) argued that the format in which the problem information is presented is of crucial importance. They reasoned that people can deal much more easily with natural frequencies, that is, frequencies not normalized with respect to base rates, than with probabilities.[4] Restated in terms of natural frequencies, the mammography problem reads (introductory text remains identical):

---

[4]Absolute frequencies are not eo ipso natural frequencies. For instance, the information in the mammography problem could also be stated in normalized absolute frequencies: a base rate of 1 in 100, a hit rate of 80 in 100, and a false alarm rate of 10 in 100. These frequencies, 1, 80, and 10, no longer carry information about the relevant base rates.

Base rate (prior probability)

Ten of every 1,000 women who undergo a mammography exam have breast cancer

Hit rate

Eight of every 10 women with breast cancer who undergo a mammography exam will test positive.

False alarm rate

Ninety-nine of every 990 women without breast cancer who undergo a mammography exam will test positive.

Question

Imagine a new representative sample of women who have had a positive mammogram. How many of these women would you expect to actually have breast cancer?

Note that not only has the representational format been changed from probabilities (expressed in percentages) to frequencies, also the calculation has become easier; equation 2.

Gigerenzer and Hoffrage (1995) found an increase of Bayesian solutions from 16% with problems formulated in the probability format to 46% when formulated in the natural frequency format. Similar results were found with laypeople (Christensen-Szalanski & Beach, 1982; Cosmides & Tooby, 1996) and experts (Hoffrage & Gigerenzer, 1998; Hoffrage, Lindsey, Hertwig, & Gigerenzer, 2000).

$$p(cancer|pos.) = \frac{\#(pos. \cap cancer)}{\#pos.} \qquad (2)$$

$$= \frac{8}{107}$$

$$= .075$$

The Ratio Intuition

How can intuition help to solve Bayesian problems? My suggestion is that several kinds of probability problems can be solved intuitively by building a ratio between a smaller and a larger number. I call this intuition the *ratio intuition*. The ratio intuition might be seen as an extension of the *intuition of relative frequency*, for which Fischbein (1975) cites ample evidence. I further argue that this intuition only works if the numbers in question represent natural frequencies (see Footnote 4).

What kinds of probability problems am I talking about? Let us consider the situation in Figure 16.1, which depicts the solution to the mammography

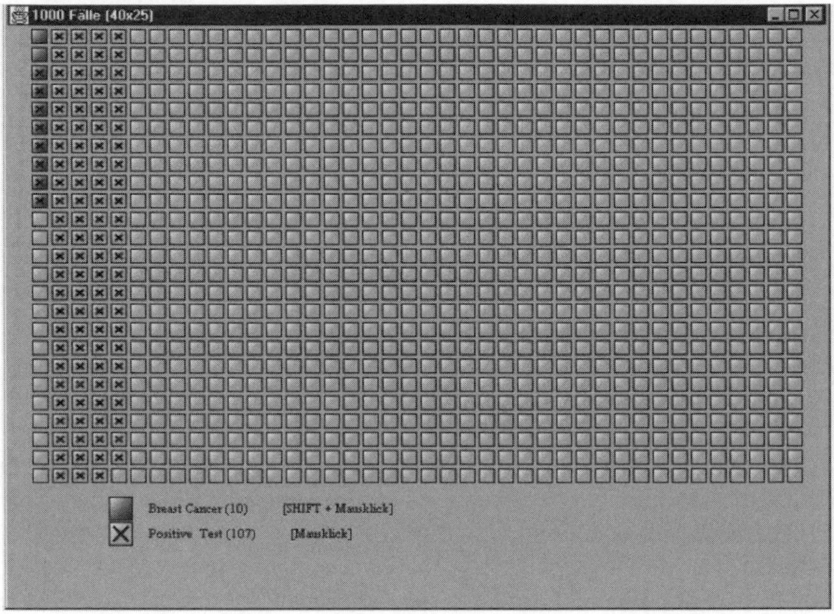

Figure 16.1　Frequency grid representation of the mammography problem. The 10 shaded squares represent the number of women out of 1,000 who can be expected to have breast cancer according to the information given in the mammography problem, and the 107 squares marked by a cross represent the number of women who can be expected to obtain a positive test result. The frequency grid was generated by using the software that accompanies a textbook on elementary probability theory (Sedlmeier & Köhlers, 2001). See text for further explanation.

problem as given by a computerized tutorial that covers the elements of basic probability theory as taught in German high schools (Sedlmeier & Köhlers, 2001).[5] The 1,000 cases (German: *Fälle*) in the problem are represented by squares. Specific squares can be shaded in the program by pressing the Shift key and clicking with the mouse on the square (German: *Mausklick*). In this way 10 squares have been shaded, representing the 1% of the women who have breast

---

[5]This program is a modification and extension of several more specific programs tested in prior experiments (Sedlmeier, 1999; Sedlmeier & Gigerenzer, 2001; see also the section on "Training Programs in High School"). The program relies heavily on flexible frequency representations, learning by doing, and immediate feedback, corresponding to three of Lovett and Greenhouse's (2000) five principles of learning (Principles 1, 3, and 5).

cancer. Out of these 10, the 8 (80% of 10) with a positive test result are marked with a cross (by clicking on the square with the mouse without pressing any other key), and so are a further 99 squares, representing the 10% of women with a false-positive test (out of 990). The ratio that has to be built to solve the mammography problem is 8/107, that is, one has to divide the 8 women who have cancer and get positive test results by all women who get positive test results (see Equation 2). This is an example of how the ratio intuition can be applied to Bayesian tasks. But the special thing with frequency representations is that the solution of Bayesian tasks does not differ from the solution of apparently simpler tasks such as finding the probability of conjunctive events or finding simple conditional probabilities. What, for instance, is the probability that a randomly chosen woman both suffers from breast cancer and gets a positive test result—the probability of a conjunctive event? Figure 16.1 would quickly give the answer: 8/10 or 80%. And what is the conditional probability that a given woman has a positive test result if she does have cancer? We already know this probability—the hit rate from the problem—but if we did not, Figure 16.1 would quickly give the answer: 8/10 or 80%.

So what we see here is that if natural frequencies are used as the representational format, probability problems that are expressed differently in the usual language of probability theory are solved in the same way.[6] The solution in all three cases above is to build a ratio that relates a smaller number to a larger number or, in other words, to calculate a relative frequency. The three cases just differ in the selection of the right reference class: all women in the sample for the conjunctive-probability problem, all women with cancer in the simple conditional-probability problem, and all women with a positive test result in the original Bayesian problem. In many cases, finding the right relative frequency does not seem to be difficult if events are represented in terms of natural frequencies: Even young children show a remarkable sensitivity in both choice and estimation tasks (Huber, 1993; Inhelder & Piaget, 1959/1964; Kuzmak & Gelman, 1986; Reyna & Brainerd, 1994).

However, there is no guarantee that the right reference class will be chosen automatically: Especially when people seek to confirm hypotheses they are already holding and if they are not restricted in the way they sample information they may tend to use biased reference classes (Fiedler, Brinkmann, Betsch, & Wild, 2000; Klayman & Ha, 1989). In addition, the

---

[6]The usual way to arrive at a Bayesian solution—p(cancer|positive result) in our example—is to use Bayes' theorem (Equation 1). The probability of the conjunctive event in our example is usually calculated as p(cancer & positive result) = p(cancer|positive result)p(positive result) = p(positive result|cancer)p(cancer), and the simple conditional probability would be calculated as p(positive result|cancer) = p(cancer & positive result)/p(cancer).

selection of a reference class is also influenced by whether people perceive base rates to be relevant and reliable (Ginossar & Trope, 1980; Koehler, 1996). If the wrong base rates are chosen, the ratio intuition would, of course, yield biased results.

Let us now turn to another type of problem that examines how well the impact of sample size on confidence judgments about proportions and means is understood.

Impact of Sample Size: Problematic Results

After several studies on the impact of sample size on statistical reasoning, Kahneman and Tversky (1972) concluded that "a strong tendency to underestimate the impact of sample size lingers on despite knowledge of the correct rule and extensive statistical training" (p. 445). One of the problems they used was the following, the *maternity ward* problem (part headings inserted for discussion only):

Introductory text

A certain town is served by two hospitals. In the larger hospital about 45 babies are born each day, and in the smaller hospital about 15 babies are born each day. As you know, about 50% of all babies are boys. The exact percentage of baby boys, however, varies from day to day. Sometimes it may be higher than 50%, sometimes lower.

Specification part

For a period of 1 year, each hospital recorded the days on which more than 60% of the babies born were boys. Which hospital do you think recorded more such days?

Answer alternatives

A. The larger hospital

B. The smaller hospital

C. About the same

What is the correct solution for this task? The question refers to the difference in the variances of empirical sampling distributions or, to be more exact, to the difference between the number of proportions that are expected to fall beyond a value of 60% in two sampling distributions, one for the larger and one for the smaller hospital. These distributions are binomial distributions with $p = .5$ (a 50% chance that a baby born is a boy) and sample sizes of $n = 45$ (larger hospital) and $n = 15$ (smaller hospital), respectively. The correct answer can be inferred from the result of a simulation shown in Figure 16.2.

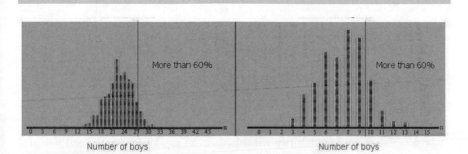

Figure 16.2 Illustration of the solution of the maternity ward task (sampling distribution version). The simulation results (relying on Bernoulli trials with $p = .5$) were obtained by using the software that accompanies a textbook on elementary probability theory (Sedlmeier & Köhlers, 2001).

The figure shows two empirical sampling distributions, consisting of 365 proportions of "baby boys" each (corresponding to the 365 days of the year). The results over a year are shown for the smaller hospital with proportions calculated from 15 "births" each (Fig. 16.2, left) and the larger hospital with proportions calculated from 45 "births" each (Fig. 16.2, right). The result in Figure 16.2 is typical: because sampling distributions with larger sample sizes can be expected to be more closely centered around the expected value (50%), the chances for proportions to deviate from the expected value beyond a given noncentral value are higher in the smaller hospital.

Participants given this and similar tasks usually (and erroneously) prefer C, that is, the option that says "no difference"; and the percentages of correct solutions are only around 20% (e.g., Kahneman & Tversky, 1972; Murray, Iding, Farris, & Revlin, 1987; Swieringa, Gibbins, Larsson, & Sweeney, 1976). These results are echoed in a summarizing statement by Reagan (1989, p. 57): "The lesson from 'sample size research' is that people are poorly disposed to appreciate the effect of sample size on sample statistics."

Impact of Sample Size Re-Examined

Already in the 1950s, Piaget and Inhelder (1951/1975) found children from the age of 11 or 12 to be sensitive to the impact of sample size on the quality of estimates. Should adults have lost this sensitivity? There is indeed evidence for this suspicion (see the previous paragraph) but could the decline be so dramatic? Apparently not—otherwise one would not expect statements like this one: "Overall, subjects did quite well as intuitive statisticians in that their judgments tended, over the experiments as a whole, to move in the direction required by statistical theory as the levels of Mean Difference, Sample size and Variability were varied" (Evans & Pollard, 1985, pp. 68–69). Gerd Gigerenzer and I took a closer look at the sample size literature and found a huge variation in solution rates (Sedlmeier & Gigerenzer, 1997). After considering several possibilities, the explanation most plausible to us was that two different types of tasks have been used in the pertinent research: one type, of which the original maternity ward task is an example, we termed a "sampling-distribution task." In 29 studies in which participants had to solve such tasks the median solution rate was 33%, a figure that can be expected by chance (if one decides randomly among the three alternatives). However, in a slightly different type of task, the median solution rate was dramatically higher: 76%. We termed this type of task a "frequency-distribution task." Here is an example, a variant of the maternity ward problem:

Introductory text

A certain town is served by two hospitals. In the larger hospital about 45 babies are born each day, and in the smaller hospital about 15 babies are born each day. As you know, about 50% of all babies are boys. The exact percentage of baby boys, however, varies from day to day. Sometimes it may be higher than 50%, sometimes lower.

Specification part

Which hospital do you think is more likely to find on a given day that more than 60% of the babies born were boys?

Answer alternatives

A. The larger hospital

B. The smaller hospital

C. About the same

Note that this task differs from the original one only in the "Specification part" but this difference seems to be a crucial one. Why? Because in this version of the task, the question is about two distributions of raw scores or "frequency distributions," the distributions of baby boys and baby girls in the two hospitals on a given day. The proportion from a single sample in the larger hospital is compared to the proportion from a single sample in the smaller hospital.

The Size-Confidence Intuition

Why is the frequency-distribution version of the maternity ward problem so much easier than the corresponding sampling-distribution problem?

Centuries ago Jacob Bernoulli argued that "even the stupidest man knows by some instinct of nature per se and by no previous instruction" that the greater the number of confirming observations, the surer the conjecture (Gigerenzer et al., 1989, p. 29). This is an early formulation of what Gerd Gigerenzer and I called the *size-confidence intuition* (Sedlmeier & Gigerenzer, 1997). The size-confidence intuition conforms to the *empirical law of large numbers* and is not a mathematical law, but it can be experienced when drawing random samples: As samples become larger, means or proportions calculated from these samples tend to become more accurate estimates of population means or proportions. This tendency may at times not hold, that is, larger samples may lead to more inaccurate results, but the law holds on average (Sedlmeier & Gigerenzer, 2000).

The size-confidence intuition makes it easy to solve frequency-distribution tasks. For instance, in the frequency-distribution version of the maternity ward task, the result from the larger hospital can be expected to be closer to the "true" 50% than the result from the smaller hospital, or—in other words—a large deviation of the proportion of baby boys from 50% is more likely in the smaller hospital. However, the size-confidence intuition is not directly applicable to sampling-distribution tasks, which explains the difference in solution rates found in the relevant studies (Sedlmeier, 1998; Sedlmeier & Gigerenzer, 1997).

One could argue that what we called sampling-distribution tasks can be solved by repeatedly applying the empirical law of large numbers. This is immediately evident to persons trained in statistics but the empirical evidence indicates that laypeople are not able to do so spontaneously. So the crucial difference for the size-confidence intuition is whether frequency-distribution tasks or seemingly similar sampling-distribution tasks are to be solved. In addition, the spontaneous use of this intuition seems to profit largely from what could be called the *dynamical frequency format*. Samples naturally come as frequencies of events but it seems to make a difference whether the sampling process is only described verbally or whether one can directly experience it. When participants had the chance to perform simulations of the sampling process with the help of a computer program, the rates of correct solutions were about 25% higher than when problems were just described to them in texts (Sedlmeier, 1998). This finding indicates that frequency representation per se does not always help automatically—the match between visual features and the perceived meaning of these features is decisive (see also Shah & Hoeffner, 2002).

There are several other explanations for why such a huge variance in the solution rates for sample-size tasks can be found in the literature. The factors responsible include the ratio between sample sizes (Murray et al., 1987), the extremity of cut-off percentages (e.g., "more than 80%" instead of "more than

60%," Bar-Hillel, 1982), the part of the distribution to which the question refers (Well, Pollatsek, & Boyce, 1990), the complexity of the problems (Evans & Dusoir, 1977), and the salience of chance factors (Nisbett, Krantz, Jepson, & Kunda, 1983). However, none of the examined factors was found to have an influence on solution rates nearly as large as the distinction between frequency- and sampling-distribution tasks suggested by the size-confidence intuition (for details see Sedlmeier, 1998; 2006).

STATISTICAL INTUITIONS AS THE RESULT OF ASSOCIATIVE LEARNING

I have just postulated the existence of two intuitions that might be helpful in solving statistical reasoning problems. Here I suggest how these intuitions might arise: They are the result of associative learning. The specific associative learning model I am proposing is the PASS (probability associator) model, which was developed to simulate probability and relative frequency judgments (Sedlmeier, 1999, 2002). I first describe how PASS works in principle and then discuss how it may account for the ratio and the size-confidence intuitions.

PASS: Learning And Representation

PASS encodes events (hereafter, "event" stands for "events," "objects," "persons," etc.) consecutively. These events may exist either in reality or in the imagination. An event is represented by its features, to which the associative learning mechanism applies. Figure 16.3 shows a simplified representation of the events needed to model the mammography problem. PASS works with distributed representations, that is, "breast cancer," "positive test," and "female" would be represented by patterns of features. For the sake of simplicity, these patterns have been compressed here to one feature each. If the feature is present, this is shown as a filled circle in Figure 16.3; if the feature is absent, the circle is empty. For instance, "Ms. A," one of the 9 women represented in Figure 16.3, does not have breast cancer, nor did she obtain a positive test result, whereas "Ms. B's" breast cancer has been correctly diagnosed.

The core of PASS is a neural network that encodes features by its input nodes, modifies the associations between features by changing the weights between nodes, and elicits reactions by producing activations at its output nodes. Learning consists in modifying the associations between the features in memory (in this simplified example, the memory consists of only three features and their associations). PASS operates in discrete time steps. At each time step, the features of the event towards which the attention is directed are encoded. Learning takes place at every time step. If features co-occur in an

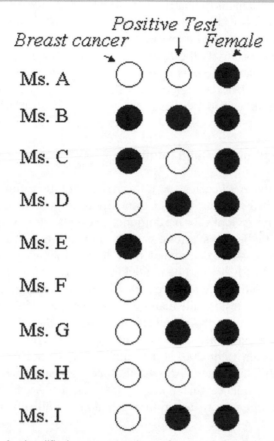

Figure 16.3 A simplified representation of part of the information from the mammography problem as used by the PASS model. Only three features ("breast cancer," "positive test," and "female") are shown per "event." Filled circles indicate that the respective feature is present, whereas empty circles indicate the absence of that feature. For instance, "Ms. A." is female but does not have breast cancer, nor has she tested positive.

event—such as when PASS encounters the featural description of "Ms. B." in Figure 16.3, the association between them is strengthened; if this is not the case, the association between the respective features becomes weaker—such as the association between "breast cancer" and "positive test" when PASS encounters the description of "Ms. A." or that of "Ms. C."[7] This learning

---

[7]PASS would use two different "forgetting rules" "for the two cases, a rule that simulates memory decay in the first case, and interference in the second.

process results in a memory matrix that is updated after every time step and that contains the association strengths between all the features in memory. When PASS is prompted with an event, that is, the features that define this event, activations occur at all output nodes (activations range from 0 to 1). The sum of these activations is taken as PASS's response. The more often features occur together, the higher is PASS's response when prompted with an event that is described by these features or at least a large number of them.

PASS's Account of the Ratio Intuition

Estimating relative frequencies and thus arriving at ratio estimates is PASS's basic task. For its estimates, PASS essentially follows the definition of relative frequency. It first looks for the conjunctive events—for example, the joint occurrences of the features "breast cancer" and "positive test" in the mammography problem—and determines their summed activation (in Fig. 16.3, only the event "Ms. B." would be treated in this way). Then it sums the activations for all events of the reference class—for example, all occurrences of the feature "positive test" in the mammography problem (5 of the 9 events in Fig. 16.3 would count as this). And finally it divides the first sum of activations by the second and takes this as an estimate of the relative frequency or ratio (see Sedlmeier, 1999, 2002; for a similar model, see Dougherty, Gettys, & Ogden, 1999). This is how PASS would solve the mammography problem. There is ample evidence that building ratio estimates can be done very quickly and is often more accurate when done intuitively (Sedlmeier & Betsch, 2002).

PASS's Account of the Size-Confidence Intuition

The explanation of the size-confidence intuition in the PASS model follows as an emergent property of the way the model learns. In PASS it is assumed that confidence judgments covary with how well the model can differentiate between different events. PASS uses the variance across the output units' activations as an index for confidence: In the beginning of the learning process, there is little variation among the activations of PASS's output units, and PASS would not be very confident in its estimates. The more variation there is in these activations after being prompted with a given event, the better PASS "knows" this event. It can be shown that the variance tends to increase with increasing sample size, thus exhibiting the size-confidence intuition (Sedlmeier, 1998; 1999). Note that there is no additional mechanism involved: The variation of output activations is just a by-product of the learning process.

Why Do We Need Training Despite Valid Intuitions?

One might now ask why training is needed when statistical problems can already be solved intuitively. According to PASS (or similar associative learning models), a problem is solved intuitively if there is a match between the way it processes information and the way the problem information is perceived. In both the mammography problem and the maternity ward problem, information about the events is not presented serially. Can the PASS model be applied to these problems at all? In the case of pictorial representations such as that in Fig. 16.1, one can argue that the squares or other symbolic representations could be nevertheless encoded serially. But what if problems are only described in a text? It seems that the crucial point for whether the PASS model applies (i.e., whether a problem can, in principle, be solved intuitively) is whether the information is transformed in a way that enables the imagination of discrete events (for recent evidence that memories develop with imagination alone, see Mazzoni & Memon, 2003). The importance of imagination in judgmental processes has been stressed repeatedly (e.g., Hogarth, 2001; Kahneman & Tversky, 1982a). So whenever one can expect that texts elicit an imagining of discrete events, either by giving prompts or as the result of specific training, one can expect intuitive judgments according to the PASS model. Let us return to the question just discussed: Training is needed to help "translate" a problem into a suitable representational format. The existence of a valid intuition alone does not automatically lead to its application: it has to be triggered first. Training can also help to increase the likelihood that valid intuitions will be triggered appropriately.

VALID INTUITIONS IN TRAINING

If the serial encoding or imagining of events is a crucial precondition for the use of statistical intuitions, as postulated by the PASS model, how should training programs be designed to make these intuitions work? The most plausible answer seems to be to make trainees learn to translate an unhelpful representational format into a format that can be expected to evoke intuitive and correct solutions. This is what we tried to do. Here, I give a short overview about the empirical evidence with Bayesian training and with training that taught the understanding of the impact of sample size.

Bayesian Training

In several studies, we tested training programs that taught participants to translate probability information into natural frequencies (Sedlmeier, 1997; 1999;

Sedlmeier & Gigerenzer, 2001). The computerized training programs consisted of two parts. The first part led trainees through the solution of two problems, step by step; in the second part, trainees could solve Bayesian problems on their own but the program gave corrections and hints and ensured that every problem could be solved correctly. Among the representational formats used were the frequency grid (Fig. 16.1) and the frequency tree (Fig. 16.4, left; *Baum* is German for "tree"). In the frequency tree training, the number of women in the reference class (here: 1,000) is divided up according to the base rate (here: 1%, that is, 10 out of 1,000 women with breast cancer—see middle part of tree) and then according to the hit rate (here: 80%, that is, 8 out of 10 women), and the false-alarm rate (here: 10%, that is, 99 out of 990 women). The results of these training programs were compared with those obtained in training programs that used the conventional probability format. In the latter, trainees were taught either to fill in Bayes' formula (Equation 1) with the appropriate values (not shown) or to fill in the right values on a probability tree (Fig. 16.4, right). Filling in the values in the probability tree works similar to the frequency tree—the only difference being that the decimal point for all numbers is moved three digits to the left (e.g., 8 becomes .008). In both the frequency and the probability tree the correct solution for p(cancer|positive result) is obtained by dividing the number in the leftmost node by the sum of this number and the number in the third node at the bottom of the tree [e.g., .008 / (.008 + .099) in the case of the probability tree]. The training regimens were held as similar as possible otherwise.

Trainees were tested immediately before and after the training, which (without the testing) took less than an hour on average. In addition, trainees were tested again 1 week and up to 3 months after the training. Figure 16.5 shows a representative result. In this study, participants were quite good with the probability formats immediately after training, but the results after 3 months show the long-term effect of using frequency formats to be clearly superior. Our results were obtained with university students, both in the United States and in Germany, as participants, but similar results were also found with high school students (Wassner, Martignon, & Sedlmeier, 2002). Comparable training regimens that did not use computerized tutorials also yielded similar results, although the absolute success rates were somewhat lower (Ruscio, 2003).

My explanation for the difference in results shown in Figure 16.5 is that the ratio intuition was more likely to be triggered by the frequency-tree representation than by the two probability representations. Is there not a much simpler explanation for this difference: Could it be that frequency representations require a lighter information-processing load than probability representations (compare Equations 1 and 2)? If this explanation holds, one should expect similar results for the frequency tree and the probability tree (but not

Frequency tree   Probability tree

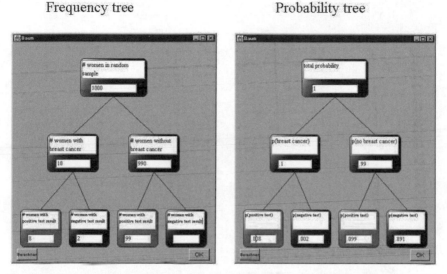

Figure 16.4 Frequency tree and probability tree, similar to those used in the original training studies. The probability tree carries the same information as the frequency tree; only the decimal point is moved three positions to the left. Screen shots are from the software that accompanies a textbook on elementary probability theory (Sedlmeier & Köhlers, 2001). The button at the lower left (*Berechnen* is German for "calculate") can be used to check whether the numbers are inserted correctly.

in the rule training) because in both cases, the simpler Equation 2 or its equivalent for probabilities can be used. However, Figure 16.5 indicates that it is not the difference in information-processing load but the difference in representational format that is decisive.

There have also been other attempts at training Bayesian reasoning, including corrective feedback (e.g., Lindeman, van den Brink, & Hoogstraten, 1988) and directing participants' attention to relevant information (e.g. Fischhoff & Bar-Hillel, 1984; Wolfe, 1995). However, the training effects in these studies were quite modest, overall (see Sedlmeier, 1999).

Training to Solve Difficult Sample-Size Problems

Apparently, there is not much need to train the understanding of frequency-distribution tasks because the size-confidence intuition yields high spontaneous solution rates. But the size-confidence intuition can be put to use to solve difficult sampling-distribution tasks by making the connection between

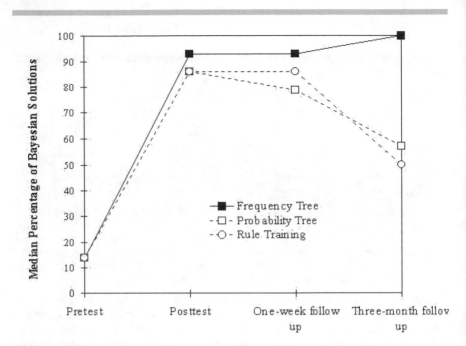

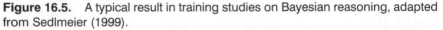

Figure 16.5. A typical result in training studies on Bayesian reasoning, adapted from Sedlmeier (1999).

frequency and sampling distributions clear. Figure 16.6 shows how this was accomplished in the training studies (see Sedlmeier, 1999, chaps. 9–11). The figure shows screen shots collected during different stages of th
e computerized tutorial (Sedlmeier & Köhlers, 2001). A dynamical frequency format was realized with the help of a virtual urn that contains a population distribution (e.g., a distribution of 50% boys and 50% girls, in the case of the maternity ward problem). The sampling process was simulated by letting a black bar with a funnel end stir the contents of the urn with random movements. After a while, the stick turned yellow and became "magnetic," thus attracting the nearest "event" (a boy or a girl, in the case of the maternity ward problem) and pulling it out (see Fig. 16.6, top). This elementary sampling process was repeated until a sample had the planned size. Figure 16.6 (middle) shows three samples of Size 15, depicting frequency distributions of boy and girl births in the smaller hospital on three arbitrary days. The proportions calculated from these samples were then put on the frame for an empirical sampling distribution—"day" by "day" in the case of the maternity ward problem. The collection of proportions finally resulted in empirical sampling distributions as

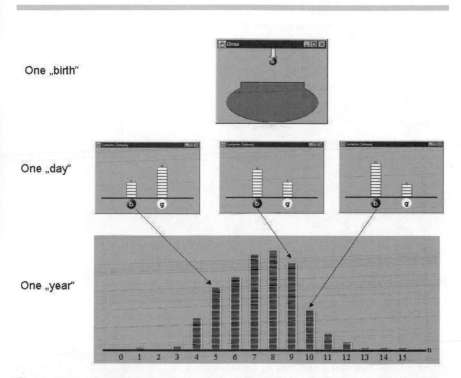

One „birth"

One „day"

One „year"

Figure 16.6   Steps ranging from sampling single results to eventually obtaining sampling distributions, using the information from the maternity ward problem. The top of the figure shows an urn that contains a population distribution of all potential births (50% boys and 50% girls). "Births" that result in either "boys" (b) or "girls" (g) are drawn one by one. The middle part shows three arbitrary days in the smaller hospital. The respective proportions of baby boys are placed onto an empirical sampling distribution (lower part) that depicts the proportions of baby boys over 365 days. Screen shots are from the software that accompanies a textbook on elementary probability theory (Sedlmeier & Köhlers, 2001).

specified in the respective problems (e.g., sampling distributions consisting of 365 days, in the case of the maternity ward problem—Fig. 16.6, bottom). Trainees could watch this process concurrently for samples of different sizes (e.g., for the small and the large hospital, see Fig. 16.2).

Similar to the Bayesian training studies, tests were administered immediately before and after the training, as well as 1 week and 5 weeks afterwards. The problems used were of the maternity-ward type (original version) and of another type in which participants had to construct sampling distributions themselves. Here is an example of the latter (adapted from Kahneman & Tversky, 1972, p. 437):

Imagine that in a certain country demographic properties in different regions are recorded. In one region (Region A) there are about 10 births per day and in another region (Region B) there are about 40 per day. Every day, the proportion of boys and girls is registered.

Please estimate the percentages of female births that can be expected in both regions over a period of 100 days. Just divide the 100 days over the categories, for each region.

Region A	*Region B*
About 10 births daily	About 40 births daily
__ Up to 5% girls	__ Up to 5% girls
__ 6% to 15% girls	__ 6% to 15% girls
__ 16% to 25% girls	__ 16% to 25% girls
__ 26% to 35% girls	__ 26% to 35% girls
__ 36% to 45% girls	__ 36% to 45% girls
__ 46% to 55% girls	__ 46% to 55% girls
__ 56% to 65% girls	__ 56% to 65% girls
__ 66% to 75% girls	__ 66% to 75% girls
__ 76% to 85% girls	__ 76% to 85% girls
__ 86% to 95% girls	__ 86% to 95% girls
__ 96% to 100% girls	__ 96% to 100% girls.

The solution rates in this type of problems are even lower than those in maternity-ward-type tasks: Usually participants' sampling distributions do not differ at all (Fischhoff, Slovic, & Lichtenstein, 1979; Kahneman & Tversky, 1972; Olson, 1976; Sedlmeier, 1992; Teigen, 1974).

Figure 16.7 shows the results for such construction tasks before and after a computerized sample-size training (Sedlmeier, 1999). Results were scored as correct if the number filled in for the middle part was larger for the larger sample and if the numbers for the extreme parts of the sampling distributions were larger for the smaller sample, and if no anomalies (e.g., bimodality) were observed. Apparently the short training (less than half an hour) was quite effective. Although the new problems presented in the testing sessions were not solved as well as the problems used in training, stable solution rates of 85% were obtained, a figure that has not been observed in the literature, so far.

To the best of my knowledge there has been only one other attempt to develop sample-size training using sampling distribution tasks (not termed so, though). This training (Well et al., 1990, Study 4) consisted of oral explanations, a demonstration of random sampling using paper slips, and a simulation on a computer screen. However, only 24% of the participants solved a sample-size task correctly afterward. Other training attempts used frequency-distribution tasks (e.g., Fong, Krantz, & Nisbett, 1986) and taught participants the rule that sample parameters approach population parameters as a function of sample size and

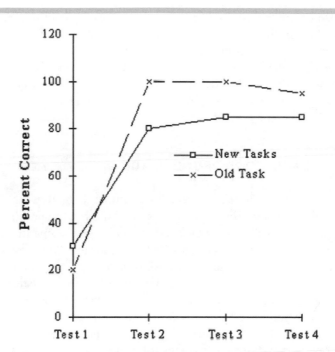

Figure 16.7   Solution rates obtained in tests on sampling-distribution problems (construction tasks) immediately before and after a sample-size training (Test 1 and Test 2), as well as 1 and 5 weeks afterwards (Test 3 and Test 4), adapted from Sedlmeier (1999).

as an inverse function of sample variability. These training attempts were moderately successful, but overall, the training effects were not larger than the differences between the spontaneous solution rates for different types of (frequency-distribution) problems (see Sedlmeier, 1999, pp. 55–60).

Training Programs in High School

The original training programs just described had been used to test different theoretical accounts of people's probabilistic reasoning skills against each other (Sedlmeier, 1999). Each theoretical account was represented by a different type of training program. The success of those program versions described above prompted us to use them as part of a curriculum for German high school students. We wrote a textbook and re-programmed the training programs—which were originally written in Common Lisp and executed on

Macintosh computers (both properties turned out to be obstacles for wider dissemination of the program in Germany)—and added some more programs that cover the whole German high school curriculum on probability theory, including significance tests and confidence intervals based on the binomial distribution (Sedlmeier, 2001; Sedlmeier & Köhlers, 2001). Textbook and software (a Java application) are currently being tested in German high schools (Wassner et al., 2002).

LIMITATIONS OF THE "INTUITIVE APPROACH"

Let me recapitulate. There is evidence that people do badly with some types of probability problems, but when changed a little bit, the problems become much easier. The explanation advanced in this chapter is that the right representational format evokes valid statistical intuitions that help people solve the respective problems. Other factors certainly also play a role but a comparison of the effect sizes found in different attempts at training statistical reasoning (as just mentioned) to those obtained with the current approach lends credence to the hypothesized working of a kind of mostly implicit knowledge I termed *valid intuitions*. I have tried to show that the connection between representational format and the working of valid intuitions is not specific to probabilistic reasoning, but that statistical reasoning is rather a special case. I have also offered an associative learning explanation for the existence of two helpful statistical intuitions, the ratio intuition and the size-confidence intuition. And finally, I have presented evidence for how these intuitions can be used in training statistical reasoning by teaching trainees to translate the information as given in difficult versions of probability problems into versions that can evoke these intuitions.

There is, of course, a limit to the intuitive approach. More complex versions of Bayes' theorem cannot be easily translated into natural frequencies and it is difficult to see how the size-confidence intuition will help in deriving the F distribution. Obviously, the approach advocated here can be very helpful at the beginning stages of learning about probability theory (such as in high school or in the first year of university) but in its current version it does not help much for more complex applications of probability theory. However, first experiences with probability theory may have decisive consequences for a student's later interest and understanding of probability issues.

I now address three other limitations of intuitive probabilistic reasoning. The first concerns the amount of transfer to other tasks obtained in our training studies, the second deals with the context for learning—the schools, and the third is about metalevel considerations: How do we know when solutions to probability problems, intuitive or otherwise, are correct?

Generalization and Transfer

How well did students generalize their solutions to other kinds of problems in our training studies? If we assume that they used valid intuitions, these intuitions were sometimes applied quite narrowly. For instance, in training studies about the probability of conjunctive events and simple conditional probabilities (not discussed here), little generalization was found. If students were trained to solve problems on the probability of conjunctive events they apparently were not able to spontaneously apply the translation skills—translating problem information into a frequency representation similar to the one shown in Figure 16.1—to conditional probability problems and vice versa (Sedlmeier, 2000). However, high school students exposed to Bayesian training as described above were able to generalize the training effect obtained for problems that had the same structure as the training problems to more complex kinds of Bayesian problems (e.g., problems with three instead of two possible outcomes and problems that dealt with extremely low probabilities; see Wassner, 2004). But the question of how well the training generalizes to other kinds of related problems has not been systematically examined yet. Anyway, it would probably be a good idea to heed Lovett and Greenhouse's (2000, p. 4) advice: "give students problems that vary in appearance so their practice will involve applying knowledge and skills in a variety of ways."

Statistical Intuitions In The Classroom

I have cited evidence that even young children possess statistical intuitions. What happens with these intuitions during school? Are they nourished and developed? If one compares the positive conclusions about children's statistical reasoning skills against the negative conclusions in the heuristics and biases literature, one might suspect that school is not that helpful. Indeed, Fischbein (1975) identified school as one of the main reasons for students' diminishing reliance on their intuition of relative frequency. According to him, schools' overwhelming emphasis on deterministic explanations about the world considerably weakens valid statistical intuitions. Recently, Joachim Engel and I went about checking Fischbein's explanation. We gave some probability problems to several classes of fifth-, seventh-, and ninth-graders who had not yet had any formal instruction in probability theory (Engel & Sedlmeier, 2004). One of the problems was this (translated from German):

A student's final grade in mathematics was "4." Which of the following statements is more likely to apply in his case?
A. He had a midterm grade of "6."
B. He has received additional tutoring in the second half of the school year and had a midterm grade of "6."

In this problem the probability of a conjunctive event (tutoring *and* midterm grade of "6") is compared to the probability of a single event (midterm grade of "6").[8] Therefore, Option B cannot be more likely than Option A. Figure 16.8 shows the results for three different kinds of schools.[9] Irrespective of type of school, the solution rates clearly decreased with amount of schooling. Even if one argues that the solution rates for the fifth-graders could be explained by guessing behavior, the systematically increasing percentage of "systematically false guesses" for the seventh- and ninth-graders are in accordance with the assumption that school has a negative effect on students' statistical intuitions. We obtained similar results in a modified version of a task originally used by Piaget and Inhelder (1951/1975). In this task, respondents had to make predictions about the distribution of snowflakes on the tiles of a garage roof by drawing the "snowflakes" on a piece of paper with grids representing the tiles. Again, the number of students who gave deterministic answers (e.g., distributed the snowflakes in a systematic way across tiles) increased with age (Engel & Sedlmeier, 2004; for similar results see Green, 1983, 1991). Informal observations indicated that especially those students who were identified by their math teachers as "excellent" usually failed in the probability tasks. Thus it seems that school might indeed overemphasize a deterministic world view.

What Counts as an Error in Statistical Reasoning?

Finally, when talking about errors and correct solutions in statistical reasoning, some words may be in order about how we determine what an error is. What is the basis for deciding whether statistical reasoning is adequate or not? How does one know that an error has occurred? Usually people's reasoning is compared against some normative rule: "The presence of an error of judgment is demonstrated by comparing people's responses either to an established fact (e.g., that the two lines are equal in length) or to an accepted rule of arithmetic, logic or statistics" (Kahneman & Tversky, 1982b, p. 124). In 1967, Peterson and Beach reviewed research that used probability theory and statistics as a framework for the study of human statistical inference and— contrary to many later researchers—concluded that "the theory of statistical inference can provide a basis for a descriptive theory of imperfect human inference" (p. 20). However, they also cautioned about the pitfalls of blind reliance

---

[8]In the German school system, grades of 1, 2, 3, 4, and 6 correspond to letter grades of A, B, C, D, and F, respectively.

[9]The school system in the German state of Baden Württemberg, where the study was conducted, divides students up after fourth grade. Some stay at the most basic level (*Hauptschule*), some change to middle level schools (*Realschule*), and others change to high-level schools (*Gymnasium*).

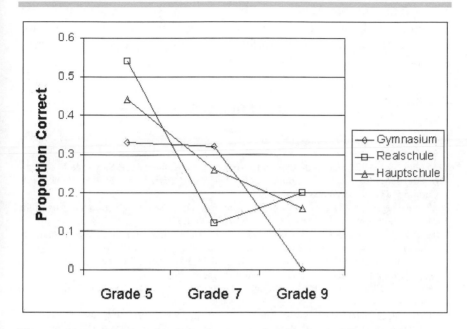

Figure 16.8 Correct solutions in a conjunctive-probability problem over the course of several school years. Results are divided up for different tracks in the German school system (*Hauptschule, Realschule, and Gymnasium*; see Footnote 8).

on theory. They stressed that discrepancies between the statistical model and participants' solutions often arise from the fact that participants' assumptions differ from the presuppositions of the model. So people might deviate from a model assumed by an experimenter but nonetheless reason rationally from the perspective of their own model, which includes additional assumptions. And indeed, the broad conclusion of negative evidence in the judgmental literature has been criticized in several respects along these lines. Apart from the fact that people might have idiosyncratic models (which might be considered normative, given some additional assumptions), statistics does not speak with one voice. Therefore, behavior that appears irrational from the perspective of one statistical theory can be regarded as being perfectly rational from the point of view of another (e.g., Birnbaum, 1983; Cohen, 1981; MacDonald, 1986). Moreover, even when there is no dispute about the right statistical theory, a normative model might be too complex for meaningful use (Sedlmeier & Kilinç, 2004).

Nonetheless, in the vast majority of probability problems that deal with everyday situations, a majority of experts (and people in general) can be expected to agree on a solution (in some cases, maybe, after some thinking). The problems discussed in this chapter very likely fall into that category. And it is in the treatment of everyday-life problems that people would profit most if valid statistical intuitions are put to use.

REFERENCES

Bar-Hillel, M. (1980). The base-rate fallacy in probability judgments. *Acta Psychologica*, *44*, 211–233.

Bar-Hillel, M. (1982). Studies of representativeness. In D. Kahneman, P. Slovic, & A. Tversky (Eds.), *Judgment under uncertainty: Heuristics and biases* (pp. 69–98). New York: Cambridge University Press.

Birnbaum, M. H. (1983). Base rates in Bayesian inference: Signal detection analysis of the cab problem. *American Journal of Psychology, 96*, 85–94.

Casscells, W., Schoenberger, A., & Grayboys, T. (1978). Interpretation by physicians of clinical laboratory results. *New England Journal of Medicine, 299*, 999–1000.

Christensen-Szalanski, J. J. J.; & Beach, L. R. (1982). Experience and the base-rate fallacy. *Organizational Behavior and Human Performance, 29*, 270–278.

Cohen, L. J. (1981). Can human irrationality be experimentally demonstrated? *Behavioral and Brain Sciences, 4*, 317–331.

Cosmides, L. (1989). The logic of social exchange: Has natural selection shaped how humans reason? Studies with the Wason selection task. *Cognition, 31*, 187–276.

Cosmides, L., & Tooby, J. (1996). Are humans good intuitive statisticians after all? Rethinking some conclusions from the literature on judgment under uncertainty. *Cognition, 58*, 1–73.

Dawes, R. M. (1988). *Rational choice in an uncertain world.* San Diego, CA: Harcourt Brace Jovanovich.

Dougherty, M. R. P., Gettys, C. F., & Ogden, E. E. (1999). MINERVA-DM: A memory process model for judgments of likelihood. *Psychological Review, 106,* 180–209.

Eddy, D. M. (1982). Probabilistic reasoning in clinical medicine: Problems and opportunities. In D. Kahneman, P. Slovic, & A. Tversky (Eds.), *Judgment under uncertainty: Heuristics and biases* (pp. 249–267). New York: Cambridge University Press.

Engel, J., & Sedlmeier, P. (2004). *Zum Verständnis von Zufall und Variabilität in empirischen Daten bei Schülern* [School students' understanding of chance and variability in empirical data]. *Unterrichtswissenschaft, 32,* 169–191.

Evans, J. St. B. T., & Dusoir, A. E. (1977). Proportionality and sample size as factors in intuitive statistical judgement. *Acta Psychologica, 41*, 129–137.

Evans, J. St. B. T., & Pollard, P. (1985). Intuitive statistical inferences about normally distributed data. *Acta Psychologica, 60*, 57–71.

Fiedler, K., Brinkmann, B., Betsch, R., & Wild, B. (2000). A sampling approach to biases in conditional probability judgments: Beyond base-rate neglect and statistical format. *Journal of Experimental Psychology: General, 129*, 1–20.

Fischbein, E. (1975): *The intuitive sources of probabilistic thinking in children.* Reidel: Dordrecht-Holland.

Fischbein, E. (1994). The interaction between the formal, the algorithmic, and the intuitive components in a mathematical activity. In R. Biehler, R. W. Scholz, R. Sträber, & B. Winkelmann (Eds.), *Didactics of mathematics as a scientific discipline* (pp. 231–245). Dordrecht, the Netherlands: Kluwer.

Fischhoff, B., & Bar-Hillel, M. (1984). Focusing techniques: A shortcut to improving probability judgments? *Organizational Behavior and Human Performance, 34,* 175–194.

Fischhoff, B., Slovic, P., & Lichtenstein, S. (1979). Subjective sensitivity analysis. *Organizational Behavior and Human Performance, 23,* 339–359.

Fong, G. T., Krantz, D. H., & Nisbett, R. E. (1986). The effects of statistical training on thinking about everyday problems. *Cognitive Psychology, 18,* 253–292.

Gigerenzer, G., & Hoffrage, U. (1995). How to improve Bayesian reasoning without instruction: Frequency formats. *Psychological Review, 102,* 684–704.

Gigerenzer, G., Swijtink, Z., Porter, T., Daston, L., Beatty, J., & Krüger, L. (1989). *The empire of chance: How probability changed science and everyday life.* Cambridge, UK: Cambridge University Press.

Ginossar, Z., & Trope, Y. (1980). The effects of base rates and individuating information on judgments about another person. *Journal of Experimental Social Psychology, 16,* 228–242.

Gould, S. J. (1992). *Bully for brontosaurus: Further reflections in natural history.* New York: Penguin.

Green, D. R. (1983). A survey of probability concepts in 3,000 students aged 11–16 years. In D. R. Grey et al. (Eds.), *Proceedings of the First International Conference on Teaching Statistics* (pp. 766–783). Sheffield, UK: University of Sheffield: Teaching Statistics Trust, University of Sheffield.

Green, D. R. (1991). *A longitudinal study of pupil's probability concepts.* Loughborough, UK: Loughborough University.

Hoffrage, U., & Gigerenzer, G. (1998). Using natural frequencies to improve diagnostic inferences. *Academic Medicine, 73,* 538–540.

Hoffrage, U., Lindsey, S., Hertwig, R., & Gigerenzer, G. (2000). Communicating statistical information. *Science, 290,* 2261–2262.

Hogarth, R. (2001). *Educating intuition.* Chicago: University of Chicago Press.

Huber, O. (1993). The development of the probability concept: Some reflections. *Archives de Psychologie, 61,* 187–195.

Inhelder, B., & Piaget, J. (1964). *The early growth of logic in the child.* (E. A. Lunzer & D. Papert, Trans.). London: Routledge & Kegan Paul. (Original work published 1959)

Kahneman, D., Slovic, P., & Tversky, A. (Eds.). (1982). *Judgment under uncertainty: Heuristics and biases.* New York: Cambridge University Press.

Kahneman, D., & Tversky, A. (1972). Subjective probability: A judgment of representativeness. *Cognitive Psychology, 3,* 430–454.

Kahneman, D., & Tversky, A. (1973). On the psychology of prediction. *Psychological Review, 80,* 237–251.

Kahneman, D., & Tversky, A. (1982a). The psychology of preferences. *Scientific American, 246,* 160–173.

Kahneman, D. L., & Tversky, A. (1982b). On the study of statistical intuitions. *Cognition, 11,* 123–141.

Kahneman, D., & Tversky, A. (1996). On the reality of cognitive illusions. *Psychological Review, 103,* 582–591.

Koehler, J. J. (1996). The base rate fallacy reconsidered: Descriptive, normative and methodological challenges. *Behavioral and Brain Sciences, 19,* 1–17.

Klayman, J. & Ha, Y.-W. (1989). Hypothesis testing in rule discovery: strategy, structure and content. *Journal of Experimental Psychology: Learning, Memory and Cognition, 15,* 596–604.

Kuzmak, S. D., & Gelman, R. (1986). Young children's understanding of random phenomena. *Child Development, 57,* 559–566.

Lindeman, S. T., van den Brink, W. P., & Hoogstraten, J. (1988). Effect of feedback on base-rate utilization. *Perceptual and Motor Skills, 67,* 343–350.

Lovett, M. C., & Greenhouse, J. B. (2000). Applying cognitive theory to statistics instruction. *The American Statistician, 54,* 1–11.

MacDonald, R. R. (1986). Credible conceptions and implausible probabilities. *British Journal of Mathematical Psychology, 39,* 15–27.

Mazzoni, G., & Memon, A. (2003). Imagination can create false autobiographical memories. *Psychological Science, 14,* 186–188.

McCormick, J. (1987, August 17). The wisdom of Solomon. *Newsweek,* 24–25.

Murray, J., Iding, M., Farris, H., & Revlin, R. (1987). Sample size salience and statistical inference. *Bulletin of the Psychonomic Society, 25,* 367–369.

Nisbett, R. E., Krantz, D. H., Jepson, C., & Kunda, Z. (1983). The use of statistical heuristics in everyday inductive reasoning. *Psychological Review, 90,* 339–363.

Norman, D. A. (1988). *The psychology of everyday things.* New York: Basic Books.

Norman, D. A.(1993). *Things that make us smart.* Cambridge, MA: Perseus Books.

Nunes, R., Schliemann, A. D., & Carraher, D. W. (1993). *Street mathematics and school mathematics.* New York: Cambridge University Press.

Olson, C. L. (1976). Some apparent violations of the representativeness heuristic in human judgment. *Journal of Experimental Psychology: Human Perception and Performance, 2,* 599–608.

Peterson, C. R., & Beach, L. R. (1967). Man as an intuitive statistician. *Psychological Bulletin, 68,* 29–46.

Piaget, J., & Inhelder, B. (1975). *The origin of the idea of chance in children* (L. Leake, Jr., P. Burrel, & H. D. Fishbein, Trans.). New York: Norton. (Original work published 1951)

Piattelli-Palmarini, M. (1994). *Inevitable illusions: How mistakes of reason rule our minds.* New York: Wiley.

Reagan, R. T. (1989). Variations on a seminal demonstration of people's insensitivity to sample size. *Organizational Behavior and Human Decision Processes, 43,* 52–57.

Reyna, V. R., & Brainerd, C. J. (1994). The origins of probability judgment: A review of data and theories. In G. Wright & P. Ayton (Eds.), *Subjective probability* (pp. 239–272). Chichester, UK: Wiley.

Ruscio, J. (2003). Comparing Bayes's theorem to frequency-based approaches to teaching Bayesian reasoning. *Teaching of Psychology, 30,* 325–328.

Sedlmeier, P. (1992). *Untersuchungen zu einem Lehr-Lernsystem zum Urteilen unter Unsicherheit* [Studies on a tutorial system concerning judgment under uncertainty]. Unpublished doctoral dissertation, University of Constance, Constance, Germany.

Sedlmeier, P. (1997). BasicBayes: A tutor system for simple Bayesian inference. *Behavior Research Methods, Instruments, & Computers, 29,* 328–336.

Sedlmeier, P. (1998). The distribution matters: Two types of sample-size tasks. *Journal of Behavioral Decision Making, 11,* 281–301.

Sedlmeier, P. (1999). *Improving statistical reasoning: Theoretical models and practical implications.* Mahwah. NJ: Lawrence Erlbaum Associates.

Sedlmeier, P. (2000). How to improve statistical thinking: Choose the task representation wisely and learn by doing. *Suggestions for the statistics classroom 28,* 227–262.

Sedlmeier, P. (2001). *Statistik ohne Formeln.* In M. Borovcnik, J. Engel, & D. Wickmann (Eds.), *Anregungen zum Stochastikunterricht* (pp. 83–95). Hildesheim: Franzbecker.

Sedlmeier, P. (2002). Associative learning and frequency judgments: The PASS model. In P. Sedlmeier & T. Betsch (Eds.), *Etc.: Frequency processing and cognition* (pp. 137–152). Oxford: Oxford University Press.

Sedlmeier, P. (2005). From associations to intuitive judgment and decision making: Implicitly learning from experience. In T. Betsch & S. Haberstroh (Eds.), *Experience-based decision making* (pp. 89–99). Mahwah, NJ: Lawrence Erlbaum Associates.

Sedlmeier, P. (2006). Intuitive judgments about sample size. In K. Fiedler & P. Juslin (Eds.). *In the beginning there is a sample: Information sampling as a key to understand adaptive cognition* (pp. 53–71). Cambridge: Cambridge University Press.

Sedlmeier, P., & Betsch, T. (2002). (Eds.). *Etc: Frequency processing and cognition.* Oxford: Oxford University Press.

Sedlmeier, P., & Gigerenzer, G. (1997). Intuitions about sample size: The empirical law of large numbers. *Journal of Behavioral Decision Making, 10,* 33–51.

Sedlmeier, P., & Gigerenzer, G. (2000). Was Bernoulli wrong? On intuitions about sample size. *Journal of Behavioral Decision Making, 13,* 133–139.

Sedlmeier, P., & Gigerenzer, G. (2001). Teaching Bayesian reasoning in less than two hours. *Journal of Experimental Psychology: General, 130,* 380–400.

Sedlmeier, P., & Kilinç, B. (2004). The hazards of underspecified models: the case of symmetry in everyday predictions. *Psychological Review, 111,* 770–780.

Sedlmeier, P., & Köhlers, D. (2001). *Wahrscheinlichkeiten im Alltag: Statistik ohne Formeln.* [Probabilities in everyday life: statistics without formula]. Braunschweig: Westermann (textbook with program on CD).

Shah, P., & Hoeffner, J. (2002). Review of graph comprehension research: implications for instruction. *Educational Psychology Review, 14,* 47–69.

Swieringa, R., Gibbins, M., Larsson, L., & Sweeney, J. L. (1976). Experiments in the heuristics of human information processing. *Journal of Accounting Research, 4,* 159–187.

Teigen, K. H. (1974). Subjective sampling distributions and the additivity of estimates. *Scandinavian Journal of Psychology, 15,* 50–55.

Tversky, A., & Kahneman, D. (1974). Judgment under uncertainty: Heuristics and biases. *Science, 185,* 1124–1131.

Wassner, C. (2004). *Förderung Bayesianischen Denkens: Kognitionspsychologische Grundlagen und didaktische Analysen.* [Advancing Bayesian reasoning: cognitive psychological foundations and didactical analyses]. Unpublished dissertation, University of Kassel, Germany.

Wassner, C., Martignon, L., & Sedlmeier, P. (2002). Die Bedeutung der Darbietungsform für das alltagsorientiete Lehren von Stochastik [The impact of representational formats on the teaching of statistics for daily life]. *Zeitschrift für Pädagogik, 45* (Suppl.), 35–50.

Well, A. D., Pollatsek, A., & Boyce, S. J. (1990). Understanding the effects of sample size on the variability of the mean. *Organizational Behavior and Human Decision Processes, 47,* 289–312.

Wolfe, C. R. (1995). Information seeking on Bayesian conditional probability problems: A fuzzy-trace theory. *Journal of Behavioral Decision Making, 8,* 85–108.

17

Adolescents' Thinking About the Risks of Sexual Behaviors

Wändi Bruine de Bruin
Julie S. Downs
Baruch Fischhoff
Carnegie Mellon University

Responsible individuals do what they can to reduce their personal vulnerability. Responsible societies teach those with limited knowledge how to achieve that goal. Adolescents are a popular target of such efforts, as they face many risky decisions for the first time in their lives. For example, 45.6% of adolescents have tried sexual intercourse by the time they are in high school (Grunbaum et al., 2002). The decision to have sex triggers additional decisions, like whether to use condoms, which 42.1% of high school students reported doing at last intercourse (Grunbaum et al., 2002). "Use condoms" can be an ambiguous option, if it is unclear how to use them correctly. Younger women seem to lack this information, because they are more likely than older women to experience condom breakage (Macaluso et al., 1999). Failing to use condoms effectively exposes teens to risks for human immunodeficiency virus (HIV) infection, other sexually transmitted infections, and unintended pregnancy (Darroch, 2001; Williams et al., 2002). If adolescents do not understand the consequences of their actions, then they may incur these risks unwittingly.

Extensive, and often expensive, programs aimed at adolescents seek to reduce their sexual risk behaviors, and the associated threats to sexual health (Albarracín et al., 2000; Kim, Stanton, Li, Dickersin, & Galbraith, 1997).

School-based sexuality education reaches more than three fourths of teens before they turn 18 years old (Kirby, 1999), supplementing the uncounted efforts by parents and other adults to provide information (DeLoye, Henggeler, & Daniels, 1993; Sigelman, Mukai, Woods, & Alfeld, 1995). Perhaps as a result, teens recognize the importance of sexual health issues (Millstein & Irwin, 1985) and worry about HIV/AIDS (DiClemente, Zorn, & Temoshok, 1987). Yet, evidence is mixed regarding the effects of these programs on risky sexual behavior (Kirby, 1999; 2002).

One potential barrier to program effectiveness occurs when educators misunderstand the decisions faced by their audience and the circumstances in which those decisions are made. Especially with regard to sexuality, teens and adults may view the same decisions very differently (Beyth-Marom & Fischhoff, 1997; Fischhoff, Bostrom, & Quadrel, 2002; Merz, Fischhoff, Mazur, & Fischbeck, 1993). In such cases, educators and policymakers may attribute teens' risky behaviors solely to underestimating risk or behaving irrationally, when, in fact, their interventions may have failed to communicate information relevant to teens' decisions.

Underestimating risks should encourage risky behaviors, if teens are reasonable but incompletely informed decision makers. Teens, like adults, tend to underestimate their risk compared to that of others, especially in situations where they (accurately or inaccurately) perceive some element of personal control (Weinstein, 1984). However, teens feel less invulnerability than do adults (Fischhoff et al., 1993), perhaps because they see themselves as having less control over their lives.

Although it might encourage underestimating risks, a perception of control is essential to seeing that choices exist. Teenage girls feel particularly little control over their sexual decisions (Amaro, 1995; Gutierrez, Oh, & Gillmore, 2000). They may be unduly influenced by older sexual partners (Kaestle, Morisky, & Wiley 2002) or by sexual partners with whom communication is poor (Crosby, DiClemente, Wingood, Rose, & Lang, 2003). If so, then knowledge about sexual risks, without knowledge about effective relationship negotiation, may have little effect on their behavior.

Beliefs about risks should not fully determine a choice. Teens, like adults, will knowingly take risks in order to gain benefits (Goldberg & Fischhoff, 2000; Goldberg, Halpern-Felsher, & Millstein, 2002; Weinstein & Fineberg, 1980). Those benefits may be determined or mediated by the social context of the choice, such as social censure, a feeling of belonging, or pride in upholding a social norm even when no one is watching. Teens may value these rewards enough to incur risks, while making reasoned choices, albeit not ones that adults may want them to make.

Without understanding how teens view their world, educators may misdiagnose what teens need to learn in order to manage risks more effectively. A mismatch between adults' messages and teens' needs may have contributed to the widespread feeling among educators that "information doesn't work," for changing teens' sexual behavior (e.g., Baldwin & Baldwin, 1988; MacHale & Newell, 1997; Winfield & Whaley, 2002). When knowledge is defined solely from the adults' perspective, it may not work simply because it is beside the point.

Messages that fail to address teens' informational needs have opportunity costs, in the sense of using time, and occupying a communication niche that could be filled better. Such messages may have direct costs if they lead teens to draw erroneous inferences or resent adults who seem to be wasting their time with simplistic, incomplete, and repetitive messages. If teens' experience and intuitions contradict those messages, they may come to mistrust the source. The same may happen if they fail to see that their concerns are addressed or feel that their right to autonomous decision making is being challenged (Midgley & Feldlaufer, 1987; Steinberg & Silverberg, 1986).

AIMING TO PROVIDE SUFFICIENT INFORMATION: USING THE MENTAL MODELS APPROACH

How much teens value information (and those who provide it) should depend on how well they feel it can help them to make effective choices. To that end, they may value quantitative estimates of the risks and benefits of possible actions, as well as qualitative information about the processes producing those effects. Such qualitative knowledge can provide the context that they need to think effectively, and to combine the often scattered bits of information that they already have. The challenge, for research and practice, is to figure out (a) what information teens need to know in order to make effective choices; (b) what they currently believe, accurately or not; and (c) what they need to learn in order to create an accurate, coherent picture of their circumstances.

In behavioral decision research terms, these steps are referred to as (a) *normative* analysis of the information relevant to the decision, (b) *descriptive* study of existing beliefs, and (c) *prescriptive* interventions designed to bridge the gaps between the descriptive reality and the normative ideal (Hastie & Dawes, 2002; von Winterfeldt & Edwards, 1986; Yates, 1990). From this perspective, the value of information is context-dependent. A fact that is critical for one choice may be less relevant for another. For example, information about HIV-prevention methods should, generally, do more to help teens make choices reducing their HIV risk than would information about how the immune system works (Albarracín et al., 2003). On the other hand, knowledgeable teens might find that a better understanding of the immune system solidifies their mental model of HIV/AIDS.

With well-structured problems, the decision analysis is straightforward: create a decision tree, estimate its parameters (i.e., the probabilities and magnitudes of outcomes), and use sensitivity analyses to determine which facts matter the most. With ill-structured problems, decision-makers must identify the factors affecting the outcomes that matter to them, so that they can create and evaluate options. We have used variants of influence diagrams (akin to Bayesian belief networks) as formal representations of the processes, capable of accommodating diverse forms of data. We have called the comparable cognitive representations *mental models* (Morgan, Fischhoff, Bostrom, & Atman, 2001), building on psychology's legacy of mental models approaches (Gentner & Stevens, 1983; Johnson-Laird, 1983; Newell & Simon, 1972; Rouse & Morris, 1986). We have applied this strategy to many risks, including topics as diverse as domestic radon (Bostrom, Fischhoff, & Morgan, 1992), mammography (Silverman, Woloshin, Schwartz, Byram, Welch, & Fischhoff, 2001), climate change (Morgan et al., 2001), electromagnetic fields (MacGregor, Slovic, & Morgan, 1994), carbon dioxide sequestration (Palmgren, Morgan, Bruine de Bruin, & Keith, 2004), paint stripper (Riley, Fischhoff, Small, & Fischbeck, 2001), *Cryptosporidium* (Casman, Fischhoff, Palmgren, Small, & Wu, 2000), nuclear energy sources in space (Morgan et al., 2001), and breast implants (Byram, Fischhoff, Embrey, Bruine de Bruin, & Thorne, 2001; Fischhoff, 1999;). Here, we describe its application to young women's risk of sexually transmitted infections.

Common theories of behavior change, such as the health belief model (Becker & Rosenstock, 1987) and the theory of planned behavior (Ajzen, 1991), have also been applied to sexual behavior. When thoughtfully applied, such linear models can provide useful predictions of sexual behavior. However, they have limited ability to distinguish among competing process models, as needed to design problem-specific interventions and generate testable topic-specific hypotheses (Dawes & Corrigan, 1974; Ogden, 2003). The mental models approach extends what is learned from linear models to identify the specific beliefs and formulations that are most relevant to the decisions of the target population and most in need of intervention.

Normative Analysis: Identifying the Relevant Information

The first step in a mental models project is to create an integrated normative assessment, summarizing the relevant research and theories regarding the factors that determine the outcomes of the focal choices. In this case, those were female adolescents' sexual decisions, which affect their risk of acquiring a sexually transmitted infection, as well as their pleasure, personal relations, and other benefits that they deem relevant. Adolescents have a well-established need to exercise autonomous decision making (Midgley & Feldlaufer, 1987; Steinberg & Silverberg, 1986). Empowering them to meet that need means helping them to understand their world and work it to their best advantage. Given the complexity of sexual decisions, young women need a broad perspective to create and evaluate options, adapt to unanticipated obstacles and opportunities, and consider the broader context that gives meaning to their lives and relationships.

Elsewhere (Fischhoff, Downs, & Bruine de Bruin, 1998), we present an integrated assessment of the factors determining the consequences of sexual choices, including the risk of acquiring a sexually transmitted infection. It was informed by our reading of the research literature and relevant theories, then reviewed by experts in public health, adolescent medicine, nursing, and psychology. Some influences on the risks of acquiring a sexually transmitted infection are well understood. These include the effects of the number and overlap of sexual partners, the kind of sexual behavior, the use of barrier protection (e.g., condoms), and patterns of disease screening and treatment (Johnson, Carey, Marsh, Levin, & Scott-Sheldon, 2003; Pinkerton, Layde, DiFranceisco, & Chesson, 2003; Roper, Peterson, & Curran, 1993). Various theories afford roles to perceived risk in the context of sexual behavior, including social cognitive theory (Bandura, 2000), the theory of reasoned action (Ajzen, 1991) and the health belief model (Becker & Rosenstock, 1987). Other influences are less well understood (e.g., the impacts of substance use and social norms) or hardly studied at all (e.g., perceived benefits). By summarizing the suite of factors that might affect the outcomes of sexual decisions, the normative assessment identifies the facts that might have value to teens facing sexual decisions.

Descriptive Analysis: Determining What Information Teens Already Have

Even relatively well-informed teens may make suboptimal choices, if gaps and errors in their beliefs undermine the value of what they know. For example, teens may recognize the value of condoms as protection against sexually transmitted infections, but see them as more relevant to casual partners than to steady ones (Fisher, Misovich, & Fisher, 1995). As mentioned, they may know about condoms, but not how to use them, or they may not realize the differences between lambskin and latex condoms (Bruine de Bruin, Downs, Fischhoff, & Palmgren, 2005). Such incomplete knowledge may account for the high rate of condom failures among young people who decide to use condoms (Crosby, Sanders, Yarber, & Graham, 2003; Macaluso et al., 1999). Teachers may fail to address these relevant details because they feel uncomfortable discussing sexually explicit topics with their students or face political pressure to avoid them (Bok & Morales, 1998).

Another form of incomplete knowledge arises when teens endorse risk-reduction practices like "abstinence" and "safer sex" without knowing exactly what the terms mean (McIntyre & West, 1992). For example, some sexually active teens use anal sex as a form of abstinence (Schuster, Bell, & Kanouse, 1996). Though having anal sex reduces pregnancy risk compared to having vaginal sex, it increases risk for HIV/AIDS. Unfortunately, "taboo" subjects, such as anal sex, are often left off the sex education curriculum (Halperin, 1999).

Even superficially correct beliefs can hide serious misconceptions. When asked whether HIV risk is affected by how often a person has unprotected sex, adolescents typically say no, arguing that "it only takes once." When asked explicitly, one third of adolescents in a diverse sample said that sex with an infected partner would lead to HIV infection "for sure" (Bruine de Bruin et al., 2005). This belief seems to reflect well-intended educational messages that warn against having sex without protection (e.g., Intermedia, Inc., 1986). In reality, however, having unprotected sex once typically does not result in pregnancy (Wilcox, Dunson, Weinberg, Trussell, & Baird, 2001). Neither is a single unsafe sexual encounter with an infected partner likely to lead to HIV transmission (Gray et al., 2001). Of course, all risks increase with repeated exposure; done often enough, small risks become big ones.

Adolescents do not seem to understand how the risks of having unprotected sex accumulate with repeated exposure (Bruine de Bruin et al., 2005). Even adults have a hard time with this concept, tending to underestimate how quickly risks accumulate, or even that they do (Linville, Fischer, & Fischhoff, 1993; Shaklee & Fischhoff, 1990). Without providing a deeper understanding about cumulative risk, emphasizing that "it only takes once" can be misleading. Most sexually active teens have had at least one negative pregnancy test by age 17 (Zabin, Emerson, Ringers, & Sedivy, 1996). In the absence of explicit instruction, they must figure out what to make of their experience. Lacking an understanding of risk increases the chances that young women who receive a negative pregnancy test will conclude that they were infertile (Downs, Bruine de Bruin, Murray, & Fischhoff, 2004). That conclusion is likely to be unwarranted, and can have serious consequences: Young women who believe that they are infertile are more likely to engage in risky behavior (Downs, Bruine de Bruin et al., 2004) Thus, the "scare tactic" of emphasizing that "it only takes once" may work more poorly than a more comprehensive approach.

These examples suggest dangers arising from inferences based on incomplete information. In order to anticipate such inferences, educators need data to let them know how their messages are interpreted and the contexts within which they are applied. The descriptive analysis of a mental models project seeks to focus educational efforts by understanding the mental models that teens bring to them, in order to ensure that messages are interpreted as intended and elaborate, rather than confound, other information that teens already have.

The normative assessment structures the descriptive analysis: in-depth "mental models" interviews with the target audience are designed to explore the depth of respondents' understanding in a form that reveals their intuitive theories and wording. These are followed by written surveys measuring the prevalence and correlates of potentially critical beliefs, as identified by the interviews. The interviews use nondirective questions (e.g., "How can this risk be avoided?") to avoid suggesting topics or terminology. Respondents are asked to elaborate on whichever topics they raise (e.g., "Can you tell me more about how that works?"), while using their intuitive formulations to the extent possible. Increasingly specific prompts draw respondents to topics in the integrated assessment that they have not addressed, reducing the risk of inadvertently neglecting to discuss things that are known. Once transcribed, the interviews are coded in terms of the variables and relationships in the integrated assessment, and analyzed to reveal what audience members already know—and still need to learn.

Affirming previous research (Amaro, 1995; Gutierrez, Oh, & Gillmore, 2000), our mental models interviews revealed that female adolescents feel little control over their sexual decisions (Downs, Murray, et al., 2004). Interviewees described sexual behavior as being largely determined by situational influences, often beyond their control, rather than seeing themselves as making explicit decisions. Some young women even said that deciding not to have sex meant deciding to avoid all situations that might lead to sex (e.g., parties).

The interviews also suggested three notable errors in teens' knowledge (Downs, Murray, et al., 2004). First, many interviewees endorsed an absolute view of risk, rather than a relative one; for example, they sometimes dismissed condoms for not being "100% effective." Second, respondents knew little about reproductive health, professing ignorance or using terms that they could not explain when asked to elaborate. Third, their knowledge about sexually transmitted infections was almost entirely limited to HIV/AIDS, which they often extrapolated incorrectly to other sexually transmitted infections. These findings suggest what young women need to learn in order to make competent decisions about their sexual health.

Prescriptive Research: Providing the Necessary Information

The intervention that we developed sought to address the educational needs just described, using an interactive video format on DVD. Video facilitates presenting topics that are more easily seen than explained (e.g., how to put a condom on; how to say no or negotiate a safer option). The interactive format allows teens to tailor their usage, exerting some control, by selecting personally relevant material from the 90 minutes of material (see www.WhatCouldYouDo.org). The technology avoids the awkwardness that teens and educators often have in talking about sexually explicit or taboo topics (Bok & Morales, 1998; Halperin, 1999), as well as ensuring a respectful tone. Extensive pretests, using think-aloud protocols with teens in the target population, sought to make the content realistic, compelling, and understandable.

The video begins by introducing a group of ethnically diverse adolescent girls, one of whom has a boyfriend, another of whom meets someone new at a party—given the evidence that teens choose differently in the contexts of "steady" and "new" relationships (Fisher, Misovich, & Fisher, 1995). In order to enhance users' ability to take control over sexual scenarios, the intervention emphasizes the identification of choice points and alternatives as each relationship progresses, allowing users to choose how the female character responds to pressure from the male character. In order to create a feeling of self-efficacy, users are asked to perform *cognitive rehearsal,* imagining what they would say or do in such a situation (Bandura, 2000; Maibach & Flora, 1993) This technique has been found to increase the perceived feasibility of executing acts that may otherwise seem difficult or daunting (Driskell, Copper, & Moran, 1994).

In addition to these focal stories, the intervention covers how and why condoms reduce risk, and demonstrates how to use them properly (on a cucumber). It addresses the gap in teens' understanding of relative and cumulative risk and the misconception that condoms are not a viable option simply because they are not 100% effective. To acknowledge the role of benefits in decision making (Goldberg & Fischhoff, 2000; Goldberg et al., 2002; Weinstein & Fineberg, 1980) and avoid ineffective threat messages (Albarracín et al., 2003), condom use is presented in terms of achieving positive outcomes (pleasure, reassurance, control) rather than in terms of avoiding negative ones (suspicion, disease).

Finally, the video presents a dramatized pelvic exam and conversations with medical experts covering basic issues of reproductive health, testing for disease, and symptoms of different sexually transmitted infections. These sections seek to create a mental model that can readily incorporate future information and structure interactions with health care professionals. For example, information about infections is embedded in a conceptual framework that distinguishes between bacterial and viral ones. That distinction is relevant, because bacterial infections can be cured with antibiotics, whereas viral infections can be treated, but not cured. Once they have this basic framework, users can choose to learn more about eight different infections. In addition to providing information, the DVD's scenes model how to conduct interactions with physicians effectively and respectfully.

We used a longitudinal randomized design to evaluate the interventions' effects on 300 female urban adolescents' (a) knowledge about sexually transmitted infections, (b) self-reported sexual risk behavior, and (c) acquisition of sexually transmitted infections. The interactive DVD was compared to two controls. One used the same content in book form; the other used commercially available brochures covering the same topics. The interventions were administered at baseline and at booster sessions 1, 3, and 6 months later. After 3 months, self-reports revealed that those in the DVD condition were significantly more likely to be abstinent than those in the control conditions. After 6 months, those in the DVD condition were significantly less likely to report having had a condom break, leak, or fall off, or having been diagnosed with a sexually transmitted infection (Downs, Murray, et al., 2004).

OBSTACLES TO SATISFYING TEENS' INFORMATION NEEDS

Misunderstanding Teens' Needs and Beliefs

The mental models procedure formalizes what many educators try to do when developing health communications: Determine what the audience already knows, then close the gaps with what they need to know, beginning with the most critical facts. Nonetheless, many communications are created without such systematic formative research (see Kim et al., 1997; McKay, 2000) or a theoretical foundation (see Kim et al., 1997; Kirby, 2002; Michie & Abraham, 2004). Instead, their content seems to reflect designers' semi-structured opinions regarding what their audience needs to be told, guided by an intuitive analysis of why previous interventions may have failed. The plausibility of relying on such "expert" judgment decreases as the distance between the designers and their audience increases. Adults may have difficulty both understanding and accepting how teens view the world, such as how teens perceive the benefits and social context of sex-related behaviors.

Formative research conducted without a systematic methodology can create an unwarranted feeling of confidence, in the same way that intuitively conducted focus groups may not justify the hopes placed in them (Merton,

1987). For example, knowledge is often assessed with questions so general that they miss the topics directly relevant to teens' decisions (e.g., the definition of "HIV" or "virus," but not the relative risks of oral, anal, and vaginal sex; Fisher & Fisher, 1992). Even tests that cover decision-relevant topics may misrepresent recipients' knowledge, if items are not understood similarly by test-takers and test-makers (Beyth-Marom & Fischhoff, 1997; Wexler, 1997). As just suggested, teens may endorse condoms, but exclude steady partners (Fisher, Misovich, & Fisher, 1995); endorse abstinence, but believe that it includes anal sex (Schuster et al., 1996); or endorse that "it only takes once," while thinking that it will take no more than once (Downs, Bruine de Bruin, et al., 2004).

Thorough curriculum planning must consider individual differences in the target audience, either to tailor messages for subgroups or to decide which message is most worthy of attention. In this case, past research has found lower knowledge scores among incarcerated youths (Bruine de Bruin & Fischhoff, 2000; Nader, Wexler, Patterson, Nckusick, & Coates, 1989), high-risk females (Millstein, Moscicki, & Broering, 1993), and minority groups (Bell, Feraios, & Bryan, 1990). Effectively addressing their varying needs requires understanding their mental models and terminology (Horan, Phillips, & Hagan, 1998; McIntyre & West, 1992; Schuster et al., 1996). Structured knowledge tests formulated in ways natural to adult researchers may underestimate the understanding of these groups, by restricting their ability to express what they know. Conversely, such tests may inflate the scores of test-savvy teens (Bruine de Bruin & Fischhoff, 2000). For example, consider the following multiple-choice item from an HIV/AIDS knowledge test used by the American Red Cross (see Bruine de Bruin & Fischhoff, 2000):

> For vaginal sex, which of the following offers the most protection against HIV infection?
>
> a. Any condom combined with a spermicide labeled at least "98% effective."
> b. Latex condoms used with a spermicide in the vagina.
> c. Latex condoms used with no lubricant.
> d. Natural condoms used with an oil-based lubricant.

The wording of this item teaches that vaginal sex creates HIV risk, which can be reduced with condoms. Test-wise respondents can also extract information from previous questions, the response scale, and other details of questionnaire design (Schwarz, 1996, 1999). The inflated scores of test-savvy populations may lead to underestimating their need for education. The real world, in which these teens must make their sexual decisions, usually does not offer the cues embedded in structured tests.

Furthermore, risk surveys may use ambiguous terms, making it difficult to interpret respondents' judgments of sexual risks. One well-studied source of ambiguity is the use of verbal quantifiers. Terms like "probable" and "likely" mean different things to different people within one context, and to the same person across contexts (e.g., Beyth-Marom, 1982; Brun & Teigen, 1988; Wallsten, Budescu, Rapoport, Zwick, & Forsyth, 1986). Using numerical probabilities eliminates some, but not all, of this ambiguity (Windschitl & Weber, 1990).

Numerical risk perceptions elicited with open-ended probability questions (asking for a number between 0 and 100%) tend to show an anomalous "blip" at 50, even for events with central tendencies far from 50%. Taking these responses at face value encourages claims that lay people exaggerate small probabilities (Black, Nease, & Tosteson, 1995; Dominitz & Manski, 1997; Fischhoff & Bruine de Bruin, 1999; Viscusi, 1993). However, research suggests that people sometimes use "fifty-fifty" to reflect epistemic uncertainty (i.e., their inability to express their feeling with a number), rather than their actual perceived risk (Bruine de Bruin, Fischhoff, Millstein, & Halpern-Felsher, 2000; Fischhoff & Bruine de Bruin, 1999; Konold, 1991). Saying "50%" allows people to give a number, as requested, without feeling that they have committed themselves to a specific answer. Even scientists may not be immune to this usage (Bruine de Bruin, Fischbeck, Stiber, & Fischhoff, 2002). Such non-numerical use of 50 can be discouraged by using distributional probability questions, asking about the percentage of people that will experience an event, rather than the probability that one person will experience it (Bruine de Bruin et al., 2000), or a numerical probability scale presenting explicit tickmarks between 0% and 100% (Fischhoff & Bruine de Bruin, 1999). Other format effects on people's reasoning with probabilities are discussed by Sedlmeier (chap. 16, this volume).

Measurement problems that inadvertently misrepresent young people's knowledge may not only misdirect educational efforts, but also obscure the relationship between knowledge and behavior. For example, such problems may underlie the common failure to find a relationship between teens' knowledge about sexually transmitted infections and their sexual behavior (e.g., Baldwin & Baldwin, 1988; MacHale & Newell, 1997; Winfield & Whaley, 2002). Correcting measurement problems should reduce noise that would obscure such a relationship. In other work, we created a knowledge test to cover decision-relevant information, using wording that reflects adolescents' intuitive understanding. The evaluation of this test showed a significant positive relationship between knowledge and condom use among sexually active respondents (Bruine de Bruin et al., 2005).

Denying Teens Sufficient Information

The political, legal, and social context of adolescent sexuality poses additional challenges, even for researchers who have conscientiously pursued other aspects of the work. Adults in a position of authority may refuse to acknowledge the recommendations that science supports (Fischhoff, 1992). Individual parents' inhibitions may mirror the omission from school curricula (Bok & Morales, 1998; Halperin, 1999). This awkwardness was portrayed on the show "Thirty-something," with a father telling his early-adolescent son that, if he ever wanted to know anything about sex, he should feel free to ask. The son's first question was, "Dad, what's 69?" The father could only say, "Uh, that's the year the Mets won the World Series."

Effective decision making requires considering the probability, and not just the possibility, of risks. Educators are sometimes pressured to limit information about the relative risk of various sexual behaviors and protective measures, for fear of seeming to condone the behaviors involved. For example, those who note the low failure rate of condoms might be accused of implying that young unmarried people can have sex, as long as it is safe. However, comprehensive sex education has not led to earlier or increased sexual activity, although it has increased condom and contraceptive use among those teens who do have sex (Jemmott & Jemmott, 2000; Kim et al., 1997; Kirby, 1999, 2002; Pedlow & Carey, 2003). Thus, giving teens frank, decision-relevant information seems to help them rather than hurt them.

Despite these findings, some aggressive "abstinence-only" programs misrepresent facts about condoms in hopes of deterring teens from sex. For example, some say that HIV can pass through the microscopic holes in condoms, without mentioning that the "mover cells" needed to escort the virus are too large to do so (Haignere, Gold, & McDanel, 1999; Novello & Paterson, 1993). Some exaggerate the infection rate among people who use condoms consistently and correctly with an HIV-positive partner, which is actually quite low (Saracco et al., 1993; de Vincenzi, 1994). Some report condom failure rates associated with incorrect and inconsistent condom use, while ignoring failure rates associated with promises to abstain (Haignere, Gold, & McDanel, 1999).

Perhaps as a result, abstinence-only programs have proven less effective in reducing risk than comprehensive sex-education programs promoting the use of condoms as well as the postponement of sexual intercourse (see McKay, 2000, and Kirby, 2002, for reviews). Moreover, teens who eventually break a "virginity pledge" are less likely than sexually active teens to use contraception at first intercourse (Bearman & Brueckner, 2001). Thus, depriving teens of information about condoms may increase their risk of pregnancy and disease. That choice might be defended as sacrificing the health of those teens who break their vows, in order to maintain the societal value of abstinence. However, that position raises empirical questions, regarding the effects of this strategy, and ethical ones, regarding its utilitarian perspective.

DISCUSSION

People make decisions based on the information that they have, and the inferences that they draw from it. If they lack critical information, their decisions will suffer. We have shown how sex education can miss critical misunderstandings in teens' beliefs. Some of these failures to communicate are willful; others reflect personal discomfort or social pressures. However, even uninhibited, unconstrained educators may misdirect their efforts, if they fail to understand teens' decisions and assess teens' beliefs adequately. Those failures not only deprive teens of needed information, but also expose them to criticism for not acting the way that adults wish – despite (seemingly) being told. Knowledge may be unrelated to behavior, if it is measured in irrelevant terms, not considering what teens need to know, in order to make the choices that they face.

Effective interventions require understanding people's choices, values, and beliefs —then providing critically missing information in a comprehensible, usable way. We have described an integrated approach to accomplishing this goal. It begins with a formal analysis of the decision and the factors determining its outcomes. It proceeds by describing current beliefs, using semi-structured "mental models" interviews, perhaps supplemented by structured knowledge test, in order to secure larger samples. It concludes with the design and evaluation of interventions for closing important gaps. We illustrated the mental models approach with a research project leading to an interactive DVD targeting female adolescents' sexual decisions, which showed good results in a randomized controlled trial (Downs, Murray et al., 2004). Despite (or perhaps because of) a tone respecting teens' need for autonomous sexual decision making (Midgley & Feldlaufer, 1987; Steinberg & Silverberg, 1986), the intervention led to increased abstinence, precisely the behavior that more manipulative approaches aim for—but often fail to achieve. It also reduced condom failures and acquisition of sexually transmitted infections.

Pursuing this approach requires casting a wide net for relevant science. Its normative analyses require understanding the facts of risks, studied by different disciplines. Its descriptive research draws on psychology's various "mental models" approaches, in order to create one suited to describing thoughts regarding the complex, poorly bounded systems. Its prescriptive interventions use whatever theory and methodology psychology can provide, in bridging the gap between what people know and need to know. The application described here suggests that information about complex, "hot" topics can be conveyed to adolescents well enough to change their behavior in positive ways.

REFERENCES

Ajzen, I. (1991). The theory of planned behavior. *Organizational Behavior and Human Decision Processes, 50,* 179–211.

Albarracín, D., McNatt, P. S., Klein, C. T. F., Ho, R. M., Mitchell, A. L., & Kumcale, G. T. (2003). Persuasive communications to change actions: An analysis of behavioral and cognitive impact in HIV prevention. *Health Psychology, 22,* 166–177.

Amaro, H. (1995). Love, sex and power. Considering women's realities in HIV prevention. *American Psychologist, 50,* 437–47.

Baldwin, J. D., & Baldwin, J. I. (1988). Factors affecting AIDS-related sexual risk-taking behavior among college students. *The Journal of Sex Research, 25,* 181–196.

Bandura, A. (2000). Self-efficacy: The foundation of agency. In W. J. Perrig, & A. Grob (Eds.), *Control of human behavior, mental processes, and consciousness: Essays in honor of the 60th birthday of August Flammer* (pp. 17–33). Mahwah, NJ: Lawrence Erlbaum Associates.

Bearman, P. S., & Brueckner, H. (2001). Virginity pledges and first intercourse. *American Journal of Sociology, 106,* 859–912.

Becker, M. H., & Rosenstock, J. M. (1987). Comparing social learning theory and the health belief model. In W. B. Ward (Ed.), *Advances in health education and promotion* (pp. 245–249). Greenwich, CT: JAI Press.

Bell, D., Feraios, A., & Bryan, T. (1990). Adolescent males' knowledge and attitudes about AIDS in the context of their social world. *Journal of Applied Social Psychology, 20,* 424–448.

Beyth-Marom, R. (1982). How probable is probable? A numerical translation of verbal probability expressions. *Journal of Forecasting, 1,* 257–269.

Beyth-Marom, R., & Fischhoff, B. (1997). Adolescent decisions about risk: A cognitive perspective. In J. Schulenberg, J. Maggs, & K. Hurnelmans (Eds.), *Health risks and developmental transaction during adolescence.* New York: Cambridge University Press.

Black, W. C., Nease, R. F., & Tosteson, A. N. A. (1995). Perceptions of breast cancer risk and screening effectiveness in women younger than 50 years of age. *Journal of the National Cancer Institute, 8,* 720–731.

Bok, M., & Morales, J. (1998). "Just say no to drugs and sex": A formula for disaster. *Journal of HIV/AIDS Prevention & Education for Adolescents & Children, 2,* 88–94.

Bostrom, A., Fischhoff, B., & Morgan, M. G. (1992). Characterizing mental models of hazardous processes: A methodology and an application to radon. *Journal of Social Issues, 48,* 85–100.

Bruine de Bruin, W., Downs, J. S., Fischhoff, B., & Palmgren, C. (2005). *Development and evaluation of an HIV/AIDS knowledge measure for adolescents focusing on gaps and misconceptions.* Manuscript in preparation.

Bruine de Bruin, W., Fischbeck, P. S., Stiber, N.A. & Fischhoff, B. (2002). What number is "fifty–fifty"? Redistributing excess 50% responses in risk perception studies. *Risk Analysis, 22,* 725–735.

Bruine de Bruin, W., & Fischhoff, B. (2000). The effect of question format on measured HIV/AIDS knowledge in detention center adolescents, low-risk adolescents, and adults. *AIDS Education and Prevention, 12*, 187–198.

Bruine de Bruin, W., Fischhoff, B., Millstein, S. G., & Halpern Felsher, B. L. (2000). Verbal and numerical expressions of probability: "It's a fifty–fifty chance." *Organizational Behavior and Human Decision Processes, 81*, 115–131.

Brun, W., & Teigen, K.H. (1988). Verbal probabilities: Ambiguous, context-dependent, or both? *Organizational Behavior and Human Decision Processes, 41*, 390–404.

Byram, S., Fischhoff, B., Embrey, M., Bruine de Bruin, W., & Thorne S. (2001). Mental models of women with breast implants: Local complications. *Behavioral Medicine, 27*, 4–14.

Casman, E., Fischhoff, B., Palmgren, C., Small, M., & Wu, F. (2000). Integrated risk model of a drinking waterborne Cryptosporidiosis outbreak. *Risk Analysis, 20*, 493–509.

Crosby, R. A., DiClemente, R. J., Wingood, G. M., Rose, E., & Lang, D. (2003). Correlates of continued risky sex among pregnant African American teens: Implications for STD prevention. *Sexually Transmitted Diseases, 30*, 57–63.

Crosby, R., Sanders, S., Yarber, W. L., & Graham, C. A. (2003). Condom-use errors and problems. A neglected aspect of studies assessing condom effectiveness. *American Journal of Preventive Medicine, 24*, 367–370.

Darroch, J, E, (2001). Adolescent pregnancy trends and demographics. *Current Women's Health Report, 1*, 102–110.

Dawes R. M., & Corrigan B. (1974). Linear models in decision making. *Psychological Bulletin, 81*, 95–106.

DeLoye, G. J., Henggler, S. W., & Daniels, C. M. (1993). Developmental and family correlates of children's knowledge and attitudes regarding AIDS. *Journal of Pediatric Psychology, 18*, 209–219.

DiClemente, R. J., Zorn, J., & Temoshok, L. (1987). The association of gender, ethnicity, and length of residence in the Bay area to adolescents' knowledge and attitudes about Acquired Immune Deficiency Syndrome. *Journal of Applied Social Psychology, 17*, 216–230.

Dominitz, J., & Manski, C. F. (1997). Perceptions of economic insecurity: Evidence from the survey of economic expectations. *Public Opinion Quarterly, 61*, 261–287.

Downs, J. S., Bruine de Bruin, W., Murray, P. J., & Fischhoff, B. (2004). When "it only takes once" fails: Perceived infertility after unsafe sex predicts condom use and STI acquisition. *Journal of Pediatric and Adolescent Gynecology, 17*, 224.

Downs, J. S., Murray, P. J., Bruine de Bruin, W., Penrose, J., Palmgren, C., & Fischhoff, B. (2004). Interactive video behavioral intervention to reduce adolescent females' STD risk: A randomized controlled trial. *Social Science & Medicine, 59*, 1561–1572.

Driskell, J. E., Copper, C., & Moran, A. (1994). Does mental practice enhance performance? *Journal of Applied Psychology, 79*, 481–492.

Fischhoff, B. (1992). Giving advice: Decision theory perspectives on sexual assault. *American Psychologist, 47*, 577–588.

Fischhoff, B. (1999). What do patients want? Help in making effective choices. *Effective Clinical Practice, 2*, 198–200.

Fischhoff, B., Bostrom, A., & Quadrel, M. J. (2002). Risk perception and communication. In R. Detels, J. McEwen, R. Beaglehole, & H. Tanaka (Eds.), *Oxford textbook of public health*. (pp. 1105–1123). London: Oxford University Press.

Fischhoff, B., & Bruine de Bruin, W. (1999). Fifty–fifty = 50%? *Journal of Behavioral Decision Making, 12*, 149–163.

Fischhoff, B., Downs, J. S., & Bruine de Bruin, W. (1998). Adolescent Vulnerability: A framework for behavioral interventions. *Applied and Preventive Psychology, 7*, 77–94.

Fischhoff, B., Parker, A. M., Bruine de Bruin, W., Downs, J. S., Palmgren, C., Dawes, R., & Manski, C. F. (2000). Teen expectations for significant life events. *Public Opinion Quarterly, 64,* 189–205.

Fisher, J. D., Misovich, S. J., & Fisher, W. A. (1992). The impact of perceived social norms on adolescents' AIDS risk behavior and prevention. In R. J. DiClemente (Ed.), *Adolescents and AIDS: A generation in jeopardy* (pp. 117–136). Beverly Hills, CA: Sage.

Fisher, J. D., & Fisher, W. A. (1992). Changing AIDS-risk behavior. *Psychological Bulletin, 111,* 455–474.

Gentner, D., & Stevens, A. L. (1983). (Eds.). *Mental models.* Hillsdale, NJ: Lawrence Erlbaum Associates.

Goldberg, J. H., & Fischhoff, B. (2000). The long-term risks and the short-term benefits: Perceptions of potentially addictive activities. *Health Psychology, 19,* 299–303.

Goldberg, J. H., Halpern-Felsher, B. L., & Millstein, S. G. (2002). Beyond invulnerability: The importance of benefits in adolescents' decisions to drink alcohol. *Health Psychology, 21,* 477–484.

Gray, R. H., Wawer, M. J., Brookmeyer, R., Sewankambo, N. K., Serwadda, D., Wabwire-Mangen, F., et al. (2001). Probability of HIV-1 transmission per coital act in monogamous, heterosexual, HIV-1-discordant couples in Rakai, Uganda. *Lancet, 357,* 1149–1153.

Grunbaum, J. A., Kann, L., Kinchen, S. A., Williams, B., Ross, J. G., Lowry, R., & Kolbe, L. (2002). Youth risk behavior surveillance—United States, 2001. *Journal of School Health, 72,* 313–328.

Gutierrez, L., Oh, H. J., Gillmore, M. R. (2000). Toward an understanding of (em)power(ment) for HIV/AIDS prevention with adolescent women. *Sex Roles, 42,* 581–611.

Haignere, C. S., Gold, R., & McDanel, H. J. (1999). Adolescent abstinence and condom use: Are we sure we are really teaching what is safe? *Health Education & Behavior, 26,* 43–54.

Halperin, D. T. (1999). Heterosexual anal intercourse: Prevalence, cultural factors, and HIV infection and other health risks, Part I. *AIDS Patient Care and STDs, 13 ,* 717–30.

Hastie, R., & Dawes, R. M. (2002). *Rational choice in an uncertain world* (2nd ed.). San Diego: Sage.

Horan, P. F., Phillips, J., & Hagan, N. E. (1998). The meaning of abstinence for college students. *Journal of HIV/AIDS Prevention & Education for Adolescents & Children, 2,* 51–66.

Intermedia, Inc. (1986). *It only takes once.* Seattle, WA.

Jemmott, J. B., & Jemmott, L. S. (2000). HIV behavioral interventions for adolescents in community settings. In J. L. Peterson, & R. J. DiClemente, (Eds.), *Handbook of HIV Prevention.* (pp. 103–127) New York Kluwer.

Johnson, B. T., Carey, M. P., Marsh, K. L., Levin, K. D., & Scott-Sheldon, L. A. (2003). Interventions to reduce sexual risk for the human immunodeficiency virus in adolescents, 1985–2000: A research synthesis. *Archives of Pediatrics & Adolescent Medicine, 157,* 381–388.

Johnson-Laird, P. N. (1983). *Mental models.* Cambridge, MA: Harvard University Press.

Kaestle, C. E., Morisky, D. E., & Wiley, D. J. (2002). Sexual intercourse and the age difference between adolescent females and their romantic partners. *Perspectives on Sexual and Reproductive Health, 34,* 304–309.

Kim, N., Stanton, B., Li, X., Dickersin, K., & Galbraith, J. (1997). Effectiveness of the 40 adolescent AIDS risk reduction interventions: A quantitative review. *Journal of Adolescent Health, 20,* 204–215.

Kirby, D. (1999). Sexuality and sex education at home and school. *Adolescent Medicine, 10,* 195–209.

Kirby, D. (2002). Effective approaches to reducing adolescent unprotected sex, pregnancy, and childbearing. *The Journal of Sex Research, 39,* 51–57.

Konold, C. (1991). Understanding students' beliefs about probability. In E. von Glasersfeld (Ed), *Radical constructivism in mathematics education* (pp. 139–156). Amsterdam, the Netherlands: Kluwer.

Linville, P. W., Fischer, G. W., & Fischhoff, B. (1993). AIDS risk perceptions and decision biases. In J. B. Pryor & G. D Reeder (Eds.), *The social psychology of HIV infection* (pp. 35–38). Hillsdale, NJ: Lawrence Erlbaum Associates.

Macaluso, M., Kelaghan, J., Artz, L., Austin, H., Fleenor, M., Hook, E. W. 3rd., et al. (1999). Mechanical failure of the latex condom in a cohort of women at high STD risk. *Sexually Transmitted Diseases, 26,* 450–458.

MacGregor, D. G., Slovic, P., & Morgan, M. G. (1994). Perception of risks from electromagnetic fields: A psychometric evaluation of a risk-communication approach, *Risk Analysis, 14*(5), 815–828.

MacHale, E., & Newell, J. (1997). Sexual behavior and sex education in Irish school-going teenagers. *International Journal of STD & AIDS, 8,* 196–200.

Maibach, E., & Flora, J. A. (1993). Symbolic modeling and cognitive rehearsal: Using video to promote AIDS prevention self-efficacy. *Communication Research Special Issue: The Role of Communication in Health Promotion, 20,* 517–545.

McIntyre, S. & West, P. (1992). What does the phrase "safer sex" mean to you? Understanding among Glaswegian 18-year-olds in 1990. *AIDS, 7,* 121–126.

McKay, A. (2000). Prevention of sexually transmitted infections in different populations: A review of behaviorally effective and cost-effective interventions. *The Canadian Journal of Human Sexuality, 9,* 95–120.

Merton, R. K. (1987). The focused interview and focus groups: Continuities and discontinuities. *Public Opinion Quarterly, 51,* 550–566.

Merz, J. F., Fischhof, B., Mazur, D. J., & Fischbeck, P. S, (1993). A decision-analytic approach to developing standards of disclosure for medical informed consent. *Journal of Products and Toxics Liabilities, 15,* 191–215.

Michie, S. & Abraham, C. (2004). Interventions to change health behaviors: Evidence-based or evidence-inspired? *Psychology & Health, 19,* 29–49.

Midgley, C., & Feldlaufer, H. (1987). Students' and teachers' decision-making fit before and after the transition to junior high school. *Journal of Early Adolescence, 7,* 225–241.

Millstein, S. G., & Irwin, C. E., Jr. (1985). Adolescents' assessments of behavioral risk: Sex differences and maturation effects. *Pediatric Research, 19,* 112A.

Millstein, S. G., Moscicki, A. B., & Broering, J. M. (1993). Female adolescents at high, moderate, and low risk of exposure to HIV: Differences in knowledge, beliefs, and behavior. *Journal of Adolescent Health, 15,* 133–142.

Morgan, M. G., Fischhoff, B., Bostrom, A., & Atman, C. (2001). *Risk communication: The mental models approach.* New York: Cambridge University Press.

Nader, P. R., Wexler, D. B., Patterson, T. L., Nckusick, L., & Coates, T. (1989). Comparison of beliefs about AIDS risk behavior knowledge: Scale development, validation, and norms. *Journal of Behavior Therapy and Experimental Psychiatry, 20,* 227–234.

Newell, A., & Simon, H.A. (1972). *Human problem solving.* Englewood Cliffs, NJ: Prentice Hall.

Novello, A., & Paterson, H. B. (1993). From the Surgeon General: U.S. public health service. *Journal of the American Medical Association, 269,* 2840.

Ogden, J. (2003). Some problems with social cognition models: A pragmatic and conceptual analysis. *Health Psychology, 22,* 424–428.

Palmgren, C., Morgan, M. G., Bruine de Bruin, W., & Keith, D. (2004). Public perceptions of carbon dioxide sequestration. *Environmental Science & Technology, 38,* 6441–6450.

Pedlow, C. T., & Carey, M. P. (2003). HIV sexual risk-reduction interventions for youth: A review and methodological critique of randomized controlled trials. *Behavior Modification*, 135–190.

Pinkerton, S. D., Layde, P. M., DiFranceisco, W., & Chesson, H. W. (2003). All STDs are not created equal: An analysis of the differential effects of sexual behavior changes on different STDs. *International Journal of STD & AIDS*, *14*, 320–328.

Quadrel, M. J., Fischhoff, B., & Davis, W. (1993). Adolescent (in)vulnerability. *American Psychologist, 48,* 102–116.

Riley, D. M., Fischhoff, B., Small, M., Fischbeck, P. (2001). Evaluating the effectiveness of risk-reduction strategies for consumer chemical products. *Risk Analysis*, *21*, 357–369.

Roper, W. L., Peterson, H. B., & Curran, J. W. (1993). Commentary: Condoms and HIV/STD prevention—clarifying the message. *American Journal of Public Health*, *83*, 501–503.

Rouse, W. B., & Morris, N. M. (1986). On looking into the black box: Prospects and limits in the search for mental models. *Psychological Bulletin, 100*, 349–363.

Saracco, A., Musicco, M., Nicolosi, A., Angarano, G., Arici, C., Gavazzeni, G., et al. (1993). Man to woman sexual transmission of HIV; longitudinal study of 343 steady partners of infected men. *Journal of Acquired Immune Deficiency Syndrome, 6,* 497–502.

Schuster, M. A., Bell, R. M., Berry, S. H., & Kanouse, D. E. (1998). Impact of a high school condom availability program on sexual attitudes and behaviors. *Family Planning Perspectives, 30,* 67–72.

Shaklee, H., & Fischhoff, B. (1990). The psychology of contraceptive surprises: Cumulative risk and contraceptive effectiveness. *Journal of Applied Psychology, 20,* 385–403.

Schuster, M. A., Bell, R. M., & Kanouse, D. E. (1996). The sexual practices of adolescent virgins: Genital sexual activities of high school students who have never had vaginal intercourse. *American Journal of Public Health, 86*, 1570–1576.

Schwarz, N. (1996). *Cognition and communication: Judgmental biases, research methods and the logic of conversation.* Mahwah, NJ: Lawrence Erlbaum Associates.

Schwarz, N. (1999). Self-reports: How the questions shape the answers. *American Psychologist, 54,* 93–105.

Sigelman, C. K., Mukai, T., Woods, T., & Alfeld, C. (1995). Parents' contributions to children's knowledge and attitudes regarding AIDS: Another look. *Journal of Pediatrics, 20,* 61–77.

Silverman, E., Woloshin, S., Schwartz, L. M., Byram, S. J., Welch, H. G., & Fischhoff, B. (2001). Women's views of breast cancer risk and screening mammography: A qualitative interview study. *Medical Decision Making, 21*, 231–240.

Steinberg, L., & Silverberg, S. (1986). The vicissitudes of autonomy in early adolescence. *Child Development, 57,* 841–851.

Thomas, M. H. (2000). Abstinence-based programs for prevention of adolescent pregnancy: A review. *Journal of Adolescent Health, 26,* 5–17.

de Vincenzi, I. (1994). A longitudinal study of human immunodeficiency virus transmission by heterosexual partners. *New England Journal of Medicine, 331,* 341–346.

Viscusi, W. K. (1993). *The risks of smoking.* Cambridge, MA: Harvard University Press.

Wallsten, T. S., Budescu, D. V., Rapoport, A., Zwick, R., & Forsyth, B. (1986). Measuring the vague meaning of probability terms. *Journal of Experimental Psychology: General, 115*, 348–365.

Weinstein, M. C., & Fineberg, H. (1980). *Clinical decision analysis.* Philadelphia, PA: Saunders.

Weinstein, N. (1984). Why it won't happen to me: Perceptions of risk factors and susceptibility. *Health Psychology, 3,* 431–457.

Wexler, S. (1997). AIDS knowledge and educational preferences of at-risk runaway/ homeless and incarcerated youth. *Children & Youth Services Review, 19*, 667–681.

Wilcox, A. J., Dunson, D. B., Weinberg, C. R., Trussell, J., & Baird, D. D. (2001). Likelihood of conception with a single act of intercourse: Providing benchmark rates for assessment of post-coital contraceptives. *Contraception, 63*, 211–215.

Williams, K. M., Wingood, G. M., DiClemente, R. J., Crosby, R. A., McCree, D. H., Liau, A., et al. (2002). Prevalence and correlates of Chlamydia trachomatis among sexually active African-American adolescent females. *Preventive Medicine, 35,* 593–600.

Windschitl, P. D., & Weber, E. U. (1999). The interpretation of "likely" depends on context, but "70%" is 70%, right? The influence of associative processes on perceived certainty. *Journal of Experimental Psychology: Learning, Memory & Cognition, 25,* 1514–1533.

Winfield, E. B., & Whaley, A. L. (2002). A comprehensive test of the Health Belief Model in the prediction of condom use among African American college students. *Journal of Black Psychology, 28*, 330–346

von Winterfeldt, D., & Edwards, W. (1986). *Decision analysis and behavioral research.* New York: Cambridge University Press.

Yates, J. F. (1990). *Judgment and decision making.* New York: Wiley.

Zabin, L. S., Emerson, M. R., Ringers, P. A., & Sedivy, V. (1996). Adolescents with negative pregnancy test results: An accessible at-risk group. *Journal of the American Medical Association, 275*, 113–117.

18

Discussion of Part III: Learning and Making Decisions With Data

Marie Burrage
Marina Epstein
Priti Shah
University of Michigan

In everyday contexts, new data change the way we understand and make decisions about the world at large. Although most of the chapters in this volume focus on the process of understanding statistical data in classroom or scientific reasoning contexts, the last three chapters in this volume consider how data influence how we perceive and make decisions about the real world. These three chapters represent three traditions for considering data in the real world. Chapter 15, by David Danks, presents a unifying framework for comparing models of how people make causal inferences from data. The chapters by Peter Sedlmeier (chap. 16) and Wandi Bruine de Bruin, Julie S. Downs, and Baruch Fischhoff (chap. 17) describe interventions designed to help people better understand statistical information. In the case of the Sedlmeier chapter, the statistical reasoning is domain-general. In the case of the Bruine de Bruin et al. chapter, the reasoning is in the context of making decisions about sexual behavior. Thus, all three chapters address the question of what people do when they encounter data.

Despite this general similarity, it is difficult to compare these chapters as they address fundamentally different questions within the realm of how people learn and make decisions with data. We have identified three dimensions along which we can situate chapters in order to understand their contributions to

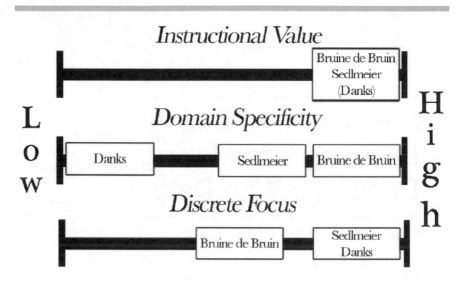

Figure 18.1 The position of the three chapters in the final section of the book along the dimensions of instructional value, domain-specificity, and relative focus on discrete versus probabilistic representations.

literature on thinking with data, illustrated in Figure 18.1. The first dimension is instructional value, the second dimension is domain specificity, and the third dimension is the relative importance of discrete, individual instances (and frequencies) versus probabilities.

The Sedlmeier and Bruine de Bruin chapters describe interventions designed to help people to better reason about and make decisions with data. Both of these chapters consider how to build on individuals' prior knowledge and intuitions into the learning and decision-making processes, thereby helping to make risk data more accessible and statistical reasoning more natural. David Danks' chapter, which describes how the Bayes Net framework can be used to directly compare different models of causal reasoning, provides a tool for researchers themselves to better understand causal reasoning. Thus, we place the three chapters along similar positions along the first dimension: they each teach adolescents, students, or researchers about an aspect of learning from data.

On the other hand, the three chapters differ on the second dimension, domain-specificity. Bruine de Bruin et al.'s chapter presents a content specific analysis of how people use data to make decisions. Their domain is risky sex behavior—they address issues of how educators can convey risk information effectively to improve adolescents' decision-making about sex behaviors. Although this intervention might serve to improve adolescents' general reasoning skills and may help them to make better decisions in other areas of their lives, the intent is to provide support for their reasoning about sex behavior. The content specificity of this intervention makes it a useful example of how people make decisions with data in real world, high-risk contexts.

Peter Sedlmeier's chapter provides specific tools to use to translate statistical intuitions into valid statistical reasoning. His intervention is targeted at two types of statistical reasoning problems: Bayesian inferences and sample size-dependent tasks. Although Sedlmeier's intervention is limited to statistical reasoning, he does not apply this reasoning to one, single domain of content. Instead, he provides examples from a wide range of real-world decision-making contexts ranging from how to avoid serving underage drinkers to writing a women's magazine article on mammography as an indicator of breast cancer. These content-specific examples are well used and help to illustrate the larger message of how to make statistical reasoning more accessible to anyone with valid statistical intuitions.

In his chapter, Danks does not provide domain specific examples of how people learn new causal inferences. Instead, he compares and contrasts a series of domain general models of causal learning. Though he acknowledges that some models might apply to certain types of learning and certain learning contexts better than others, this chapter does not focus on modeling learning in one or another domain of content. Therefore, Bruine de Bruin's chapter is the most domain-specific followed by Sedlmeier's chapter, and then Danks' chapter.

People often experience information in discrete instances and, in order to "see the bigger picture," must translate it into probabilistic representations or causal models. The three chapters in this section can be classified in terms of their focus on either discrete instances and individual experiences with data, or cumulative and probabilistic representations. Bruine de Bruin et al.'s chapter takes into account that people's experiences of data are on a day-by-day, event-by-event basis and that they must translate and compile this new information along with prior knowledge into meaningful representations. However, this is only one of the many data interpretation processes that this chapter focuses on. The Sedlmeier chapter most directly addresses the issue by providing specific tools for converting frequency representations into valid, probabilistic representations. Finally all the models described by the Danks chapter focus on causal learning resulting from experiences with individual instances. Thus, the data considered in the Danks and Sedlmeier chapters focus most on discrete, individual instances versus probabilities.

In summary, although the three chapters in the final section of *Thinking with Data* all concern learning from and making decisions about data, the three chapters differ along the dimensions of instructional focus, domain-specificity, and discreteness. In the following section we consider each individual chapter separately. For each chapter, we first provide a brief discussion of the main contributions of the chapter, followed by a discussion of the questions raised by the research presented and possible future directions. We consider the chapters in the order presented in the book.

THINKING ABOUT CAUSATION

In chapter 15, David Danks compares and contrasts multiple models of causal reasoning, including associationist models and Bayes net models. The following is the modeled process: An existing causal structure is presented with a set of cases observed at one time or in summary form. The influence of each potential cause on each potential effect is determined. Throughout the process, prior knowledge to can be used to label variables as causes or effects.

Danks does not make the argument that one model best explains causal learning under all circumstances. Instead, he focuses on similarities between the models and ways that they correctly capture learning strategies used in different contexts. He does not delve into the question of which theory best fits empirical data, a question of concern to psychologists and educational researchers, but not within the realm of this primarily philosophical review. Instead, Danks provides us with useful tools with which to approach research questions in fields such as cognitive and developmental psychology. Researchers such as Alison Gopnik have taken Danks' work on Bayes nets into the laboratory, and have found empirical support for this type of model. This team's work is an example of the ways in which the educational and psychological research communities can use Danks' excellent review of causal learning models to inform their thinking about their own work.

Danks' chapter presents Bayes nets as a "normative framework for representing causal structures" (p. 371). He also shows that Bayes nets are a powerful way to represent other existing psychological theories, and that, indeed, many models have been developed using their probabilistic structure.

One such theory uses Bayes net learning algorithms to computationally model causal learning. The algorithms are used to derive predictions about how people learn to reason about causal relationships. For example, Alison Gopnik and colleagues have done work on causal Bayes nets as a psychological model of children's learning (for a review, see Gopnik et al., 2004). They created a task called the "blicket detector" during which children must draw causal inferences about which objects have causal power to make a "blicket machine" go (these are called "blickets") and which do not. Children's performance in a range of different experiments using versions of the "blicket detector" task suggest that they use learned causal maps in order to make decisions about causal relations among events. These causal maps are consistent with Bayes net formalism and causal Bayes nets can accurately predict children's performance on these types of tasks (Nazzi & Gopnik, 2000).

Danks points out that Bayes nets are not necessarily a substitute for other theories of causal reasoning. He emphasizes that they can be used in conjunction with other theories and can even provide a structure for understanding other theories. One thing that Bayes nets uniquely offer is extra power during the learning process by taking into account preliminary learning steps that occur prior to the initial parameter learning step used by other models. Bayes nets give us a new way to understand older models of causal reasoning, and, in doing this, they have led to research projects such as Gopnick et al.'s, which is aimed at measuring their empirical accuracy.

We hope that Gopnick et al.'s work will encourage other researchers in education, psychology and related fields to consider the models that Danks presents as potential tools for use in empirical contexts. In the final section of their 2004 review, Gopnik and colleagues contend that their application of Bayes nets to causal learning in children raises a whole range of additional experimental and computational questions. For example, how do children use specific kinds of prior knowledge in combination with formal reasoning? They also acknowledge that their experiments do not provide definitive evidence for a particular method of causal learning. In fact, they suggest that other models such as associationist models could be modified to produce similar results. Therefore, the relationship between models of causal reasoning warrants further investigation. Future research might work to identify which models provide the best representation of causal reasoning given different types of data or causal reasoning tasks. Empirical data clarifying the relationships between the models would be useful for those who wish to understand further the larger framework that Danks' paper so carefully lays out.

THINKING ABOUT BAYESIAN INFERENCES AND SAMPLE SIZE

Since the publication of Kahneman and Tversky's seminal work (e.g., Tversky & Kahneman, 1974) identifying human errors in judgment, there has been a long tradition of trying to find the underlying explanation for why human beings have difficulty with statistical reasoning in everyday contexts. In his chapter, Sedlmeier suggests that rather than statistical reasoning being naturally difficult, individuals hold valid statistical intuitions. However, the reason that individuals have difficulty with certain statistical reasoning tasks is that tasks are often framed in terms of difficult to understand probability representations rather than in terms of frequency. In his chapter, he argues that frequency representations are more natural and allow individuals to base their reasoning about probability on discrete, everyday experiences. He also provides a computational model called PASS in which he describes how storing frequencies of events helps individual understand probability judgments.

Evidence for his assertion that frequency-based representations are more natural and meaningful than probability-based representations is that when problems are framed in terms of frequency-based thinking, student performance on statistical reasoning tasks improves dramatically. This improvement occurs even on more complex transfer statistical reasoning problems performed well after the intervention. Sedlmeier focuses on two types of common statistical reasoning problems: those that require making Bayseian inferences (e.g., considering base rates), and those that require making inferences based on sample size (e.g., involve recognizing that one can be more confident in larger samples).

One question that arises from Sedlemeier's work is what aspect of this training and reframing of statistical reasoning problems is helping students solve them. Is it really that we have statistical intuitions based on a frequency-based associative learning system? Or are the frequency representations that Sedlmeier trains students to use less cognitively demanding to deal with for other reasons? There are several differences between the frequency representations and the probabilistic representation used in Sedlemeier's studies. Consider, for example, the common Bayesian reasoning problem about base rates in diagnoses. The traditional representation of the problem looks like this:

- The probability that a randomly chosen woman who undergoes mammography will have breast cancer is 1%
- If a woman undergoing mammography has breast cancer, the probability that she will test positive is 80%
- If a woman undergoing mammography does not have breast cancer, the probability that she will test positive is 10%

This representation does not explicitly state that the number of false alarms is higher than the number of hits. Furthermore, the problem requires a relatively complex calculation

$$
\frac{p(\text{cancer})p(\text{pos/cancer})}{p(\text{cancer})p(\text{pos/cancer}) + p(\text{no cancer})p(\text{pos/no cancer})}
$$

In Sedlmeier's frequency representation of the problem, the following information is provided:

- Ten of every 1,000 women who undergo mammography have breast cancer
- 8 of every 10 women with breast cancer who undergo mammography will test positive
- 99 of every 990 women without breast cancer who undergo mammography will test positive.

This example explicitly provides the key piece of information: there are 99 false alarms and 8 hits, and thus it highlights the influence of base rates. Furthermore, the mathematical calculation is trivial.

Perhaps the new representations are useful because they provide scaffolding, forcing people to confront what they might otherwise ignore (sample size, base rates). Additionally, they make calculations much easier. Further research that specifies what aspects of Sedlemeier's effective instructional strategies are beneficial would be very interesting.

In addition to demonstrating the effectiveness of Sedlmeier's statistical reasoning interventions, Sedlmeier presents some intriguing data in his chapter about the development of statistical reasoning in middle school children that also warrants future research. In his study, younger students (fifth-graders) outperformed older students (ninth-graders) on reasoning problems that involved the conjunctive fallacy. Sedlmeier argues that schools may train individuals to be more deterministic rather than probabilistic thinkers. Furthermore, students who are considered better at mathematics are most likely to make errors. This result is interesting, and further exploration of a typical mathematics curriculum to understand the source of this possible effect seems to be warranted. Another possibility, however, is that the result is some sort of artifact. For example, it is possible that students learn, over time, to select more complex answers over simpler ones, a strategy that is not effective for conjunctive fallacy problems. Or, younger students may not use the complex sentences for the conjunctive choice. Finally, younger students may not have schemas that lead them to selecting the wrong answers in conjunctive reasoning problems (e.g., they may not select "Linda is a feminist and a bank teller" in the common conjunctive fallacy example if one does not know what a *feminist* is or that individuals who are politically active in certain ways are more likely to be feminists in our culture).

In summary the Sedlmeier chapter presents a highly effective method for teaching statistical reasoning built on what he argues are statistical intuitions that individuals have from interacting in the real world. Future research on the underlying mechanisms leading to the success of his intervention, as well as on the surprising developmental trajectory of children in typical school contexts, are possible future directions to take this research.

THINKING ABOUT RISKS AND BENEFITS
OF SEXUAL BEHAVIORS

In the final chapter under consideration, Bruine de Bruin et al. describe an intervention for helping teens think about risks and benefits of sexual behaviors and make decisions about sexual behaviors. Their intervention, a DVD viewed by teens, is based on a mental models approach in which they initially assess teens' beliefs about HIV/AIDS and compare teens' understanding with expert models. By using this approach, they are able to identify gaps and misconceptions that may influence teens' decisions about sexual behavior, and attempt to close these critical gaps and thus improve decision-making. This approach appears to be quite successful. Teens who viewed the DVD were more likely to be abstinent, less likely to report problems with condom use (e.g., a condom breaking or falling off), and less likely to have a sexually transmitted infection 3–6 months later than those in the control group.

The main strength of this intervention is in its mental model approach that seeks to identify what information and skills adolescents already possess, as well as what their specific needs are. Thus, instead of being researcher-driven, the authors emphasize the need to make a concerted effort in learning about the "reality" of adolescent lives acknowledging that cultural and personal factors (such as difficulty resisting pressure to have sex from older partners) play a role in sexual decision-making.

The research presented here is an exciting demonstration that improving understanding of risk and benefits in a particular context can lead to improved decision-making in that context. Given the importance of this topic, there are several questions that arise from this study that might lead to better understanding of adolescents decision-making about sexual behavior, and, more generally, their thinking about data. First, we discuss what factors might influence adolescents' decision-making about sexual behavior and consider characteristics of instructional interventions, some of which are already incorporated in the Bruine de Bruin intervention, that go beyond the mental models approach. Then, we briefly discuss how the Bruine de Bruin intervention provides insights not only for adolescents' reasoning about risks and benefits in the context of sexual behavior, but also about risks and benefits in other contexts.

The DVD intervention in this study focuses mostly on adolescents' misconceptions and gaps in knowledge. It is possible that other factors also lead to faulty decision-making and that incorporating additional factors may improve the effectiveness of the intervention. One possible issue that arises is the degree to which errors in decision-making are caused by inconsistent or incomplete information, poor understanding of facts, or faulty application of facts (e.g., condoms are not 100% reliable, therefore are not useful). It is possible that adolescents' decision-making relies on a more experiential system, heuristics, prior beliefs and intuition (see Klaczynski, 2004 for review of literature on adolescent decision-making). Thus strengthening adolescents' knowledge base and cognitive toolbox may be only a partial solution to improving sexual decision-making.

Another possible area of disconnect for adolescents between knowledge and decision-making is the cultural context that discourages sexual behaviors among adolescents. Correct information regarding condom effectiveness coupled with the correct judgment on the appropriateness of condom use may still not increase intended behavior (e.g., use of condom) if issues of availability, cost, and safety of acquiring and storing contraception are at play. These issues must be acknowledged and addressed by the intervention.

In addition to issues regarding the effect of knowledge versus other factors on adolescent decision-making, there is some variability in the methodological choice of outcome variables in the sexual behavior decision-making literature. Although decision-making is commonly acknowledged to be a multistep process (e.g., Byrnes, 2004), sexual decision-making is often treated as a single outcome variable (such as on bottom-line averages such as acquiring an STD or getting pregnant). Such reductionistic approaches may mask progress steps that are made toward normative choices (such as considering and purchasing contraception) highlighting instead only the eventual outcome (failure to use a condom). It would be interesting if even larger gains were found in these substeps, and whether it would be effective to evaluate how interventions might focus specifically on these substeps. The intervention in this chapter does exactly that, by providing females examples and suggestions to assure that they are able to implement the choices they make (e.g., by teaching them explicitly how to discuss these issues with their partners).

This last example suggests that it is important to consider role of culture in the options afforded to adolescents (in particular females). Specifically, women from patriarchal cultures that afford less power to women than men may have a difficult time negotiating safer sexual decisions with their partners (e.g., Landrine, 1998; Paternostro, 1999). Although the current intervention makes an attempt to resolve this issue via the examples of concrete conversations between women and their partners, another possible approach would be to involve male partners in interventions of this kind. Traditionally, the role of males in sexual decision-making is often ignored or underestimated. Although adolescent girls often bear the brunt of poor sexual decision-making (e.g., with regards to unwanted pregnancy), not involving their male counterparts in teaching healthy decision-making is unlikely to promote sexual communication or improve choices made as a couple (Tolman, Striepe, & Harmon, 2003; Tolman, Spencer, Harmon, Rosen-Reynoso, & Striepe, 2004).

Bruine de Bruin et al. point out that the effectiveness of interventions such as the one in this study is based on how trustworthy adolescents consider the information that they are give. If they do not trust information or the source of that information, they are unlikely to incorporate it in their decision-making. One way that they may not trust information is if they feel they are not getting a complete story, and that the individuals creating the intervention have a particular agenda. The Bruine de Bruin et al. chapter intervention explicitly addresses this issue of trust of information in a number of ways, such as providing complete information and trustworthy characters teens relate to. Another factor that recent studies suggest may be related to trustworthiness of quantitative data is the format in which data are depicted. Individuals are more likely to use information to make decisions when that risk/probability information is presented in graphs rather than numerically, perhaps because they find this information more trustworthy and salient (e.g., Chua, Yates, & Shah, 2006; Fagerlin, Wang, & Ubel, 2005). Future research on what kinds of information and formats adolescents find valuable, trustworthy, and scientific may be useful in designing effective interventions for teens.

A final issue that arises is the degree to which interventions of sexual behavior in teens needs to be tailored for different individuals. Much research in the medical decision-making literature has recently focused on tailoring decision-making to the needs of the individuals making the decisions (Hibbard, Slovic, & Jewett, 1997). Specifically, these studies suggest that individuals who differ in background experiences and knowledge, as well as in statistical reasoning and numerical literacy skills, may require different kinds of knowledge and skills to make a decision. In the case of adolescent decision-making specifically, factors such as whether an individual is heterosexual or homosexual, has a current partner, cultural backgrounds and beliefs may all play a role.

In addition to possible factors that might influence the effectiveness of the intervention described in this chapter and other possible interventions for teaching adolescents about risks and benefits of sexual behavior, the current chapter opens up several possibilities regarding teaching of statistical reasoning to adolescents in general.

One possibility is that by teaching adolescents about cumulative risk in the context of sexual behaviors, a topic of interest to adolescents, they might be encouraged to apply this understanding of cumulative risk in other contexts (e.g., drunk-driving, wearing seatbelts, and so forth). It may be interesting to conduct studies that examine whether this new statistical understanding transfers to new contexts. Transfer may be facilitated by explicitizing some of the misconceptions that students have had. For example, students may be asked to consider how their thinking about cumulative risk may have changed and consider how this new understanding might apply to other contexts. This type of intervention may also help students think more critically about information in the media or in school. By asking students to evaluate the data given to them and to be cautious about drawing conclusions from individual instances or anecdotes, they may learn to reason more effectively in a variety of contexts.

Thus, it is possible that although this intervention is intended to be domain-specific, adolescents' new understanding of risk and interpretation of data has the possibility to applying to new contexts. Our own recent research suggests that this may be possible. In one study, we examined how experts in history, mechanical engineering, cognitive, and social psychology reasoned about data presented to them (Shah, Freedman, & Watkins, 2003). In this study, individuals were influenced by their own disciplinary norms in evaluating data outside of their domain. Cognitive psychologists, for example, attempted to identify mechanistic explanations for data, social psychologists were particularly skilled at considering alternative explanations, mechanical engineers noticed quantitative anomalies, and historians questioned the operationalization of variables.

In summary, the Bruine de Bruin study provides an excellent example of an intervention to train adolescents about risks and benefits of sexual behaviors and, at the same time. Two questions ripe for empirical research include the examination of other possible factors that may influence adolescent decision-making, as well as considering the potential of this intervention for teaching more domain-general statistical literacy skills.

CONCLUSION

The three chapters in the final section of *Thinking with Data* provide a wide range of useful tools for thinking about how people learn about and make decisions with data in the real world. Although the three chapters are products of different areas of research and indeed different disciplines, they each inform our understanding about the structures that underlie human reasoning abilities. In fact, because they each bring a unique perspective to the topic, they ultimately provide us with a complex picture of cutting-edge work in the field.

ACKNOWLEDGMENTS

We would like to thank Dan Willig for help in creating Figure 18.1 and Aysecan Boduroglu for comments on an earlier version of this chapter. We are very grateful to the authors of the three chapters that are the subject of this discussion for sharing their work and for engaging and thoughtful discussion at the symposium.

REFERENCES

Byrnes, J. P. (2005). The development of self-regulated decision making. In J. E. Jacobs & P. A. Klaczynski (Eds.), *The development of judgment and decision making in children and adolescent.* (pp. 5–38). Mahwah, NJ: Lawrence Erlbaum Associates.

Chua, H., Yates, J. F., & Shah, P. (2006). Risk avoidance: Graphs vs. numbers. *Memory & Cognition, 34*(2), 399–410

Fagerlin, A., Wang, C., & Ubel, P. A. (2005). Reducing the influence of anecdotal reasoning on people's health care decision: is a picture worth 1000 statistics? *Medical Decision Making, 25,* 398–405.

Gopnick, A., Glymour, C., Sobel, D. M., Schultz, L. E., Kusnnir, T., & Danks, D. (2004). A theory of causal learning in children: Causal maps and Bayes nets. *Psychological Review, 111,* 3–32.

Hibbard, J. H., Slovic, P., & Jewitt, J. J. (1997). Informing consumer decision in health care: Implications from decision-making research. *The Milbank Quarterly, 75,* 393–414.

Klaczynski, P. A. (2005). Metacognition and cognitive variability: A dual-process model of decision making and its development. In J. E. Jacobs & P. A. Klaczynski (Eds.), *The development of judgment and decision making in children and adolescent.* (pp. 39–76). Mahwah, NJ: Lawrence Erlbaum Associates.

Landrine, H. (1998). Cultural diversity, contextualism and feminist psychology. In B. K. Clinchy & J. Norem (Eds.), *The gender psychology reader* (pp. 78–103). New York: New York University Press.

Nazzi, T. & Gopnik, A. (2000). A shift in children's use of perceptual and causal cues to categorization. *Developmental Science, 3,* 389–396.

Paternostro, S. (1999). *In the land of God and man.* New York: Plume Books.

Shah, P., Freedman, E., & Watkins, P. (April, 2003). *The influence of prior content knowledge and graphical literacy skills on data interpretation.* Paper presented at the 2003 annual meeting of the American Educational Research Association, Chicago, IL.

Tolman, D. L., Striepe, M., & Harmon, T. (2003). Gender matters: Constructing a model of adolescent sexual health. *Journal of Sex Research, 40,* 4–12.

Tolman, D. L., Spencer, R., Harmon, T., Rosen-Reynoso, & Striepe, M. (2004). Getting close, staying cool: Early adolescent boys' experiences with romantic relationships. In N. Way & J. Y. Chu (Eds.), *Adolescent boys: Exploring diverse cultures of boyhood* (pp. 235–255). New York: New York University Press.

Tversky, A., & Kahneman, D. (1974). Judgment under uncertainty: Heuristics and biases. *Science, 185,* 1124–1131.

Author Index

453

Subject Index